Other Guides in the
Discovering Historic America Series

NEW ENGLAND
THE MID-ATLANTIC STATES
THE SOUTHEAST

Text:

Vicki Brooks
Michael Fiore
Martin Greif
Lawrence Grow

Design:

Frank Mahood
Donald Rolfe

Cover illustration: *Mission San Xavier del Bac, Tucson,
AZ; courtesy, Arizona Office of Tourism.*

DISCOVERING HISTORIC AMERICA

CALIFORNIA & THE WEST

General Editor: S. Allen Chambers

E.P. DUTTON & CO., INC. · *NEW YORK*
1982

Published in the United States by E.P. Dutton, Inc. 2 Park
Avenue, New York, N.Y. 10016

Library of Congress Catalog Card Number 82-71548
ISBN: 0-525-93246-1 Volume 2

Published simultaneously in Canada by Clarke, Irwin &
Company Limited, Toronto and Vancouver

10   9   8   7   6   5   4   3   2   1

First Edition

Contents

Introduction

EACH of the titles in the *Discovering Historic America* series brings together the rich and varied resources available to the traveler in an historic region of the United States. In whatever season of the year, the traveler may journey into a past that is alive today and not an ocean or oceans away from home. History may have begun on the other side of the Atlantic or Pacific, but it is abundantly and colorfully displayed in the highways and byways of rural and urban America, in historic homes, museum villages, state and national parks, inns and churches, courthouses and city halls, hotels and restaurants, museums and libraries, battlefields and archaeological sites, mills and manors.

This comprehensive guide to historic California and the West, organized state by state, and within each state from south to north, offers the traveler hundreds of opportunities to step away from the frenzied pace of everyday life — to enjoy the quiet of a picturesque seaside inn, to trace the path of pioneer forebears, to experience the delights of a ride in a horse and buggy or a steam-driven train, to discover our heritage in the traditional arts and crafts. For families with small children *Discovering Historic America* provides useful information on activities which are not only entertaining but educational, whether on a day trip, weekend, or extended vacation. For every traveler there is a rich selection of historical treasures to be explored and enjoyed in almost every corner of the five tradition-rich states that make up the region.

Many of the places described in this book are listed in the National Register of Historic Places; some are also official National Historic Landmarks. These listings have been supplemented with historical museums, reconstructions such as museum villages, excursion railroad lines, traditional craft workshops, state and national parks, and monuments of historic interest. And there are, of course, hundreds of historic properties included here which have yet to reach the official listings in Washington or elsewhere.

For the traveler heading out from one of the major metropolitan areas of California and the West, a one-volume guide which includes information on all of these features in addition to a selection of historic inns, hotels, and restaurants is of considerable value. Whether a trip is undertaken as a family activity or as a get-away-from-it-all escape for a weekend or a week, there is much pleasure to be gained in discovering the treasures of this historic region. Discerning travelers, dismayed by today's slick commercial tourism, will delight in the authentic and will find exploration of America's past a satisfying experience.

Dozens of people associated with the region's many historical societies, preservation organizations, and tourist authorities have provided generous suggestions and source material for this volume. In addition, the records of the National Register have been made available for checking facts. Although it is impossible to name everyone who has offered assistance, several people merit very special thanks. I wish particularly to thank Mrs. Colette Eady of the National Register staff for answering the many questions regarding the whereabouts of pertinent information on historic properties; thanks also, to Alicia Bremer-Davis, Utah Travel

Council, Salt Lake City; Dan E. Burke, Utah Arts Council, Salt Lake City; Aaron Gallup, architectural historian, Office of Historic Preservation, Department of Parks and Recreation, State of California; J. G. Simpson of the Hawaii Visitors Bureau; John Townsend, supervisor, Visitors Information Center, Greater Los Angeles Visitors & Convention Bureau; Stephen F. Tripp, public relations coordinator, Arizona Office of Tourism; the staff of the California Collection, Los Angeles Public Library; and the staff of the Nevada Historical Society at Las Vegas.

How to Use This Guide

Discovering Historic America: California & the West is a useful book to consult and a very easy book to use. It is organized by state, starting with California, and ending with Hawaii. The states are further broken down into geographic regions. Utah and Nevada, for example, are divided into southern and northern sections. These smaller areas make the planning and execution of trips easier and enable the traveler to choose from a wide variety of historic sites and attractions concentrated within a self-contained geographic region. California, the largest of the states, is also divided into southern and northern regions, with each of these appearing as a separate chapter, the southern coming first. Southern California is in turn divided into seven sub-regions, and northern California into six. A state map, with two for California, indicating the key regions within, appears at the beginning of each chapter of the book. The listings for each of these regions are broken down by town and city in alphabetical order.

Information on the historical, architectural, or other cultural significance of a place is given along with essential facts on hours of operation, address, telephone number, and admission fee if any. Some of the historic places listed and described remain in private hands, but are still accessible for viewing from the public way or are open on special days for group tours. These are so designated.

Special letter codes and symbols are used with many of the listings. **NR** means that the property has been nominated and accepted as an historic property by the National Register of Historic Places, National Park Service, Washington, D.C. **NHL** is the designation for a National Historic Landmark, an honor reserved by the National Park Service for properties or geographic districts of exceptional significance to the nation. All these landmarks are automatically included in the National Register. Places of special interest to families with children are marked with the symbol ♛.

Listings of lodging and restaurants are included at the end of each state's entries. Only properties which can be considered historic to a significant degree have been included. In every case, modern improvements have been made, but these have been designed with consideration for the architectural integrity of the original building.

The cost of lodgings has been rated on the following scale based on the average daily single room rate: **I** = inexpensive, $25 or under; **M** = moderate, $40 or under; **E** = expensive, over $40. The cost of meals has been rated on the following scale based on the average dinner price: **I** = inexpensive, $7.50 or under; **M** = moderate, $12.50 or under; **E** = expensive, over $12.50. Other abbreviations used in the lodging and dining sections are the following: **MAP** = modified American plan, **EP** = European plan, **AE** = American Express, **CB** = Carte Blanche, **D** = Diners Club, **M** = Mastercharge, **V** = Visa, and **PC** = personal checks accepted.

Although every effort has been made to insure the accuracy of addresses, telephone numbers, hours of operation, and admission fees appearing in this book, these are all subject to change over time. In planning a trip, it is always wise to call or write ahead for the latest information.

CALIFORNIA & THE WEST

1. CALIFORNIA

Southern California

IT is often said that southern California leads the nation in technology and popular culture, that what is found there *now* will be the norm for the rest of the country five or ten years *hence*. To experience the future, one is told, go to southern California. The only problem with this piece of folk wisdom is that it isn't true. Freeway city, Los Angeles itself, is uniquely different from the rest of the United States. But this singularity does not stem from an advance look at the future, but from its special history and geography.

Except in the desert areas, southern California has a year-round temperate climate. Because of this, much more is made of the outdoors than in most other parts of the United States. The emphasis on outdoor living has been present since the early 19th century, when homes were built of adobe bricks and arranged around a courtyard. The California ranch house has an old and noble lineage.

Of the twenty-one missions established by the Franciscan fathers in the 18th and early 19th centuries, nearly all are found in the southern section of the state along El Camino Real (The King's Highway), now partially paralleled by CA 101. The Spanish, and later the Mexicans, attempted to establish their presence in the cooler north, but only succeeded in gaining a tenuous hold in a few settlements before the wave of American fortune seekers swept away competing foreign interests in the 1840s.

The extent of the influence of the Hispanic tradition can be seen today in such communities as San Juan Bautista, Monterey, and Santa Barbara. It has been preserved in Los Angeles's El Pueblo quarter and in San Diego's Old Town. It is present, too, in the many neighborhoods of Mission Revival and Spanish Colonial Revival buildings—homes, markets, churches, railroad stations, all with the distinctive stepped gable, tile roof, and stucco or plaster facade.

The other tradition which has shaped southern-California culture is the emphasis on the new. Separation from the East Coast and Europe by thousands of miles has had an effect on the work of architects, designers, and artists. Irving Gill, Rudolph Schindler, the Greene brothers, and Frank Lloyd Wright produced most of their early adventuresome work in southern California. To this list one must add the many lesser-known designers of thousands of Art Deco and Moderne homes, stores, and office buildings found throughout the region.

Southern California is another country, even to Californians of the north. It has been presented as a separate entity in this volume. The line between north and south has been drawn below San Francisco Bay and San Mateo County in the northwest and the Sierra Nevadas in the northeast. The two regions, naturally, overlap. Monterey and Carmel, for example, can be reached much more easily from San Francisco than from Los Angeles, but these two towns are historically related to those of the south along the mission trail. In the pages that follow, southern California is broken down into seven sub-regions starting with San Diego and Imperial counties in the south and ending with Inyo County in the northeast.

Strathearn Home, Simi

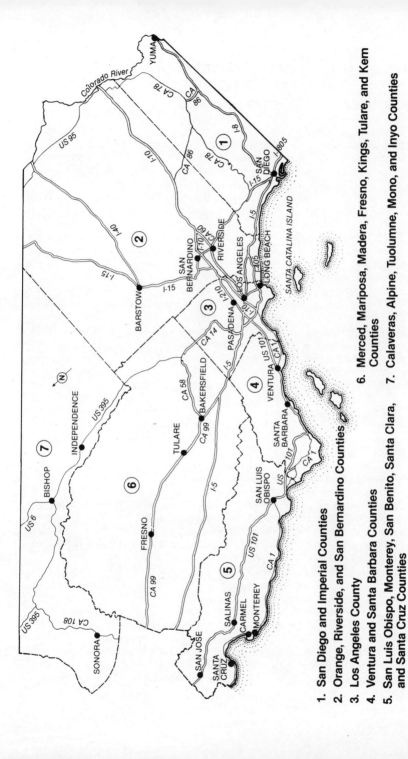

1. San Diego and Imperial Counties
2. Orange, Riverside, and San Bernardino Counties
3. Los Angeles County
4. Ventura and Santa Barbara Counties
5. San Luis Obispo, Monterey, San Benito, Santa Clara, and Santa Cruz Counties
6. Merced, Mariposa, Madera, Fresno, Kings, Tulare, and Kern Counties
7. Calaveras, Alpine, Tuolumne, Mono, and Inyo Counties

San Diego and Imperial Counties

The two most southern counties of California, both bordering on Mexico and sharing an Anglo-Hispanic culture, nonetheless present a striking study in contrasts. In the west, in San Diego County, are mountains, national forests, and the seashore. In the east, in Imperial County, there seems to be a surplus only of sandy soil. The western region was cultivated as early as the 18th century by the Franciscan fathers and Spanish ranchers; cultivation of the land to the east had to await the development of proper irrigating techniques in the 20th century. Consequently, San Diego County is rich in history today and Imperial County is very poor. When one searches for the historic in this corner of California, all paths lead immediately to the city of San Diego and its surrounding communities. It is the fastest growing area of the state, a result in part of its fine climate and cultural resources.

Coronado

HOTEL DEL CORONADO, 1500 Orange Ave., 1887-88. This spectacular seaside resort hotel provides as good an introduction to historic southern California as any establishment that one could possibly conjure up. Almost everything in its appearance — turrets, cupolas, pillars, geegaw gingerbread — suggests the richness and eclecticism of late-Victorian American architecture. The Del, as it is locally known, was designed by James W. Reid and Merritt Reid and is situated on a peninsula across from San Diego and continues to serve as that city's most exclusive social address. It is said that the Duke of Windsor first met Mrs. Simpson here in 1920. Nearly every modern U.S. president has visited the Del, and it has appeared in "pictures," most notably as a setting for Billy Wilder's *Some Like It Hot.*

Modernization has been necessary over the years, this consisting principally of the removal of fireplaces and the installation of bathrooms. The basic spaces, however, remain much as they were nearly 100 years

ago. The Crown Room, the Coronet Room, and the main lobby area are almost untouched. One part of the complex which has been moved from its original site is the pyramidal **boathouse** with a belvedere

atop the roof. This used to stand further offshore; it now serves as a restaurant and has been completely renovated. NR, NHL.

For further information regarding accommodations, consult the listing under Lodging and Dining.

La Jolla

LA JOLLA WOMAN'S CLUB, 715 Silverado St., 1914. No other 20th-century archi-

tect has more smoothly and creatively combined the Mission Revival style with the modern than Irving Gill. He worked almost entirely in that most contemporary of mediums, reinforced concrete. The Woman's Club is one of his most successful buildings, and one of many Gill works still standing in the wealthy community of La Jolla. The land and building were donated to the club by Ellen Browning Scripps, a writer and member of the philanthropic publishing family. La Jolla was established in 1887 as a well-bred outpost of wealthy San Diegans. Other buildings designed by Gill include the **Bishop's School for Girls** complex, 7607 La Jolla, 1909-16; **La Jolla Community Center,** 615 Prospect, 1914; and **Scripps House** (La Jolla Museum of Contemporary Art), 700 Prospect, 1913. NR.

Oceanside vicinity

SAN LUIS REY MISSION CHURCH, Mission Ave. at Rancho del Oro, 1811-15, restored 1893. The second mission in a chain of 21 Franciscan outposts extending up the coast, San Luis Rey is among the most simple in design. This simplicity adds greatly to its stature. The mission was first established in 1798, and a small adobe chapel was built at that time. By the late 1800s, long after the mission had been secularized, the buildings had fallen into such disrepair that complete rebuilding was called for. In 1893 the renewed mission was rededicated as a Franciscan college. NR, NHL. Open M-Sa 9-4, Su 12-4. $1 adults, 50¢ juniors 12-18, 25¢ children 6-11. (714) 757-3651. ♿

Oak Grove

OAK GROVE BUTTERFIELD STAGE STATION, 13 miles NW of Warner Springs, CA 79, 1858. The northern section of this adobe building is the original stage station on the Butterfield Overland Mail Route which operated from 1858 to 1861. St. Louis and Memphis were the eastern terminals of the route which began in San Francisco. NR, NHL.

Pala

ASSISTENCIA DE SAN ANTONIO DE PALA, Pala Mission Rd., 1816. Pala was founded by Mission San Luis Rey to serve the Indians of the backcountry ranchos. By the late 1800s, the condition of the buildings, including the chapel, had deteriorated badly. The chapel was restored before the area was designated as part of an Indian reservation in 1903. Since that time the whole complex of buildings, including the only freestanding *campanario* or bell tower in the chain of Franciscan missions, has been refurbished. The branch mission still serves its Indian community, and a school run by the fathers has been part of the scene for many years. A small **museum** features relics of the mission and Indian-carved statues. The museum and chapel are open daily except M, 10-3. (714) 742-3317.

San Diego (see also Coronado)

One of America's fastest growing cities, San Diego has nonetheless managed to preserve a substantial number of its historic buildings. The losses have been primarily among the more modern buildings such as those designed in the early 1900s by Irving Gill and which have not acquired the patina of antiquity. Anything vaguely Spanish Colonial or Mission-like in style has been accorded protection for many years. Such historical shrines as the mission church, the Presidio, and the Old Town buildings are the focus of much attention and loving care. They are reminders of the days in the 18th- and early 19th-centuries when San Diego was foremost an Hispanic town.

San Diego's later history as a cultural center is reflected in the buildings of Balboa Park built for the Panama California International Exposition in 1915 and the 1935 California Pacific International Exposition. A number of prominent architects were responsible for the design of the buildings, but the Spanish Colonial Revival style emerged as the predominant one for exhibition buildings, botanical gardens, and other facilities.

BALBOA PARK, bounded by Upas, 6th, and 28th Sts. and CA 94. This is a 1,400-acre complex of which 320 acres were first set aside by the city in 1868. Most recently it has become famous as the site of the zoo and its award-winning children's exhibits. The locale of the two major national exhibitions of 1915 and 1935, Balboa Park has received more attention from landscapers, architects, and artists than any other section of the city. Buildings that were meant to be temporary facilities for fairgoers were, in many cases, used later to house permanent exhibits. Do not miss the important features of the park that are listed below:

The San Diego Museum of Art is housed in the Spanish-Renaissance Fine Arts Building designed by Bertram Goodhue in 1915. NR. Open daily except M, 10-5. $1 adults, 50¢ students under 16. (714) 232-7931.

The **San Diego Aero-Space Museum** is installed in the former Ford Motor Co. building designed by Walter Dorwin Teague for the 1935 fair. The entrance pavillion is cylinder-shaped and rises 90 feet. This is backed up by the main exposition hall, a circular space with a fountain in the shape of a Ford V-8 insignia in the center. The history of transportation is depicted in a mural which wraps around the upper walls of the exhibit area. The museum also houses the **N. Paul Whittier Historical Aviation Library.** NR. Open daily 10-4:30. $2 adults, 50¢ children. 🏃 (714) 234-8291.

The **House of Charm** was built for the 1915 fair and now houses the **San Diego Hall of Champions,** a sports history museum. Open M-Sa 10-5, Su 12-5. Free. (714) 234-2544. 🏃

The California State Building, designed by Bertram Goodhue for the 1915 fair, is now used for the **Museum of Man.** It is a Spanish Baroque building of the kind that Goodhue felt was much superior in design to that designated "Mission." The museum is rich in Indian artifacts and Mayan culture. Open daily 10-4:30. $1 adults, 50¢ students, 25¢ children 6-16. (714) 239-2001.

The grounds of the park are noted for their beauty. The landscaping for the 1915 fair was to have been undertaken by the famous Olmstead firm, and although it did not carry out the work, much of the Olmstead design was executed by others. The **Botanical Garden** is a vast, airy space of exceptional grace well worth a visit.

U.S. GRANT HOTEL, 326 Broadway St., 1910. This hotel, designed by San Diego architect Harrison Albright and established by Ulysses S. Grant, Jr., the president's son, was once the center of social and political activity in town. It remains a convenient and well-preserved meeting place and hostelry. (See Lodging and Dining for further information regarding accommodations.) Many of the original exterior decorative details have been covered over, but enough of the elegant fabric remains to make the Grant an important downtown landmark. NR.

HISTORICAL SHRINE FOUNDATION, 2482 San Diego Ave. Two important buildings near the Old Town San Diego park district (see below) are owned and maintained by this non-profit preservation society. Both of these residences—the **Whaley House,** the corner of San Diego and Harney Sts. 1856; and the **Derby-Pendleton House,** next door on Harney, 1851—are built in the Greek Revival style. The clapboard Pendleton House is said to have been shipped from Maine around the Cape. Both homes are furnished with antique furniture from the 1850s and '60s. Each is open W-Su 10-4:30. Whaley House: $1.50 adults, $1.25 senior citizens, 75¢ juniors 12-16, 40¢ children 5-11. Derby-Pendleton House: 75¢ adults, 60¢ senior citizens, 50¢ juniors, 40¢ children 5-11. (714) 298-2482.

LONG-WATERMAN HOUSE, 2408 First Ave., 1889. A finer example of Queen

Botanical Garden, Balboa Park

Anne architecture would be hard to find in southern California. It is a three-story frame building with decorative shingling. Its roof is pierced at one side with a third-story turret with an open porch, and at the other side with a gabled attic bay. The wraparound first-floor porch is perfectly worked with turned supports and elaborately carved elements. Private, but visible from the street. NR.

MISSION SAN DIEGO DE ALCALA, 10818 San Diego Mission Rd., 1808-13, 1931. The first of California's 21 missions, founded in 1769 by Father Junipero Serra, was moved from its original location on Presidio Hill in 1774 to what was a better agricultural area. The present church is the fourth one erected and was almost completely rebuilt in 1931. At that time, only the facade and a small part of the sidewalls were still standing. Since 1941 it has served as a parish church. A **museum building** on the grounds displays manuscripts and other artifacts relating to the mission. The 46-foot bell tower or *canpanario* is the mission's most striking architectural feature. NR, NHL. Open daily 9-5. $1 adults. (714) 283-7319.

OLD TOWN SAN DIEGO STATE HISTORIC PARK, bounded by Juan, Twiggs, Congress, and Wallace Sts., 19th century. The **Visitor Center** for this complex of buildings is located at 2645 San Diego Ave. Restoration of the remaining buildings from San Diego's 1821-72 Mexican-American period and the reconstruction of others began in earnest in the 1960s after a spurt of interest in the 1930s. The state of California has sponsored most of the necessary work in what is one of San Diego's earliest neighborhoods. Until the mid-19th century, it remained distinctively Mexican in character with a large open plaza surrounded by one-story adobe buildings. After 1846 and the American occupation, frame construction began to supersede that of clay, and the scale of the old town changed. Today there are nine buildings dating from the period 1829-1865 which can be toured.

La Casa de Estudillo, 4000 Mason St., 1827-29. Of four adobe buildings in the area, this is the most famous and was the first to be restored in the 20th century. Jose Antonio de Estudillo, a distinguished official under both the Mexican and American governments, built the U-shaped home around a courtyard. The hand-hewn beams are lashed together with rawhide thongs. A one-story veranda extends around the three inner courtyard sides. The house is also known as "Ramona's Marriage House," a reference to the heroine of Helen Hunt Jackson's romantic novel *Ramona* (1884). The house has nothing to do with the California potboiler which was penned in a New York City hotel room.

Casa de Machado y Stewart, Congress St., 1829. The Stewart family, related by marriage in the 1840s with the Machados, occupied this adobe until the late 1960s. It is covered with clapboards, presumably of a much later date than its erection.

Casa de Machado y Silvas, San Diego Ave., c. 1830. This is a single-story adobe laid out in a U plan with a patio and garden at the rear.

Casa de Bandini, Calhoun St., 1829. The building is a two-story adobe with a full first-story porch and second-story balcony. The Greek Revival wood detailing of the windows and doors is probably a result of later American modification.

Mason Street School, 1865. A frame building, it is marked with the characteristic Greek Revival stylistic elements favored by mid-century Anglo builders.

San Diego Union Building, San Diego St., 1851. This single-story wood frame building began life as the **Casa de Altamahino** and became the first home of San Diego's leading newspaper in 1868. It has been restored to that period with the basic equipment of an old-fashioned newspaper.

Seeley Stables, Calhoun St., c. 1869. These buildings have been reconstructed as they appeared in the days when Alfred L. Seeley began the San Diego-Los Angeles Stage Line. A collection of horse-drawn vehicles and Western Americana is housed here.

The buildings in the park are open daily; winter, 10-5, and summer, 10-6. There is no charge except for the Casa de Estudillo and Seeley Stables. A single fee of 50¢ for adults and 25¢ for senior citizens and children is valid for both museums. (714) 294-5183 for further information.

SANTA FE DEPOT, 1050 Kettner, 1915. The atmosphere here is much more like that of a cloister than a railroad station.

The waiting room of the Spanish Colonial Revival building designed for the 1915 exposition is remarkably cool, and chaste. The simple white Colonial walls are broken only by arched side entrances. The station was designed by the firm of Bakewell and Brown. The towers which flank the massive arched entrance are topped with domes overlaid with blue and yellow tiles in zig-zag patterns and crowned with tiled lanterns. NR.

SAN DIEGO MARITIME MUSEUM, 1306 N. Harbor Dr. Three shops form the historic fleet berthed at this site. The most famous is the 1863 *Star of India,* a three-masted, iron-hulled vessel. An English-built ship, it was last used as an Alaskan salmon bark. Restoration began in 1959. It is considered the oldest iron-hulled merchantman afloat. NR, NHL. The other ships which can be visited are the steam ferry *Berkeley* (1898), which houses exhibits, and the steam yacht *Media* (1904). The museum is open daily 9-8. $2.50 adults; $2 senior citizens, juniors 13-17, and military; 50¢ children. (714) 234-9153.

SAN DIEGO PRESIDIO, Presidio Park, 1769. The Presidio is San Diego's most historic site, the first permanent European settlement on the Pacific coast of the United States. It was also here that the first mission, San Diego de Alcala, was founded by Fray Junipero Serra. Little remains of the early settlement on the hill except for the outlines of the bastion's adobe foundations. By the 1830s the mission had been moved elsewhere (see Mission San Diego de Alcala), and the fort and its quarters had been abandoned for the Old Town quarter below.

A decision was made in the early 1900s to leave the site as it was and not to attempt an historical reconstruction. Rather, the San Diego Historical Society erected the **Serra Museum, Library and Tower Gallery** in the park to house exhibits and manuscript materials on the early settlement. The handsome Spanish Colonial Revival building dates from 1929 and was designed by William T. Johnson. The museum is open M-Sa 9-4:45, Su 12-4:45. $1 adults, 50¢ children. (714) 297-3258.

SPRECKELS THEATER BUILDING, 123 Broadway, 1912. This is one of San Diego's Beaux-Arts commercial buildings designed by Harrison Albright, also the architect of the U.S. Grant Hotel. The theater, restored in 1964, is better known for its interior decoration than for its exterior. The painted stage and ceiling scenes by Emil T. Mazy and the paintings by Arthur Hurlt in the lobby area are noteworthy. NR.

VILLA MONTEZUMA (Jesse Shepard House), 1925 K St., 1887. Jesse Shepard was a most unusual man, and the late-Victorian house he had built is without equal in America. A spiritualist, musician, and writer, Shepard settled in San Diego in the 1880s with his devoted companion, Lawrence Tonner. He quickly gained the confidence of the community's wealthy social set, and members of this local aristocracy helped finance the building of Villa Montezuma, designed by the local firm of Comstock and Trotsche. Basically it is a frame two-story house, but added to this structure were thousands of elements that transformed it into a visually dazzling concoction. The roof line is punctuated with turrets and towers, the tallest having a reverse curve dome. The exterior walls are covered with a wide variety of pattern shingles —diamond, round, square, fishscale— tongue and groove paneling, half-timbering, and a bas-relief wood plaque. The interior rooms are every bit as fanciful as the exterior spaces.

Only the finest materials—walnut, Lincrusta-Walton, ceramic tile, and art glass were used in the house. The music room occupies the east side and includes a most unusual ceiling of Lincrusta-Walton overlaid with redwood strips, and circular art-glass windows with portrait heads of Beethoven, Mozart, Rubens, and Raphael. Adjoining this room is the drawing room with yet more art glass portrait windows (heads of Shakespeare, Goethe, Corneille). Other rooms include the Red Room, (Shepard's bedroom), the Gold Room (used as a library), the Blue Room (Tonner's quarters), and the dining room. The second floor was never used for living purposes but was a catch-all museum of Shepardiana. A room in the main tower, reached from the second story, was Shepard's inner sanctum and from this perch he could survey San Diego from all four sides. After he left San Diego, Shepard became world-famous as the writer "Francis Grierson."

Villa Montezuma is owned and maintained by the San Diego Historical Society. NR. It is open Tu-F and Su 1-4:30. Free. (714) 239-2211.

San Diego vicinity

CABRILLO NATIONAL MONUMENT, off US 101, Point Loma, 1542. The remarkable voyage of discovery of Juan Rodriguez Cabrillo, a Portuguese mariner, is commemorated here. The first landing of Europeans on this part of the New World took place on September 28, 1542. The expeditionary force consisted of two ships, the *San Salvador* and the *Victoria,* and Cabrillo only anchored in San Diego for a few days before heading north, eventually reaching the southern Oregon boundary.

The park consists of some 80 acres and includes a modern **visitor center** with exhibits explaining Cabrillo's voyage. A glass-enclosed "view building" is found within the center that provides a spectacular view of the harbor and city. The oldest building in the park is the original **Point Loma Lighthouse** (1854). A rectangular stone bulding with a tower rising from the center of the roof, it is one of the first eight lighthouses built on the Pacific coast by the American government soon after the California territory had been annexed. The tower is built with a balustraded deck and glass-enclosed lantern. 👬

A walkway from the old lighthouse leads to the **"whale overlook,"** a place where one may occasionally spot the ten-to fifteen-foot telltale geyser of a gray whale. From December through February, hundreds of these creatures migrate from the Arctic Ocean to Baja California. NR.

JOHNSON-TAYLOR RANCH HEADQUARTERS, Black Mountain Rd., Rancho de los Penasquitos, 1862, 1887, 1913. This is one of the few surviving adobe and frame ranch houses dating from the mid-19th century. George Alonzo Johnson began construction of his house at the Rancho de los Penasquitos in 1862; in 1884 it was converted into a hotel by Col. Jacob Taylor, a wealthy cattleman. Later is was turned to use as a bunkhouse for cowboys. In 1974, San Diego County purchased the property, and restoration work has been underway on the complex since that time. There are beautiful palm, pepper, eucalyptus, and sycamore trees on the grounds, and a stream passes close to the U-shaped main bulding and its courtyard and various adobe and frame outbuildings. Since the north San Diego neighborhood where the headquarters is located is one of the fastest growing commercial districts in the area, the historic park will supply needed green acres. NR.

Spring Valley

HUBERT H. BANCROFT RANCH HOUSE, Memory Lane, off Bancroft Dr. and CA 94, 1856. Western historian Bancroft couldn't have chosen a more congenial setting for writing the story of the settling of the frontier. His one-story adobe house, lived in from 1885 until his death in 1918, is now maintained by the Spring Valley Historical Society. NR, NHL. It is open F-Su 1-4. Free. (714) 469-1480.

Yuma Crossing (see Yuma, Arizona)

Old Officers' Quarters, Fort Yuma

Orange, Riverside, and San Bernardino Counties

The three counties adjoining Los Angeles County to the south and the west encompass both the ocean and the desert. This is an enormous area extending from the Nevada and Arizona state lines to the old Franciscan mission trail along the Pacific. At least 75 percent of the territory is off-base to the visitor as it is used for military purposes or is otherwise inaccessible. Joshua Tree National Monument covers a considerable area, as do state and national forests, and Indian reservations. Orange County is the smallest of the three counties and the one most familiar to tourists. For over 100 years it has been a promised land for seekers of a better life. Until the post-World War II period, the county was probably best known for its citrus production; since then the groves have given way to acres of ranch-style homes and such attractions as Disneyland and Knott's Berry Farm. The remaining "old" features of the manmade landscape date primarily from the early 1900s. The same situation applies to the western areas of Riverside and San Bernardino counties closest to Los Angeles. Until fairly recently, even antique 20th-century buildings were not safe from the developer. Now they are receiving

some official protection and their value as cultural resources is recognized.

Anaheim

Now the home of Disneyland, a major sports stadium, and a mammoth convention center, Anaheim is almost completely new. The core of the old city has been rebuilt several times since its founding in the late 1850s by the Los Angeles Vineyard Society, a crew of northern California German vintners who later switched to the cultivation of oranges. They were successful at raising both crops, but Los Angeles encroached more and more upon their land. Now there is only one remaining building which tells the story of this disciplined communal society named for the river (Santa Ana) and the German word for home (*heim*).

MOTHER COLONY HOUSE (Hansen House), 414 N. West St., 1857. The building was moved to this location from its original site on N. Los Angeles St., a principal artery. Like many other early Anglo California residences, the style is Greek Revival and more suggestive of the East than the romantic Wild West. George Hansen was the community's founder.

There was a time when you couldn't leave or enter Anaheim without passing through one of four gates in a wall or fence of willow poles surrounding the community. The barricade was meant for keeping out herds of wild cattle. A historic **plaque** commemorates the site of the most important entrance, the north gate, on the main road to Los Angeles, at Los Angeles and North Sts.

Another chapter in Anaheim's cultural history and that of most other southern California towns unfolded in the early 1900s. The Mission style swept the popular architectural sweepstakes. Almost everywhere homes and commercial buildings were designed with stucco and frame or concrete walls in imitation of the old Franciscan missions then crumbling away. At first the style was reminiscent of the early buildings, with curvilinear stepped gables, an arcade or cloister, and perhaps even a tower. By the 1920s a more sophisticated and ornate version, known as the Spanish Colonial Revival, had taken hold of the popular imagination. The red tile roof and the distinctive stepped gable was retained, but everything was embellished in some way. Anaheim's only National Register landmark, the **Pickwick Hotel**, is a classic example of this form:

PICKWICK HOTEL, 225 S. Anaheim Blvd., 1926. This was once Anaheim's grand hotel and the only significant Spanish Colonial Revival building built during the '20s. It derived its name from the fact that it also served as the terminal for the Pickwick Stage Company's bus line to San Diego. Now showing its age, the Pickwick is a prime candidate for restoration. It takes some imagination to envision the day when this was the community's leading hotel and restaurant. When it opened in 1926, the Anaheim *Gazette* praised its "spaciously and exquisitely appointed lobby where the soft glowing lights blend well with the golden-tinted stucco walls and ceiling. A comfortable lounging and reading room is equipped with overstuffed chairs and electric lamps." NR. (714) 535-9042.

Banning

MALKI MUSEUM, Morongo Indian Reservation, 11-795 Fields Rd. The Morongo reservation is one of the largest in southern California. Tribal artifacts, especially those of the Cahuilla Indians, are displayed in the museum. Open Tu-Su 1-5. Free. (714) 849-7289. ♦♦

Chino vicinity

YORBA-SLAUGHTER ADOBE, 5½ miles S of Chino at 17127 Pomona Rincon Rd., 1850s. This adobe ranch house now serves as a branch museum of the San Bernardino County Museum. The area used to be one of immense ranches, including the 47,000-acre Rancho del Chino. The house is open Sa 10-5 and Su 1-5. Free. (714) 825-4825.

Desert Hot Springs

CABOT'S OLD PUEBLO MUSEUM, 1913. It you're on your way to Palm Springs or the Joshua Tree National Monument, you might want to stop over at this unusual site. Cabot Yerxa discovered the natural hot springs and built himself a 35-room Hopi-style building out of earth and cast-off materials. The exhibits center around Indian artifacts and handicrafts. Open W-M 9:30-4:30. $1 adults, 50¢ children. (714) 329-7610. ♦♦

If early Indian culture is of interest to you, another interesting place to visit is the **Palm Springs Desert Museum.** Over 1,500 artifacts are housed in the building, located at 101 Museum Dr. Palm Springs, now much more than a millionaire's hide-away, is almost surrounded by Indian reservations, the Agua Calienta reservations being the largest. The museum is open late Sept-June, Tu-Sa 10-5, Su 1-5. $1.50 adults, no charge for students and children. (714) 325-7186.

Fullerton

Fullerton is a small city and, like other Orange County communities, was once a center of fruit cultivation, but has become part of the Southern California suburban

Dining Room, Yorba-Slaughter Adobe, Chino

sprawl. The first Valencia oranges grown in the county were planted at **Gilman Ranch,** a site which has been preserved by the city and California State University at Fullerton. The **Fullerton Arboretum** is located here as well as the three historic sites that follow:

DR. GEORGE CLARK HOME AND OFFICE (Heritage House), Fullerton Arboretum, California State University campus, 1894. The doctor's office and a pharmacy, as they might have appeared in the 1890s, can be seen here along with a general collection of Victorian furniture and furnishings. The house is open each Su 2-4 and at other times by appointment. Free. (714) 773-3579.

MUCKENTHALER HOUSE, 1201 Malvern Ave., 1923. The home of Walter and Adella Muckenthaler was given to the city of Fullerton by their son, Harold, for use as a cultural center. It is an impressive example of Spanish Colonial Revival architecture and is handsomely situated on the 8½ remaining acres of an 80-acre estate. Most of the mansion is used for art exhibitions and workshops. Open Tu-Su 12-5. Free. (714) 738-6595.

MUSEUM OF NORTH ORANGE COUNTY, 301 N. Pomona Ave. Local history and Indian culture are among the major concerns of this facility. Special programs and displays—both permanent and rotating—are devoted to subjects of historical interest. Open Tu-F 10-3, Sa 10-5, Su 12-5. Free. (714) 738-6545.

Joshua Tree National Monument

The park, named for the abundant stands of this spiney tree of the lily family, stretches for miles across parts of eastern Riverside and San Bernardino counties. It is primarily desert land and is formed of two ecosystems—the Colorado desert to the east and the somewhat cooler Mohave desert in the west. Five oases of fan palms dot the park. A great deal of the park has been designated as a wilderness area and will never be explored by the average visitor. There are both paved and dirt roads that lead into some of the most interesting manmade and natural areas, as well as hiking trails. Unless you are approaching the monument from the south and west, it makes most sense to enter the area from

CA 62 and at the **Oasis Visitor Center** just east of Twentynine Palms. Here one can gather information on the present accessibility of some of the major sites.

In the late 19th century the desert area became the focus of considerable gold mining activity, and work continued in one of the mines until 1961. Desperadoes were of course attracted to the glitter of gold, and they also found the wilderness a useful sanctuary from the law. In the 1930s homesteaders attempted to stake out new lives in the desert. Almost all of these attempts at taming nature have been defeated by time and the elements. Only traces of human activity remain, most of them in a ruinous state which enhances their romantic nature. Three sights within the park are particularly recommended:

DESERT QUEEN MINE. This gold mine dates from the 1890s. The ruins of a stone house are located on one hillside, and opposite can be found the cast-off equipment, rusting pipe, scrap lumber, and other debris.

LOST HORSE MINE. Developed by the Ryan family in the 1890s, this was the most profitable of the gold deposits in the area.

KEYS DESERT QUEEN RANCH, 1894. The home of well-known rancher and miner William Keys is still standing amidst a complex which includes a schoolhouse, windmill, mining equipment, and other farm buildings.

Information regarding the monument and the previously mentioned sights can be obtained from the Twentynine Palms Oasis Visitor Center, Joshua Tree National Monument, 74485 National Monument Dr., Twentynine Palms 92277. The center is open daily 8-5. (714) 367-7511.

La Habra

LA HABRA CHILDREN'S MUSEUM, 301 S. Euclid, 1923. A Mission Style Union Pacific railroad depot is the perfect setting for this municipal museum. It is devoted almost exclusively to the kinds of things which especially intrigue children — trains, airplane models, a live bee observatory. There is a model train village and full-size railroad cars to explore. It isn't Disneyland, but it's probably more real, and the admission fee is only $1 for adults and 50¢ for children. La Habra is just north of Fullerton on the Los Angeles county line. The museum is open Tu-Sa 10-4. (213) 694-1011.

Lake Elsinore

CRESCENT BATHHOUSE, 201 W. Graham Ave., 1887. Healthful hot springs were discovered here in the 19th century, and a resort hotel-spa was just what Victorian doctors ordered. The bathhouse is now a store called "Chimes" which specializes in antiques, but the building is very much intact. It is a highly fanciful two-story structure in what might be called a Moorish design with decorated arches between columns. A color scheme of red, yellow, and green emphasizes the fantastic spirit of the place. Frank Ferris was the architect, and he and Franklin Heald, a founder of Elisinore city, established the health resort. The lake is the only fresh water body in southern California, and the nearby springs were valued by the Indians long before eminent Victorians began making pilgrimages to the bathhouse. NR.

Modjeska

MODJESKA'S HOME, Forest of Arden, 0.7 miles to the left from the junction of the Santiago Canyon Rd. and the Modjeska Grade Rd., 1888. Anyone with a flare for the dramatic will appreciate the career of the Polish actress Helena Modjeska and the setting of her hideaway, surrounded by the Cleveland National Forest. Fame was achieved in the 1870s and '80s with a series of national tours featuring the plays of Shakespeare. Mme. Modjeska attempted to found a colony of Polish artists here in 1876, but this attempt failed. Twelve years later Stanford White designed a home for her on the property named after the setting of Shakespeare's *As You Like It,* played so often by the famous thespian. The property is private, but visible from the public way.

Newport Beach

Newport Beach is best known for its harbor full of yachts and its seafood restaurants. Little known is one of the masterpieces of the International Style in America located here:

LOVELL BEACH HOUSE, 1242 W. Ocean Front, 1926. The creation of architect R.M. Schindler, an Austrian who came to America in 1913, the house is built of reinforced concrete and is suspended above the beach on five frames. To so cantilever the two upper floors of a house was a revolutionary concept at the time. The frames or supports are left exposed, and the open-air area around them at ground level forms a patio. The two-story living area above projects over the frames and provides a spectacular view of the ocean. An upper level sleeping porch was originally left open, but this has since been enclosed. The beach house is now crowded in by other buildings at each side, but it still stands out as a singular creation. NR. Privately owned.

ORANGE EMPIRE RAILWAY MUSEUM, 2201 South A St. An 1880 general store from the old community of Pinecate serves as the center for this railroad buffs' paradise. Pinecate was the original settlement a mile and a half away on the area's first railroad line (Santa Fe) from Chicago to San Diego. On display are steam and diesel locomotives, streetcars, interurban cars, trolleys, and freight and maintenance cars. Open daily 9-5. Free. (714) 627-2605.

The newer settlement of Perris was established by the Southern California railroad in 1886. These were the days when as many as a dozen gold mines were in operation in the area. While in Perris, a stop at the c. 1887 **railroad station**, on 4th St. near D, is well worthwhile. It is a rather charming Queen Anne brick design with an open tower or belvedere.

Rancho Cucamonga

It is hard for an Easterner to believe that such a place exists and is not a joke. Jack Benny used to go on and on about the town's Santa Fe railroad station. In any case, however crazy it sounds, Cucamonga is for real, and has had something of a history as a wine-making center; both Virginia Dare and the Cucamonga Rancho Winery (Thomas Vineyards) have been located here. The **Virginia Dare winery,** Haven and Foothill Blvd., is a Mission Revival ruin. **Thomas Vineyards,** 8916 Foothill Blvd., operates a museum and offers a self-guided tour. The building has been restored at various times, and parts of it are thought to be more than 125 years old. The vineyards were established in 1839. The museum is open daily 9-6. Free. (714) 987-1612.

JOHN RAINS HOUSE (Rancho Cucamonga), 7869 Vineyard Ave., 1860-61. The residence is believed to be the oldest fired-brick building in San Bernardino County. It is now maintained as a museum by the county. Among the most interesting features is an early air conditioning system which consisted of a system of ducts under the floor through which cool water from a creek was forced into the rooms. There is a large patio in the center of the complex formed by the main house and two wings. NR. Open W-Su 12-4. Free. (714) 989-4970.

Redlands

Redlands is a prosperous, attractive small city that has managed to escape many of the depressing effects of economic development so noticeable in the West. Thanks to the beneficence of the Smiley brothers

(Alfred and Albert) beginning in the early 1900s, the streets are lined with superb plantings, and private and public spaces are uncommonly beautiful. Their example has been imitated by others since that time. The County Museum is headquartered in Redlands and the University of Redlands has played an important role in maintaining a strong cultural presence.

SAN BERNARDINO COUNTY MUSEUM, 2024 Orange Tree Lane. Primarily a natural history museum, this institution also houses general historical materials in its library and exhibit areas. Several historic buildings — including the Yorba-Slaughter Adobe in Chino and the John Rains House in Rancho Cucamonga (see previous listings), as well as the San Bernardino Assistencia (see following listing) — are administered by the County Museum. Open Tu-Sa 9-5, Su 1-5. Free. (714) 825-4825.

SAN BERNARDINO ASSISTENCIA, 26930 Barton Rd. (at Mountain View Ave.), 1830, 1927-37. Also known as the Asistencia de San Gabriel, the chapel here served as an outpost of the Mission of San Gabriel Arcangel for Rancho San Bernardino in the early 19th century. The headquarters of the more than 40,000-acre ranch was also located here. The remaining buildings are, for all intents and purposes, reconstructions. The San Bernardino Historical Society had the mission buildings rebuilt. The Asistencia is open W-Sa 10-5 and Su 1-5. Free. (714) 793-5402.

Redlands has a number of Mission Revival homes which are almost as interesting as those which have been restored. Of special note is the **Holt House,** 405 W. Olive, 1903, and the **Burrage House,** 1205 Crescent, 1900-01. Both are private but can be viewed from the public way.

A.K. Smiley Public Library, 4th and Eureka, one of the Smiley family gifts to the city, is also a Mission Revival building dating from 1898. It is situated in **Smiley Park,** a pleasantly landscaped area which also includes the **Lincoln Memorial Shrine** (1932).

A. K. Smiley Public Library, Redlands

Riverside

Riverside, simply named for its position along the Santa Ana, was not formally laid out until the 1870s. Once the center of navel orange cultivation, Riverside became enormously prosperous and fashionable. In architecture the citizenry's taste first embraced the Queen Anne style, but by the early 1900s this was almost entirely replaced by the Mission Revival and, a bit later, by the Spanish Colonial Revival. The local popularity of both of these stylistic movements can be traced in part to the example set by the Mission Inn, one of southern California's key landmark buildings. This is but part of the Riverside story, however, as the whole city embraced red tile, stucco, and the stepped gable as the traditional mode by the 1920s.

ALL SOULS UNIVERSALIST CHURCH, 3657 Lemon St., 1891-92. The oldest Universalist or Unitarian church west of the Rockies is a reminder of the role played by New England settlers in the development of southern California. Also known as the "Red Sandstone Church" and the "Elegant Little Church," All Souls is Norman Gothic in style and was built entirely of Arizona red sandstone. Oak was used for the doors, pews, pulpit furniture, and interior trusses; marble was laid for the floors. NR.

HERITAGE HOUSE (Bettner House), 8193 Magnolia Ave., 1890s. This white frame mansion, built in a combined Queen Anne-Colonial Revival style, serves as a

branch history center of the Riverside Municipal Museum. It was built by the widow of James Bettner, a founder of the California Fruit Growers Exchange, and is furnished today much as it was in the early 1900s. NR. Open Tu and Th 12-2:30, Su 12-3:30. (714) 787-7273.

MISSION INN, 3649 7th St., 1890-1901, 1929. Many a noted southern California architect who worked in the Mission Revival or Spanish Colonial Revival style lent his hand at some part of the Mission Inn, including Arthur B. Benton, Myron Hunt, Elmer Grey, and G. Stanley Wilson. Frank A. Miller was the man who started it all by buying the Glenwood Inn in 1901. Within thirty years, the largest Mission Revival building in California had taken shape. The oldest parts of the inn are the lobby and the two wings extending along Orange and Main Sts. An open patio stands at the center of the complex. Around the courtyard can be found such features as the St. Francis Chapel with an 18th-century Spanish altar screen, bell towers, and cool flagstone-floored cloisters. The main public rooms are lavishly decorated with antique furnishings and paintings from around the world; nine Tiffany windows, intended in 1906 for a New York City church, are installed in the building. In recent years the inn has been revamped to include offices and shops in addition to hotel rooms and restaurants. Guided tours of the complex are given daily 11:30 and 2:30; the admission is $2 for adults and 75¢ for children

5-11. For additional information about hotel facilities, consult the listing under Lodging and Dining. NR, NHL. (714) 784-0300. 🏛

SHERMAN INDIAN MUSEUM, 9010 Magnolia Ave., is located in the Sherman Indian High School's administration building. This is the last of a group of Mission Revival structures designed for the school, formerly known as the Sherman Institute, devoted to the education of young Indian males. Indian culture is, of course, the focus of the displays. Open June-Aug, M-F 1-3:30; remainder of year, M-F 1-4. Donations accepted. (714) 359-9434. 🏛

San Juan Capistrano

The famous swallows keep coming back to the old mission on March 19th (St. Joseph's Day), having departed there on schedule, October 23rd (St. John's Day). And so do the tourists. Excluding Hollywood and the Anaheim of Disneyland, there is probably no better known or more popular town in California than San Juan Capistrano. This makes things somewhat difficult for visitors who prefer a less commercial and crowded approach to traveling and history. But San Juan Capistrano is still worth it, and one's visit should start at the mission itself:

MISSION SAN JUAN CAPISTRANO, Camino Capistrano and Ortega Hwy., 1777-1816. Only ruins exist of the great sandstone church finished in 1806; it was destroyed six years later by an earthquake. The building was to be the centerpiece of the seventh of the Franciscan coastal missions. The building was erected in the form of a cross, 180 feet long and 90 feet wide; there were seven domes, a bell tower visible for ten miles, and an arched roof. It is the ruins, however, that have so entranced the visitor over the years. The stone arches and doorways are beautifully carved and have a striking romantic and poignant quality which derives from their having no real function. Despite the fact that the church is now in the process of being copied, no one can lessen the picturesque qualities of the original ruins. The swal-lows probably won't want to have anything to do with the reproduction and will continue to roost in the old campanario wall.

Saved from destruction all of these years is the original **adobe chapel**, a building nearly 30 years older than the ruined church. It was last restored in the 1920s and also serves as a museum. The chapel, living quarters, and other adobe buildings form three sides of a quadrangle. NR. Open daily 7-5. $1 admission. (714) 493-1111.

MIGUEL PARRA ADOBE, 27832 Ortega Hwy., c. 1841. Originally a farmhouse, the Parra adobe is probably the least altered example of this type of early construction in Orange County. It is a symmetrical one-story building with pedimented windows and door which show some "Yankee" stylistic influence. The builder and first owner, however, was an Indian and the house is located in an area granted to the natives in 1841. Suburban sprawl has been enveloping most of the historic mission area where this home is located, and the city of San Juan Capistrano has developed plans to use the house as an Indian cultural center. NR.

Santa Ana

CHARLES W. BOWERS MEMORIAL MUSEUM, 2002 N. Main St., 1931-36. Santa Ana's downtown was shaken to pieces in a 1933 earthquake, and real estate developers have picked over many of the remaining pieces dating from the Mission Revival and Queen Anne periods. The museum is almost pure Spanish Colonial Revival inside and out. It is a rich depository of Indian objects and lore and displays material on 19th- and 20th-century art and transportation as well as on the history of Orange County's citrus industry. Main gallery open Tu-F 1-5, Sa 9-5, Su 12-5; other galleries, Tu-Sa 9-5, Su 12-5. Free. (714) 972-1900.

Twentynine Palms. (See Joshua Tree National Monument)

Yorba Linda

RICHARD NIXON BIRTHPLACE, 18061 Yorba Linda Blvd., 1912. The 37th President was born here in 1913, the year after his father, Frank, completed the one-story frame cottage. It is probably the most humble home the ex-president has lived in since. NR, NHL.

San Clemente, also in Orange County, is a town on the coast, and the Nixon property there, after having been stripped of many of its controversial presidential perquisites, has been sold to another private owner. The **Nixon Museum** in San Clemente has closed its doors but is expected to reopen in a facility to be shared with Ole Hanson, a founder of the town.

Los Angeles County

Los Angeles County defies description. It encompasses dozens of communities of which the city of Los Angeles is only the largest. The city spreads over 458 square miles—from the San Gabriel Mountains in the north to the harbor at San Pedro in the south. But this area, big as it is, only represents roughly one-tenth of the square mileage of Los Angeles County. The county is just about as large as the state of Connecticut, and, in many ways, it is more diverse in its features than the New England state.

It often appears that everything is new in

the Los Angeles area, and perhaps that is an image which is cultivated, since it is by no means an accurate one. Los Angeles is an old city, although not the oldest in the county. San Gabriel was founded ten years earlier, in 1771. The Spanish tradition in architecture has been avidly celebrated since the early 1900s, and there are striking reminders of this to be seen today in adobe dwellings, ranchos, mission churches, early commercial buildings, as well as in later revival style homes and offices.

There is another Los Angeles which may not be quite as sacred in the canons of history, but it is every bit as interesting and inspired a tradition as the Hispanic. This is the Los Angeles of the early 20th century—of the movies, of big business, of an opulent modern life style. Nowhere else in America were architects given quite so free a hand in the 1920s and '30s to design buildings free of classical restraints. It was then, too, that the first truly modern American city was planned around the automobile, that the freeway system killed the concept of a downtown. Ever since then Los Angeles has tried to resurrect her center city, but the center will not hold. There are too many satellite communities along the broad boulevards and freeways which have their own attractions.

It is for this reason that Los Angeles County is approached *regionally* in this book rather than on a strict city and county basis. In Los Angeles County city runs into county and vice versa, and the mix is almost always changing.

Angelino Heights and Highland Park

Located to the northwest of downtown Los Angeles these early suburban and now city neighborhoods have had a rough time holding on to some semblance of their historic character. The Angelino Heights section has been cut off by both the Hollywood and Pasadena freeways from related neighborhoods. Yet many fine Victorian homes remain, and these are being slowly reclaimed from neglect. Highland Park, further to the northeast, was established in part during the late 1800s along the Arroyo Seco, and as early as the 1930s the residents suffered the indignity of seeing the Pasadena Freeway plowed through the area. There is nothing quite like a window full of expressway to look out upon, but Highland Park has managed to hold on to some of its Colonial Revival and Craftsman homes and bungalows which are tucked away on streets well removed from the freeway. What might be termed an old-house sanctuary—Heritage Square—has become established in the area for the purpose of taking in Victorian waifs no longer wanted elsewhere.

CARROLL AVENUE, 1300 Block, Carroll Ave. between Edgeware and Douglas Sts., 1880s. Visitors are often taken to Carroll Avenue's row of Victorian buildings in Angelino Heights to prove that preservation has a constituency in Los Angeles. Well, it's true—sort of. There are nine buildings all together. Among the notable are the **Aaron Phillips House,** 1300 Carroll, c. 1887; the **Innes House,** 1329 Carroll, 1887-88; and the very decorative

Sessions House, 1330 Carroll, 1888, designed by Joseph Cather Newsom. All three are frame Queen Anne residences with varying degrees of ornamentation.

If you are in the Angelino Heights area, there is no reason to stop only along Carroll Ave. There are other Queen Anne mansions worthy of respect as well as a good collection of early 20th-century buildings—Colonial Revival, Craftsman, and Pueblo Revival in style. The **Atwater Bungalows** at 1431 and 1433 Avon Park Terrace, 1931, were designed in an exaggerated version of the Pueblo Revival style, which originated in New Mexico. Vigas or beams project from exterior walls at odd places; the walls are heavily stuccoed in the manner of a frosted wedding cake. The architect, Robert Stacy-Judd, was surely a master of the Los Angeles manner, a romantic or theatrically exaggerated interpretation of a traditional style.

HERITAGE SQUARE, 3800 block of N. Homer St., 1875-85. Heritage Square lies S of the Pasadena Freeway off Ave. 43, and it is here that several Victorian homes have been moved and restored. The **Mount Pleasant House,** 1875-76, is the earliest building and was well restored in 1976-77. The architect of this Italianate frame landmark with redwood clapboarding was Ezra Kysor, who also designed St. Vibiana's Cathedral and several of the N. Main St. buildings in El Pueblo State Historical Park. The **Hale House,** c. 1885, is what Californians term a Queen Anne-Eastlake building. This is essentially a fussy, heavily

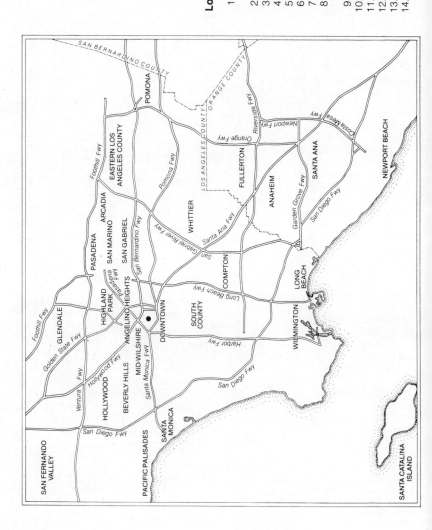

Los Angeles County detail

1. El Pueblo de Los Angeles State Historic Park
2. Los Angeles Public Library
3. Bradbury Building
4. Southwest Museum
5. Lummis House
6. Civic Center District
7. Gamble House
8. Los Angeles State and County Arboretum
9. Missoin San Gabriel Arcangel
10. Hollyhock House
11. Crossroads of the World
12. Doheny Estate
13. Pio Pico Casa
14. Will Rogers State Historic Park

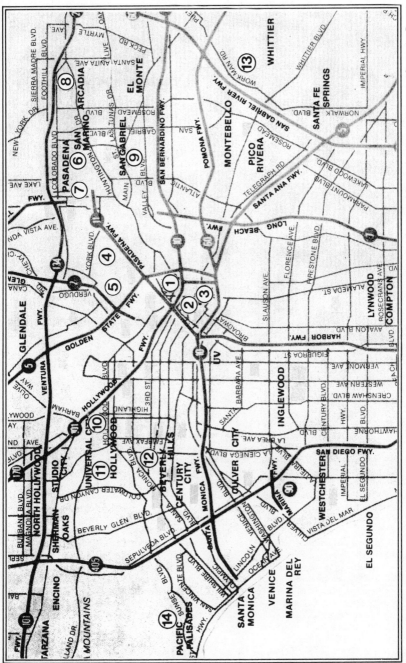

ornamental approach to the Queen Anne style. It is expressed particularly in the supporting members of porches, in balusters, and in lattice work. The entrance porch of the Hale House, for example, has heavy turned posts, curved wood bracket caps, and milled balusters. Above the entrance to the porch is a pediment with a U.S. shield and a profusion of floral ornamentation. The interior of the house is similarly elaborate. NR.

The Heritage Square houses may be toured on the first and second Sundays and third Wednesday of each month, 11-3. $1 adults, 50¢ children and senior citizens. (213) 222-3150.

LUMMIS HOUSE (El Alisal), 200 E. Ave. 43, 1897-1912. Charles Lummis (1859-1928), author and founder of the Southwest Museum (see following listing), built his own Craftsman style house from Arroyo stone boulders. It is now the headquarters of the Historical Society of Southern California. The house features built-in furnishings, an Art Nouveau fireplace designed by Gutzon Borglum (the famous sculptor of Mt. Rushmore), Indian artifacts, and personal memorabilia. The museum is open Su-F 1-4. Free. (213) 222-0546.

SOUTHWEST MUSEUM, 234 Museum Dr., 1912. One of the least known of the Los Angeles area cultural institutions, this is a museum not to be missed. You can enter the Mission style complex through a Mayan temple entrance at the base of a hill. This will take you, via a 250-foot long corridor, to an elevator which rises up through the hill to the museum proper. There are various exhibition areas which present comprehensive displays of such subjects as Indian baskets, blankets, and pottery. Special attention is also given to the Spanish Colonial and Mexican provincial periods of California history. Open 1-4:45 Tu-Su. Free. (213) 221-2163.

The Southwest Museum also maintains the **Casa de Adobe**, at 4603 N. Figueroa St., a 1917 recreation of a Mexican provincial building built around a patio. Artifacts from this early 19th-century era are displayed here. Open W, Sa-Su 2-5. Free. (213) 221-2163.

Beverly Hills

In the public imagination Beverly Hills is luxury itself. Rodeo Drive, the Beverly Hills Hotel, the Beverly Wilshire: the impression is one of expensive shops, elegant appointments, immaculately manicured grounds, an air of celebrity. Actually, Beverly Hills is a city within a city, completely encircled by the metropolis from which it was born. In 1914, when the fashionable community was incorporated, there was not the high concentration of wealth seen today on the shopping boulevards and residential avenues. Movie personalities didn't begin to settle in Beverly Hills until after the area had been discovered by more common folk—doctors and lawyers, solid business types.

The world has grown a bit more sophisticated since the days when Beverly Hills was most famous as the home of movie stars. With the exception of such overgrown Dick-and-Jane houses as Pickfair,

most celebrity roosts are likely to remind you of your Uncle Arnold's house back home. Not a single movie star's home, incidentally, is an official landmark. Still, tracking down the houses of the stars can be fun. The Beverly Hills Visitors and Convention Bureau will be glad to help. It is located at 239 S. Beverly Dr. (213) 271-8174.

DOHENY ESTATE/GREYSTONE, 905 Loma Vista Dr., 1923. Nestled in a lovely hillside park, this extravagant 55-room mansion was built as a gift by millionaire oilman Edward Doheny for his son. Tudor styling dominates the stone mansion, designed by architect Gordon Kaufmann in 1923, and the estate owes its affectionate second name to the house's grey slate roof. Greystone's 16.8 acre grounds were originally part of a 400-acre ranch owned by

Doheny, Sr., an oil millionaire. The estate once included stables, a lake, tennis courts, and kennels; these have been sacri-

ficed for parking lots. NR. Although the interior of the main building is not accessible, the grounds are open free to the public from 10-6, daily. The estate also features guided tours of the grounds, and a summer concert series. (213) 550-4864.

SPADENA HOUSE, 516 Walden Dr., 1921. The whimsical thatched-roof residence, best characterized as late Hansel and Gretel, was originally designed by Henry Oliver as a movie set. Its steep roofline provides a refreshingly odd sight in a neighborhood of conventional houses. A succession of private owners have been interested in preserving this monument to the crazed eclecticism found only in southern California. Private but can be viewed from the street.

VIRGINIA ROBINSON ESTATE, 1008 Elden Way, 1908-11. Generally considered the first modern residence in Beverly Hills, this Beaux Arts estate was the home of Mr. and Mrs. Harry Winchester Robinson and was designed by Nathaneal Dry-

Entry, Virginia Robinson Estate, Beverly Hills

den, Mrs. Robinson's father. "In 1911, when we built the house," Mrs. Robinson wrote, "Beverly Hills consisted of barley fields and one small real estate office about a mile from the house." The highlight of the Robinson residence is the playhouse pavilion added in 1924. Based on such late Renaissance buildings as the Cortile de Belvedere, the pavilion is related to the main building through a series of integrated steps, terraces, and landscape effects. An outstanding feature of the pavilion is the sliding, windowed doors which open onto a reflecting pool, creating a gazebo-like effect. NR. Private, but can be viewed from the street.

Downtown Los Angeles

It is hard for many people to believe it but, yes, there still is a downtown Los Angeles. The first settlement in what is now the city occurred in the area occupied by El Pueblo de Los Angeles State Historic Park in the downtown section just north of the Santa Ana Freeway. Gradually business drifted further south along the presently numbered east-west streets and named north-south streets. The whole area resembles something of an oasis, being hemmed in and separated from the rest of the city by the Santa Ana, Harbor, and Santa Monica freeways. Downtown bustles during the day with the activity of major business corporations and financial institutions; at night the streets are quite dead except for a smattering of tourists staying in downtown hotels who cannot quite find their way to the livelier haunts of Beverly Hills and the mid-Wilshire area to the west. Sightseeing in downtown LA is very much a daytime activity, and there is much to enjoy. Except for the remaining Hispanic landmarks of the state park, the style of the historic buildings is turn of the century to 1930s modern.

BRADBURY BUILDING, 304 S. Broadway, 1893. You would never know from the bland exterior that a highly imaginative, glass-roofed inner court lies at the heart of this building. The visual delight is created by the unique design of the five-story open court. The space is defined by ornate ironwork balconies, stairways, and elevator cages. Other materials which endow this space with interest are the marble stairs, Mexican tile courtyard floor, and wood paneling. The architect was George H. Wyman. NR. Open during regular office hours.

Bradbury Building

Two blocks down Broadway is the Arcade Building, #542, 1922-23. The floor-through arcade to Spring St. provides an inviting change in the row of buildings in this block. The design with a skylight is particularly well carried out. Open during regular office hours.

EL PUEBLO DE LOS ANGELES STATE HISTORIC PARK, Los Angeles Plaza, c. 1800-present. There are ten historic buildings within this park which was the site of the founding of Los Angeles. In addition to these buildings, some 70 shops and restaurants line the reconstructed red brick Olvera St. The most important of the historic buildings is the **Avila Adobe**, 14 Olvera St., the oldest existing house in Los

Angeles. Originally it was a one-story, L-shaped patio house with fifteen rooms opening up on the inner space. In 1870 an earthquake resulted in the loss of half of the building. The adobe was rescued from complete neglect in the 1920s, and now it is furnished with antiques and period reproductions from the 1830s and '40s. NR. Open Tu-F 10-3, Sa-Su 10-4:30. Free. (213) 680-2526.

The **Church of Our Lady of All Angels,** 535 N. Main St., was founded in 1818-22, the successor to a chapel. The new church was an *asistencia* or branch of the Mission of San Gabriel, Arcangel. Today's building dates from 1861 and was partly constructed from the materials used earlier. The 1861 building was enlarged in 1912 and given a more Hispanic appearance. A classic example of early mission architecture it is not, but this building, also known as the Plaza Church, remains the oldest religious structure in the city. Open for worship daily.

The other historic buildings in the park include the **Fire House No. 1,** Old Plaza and

Los Angeles Sts., which houses a fire-fighting museum. Open M-F 10-3 and Sa-Su 10-4:30. Free.

The Italianate **Masonic Temple,** 416 N. Main, 1858, has been completely restored with furnishings originally brought from the East by clipper ship. Open Tu-F 10-3. Free.

The **Pelanconi House,** 17 W. Olvera St., 1855-57, one of the first brick buildings in the city, is now the home of the La Golondrina Cafe. Open Th-Tu 11-10.

Three other buildings are closed to the public at the present time but are expected to be reopened in the future. These are the

Italianate **Pico House,** 1870; the **Theater Mercedes,** Los Angeles's first theater building, 1869; and the **Sepulveda House,** 1887, a two-story brick building built originally as a hotel and restaurant.

For information regarding these buildings and park activities, call (213) 628-1274. The park is open Tu-F 10-3, Sa-Su 10-4:30. There is no admission fee to any of the buildings.

LOS ANGELES CENTRAL LIBRARY, 630 W. 5th St., 1925. Bertram Goodhue's masterpiece is now under attack from those who wish to make more profitable

Kiosko bandstand, El Pueblo de Los Angeles State Historic Park

use of the site. It is a highly unified complex which incorporates sculptural elements, a central three-story penthouse crowned with a pyramidal pinnacle, entrance pylons, and mosaic tile designs. The grounds are beautifully landscaped and form an integral part of the overall design of the property. The interior is richly decorated with murals and frescoes. The children's wing, for example, features N.C. Wyeth murals. Open M-Th 10-8, F-Sa 10-5:30. Free. (213) 626-7461. ⚐

MILLION DOLLAR THEATER (Edison Bldg.), 307 S. Broadway, 1917. A combination auditorium and office building, the Million Dollar is at the beginning of the Broadway theater district. One of the earliest movie palaces, the auditorium is extremely well preserved and includes the original proscenium, organ screen, hanging lamps, and terra-cotta detail work. William L. Wollett was the designer of the interior; A.C. Martin was the architect of the building. The exterior combines Spanish Renaissance architectural motifs with eye-catching eclectic details including theatrical figures, decorative pendants, and spiral columns. NR. Open as a movie theater.

Los Angeles Public Library

PERSHING SQUARE AREA, bounded by 5th, Hill, 6th, and Olive Sts., 1920s. Pershing Square, named after the World War I general, is a most welcome five-acre spot of green in the midst of the downtown grid pattern. On its west side stands the remarkable **Biltmore Hotel,** designed by the firm of Schultze and Weaver in 1922-23. In style, the building can only be called a combination of Beaux Arts and 16th-century Italian. It is a true palace that any world capital would jealousy safeguard. For information regarding accommodations, consult the listing under Lodging and Dining.

ST. VIBIANA'S CATHEDRAL, 114 E. 2nd St., 1871-76, 1922. This central edifice of the Los Angeles Roman Catholic community is almost as old a building as Our Lady of All Angels in El Pueblo State Historical Park. The church was clearly meant to be a copy of Puerto de San Miguel in Barcelona, Spain. The architect was Ezra F. Kysor who also designed the Pico House and Theater Mercedes in the historical park. Improvements in the design of the facade were made by John C. Austin in 1922. St. Vibiana is a rather obscure early Christian martyr. Open for worship.

SPRING STREET FINANCIAL DISTRICT, from 354 to 704 S. Spring St., 1902-31. Twenty-six buildings lining both sides of S. Spring for a little more than three blocks constitute a significant architectural complex. Although there are several hotels along the street, the buildings are primarily financial. Spring St. has long been known as the "Wall Street of the West," and the buildings, whether classical or more modern in style, are monumental and conservative in design. The financial district quickly grew from north to south in the early 1900s. Both the **Continental Building** at #408, considered the city's first skyscraper, and the **Banco Popular** (formerly the Herman Hellman Building) at 4th and Spring date from 1902. Other buildings of importance are **Barclay's Bank** at #639, built in 1919 as the **Los Angeles Stock Exchange.** The **Pacific Stock Exchange building** at #618 was built in 1929.

Of the three hotels in the area, one, the **Alexandria** at 210 W. 5th, continues to offer first-class accommodations to the visitor. Its restored Palm Court has been a gathering place since 1906. For further information, consult the listing under Lodging and Dining.

Eastern Los Angeles County

Located east of the city limits are some of the oldest and most prosperous communities in the Los Angeles area. The settlement at San Gabriel around the mission predates El Pueblo de Los Angeles by ten years. Scattered throughout the San Gabriel valley are other early adobe structures, the remnants of ranching days. The towns of Pasadena, South Pasadena, San Marino, and Pomona are much newer communities and were founded as agricultural and resort centers in the 19th century. These are towns rich in historical and cultural landmarks of high-Victorian and early 20th-century affluence. Many of the homes are splendid Spanish Colonial Revival or Craftsman mansions; the public buildings are sometimes Beaux Art palaces of classical good taste. Pomona, way to the east on the San Bernardino county line, has

slipped somewhat in cultural status, but the Pasadena area remains extremely well preserved.

Arcadia

LOS ANGELES STATE AND COUNTY ARBORETUM, 301 N. Baldwin Ave. Located on these wondrous 127-acre grounds, once part of the Rancho Santa Anita of Elias Jackson "Lucky" Baldwin, is the **Queen Anne Cottage and Coach Barn,** the **Hugo Reid Adobe,** and the **Santa Anita Depot.** Just across the way is the Santa Anita thoroughbred race track. If one were to choose any location outside of the city to visit, this is certainly one of the most attractive and varied in its features. The expense is probably one-tenth that of less interesting commercial attractions.

Queen Anne Cottage, Arcadia

Western historian Hubert Bancroft, who wasn't easily impressed by the estates of the rich, was carried away in 1892 when visiting Rancho Santa Anita: "The scene is one of fairy-like loveliness; not only the little bijou residence and its surrounds, but the entire estate, with its groves and vineyards, its golden fruit and waving harvests, its shaded drives and vistas of mountain peak and valley, carrying the beholder into an ideal region, calm and peaceful as the fabled realm of Rasselas, where soft vernal airs induce forgetfulness of the din and turmoil, the crowded streets and selfish intensity, of city life."

Baldwin chose to live in the **Hugo Reid Adobe,** which may date from the 1840s; it has been restored in recent years and is named for its first occupant. Across from this building, on the other side of a small lake, is a guesthouse designed by the architect A. A. Bennett. This is the **Queen Anne Cottage** (1885), so-called because of its high-Victorian profile. It is actually a Stick Style building with Eastlake detailing.

Bennet also designed a matching **coach barn.** The character of these buildings is highly fanciful. The cottage features many imaginative details such as lacey screened panels across the wrap-around veranda and a picturesque tower crowned by a belvedere. The building has been termed, in fact, "an overscaled gazebo" as it is an ideal place from which to view the spectacular surrounding gardens. The interior of the cottage is marked by similarly imaginative touches — stained glass windows, plaster medalions, alcove moldings, and niches; black walnut interior doors and marble mantels; encaustic tiles in the entry. The building was restored in the 1950s to its 1885-1909 condition. It is furnished with appropriate period antiques.

The gardens will never be as spectacular as they must have been when Bancroft visited them, but they remain very pleasurable. The lake is much as it was originally landscaped: a whimsical wood boathouse has been built. Among the impressive specimen trees are the tallest grove of Mexican fan palms in the continental United States, a 160-foot blue gum eucalyptus, an English oak planted in 1876, and venerable black walnuts, gingkoes, cypress, elms, and persimmons.

A recent addition to the grounds is the **Santa Anita Depot,** the 1889 Santa Fe Railroad station. It has been restored and fitted out appropriately. NR.

The grounds and buildings are open daily 9-4:30. $1 adults, 50¢ juniors 5-17, free for children under 5. Free admission third Tu of each month. Tram tours, $1. (213) 446-8251.

Glendora

GLENDORA BOUGAINVILLEA, 400 block of E. Bennett Ave. and 300 block of N. Minnesota Ave., late 1800s. After seeing the former Baldwin Ranch at Santa Anita, the largest growth of bougainvillea in the continental United States may not seem very impressive. But it most certainly is. The flowering plants cover the lower part of 25 90-foot palm trees which spread for 600 feet along Bennett Ave. and 600 feet along Minnesota. The magenta to purple-colored blooms can be seen throughout the year with the heaviest blooms in December, May, June, and July.

Bougainvillea, discovered in South America by Louis Antoine de Bougainville in the mid-18th-century, was brought to California and Florida in the 1870s. NR.

Pasadena and South Pasadena

W. T. BOLTON HOUSE, 370 W. Del Mar Blvd., 1906. This is the second house that the famed architectural firm of Greene and Greene built for Dr. Bolton, and, unlike the first, it has survived intact. Now in the process of being carefully restored, the Del Mar house displays some of the essential elements of the Greene brothers' style. The building is sheathed in wood shingles, and the eaves of the gently sloping roof generously overhang the walls; the rafters are exposed beneath the eaves. Window sills and lintels project and beams and joists extend beyond the corners of the house. By no means as ambitious or expensive a project as the Gamble House (see la-

ter listing), the Bolton House nevertheless follows in design the basic Craftsman aesthetic—form follows function—preached most vehemently by the Greenes. The two-story curved stairwell bay was added in 1929 by Garrett Van Pelt and is in keeping with the rest of the structure. Last used for storage by Ambassador College, the Bolton House is once again back in private hands. NR.

CIVIC CENTER DISTRICT, roughly bounded by Walnut and Green Sts., Raymond and Euclid Aves., 1910-32. The most important buildings in this gracious and inspiring public area date from after 1922. This is when a city planning commission decided that Pasadena deserved a new public library, city hall, and civic auditorium and that these buildings should be so disposed as to create an ideal City Beautiful type of arrangment. The architects—Myron Hunt and H. C. Chambers for the **Public library,** John Kaewell and Arthur Brown for the **City Hall,** and Edwin Bergstrom, Cyril Bennett, and Fitch Haskell for the **Civic Auditorium**—succeeded brilliantly in designing imposing but inviting Mediterranean Renaissance

Civic Auditorium

City Hall, Pasadena

buildings. The library (1925) is situated at the end of Garfield Ave. on Walnut St. City Hall (1925-26), with an open courtyard and impressive dome, fronts on a large open plaza at the end of Holly St. on Gar- field Ave. The Civic Auditorium (1931-32) lies one block beyond the opposite end of Garfield from the library. As one architec- tural historian has written, "Unlike other areas in the city, truly a place for people—

to walk, to picnic and sunbathe, and to sit with friends among the trees and enjoy the open vistas." NR.

GAMBLE HOUSE (Greene and Greene Library), 4 Westmoreland Pl., 1908. The most famous of Henry and Charles Greene's buildings serves most appropriately as a library and research center devoted to their work. The three-story shingled building is many layered with eaves, beams, and rafters projecting in almost every direction. The interior spaces were superbly crafted, principally in wood —teak, redwood, mahogany, maple, and cedar. Everything that went into the house, including furniture, lighting fixtures, and hardware, was designed by the Greenes. It is now jointly maintained by the University of Southern California and the city of Pasadena. Open for tours Tu and Th 10-3, and the last Sa and Su of each month 12-3. $3 adults, free for high school students and children. (213) 793-3334.

This neighborhod should be designated a national historic district of houses designed by Greene and Greene and by such contemporaries as Myron Hunt or Frank Lloyd Wright (see next listing). There is an

Gamble House, rear view, Pasadena

aesthetic unity about the neighborhood which is rarely discovered today in most urban areas. Next door to the Gamble House at 2 Westmoreland Pl. is the **Cole House,** a Greene and Greene building now used as a parish house for the New Neighborhood Church. Along **Arroyo Terrace,** into which Westmoreland runs, are only Greene and Greene Craftsman bungalows —six houses in all, which were built between 1901 and 1907. Along **North Grand St.** are nine other landmark houses, including Myron Hunt's own house, at #200, and the largest of the Greene and Greene commissions, the **Duncan-Irwine House** at #240. All these homes are privately owned.

MILLARD HOUSE (La Miniatura), 645 Prospect Crescent, 1923. Frank Lloyd Wright's only Pasadena house, set in a ravine, is not easy to see, but a view from Rosemont Ave. is possible. A two-story steel-frame house built up of concrete blocks, it combines in style both Prairie School and later Wrightian elements. NR.

HOTEL GREEN and CASTLE GREEN APARTMENTS, 50 E. Green, 1898, 1903. The apartments are all that remain of this once-great Pasadena resort hotel. This is just the kind of elegant facility which so appealed to wealthy visitors in the 1890s, many of whom decided to stay in the area. The Moorish and Spanish Colonial Revival building has been renovated for senior citizen housing.

PASADENA HISTORICAL SOCIETY MUSEUM (Fenjes Mansion), 470 W. Walnut St., 1905. This house originally belonged to the Curtin-Paloheimo family and later became the residence of the Finnish Consul in the Los Angeles area. A curious combination of Finnish folk art artifacts and objects from early Pasadena history are exhibited on the property. The museum sits on four handsomely landscaped acres. Located on the grounds is **Sauna House,** a replica of a 16th-century Finnish farmhouse. Open Tu, Th, and last Su of each month 1-4. $1 adults, 50¢ children. (213) 577-1660.

PASADENA PLAYHOUSE, 39 S. El Mo-

lino Ave., 1925. At the height of the "little theater" movement of the 1920s and '30s, the Pasadena Community Playhouse was one of the most vital centers of drama in the United States. The famous theater and school is now boarded up, but there is hope that it will find a new patron and life. The building is one of the most charming Spanish Colonial Revival structures in the area. It was designed by Los Angeles architect Elmer Grey and includes a 700-seat main auditorium and three 50-seat theaters. NR. It is now owned by the city of Pasadena.

HUNTINGTON-SHERATON, 1401 S. Oak Knoll, 1906, 1913. Built as the Wentworth, this is the last of Pasadena's still-operating great resort hotels. Charles Whittlesey was responsible for the original design and Myron Hunt and Elmer Grey for the additions. For further information regarding accommodations, consult the listing under Lodging and Dining.

VISTA DEL ARROYO HOTEL (1920-21, 1930-31) AND BUNGALOWS (1920-38), 125 S. Grand Ave. This towering landmark on the Pasadena scene last served as a hotel in the late 1930s. During World War II it was an Army hospital, and now it is scheduled to become the new home of the U.S. Court of Appeals. Along with the Huntington-Sheraton and the Green, it was one of the major Pasadena winter resort spas. The north wing was built in 1920-21, and the main building with its impressive tower ten years later. The individual bungalows, joined by landscaped walkways, were private properties used primarily during the winter season by wealthy families from the Midwest and East. The future of these small buildings is uncertain, and the condition of the once beautifully kept grounds is deplorable. The great beige stucco and red tile roofed building, however, is impossible to overlook from either an artistic or purely visual standpoint. NR.

WRIGLEY ESTATE (Tournament House), 391 S. Orange Grove Blvd., 1911. This vast Spanish Colonial-Mission style mansion now serves as the headquarters of the

Vista del Arroyo Hotel and Bungalows, Pasadena

Tournament of Roses Association. It was originally the home of the Wrigley family of Chicago. The building is particularly noted for its lavish style, symbolic of the manner in which Pasadena's millionaire families once lived. The house is open for tours Feb-Sept, W 2-4. Free. The garden is open daily. (213) 449-4100.

SOUTH PASADENA HISTORIC HOUSES: **Wynate**, 851 Lyndon St., 1887; **Garfield House**, 1001 Buena Vista St., 1904; **Howard Longley House**, 1005 Buena Vista St., 1897; and **Miltimore House**, 1301 S. Chelten Way, 1911. In the days when such things were important, South Pasadena was *dry,* a center of Anti-Saloon League principles. Residents have recently had a bigger battle on their hands—fighting off the designs of the state highway department for a Long Beach freeway that would mean the destruction of at least the Buena Vista St. houses. Both the Garfield and Longley Houses are Greene and Greene designs, the former built for the widow of President James Garfield, who lived here between 1904-18. The Miltimore House is a creation of Irving Gill and displays his clean Mission-derived modern design. Wynate is one of the rare late-Victorian

houses to have survived the march of progress in the Pasadena area. Its second and third floors are completely covered with fishscale shingles. Built as the home of South Pasadena's first mayor, it was a frequent stopping-off place for naturalist John Muir. A lemon eucalyptus tree he planted on the grounds is still standing. All of the buildings are NR and private, but may be viewed from the public way.

Pomona

PALOMARES ADOBE, 491 E. Arrow Hwy., 1854, 1939. This 13-room building, much larger than it looks at first, is most famous as a former San Bernardino stagecoach stop. It was built for Don Ygnacio Palomares on land that was part of the Rancho San Jose in the rich eastern San Gabriel valley. The house is furnished with period antiques and features a fine collection of Indian artifacts, including baskets. Open Tu-S 2-5. $1 adults, 50¢ juniors 12-21, free for children under 12. (714) 620-2300.

PHILLIPS MANSION, 2640 W. Pomona Blvd., 1875. This monumental Second Empire mansard roof brick house was built for Louis Phillips, a pioneer developer of Pomona. It must have been a very stylish residence in the days when Pomona, named for the Roman goddess of fruit, was an important center of citrus production. The Pomona Valley Historical Society has wisely preserved the mansion from destruction. It is open for tours on the first Su of each month from 2-5. NR. (714) 622-2043.

LA CASA PRIMERA DE RANCHO SAN JOSE, 1569 N. Park Ave., 1837. As its name says, this sod and adobe building was the first residence raised on the vast territory of the Rancho San Jose. It was built for Don Ygancio Palomares who later resided in the Adobe de Palomares (see previous listing). It is maintained by the Pomona Valley Historical Society and is open every Su 2-5. NR. (714) 622-7715.

San Gabriel

MISSION SAN GABRIEL ARCANGEL, Junipero St. and W. Mission Dr., 18th and 19th centuries. The first religious settlement in the Los Angeles area and the fourth mission to be established in the Franciscan chain, the San Gabriel building is unlike any other of its sister churches. The main facade is a side wall, and there are Moorish elements present in the buttresses and windows. The adobe building resembles a fort, and parts have been rebuilt after suffering earthquakes and neglect. The present building dates roughly from the late 1700s. San Gabriel was once a rich mission with vast acreage in the San Gabriel valley. A visitor in 1826 described the scene: "They have large vineyards, apple and peach orchards, and some orange and some fig trees. They manufacture blankets and sundry other articles; they distill whiskey and grind their own grain, having a water mill of a tolerable quality;

they have upwards of 1,000 persons employed, men, women, and children, Inds. of different nations." (See also next listing.) NR. Open daily 9:30-4. $1 adults, 50¢ children, no charge for students. (213) 282-5191.

San Marino

EL MOLINO VIEJO, 1120 Old Mill Rd., c. 1816. The mill is maintained by the California Historical Society as an historical museum. It was once part of the San Gabriel Mission property and served at one time as a flour mill and at another as a lumber mill. It is a very picturesque building and was restored in 1928 as a house. NR. Open Tu-Su 1-4. Free. (213) 449-5450.

HUNTINGTON GALLERY (1910) AND LIBRARY (1925), 1151 Oxford Rd. The Henry E. Huntington estate of 207 acres was formed in the early 1900s after Huntington gave up control of the Southern Pacific railroad and devoted his time to real estate, electric power development, and art collecting. His neo-classical residence, designed by Myron Hunt and Elmer Grey, is now the gallery which houses such masterpieces as Gainsborough's *Blue Boy* and Lawrence's *Pinkie*. Hunt and H. C. Chambers were the architects of the later library building, which is home for one of the greatest English and American book and manuscript collections in the world. The gardens, begun in 1904 and including 17th-century Italian sculpture and a Shakespearean garden, are justly famous. There is also a remarkable desert garden. The burial place of the railroad tycoon is a family mausoleum on the grounds which was designed by John Russell Pope. Open Tu-Su 1-4:30. Reservations are required for Su visits. Free. (213) 681-6601 (from Los Angeles), (213) 793-6141 (from Pasadena-San Marino).

Glendale

Beginning in the 1880s, the farming town of Glendale began to spread across the former Rancho San Rafael, the first land grant to have been made by the Spanish authorities in 1784 to the Verdugo family. The Southern Pacific Railroad brought the area within convenient commuting distance of Los Angeles, and, when the Pacific Electric Railroad was extended to Glendale, city and suburb became almost indistinguishable.

Glendale is now perhaps best known as a center of aircraft production and electronic equipment manufacture. Its most historic property—although not cited officially as such—is Forest Lawn Memorial Park, if only because it contains within its sculptured acres so many figures from the past, including Clark Gable and Carole Lombard, Aimee Semple McPherson, and Theodore Dreiser.

CASA ADOBE DE SAN RAFAEL, 1330 Dorothy Dr., 1865-71. The simple hacienda-type adobe home was erected by the one-time sheriff of Los Angeles County, Tomas Sanchez, whose wife, Maria Sepulveda, inherited part of the vast Rancho San Rafael—the original 36,000-acre land grant made in 1784 by King Charles II of Spain. Married at the age of thirteen, Maria Sepulveda bore 21 children in this house, and today cooking utensils and other relics from her day are preserved within. The modest dwelling stands in a two-acre city park planted with orange, fig, lemon, and avocado trees. The house itself is nestled in a grove of eucalyptus, and a view from the windows of the adobe offers a commanding panorama of the Verdugo hills in the background. Operated by the Glendale Parks and Recreation Division, the house and gardens are open to the public W and Su 1-4 during the summer. Free. (213) 956-2000.

THE JAMES DANIEL DERBY HOUSE, 2535 Chevy Chase Dr., 1926. Designed by Frank Lloyd Wright's son, Lloyd Wright, the house is one of six which employs a system called knit-block construction. Concrete blocks were cast in a mold of an abstract design from nature. The textured blocks which resulted were then knitted together with steel rods. The elder Wright has acknowledged the fact that the idea for the reinforced block construction originated with his son, though both architects eventually practiced the design for nearly a decade. Few would argue that both the material and the system of construction are suitable for the semi-arid climate found in southern California, and the ornamentation created by the textured blocks, while undoubtedly inspired by pre-Columbian or Mayan architecture, is certainly unique enough to appear right at home with the numerous examples of architectural eclecticism scattered throughout the Los Angeles area. NR. The road to the house has recently been widened, thus afffording an excellent view of this private residence.

Hollywood

Hollywood. The starry-eyed land of make-believe where ambitious bit-actors once dreamed of signing their names in the wet pavement of Sid Grauman's Chinese Theater. While Hollywood's history is undeniably connected with the westward migration of the movies, there was a time, long after the area had been peopled by the Cahuenga Indians, and later the Mexicans, that teetotaling Methodists—who farmed the land and liked it just the way it was—recoiled at the idea of being invaded by the Sodom and Gomorrah of Eastern showpeople. But once the Nestor Film Company brought the movie business to the "drowsy little resort village" in 1911, *the future was set. The town's name itself was a portent of the Dream Factory to come. The wife of the area's largest 19th-century real estate speculator had appropriated it from an Eastern country estate becaue she liked its sound! If limited to movieland itself, a trip to Hollywood invariably disappoints. Try to take in some of the historic sights that are older than the Chinese Theater's dried cement.*

CAMPO DE CAHUENGA, 3919 Lankershim Blvd., North Hollywood. A 1923 replica of a six-room adobe house now occupies the site where Mexican General Andres Pico signed the treaty which surrendered his forces to Lt. Col. John C. Fremont on Jan. 13, 1847. The treaty effectively ended California's participation in the war between the United States and its neighbor to the south. In the main room are documents related to the historic signing, as well as oil portraits of the opposing commanding officers. M-F 8-3. Free. (213) 760-9239.

CROSSROADS OF THE WORLD, 6671 Sunset Blvd., 1936. Although this unique shopping mall is less than 50 years old, it remains an important design statement of Hollywood in the '30s. Designed by the noted southern California architect, Robert V. Derrah, the complex features a series of streetscapes from around the world, interspersed with shops and united by carefully planned walkways and landscape elements. A classic example of 1930s Streamline Moderne, its primary architectural feature is a Moderne ship with a vertical pier supporting a revolving globe. The ship, exhibiting smooth, curved corners, railings, and porthole windows, gives the illusion that a vessel has indeed lost its way in the Hollywood Hills and come to moor on Sunset Blvd. Though the shops possess an international flavor, the overall effect is pure Hollywood fantasia. The City of Los Angeles has gone so far as to proclaim Crossroads of the World as a historic-cultural monument. NR. (213) 463-5611.

MANN'S CHINESE THEATER (formerly Grauman's Chinese Theater), 6925 Hollywood Blvd., 1927. The gala premiere of Cecil B. DeMille's *King of Kings* on May 18, 1927, was also the opening night for Sid Grauman's famed Chinese Theater. While the Oriental architecture and lavish décor created by architects Meyer and Holler are impressive in their own right, the exotic styling and dramatic scale are but a fraction of its appeal. Tradition relates how Norma Talmadge accidently stepped in the wet cement on the theater's opening night, and since then more than 160 movie stars have filled the courtyard with their footprints, handprints, signatures, and even an occasional paw print. A popular tourist attraction and arguably the

most famous landmark in Hollywood, the theater remains one of the leading movie houses in the city and is still the location of major film premieres. (213) 464-8111. ♔

Just down the boulevard at No. 6708 is the **Egyptian Theater,** another of Sid Grauman's architectural fantasies. A reproduction of the Temple of Thebes in plaster, the theater has witnessed a new multi-theater addition, but old-time Hollywood aficionados may still recall the gilded days when usherettes were dressed as Cleopatra. (213) 467-6167.

PANTAGES THEATER, 6233 Hollywood Blvd., 1929. The zigzag grillwork and the stately Egyptian figures which line the roof are the design products of B. Marcus Priteen. The elaborate exterior is nicely complemented by the fabulous Art Deco interior decoration by Anthony Heinsbergen. For many years the Pantages spotlighted the Academy Awards presentation, but recently Oscar has given way to stage plays and musicals. (213) 469-7161.

SCHINDLER HOUSE, 833 N. Kings Rd., 1921. During the '20s the influential architect Rudolph Schindler designed this double residence for himself and his engineer friend Clyde B. Chase. Schindler's construction techniques on this house were novel for the day and featured modular concrete wall slabs which were poured, then tilted into their vertical position. These massive, solid walls are relieved by narrow slits of glass between. The architect also experimented with floor-to-ceiling glass and numerous other spatial techniques including open-air sleeping lofts. The house is maintained by the Friends of the Schindler House and is accessible once one manuevers around the dense front foliage. NR.

WRIGHT HOUSES: The master builder Frank Lloyd Wright and his son Lloyd were together responsible for numerous houses in the Los Angeles area and throughout southern California. Although noted for his midwestern Prairie designs, the elder Wright experimented heavily with the knit-block construction developed by his son and perfected in these unique West

Coast contributions to modern architecture. When examined as a group, these massive block affairs can become tedious, but the Mayan and vaguely oriental motifs which adorn their surfaces offer a refreshing contrast to the Spanish-influenced architecture found throughout southern California. Among the Wright houses not to be missed by the traveler are the following:

Hollyhock House, 1916-22, located in a thick grove of olive trees known today as **Barnsdall Park,** was the first house in Los Angeles designed by Frank Lloyd Wright. The residence was part of a projected 36-acre cultural complex commissioned by Mrs. Aline Barnsdall, an oil heiress. Only this building—which appears to have been inspired by a Mayan temple—and a second structure, Residence A, survive today. The latter building is much closer to the Prairie Style houses for which Wright is noted. The deed which handed the houses and surrounding acreage over to the city in 1927 stipulated that the park and art center remain intact. The City of Los Angeles Department of Cultural Affairs today maintains the park as a shady oasis from the hot sun of the flatlands, and its cultural importance increased in 1971 with the completion of the Los Angeles Municipal Art Gallery on the grounds. NR. The Gallery is open Tu-Su 12:30-5, while the park is open daily 9 am-10 pm with no admission fee. In addition, an interesting guided tour of the Hollyhock House is offered Tu and Th, on the hour, from 10-1; and the first Sa of each month, on the hour, 12-3. (213) 662-7272.

Ennis House, 2607 Glendower Ave., 1924, located at the crest of one of the famed Hollywood hills, this massive Mayan-style house is the most monumental of Frank Lloyd Wright's experiments with knit-block construction. Variously labelled as a mausoleum, a Mayan temple, and a palace, it has been carefully restored by the owners. NR. Privately owned, but visible from the public way.

Samuel Freeman House, 1962 Glencoe Way, 1922. Tucked in the hills overlooking the Hollywood Bowl, the Freeman House is another of Frank Lloyd Wright's knit-block structures exhibiting Mayan influences. The lighting effects in this two-story hillside house are particularly noteworthy and are achieved through clerestories over the living room, large corner windows, French doors, and holes pierced in some of the concrete blocks. NR. Privately owned, but visible from the public way.

John Sowden House, 5121 Franklin Ave., 1926. Lloyd Wright designed this unusual house which is raised above the street and reached via a scissor staircase. The dark cavernous entrance is topped by a star-shaped opening in the cast concrete blocks, with plain stucco walls on both sides. NR. Privately owned, but visible from the public way.

Storer House, 8161 Hollywood Blvd., 1923. Another Frank Lloyd Wright knit-block design with the characteristic Mayan motifs, Storer House is situated on a hillside and features five separate floor levels. A two-story living room opens out onto the front and rear terraces, while on the street facade an interesting effect is created by a series of narrow windows divided by vertical bands of textile blocks. NR. Privately owned, but visible from the public way.

Sowden House

Long Beach and Wilmington

Long Beach is built along a wide ocean beach, with picturesque views of the Palos Verdes Hills and Catalina Island among its natural features. In its early days it was chiefly residential and a favored year-round pleasure and health resort. Once a trading point for Indian tribes, Long Beach was settled in 1840 and subdivided as Willmore City in 1881, when it was perhaps best known for its inadequate horse-car line, the "Get Off and Push Railroad." The community was re-named Long Beach when real-estate speculator W. E. Willmore's development went bankrupt in 1888. With the discovery of oil in 1921 the city rapidly became industrialized, although steps were taken to preserve its residential character. In 1933 much of Long Beach's past was tragically lost in a major earthquake.

Wilmington, while actually a part of Los Angeles, is close enough to Long Beach in terms of distance and historical background to warrant equal billing with its larger neighbor. First named New San Pedro, the community was founded by Phineas Banning, whose residence and the adjoining park named in his honor provide the area with its primary points of interest. Banning was also instrumental in developing Wilmington's harbor. Like other communities surrounding Los Angeles, the town was connected to the big city, first by the rail lines in 1869, and ultimately by the encroachment of LA's urban sprawl.

BANNING HOME, 401 E. M St., Wilmington, 1864. This 24-room Greek Revival home was built in 1864 for General Phineas Banning, Wilmington's founder and an important figure in the 19th-century development of southern California's transportation systems. The clapboard exterior is constructed of lumber from the Mendocino coast, with Belgian marble and European colored glass adding a touch of international luxury. The house is decorated with many period furnishings and mementos from Banning's business interests, which included stage lines, a fleet of ships, and the first railroad in southern California. Most of the rooms have high ceilings and fireplaces. The Banning family lived here until his death in 1885. The property was left to the city in 1927.

The present 20-acre **Banning Park,** the featured attraction in Wilmington, is but a fraction of the once spacious grounds which surrounded the house in the late 1800s, when a long row of eucalyptus formed a path to the house and gardens of flowers and shrubs were prominent. NR. Access to the house is by tour only: W, Sa, and Su at 12, 1, 2, 3, and 4. Free. (213) 548-7777.

DRUM BARRACKS, 1053-55 Cary Ave., Wilmington, 1862. Established as the U.S. Military Headquarters for Southern California, Arizona, and New Mexico, the Drum Barracks served as a supply house and military garrison for some 7,000 Union Army soldiers in a state which was largely sympathetic to the Confederate cause. The site was also the terminus for camel pack trains operated by the Army until 1863. Today the officer's quarters, a beautifully restored, two-story building with two smaller wings, remains the only major Civil War landmark in California. Wilmington's most prominent citizen, General Phineas Banning, served at the barracks during the 1860s. NR. Call for schedule. $1 adults, 50¢ students, 25¢ children. (213) 518-1955. ♦♦

RANCHO LOS CERRITOS, 4600 Virginia Rd., Long Beach, 1844. Generally recognized as one of the most impressive of the surviving adobe ranch houses in the southern part of the state, Los Cerritos ("Little Hills") was built by Don Juan Temple on part of the 1784 Nieto land grant.

Hailing from Massachusetts, Temple was one of a group of Yankees whose decision to brave the sparse and unsettled territory of the West proved to be a financial gold mine. Temple prospered as a pioneer merchant, property owner, and rancher, and his rancho was the sight of festive bullfights and rodeos before prolonged droughts during the 1860s brought an end to those romantic days.

The house was subsequently bought and enlarged by the Bixby family, and restored furnishings on the premises today date from this period. Exhibition areas include the children's room (complete with dolls and toys), the weaving room, and the foreman's bedroom. The exhibit wing features materials related to the various aspects of rancho life, and a research library. The exterior, a combination of Monterey styling (with a two-story veranda) and a traditional Mexican hacienda plan enclosing a central courtyard, has likewise been faithfully restored down to its brick foundations and thick adobe walls. NR, NHL. Open W-Su 1-5. Free. (213) 424-9423. ♦♦

PACIFIC COAST CLUB, 850 E. Ocean Blvd., Long Beach, 1925. When the City of Long Beach decided it needed a social-athletic club during the early 1920s, the prominent architectural firm of Curtlett and Beelman was chosen because its plan expressed the philosophy of the founding club members. The Norman style chosen by the architects was designed to capture the spirit of a fortress, a castle which brought with it an "elegant leisure which fostered the arts, patronized the letters, and amused itself with diversions." Indeed, the fourteen stories of this massive structure look particularly fortress-like when viewed from the ocean, and the building has over the years become a visual landmark in Long Beach. NR. Private club, visible from the street.

QUEEN MARY, Pier J, Long Beach, 1934. If Arizona can have London Bridge, Long beach might as well have the glory of the British Cunard Line which carried the famous and infamous across the North

Atlantic from 1934 until retirement from service in 1964. The city purchased the liner—the epitome of sleek Art Deco luxury—as a combination convention center, restaurant, and hotel. There are five dining facilities and 400 rooms to choose from. One needn't be a guest or diner, however, to tour the magnificent ship. A three-hour tour of the *Queen Mary* includes both passenger and operational areas as well as the Jacques Cousteau "Living Sea Marine Museum," other exhibits, and "Sea Probe" which introduces one to the excitement of exploring the world beneath the waves. Open daily 10-5. $6.75 adults, $4 children 5-11. Group rates. (213) 435-4733. 🏃

RANCHO LOS ALAMITOS, 6400 Bixby Hill Rd., Long Beach, 1806. Like the Rancho Los Cerritos, this single-floor adobe structure was built on land which was part of the original 1784 Nieto land grant. In 1881 the property fell under the ownership of the Bixby family, who maintained a portion of the property until it was given to the City of Long Beach in 1968. Although the house has been enlarged several times since its construction, the antique furnishings of the interior date from the late 19th century, quietly and faithfully recalling the past years of glory. The prop-

erty also includes a five-acre garden, a foreman's house, blacksmith's shop, and dairy and horse barns. The raising of horses, sheep, and cattle was one of the principal businesses on the 29,000-acre spread. Open W-Su 1-5. Free. 🏃 (213) 431-2511.

S.S. CATALINA (Great White Steamer), Berth 96, Long Beach Harbor, 1924. In 1923, William Wrigley held a contest to design and build a passenger vessel to service the ever-increasing tourist trade to the popular resort island. The result was this magnificent ship, billed at the time as the "Million Dollar Ferryship to Fairyland." Painted white from her waterline to the bridge, the vessel was luxuriously outfitted with three passenger decks, boasting all the comforts and conveniences, including a ballroom with live orchestra and a salon deck with leather upholstered chairs. Right through the Depression years weary city folk would make their way by trolley to the boat terminal at Wilmington, where they eagerly boarded the *Catalina* or one of her two sister ships, each making two daily trips during the peak summer months. After 52 years of service, this grand old lady has come to rest in Los Angeles Harbor, where she can be viewed at Berth 96.

S. S. Catalina

The gradual lengthening of Wilshire Boulevard from downtown Los Angeles to the Pacific Ocean is graphic evidence of the city's linear sprawl over the decades. Named after H. Gaylord Wilshire, a real estate entrepreneur from Ohio, the boulevard traverses many diverse neighborhoods, from low-income immigrant settlements to the ostentatious "Miracle Mile" shopping district. For the purposes of this guide, however, mid-Wilshire is defined as the area roughly bounded by Robertson St. on the west, Melrose St. on the north, and Freeways 10 and 11 along the southeast.

Aside from a short-lived period of notoriety as an oil-producing area around the turn of the century, the mid-Wilshire area receives its character largely from its association with the famous thoroughfare. Most of Wilshire's historic sites are limited to several fine examples of Art Déco commercial architecture—high rises and department stores dating from the '20s and '30s. Some eclectic examples of southern California bungalows are located to the north of Wilshire Blvd. and west of Western Ave. While these date to the first decades of this century, earlier examples of the Victorian Queen Anne style have faithfully been preserved further east off the boulevard in the MacArthur Park vicinity. Both these areas offer a pleasant retreat from commercial distraction.

BULLOCK'S WILSHIRE BUILDING, 3050 Wilshire Blvd., 1928. At the time of its construction, local newspapers referred to this majestic Art Déco masterpiece as a "temple of merchandizing." The first major "suburban" department store to move outside the downtown Los Angeles area, it proved to be a resounding success for entrepreneur John G. Bullock. Still one of the most elegant stores in the city, its six-story tower of buff terra-cotta and copper bands stands as perhaps the finest example of Art Déco architecture in the city.

Architects John and Donald Parkinson spared no expense in commissioning the finest decorators to adorn the interior. The unique organization of the store, one of the first merchandizing establishments to create separate stores within each department, is highlighted by display cases made of English laurel and rosewood, crystal chandeliers, and walls of rose marble. Original art works located throughout the store include an abstract wood mural by G. Stojana in the Sportswear Shop, and a painted glass ceiling by Herman Sachs in the fifth-floor Tearoom, where luncheon fashion shows are still offered the genteel shoppers. Tearoom open for lunch only, M-Sa. (213) 382-6161.

FREDERICK MOOERS HOUSE, 818 S. Bonnie Brae St., 1894. During the 1890s Los Angeles experienced a building and population boom. Some of the city's finest Victorian dwellings provide evidence of this expansion, and line the south end of this residential street from the 800 through the 1000 blocks. The Mooers House, a Queen Anne gem, was the one-time residence of Frederick Mitchell Mooers, the discoverer of the famous 19th-century Yellow Aster Gold Mine. Today this regal example of domestic architecture at its most ornate—complete with expansive veranda and Victorian carpentry—is one of the most widely photographed houses in the city. But don't allow your tour of this magnificent turn-of-the-century district to end here.

Continue on down Bonnie Brae until number 824, a home which cannot be overlooked because of its fanciful tower. Other imaginative examples of the Victorian craftsman's passion for decorative detail are to be seen at numbers 1026 through 1053. The Mooers House is on the National Register, but, like all the houses along the street, it is private and visible only from the street.

PAN-PACIFIC AUDITORIUM, 7600 Beverly Blvd., 1935. Originally built for the National Housing Exposition to further the "New and Better Housing" movement in Los Angeles, this futuristic design hails from the drawing boards of two young area architects, Walter Wurdeman and Welton Becket. Constructed as a large exhibition space, the building is a classic example of Streamline Moderne architecture, a style which epitomized the popular notions of 20th-century modernism evidenced during the '30s.

The building, with its smooth rounded corners and curved projecting wings highlighted with metal ship railings, is a superb example of how the style borrowed its imagery from mechanical and industrial objects and the streamlined transportation of the day. The unique entrance design is perhaps the most exciting feature of the auditorium, consisting of four rounded pylons which slice through projecting overhangs and emerge as four monumental flag pole towers. As a professor of architecture at UCLA has noted, the sense of movement conveyed by this massive structure is undeniable: ". . . some of the power of the West Facade comes from the sense it conveys of some kind of great engine 'pulling' the rest of the building along." In recent years the building has become vacant, and a proposed park on the site may threaten this landmark with demolition. NR.

WILTERN-PELLISSIER BUILDING, 3780 Wilshire Blvd., 1931. With its blue-green terra-cotta tower glistening in the southern California sun, this superb Art Déco building rises deceptively high above Wilshire Blvd., aided visually by the slender vertical bands and recessed windows which were common characteristics of high rises in this design mode. In addition to the tower, the structure includes shop and office sections. The former Warner Bros. **Western Theater** (now the Wiltern), its foyer diagonal to the street, provides an exciting highlight. The only Art Déco styled movie palace designed by renowned theater architect, G. Albert Lansburgh, the lobby has fortunately retained most of its original fixtures and furnishings, including a foyer with numerous glass chandeliers, painted ceilings, and floral wrought-iron staircases. The theater's pipe organ is the largest theater organ still in use in the United States. NR.

WILTON HISTORIC DISTRICT, S. Wilton Pl., S. Wilton Dr., and Ridgewood Pl., 1907-25. Developed during the first decades of the 20th-century, this largely untouched residential area was planned exclusively for upper-middle-class, single-family dwellings. Largely comprised of two-story Craftsman bungalows and later Colonial Revival residences, about half of these structures date to just before the First World War. This concentrated period of building, coupled with the relative scarcity of alterations and intrusions, has resulted in an unusually homogeneous neighborhood. In addition, the unusual configuration of the streets has provided builders with interesting landscaping possibilities, outdoor effects such as pergolas, courtyards, terraces, and gardens which highlight the region's interesting vistas. The fact that Wilton Place is still a well-traveled north-south route has encouraged the continued viewing of these private residences by passers-by. NR.

Pacific Palisades

WILL ROGERS STATE HISTORIC PARK, 14253 Sunset Blvd., c. 1926. 187 acres of chaparral-covered hills form the backdrop for the home of the beloved cowboy-humorist Will Rogers. The popular performer and humanitarian who "never met a man he didn't like," resided here from 1924-35, and the interior features memorabilia from his active and multifaceted career. The main house is a basic frame structure with shingled roof, over-hanging eaves, and wide verandas, with the stable, corrals, and riding and roping areas located just to the north. An adjacent visitor center presents a short film on Rogers' life narrated by friends and family, and the nearby polo field, a remnant of Will's favorite pastime, is still the site of matches on Saturday afternoons in the summer. NR. Park: summer, daily 7-7; winter, daily 8-5. Museum: daily 10-5. $2 per car. (213) 454-8212. 🏃

Known locally simply as "the Valley," the San Fernando area is very much a part of the city, but is physically cut off from the main basin by the Santa Monica mountains. Its great period of development has occurred since World War II, although annexation by the city of every community but the village of San Fernando took place in the early 1900s. It is an enormous region, largely flat in topography and made up of small communities. Among the better known are Encino, Mission Hills, Sherman Oaks, Van Nuys, Canoga Park, and Woodland Hills. The Valley is not an historian's paradise or a culture maven's delight, but is rather a middle-class haven of ranch-style homes laid out on what was very productive farm land. Here and there are remnants of the past—adobes that served as pioneer homes in the 19th century.

Calabasas

LEONIS ADOBE, 23537 Calabasas Rd., c. 1844-46. The date given is for the early part of the house; it was extensively remodeled in 1870 by Miguel Leonis. The house has been restored to this later period with appropriate furnishings. Also included on the grounds are a barn, windmill, blacksmith shop, and other ranch buildings. The restoration work took place in 1966 and was expertly done. Leonis, a prominent valley rancher, was nicknamed the "King of Calabasas," and he fashioned himself a Monterey-style ranch house with a fancy second floor wraparound porch. NR. Open W, Sa-Su 1-4. Donations accepted. (213) 346-3683.

Encino

RANCHO EL ENCINO (Los Encinos State Historic Park), 16756 Moorpark St., 1849, 1872. There are four buildings in the park: Osa Adobe, the Garnier Residence, a food storage structure, and a sheepherder's hut. The earliest, the one-story adobe, has a covered porch on three sides and was built by Don Vincente de la

Osa. After Eugene Garnier bought the ranch in 1869, he built a two-story limestone house and added the outbuildings. A Basque settler, Garnier transformed El Encino into a vast sheep ranch. A lovely spring-fed lake is also on the five-acre grounds. NR. Tours W-Su 1-4. 50¢ adults, 25¢ juniors 6-17, free for children under 6. (213) 784-4849.

Mission Hills

MISSION SAN FERNANDO REY DE ESPANA, 15151 San Fernando Mission Blvd., 1810-22, 1974. Founded in 1797, the San Fernando mission was part and parcel of the vast Rancho Encino. Of the early buildings, only the priests' house (or the convento) has survived intact. In 1818 an earthquake destroyed the first church and most of the other buildings that made up the original quadrangle. The church was rebuilt, of course, but soon after the property of the Franciscan missions was expropriated by the Mexican government in the 1830s, the church fell into ruins. Its rebuilding did not occur again for almost 100 years, in 1935. By that time the traces of the original design were very dimly observable and were difficult to follow. Once again, in 1971, an earthquake caused so much damage that reconstruction was necessary. What was copied was the 1935 model. This strange history is well recorded in a small **museum** close to the convento and its garden. Open M-Sa 9-5, Su 10-5, last tour, 4:15. 75¢ adults, 25¢ for juniors 7-15, free for children under 7. (213) 361-0186.

ANDRES PICO ADOBE (Romulo Pico Adobe), 10940 Sepulveda Blvd., 19th century. The two-story house stands on land which was once part of the San Fernando mission, and the original one-story residence, to which a second floor was later added, may have been a mission building. Further changes were made in the 1930s by Dr. M.R. Harrington who also directed the reconstruction of the mission. The house suffered structural damage in the

1971 earthquake but did not have to be rebuilt. The building is now maintained in proper fashion by the San Fernando Valley Historical Society and serves as its headquarters. Indian artifacts, costumes, paintings, and various decorative objects of historical interest are exhibited. NR. Open W-Su 1-4. Free. (213) 365-7810. 🛉

San Fernando

LA CASA DE LOPEZ ADOBE, 1100 Pico St., 1882. The Hispanic-American mode of building in adobe is shown here to have persisted well into the last years of the 19th century. The walls of the Lopez adobe are two-feet thick and have survived earth tremors. The two-story wraparound porch is fashioned in the Monterey style which became very popular in the late 1800s. The railings, balustrade, and posts suggest strong Eastlake influence, a decorative approach as appropriate at the time for a Queen Anne house as for an adobe. Open W and Sa 11-3, Su 12-3. Free. (213) 365-9990.

Santa Catalina Island

The famed island resort is located a mere 30 miles southwest of the mainland and has been visited by hordes of Los Angeles County residents seeking a brief weekend vacation ever since the area was developed as a pleasure resort in the 1890s by William Banning, the son of Phineas Banning.

The island reached its peak as a tourist spot during the Depression years, when three ships bulging with passengers made two trips daily to the island (see listing for S.S. Catalina in Long Beach). William Wrigley owned the island for a time, even using the island's balmy climate as the spring training site for his Chicago Cubs. Fortunately, the island is still largely under private ownership, and except for the small town of Avalon, the island's coastline and interior are still green oases — excellent for hiking enthusiasts and everyone who loves the sand and sea.

Year-round boat service is provided to the island from the ports of Long Beach and San Pedro. The voyage takes less than two hours, and five trips are offered daily during the summer months. Reservations are advisable: from Los Angeles phone (213) 775-6111; from the Harbor area, (213) 832-4521; from Orange County (714) 527-7111. In addition, a fifteen-minute seaplane flight from Long Beach airport to Avalon is available by calling (213) 420-1883. Finally, Catalina Airlines flies helicopters regularly from San Pedro on the mainland. For reservations from Los Angeles call (213) 775-7107; from Orange County call (714) 827-7700.

ZANE GREY PUEBLO HOTEL, 199 Chimes Tower Rd., Avalon (Santa Catalina Island), 1926. Originally the home of noted Western author Zane Grey, the hotel is located high on a knoll overlooking Avalon Bay. It affords visitors the same quiet isolation sought by the famed author, yet is just three blocks from the beach and the shops of Main St. Fashioned after the Indian homes which appear so frequently in his novels, it was here that Grey spent his later years in relative seclusion, writing and fishing until his death in 1939. A bit of folklore attached to the building's construction recalls that goat's milk was added to the mortar for strength. In any case, the pueblo has weathered the test of time well, and today the modest furnishings are complemented by modern conveniences. (See Lodging and Dining for information regarding accommodations.)

South County

Whittier. Compton. Industry. As these unobtrusive town names imply, this area of the Los Angeles Basin, which includes southern sections of Los Angeles proper, is an amorphous section of industrial districts which interlock with each other in the confusing jigsaw puzzle which comprises Los Angeles. Certainly the area's history is largely locked into the land booms of this century, but, as in the rest of the state, there are still well-preserved remnants of the Spanish-settlement days. Several adobe ranch houses remain to remind the tourists and working-class residents of the area that these haciendas were once the only outposts of civilization amid the unspoiled expanses of the ranchos. The Somerville (Dunbar) Hotel, however, brings the history of the area back into the post-World War I period. As the first hotel in America built specifically for blacks, it attests to the great ethnic importance of South County, with the largest concentration of black residents in Los Angeles.

Compton

DOMINGUEZ RANCH ADOBE, 18127 S. Alameda St., 1830. Manuel Dominguez was a public official whose career spanned both the Mexican provincial and American colonization periods of California history. The adobe was built for his use on the family's Rancho San Pedro, the first Spanish royal land grant of 75,000 acres which had been made to his uncle, Juan Jose, in 1782. The building follows the traditional U-shape and has a tile gabled roof and a front center courtyard bordered by an arcade. Some Misson Revival remodeling work was undertaken in the early 1900s. The adobe was the center of some Mexican War activity and was briefly occupied by U.S. forces. The Claretian Order maintains the buildings as an historical museum on the grounds of the Dominguez Memorial Seminary. NR. Open Tu-W 1-4, and the 2nd and 3rd Su of each month, 1-4. Free. (213) 631-5981 or 636-6030.

Industry

JOHN A. ROWLAND HOUSE, 16021 E. Gale Ave., 1855. Rowland and his friend William Workman led the first wagon train of Yankees into the Los Angeles area

in 1841, settling on the enormous Rancho La Puente which they shared for a while. When finally divided, Workman constructed his **adobe** on what is today E. Don Julian Rd. (entrance on Proctor at El Encanto). Not far away Rowland built the first brick home in the San Gabriel Valley, and still one of the oldest fired-brick houses standing in southern California. Many of the rooms contain original furnishings, while the adobe cookhouse features cooking utensils dating from the turn of the century. Operated by the La Puente Valley Historical Society. NR. Oct-July and 1st Su of each month, 1-4. Free. (213) 336-7644.

La Mirada

McNALLY'S WINDERMERE RANCH HEADQUARTERS, San Cristobal and San Esteban Sts., 1890s. Andrew McNally (of Rand McNally Co.) formed the Windermere Ranch in 1890, using new methods of tenant farming and crop production for the first time in southern California. Relying heavily on Japanese immigrants to work the fields, McNally made his workers feel right at home by constructing Japanese quarters, planting many exotic species of trees, and turning loose hundreds of exotic birds on the grounds. The ranch also received notoriety for its luscious olive trees, many of which now adorn several of Los Angeles' well-known public places. Of the three remaining buildings dating from the period when the ranch was formed in the 1890s, two of these, the foreman's house and the McNally Mansion, remain in their original condition. They are part of a three-acre complex within Neff Park, all that remains of the once grand ranch land and one of the few historic sites to survive La Mirada's development boom. NR. 👬

Los Angeles

SOMERVILLE HOTEL (Dunbar Hotel), 4225 S. Central Ave., 1928. This four-story brick hotel with a Spanish Colonial flavor is not much of an architectural feast; its significance, however, stems from its historical ties to the black community in the county. Through the efforts of the leading black citizen, Dr. John Alexander Somerville, the structure was financed and constructed by blacks who found prejudice a major obstacle in their search for traveling accommodations. It was the site of the first NAACP convention in 1928, and during its heyday in the '30s almost every prominent black passing through Los Angeles stayed here—including many now famous black entertainers. A local community organization called the Museum in Black is making an effort to preserve this landmark as a cultural center. NR.

Whittier

PIO PICO CASA, 6003 Pioneer Blvd., Whittier, 1850. A young Mexican revolutionary during the state's Mexican period of the first half of the 19th century, Don Pio Pico was a key figure in the political turmoil of the day. After leading a revolt which vaulted him into the governor's chair for a short time, he was forced to flee, but returned to share in the prosperity of California's oil strikes. This two-story hacienda contains thirteen rooms, many of which feature two-foot thick adobe walls. The U-shaped plan of the mansion surrounds the obligatory well in the central courtyard, and today the house has been restored to its 1870s ambience by the state of California. NR. W-Su 1-4. 50¢ adults, 25¢ children. The surrounding Pio Pico State Historic Park is open W-Su 10-5. 695-1217. ♿

Ventura and Santa Barbara Counties

Ventura and Santa Barbara counties lie along the coast in an almost east-west direction, with the Sierra Madre and San Rafael mountains to the north. Despite enormous economic growth since World War II, the area remains one of the most scenically attractive and socially desirable in the United States. It is in the northern section of Santa Barbara County that the President of the United States has his ranch which he so prefers to the White House. Once you have visited the area, you will easily understand why those who could afford to do so have established roots here.

The history of the region begins with four missions—San Buenaventura in Ventura; Santa Barbara, located in that city; Santa Inez, near Solvang; and La Purisima Concepcion, in the Lompoc area—which were established in the late 18th and early 19th centuries by the Franciscans. Despite the fact that the power and affluence of the missions was short-lived, not lasting beyond the mid-19th century, they set a cultural style in art and architecture which is still celebrated today. This is most marked in the expensive environs of Santa Barbara and Montecito, but traces of the Mission style can also be seen in the highly developed sections of the Santa Clara Valley of Ventura County which adjoins the exploding metropolis of Los Angeles.

Lompoc

FABING-McKAY-SPANNE HOUSE, 207 N. L St., 1875. Old-time movie fans will best remember Lompoc as the setting for W. C. Fields's *The Bank Dick,* but the city and valley of this name have more to offer. The Fabing-McKay-Spanne House serves as the **Lompoc Valley Historical Society museum.** An old house by California standards, it displays artifacts and antique furnishings of the still-largely agricultural region. Open the fourth Sunday of each month. Donations accepted. (805) 736-5044.

Lompoc vicinity

LA PURISIMA MISSION STATE HISTORIC PARK, 4 miles E of Lompoc near intersection of CA 1 and 150, early 19th century, 1935-42. The first mission was established in the town of Lompoc in 1787 by Father Fermin de Lasuen but was de-

La Purisima Mission

stroyed by an earthquake and devastating rains in 1812. By 1818 the complex had been completely rebuilt on this new site in the valley. Like those of other Franciscan missions, the buildings began to fall apart after they were expropriated by the Mexican territorial government in 1834. Not until the state moved in during the 1930s was there a concerted attempt to draw the community back together again. Unlike those in many other missions, the buildings were not arranged in a quadrangle, but were lined up in single-row fashion along the valley floor. This scheme was followed in the state's rebuilding of the church, fathers' residence, shops, and soldiers' quarters. NR, NHL. Open Oct-May, daily 8-5; June-Sept, daily 9-6. 50¢ adults, 25¢ children 6-17 and senior citizens 62 and over. (805) 733-3713.

Newbury Park

EL GRANDE HOTEL (Stagecoach Inn Museum), 51 S. Ventu Park Rd. (P.O. Box 1692, Thousand Oaks, CA 91360), 1876. Completely reconstructed after a fire in 1970, the El Grande was originally built as an important link in a coastal stagecoach line. The Conejo Valley Historical Society maintains this building as a local history museum with displays on the Indian, Spanish-Mexican, and Anglo-American cultures from 1846-1930. Open W-F and Su 1-4. Free. Donations accepted. (805) 498-9441.

Port Hueneme

CIVIL ENGINEER CORPS-SEABEE MUSEUM, Naval Construction Battalion Center. The history of such military units as the Seabees is often overlooked; what these groups have accomplished may be more permanent in the long run than most military activities. Displayed here are weapons, uniforms, models of equipment, handmade native tools, unit plaques and flags, and artifacts from Antarctic and Alaskan missions. Open M-F 8-4:30, Sa 9-4:30, Su 12:30-4:30. Free. (805) 982-5163.

Santa Barbara

It would be difficult to find a community where more has been done to make a visit an agreeable experience. Santa Barbara has pleasantly mixed the old and new without adopting the Disneyland approach. It is an expensive place in which to stay, but the cost of visiting its sites is nominal. Like some of New England's most attractive villages, Santa Barbara has "colonialized" itself in the 20th century. In this case the "colonial" styles are, of course, Mission Revival or Spanish Colonial Revival. The former, a simple adobe approach to architecture, was favored from the 1890s to the 1920s. With a great mission intact and right at hand, no one had to search for a model to follow. By the 1920s the somewhat rustic Mission Revival-Craftsman style was being reinterpreted in a more Mediterranean or Hispanic manner. The lead had been established by Bertram Goodhue at the 1915 Pacific California International Exposition at San Diego. Santa Barbara's great interpreters of the new Spanish baroque mode were James Osborne Craig, who designed the El Paseo complex, and George Washington Smith. Among the masterpieces of the Spanish Colonial Revival style with its greater degree of ornamentation are the Fox Arlington Theater and the Santa Barbara County Courthouse, both from the 1929-30 period.

A visit to the Santa Barbara area should really start with the mission and not the downtown area.

MISSION SANTA BARBARA, 2201 Laguna St., 1786. Although greatly restored after an earthquake in 1926, and again in 1953, the mission is substantially as built during the period 1812-20. Santa Barbara was the only one of the 21 Franciscan missions not to be secularized by the Mexican decree of 1833. It was the "queen" of the missions, the Franciscan capital, and the see of the first Spanish bishop. A seminary (St. Anthony's) was established here in the 19th century, and its buildings, much more recent, rise up from behind the main church. The **museum and library** house great treasures, in-

cluding the original altar and 17th- and 18th-century paintings. NR, NHL. M-Sa 9-5, Su 1-5. 50¢ adults, free for children 16 and under. (805) 682-4713.

For information on all the tours available in the Santa Barbara area, contact the Santa Barbara Conference and Visitors Bureau, P.O. Box 299, Santa Barbara, CA 93102, or call them at (805) 965-3021. The office is located at 1301 Santa Barbara St. and is open seven days a week. A walking tour of the old downtown area called the "Red Tile Tour" is recommended for every visitor. Among the highlights are:

EL PASO, Anacapa and De la Guerra Sts., 1922-23. This is a pedestrian shopping mall built around two historic buildings, the **Casa de la Guerra**, 11-19 E. De la Guerra, 1819-26; and the **Orena Adobes**, 29 E. De la Guerra, 1849 and 1858. Jose de la Guerra was the commandant of the Santa Barbara Presidio and was Spanish-born. To what extent the modern architect of El Paseo, James Osborne Craig, succeeded in creating a bit of the old Mexican territory is questionable; the atmosphere is somewhat more like that of Seville. But in any case, the mall is very pleasant and a successful early recycling of landmark buildings in a new framework. NR.

COVARRUBIAS ADOBE (1817) and HISTORIC ADOBE (1836), 715 Santa Barbara. These two early adobe residences adjoin each other, the latter having been moved to this site from its original one at State and Carrillo Sts. in 1922. The last Mexican territorial assembly met in the L-shaped Covarrubias Adobe in July, 1846; the Historic Adobe was made famous by the fact that it was Col. John C. Fremont's headquarters when Santa Barbara was taken by the Americans in December of that year. Both buildings are owned by the Santa Barbara Historical Society. They are open Tu-F 12-5, Sa-Su and holidays 1-5. Free. (805) 966-1601.

SANTA BARBARA COUNTY COURTHOUSE, 1120 Anacapa St., 1929. Considered by one and all as the outstanding model of the Spanish Colonial Revival style in California, the courthouse was designed by the firm of William Mooser and Co. It consists of three adjoining buildings which together resemble a grandee's palace. The interior murals by Dan Sayre Groesbeck, depicting the history of the area, are thought to be as important as the building itself. NR. Open M-F 8-4:45, Sa-Su and holidays 9-4:45. A guided tour is offered each Friday at 10:30. Free. (805) 966-1611.

SANTA BARBARA HISTORICAL SOCIETY BUILDING, 136 E. De la Guerra St. Artifacts — costumes, paintings, documents, mementos — from the city's four eras: Indian, Spanish, Mexican, and American — are housed here. The society has a regular program of guided tours and lectures which are open to the public. The library is an important genealogical research facility. Open Tu-F 12-5, Sa-Su and holidays 1-5. Free. Donations accepted. (805) 966-1601. 🛉

SANTA BARBARA PRESIDIO, roughly bounded by Carrillo, Garden, De la Guerra, and Anacapa Sts., 1788-1860. The Santa Barbara Presidio was the fourth and last California fort to be founded (on Apr. 21, 1782) by the Spanish on the California coast. Contrary to general belief, most of the Presidio has not survived. Two of the buildings which made up the original adobe quadrangle — **El Cuartel**, 122 E. Canon Perdido, part of the guards' quarters, and **La Caneda Adobe**, 123 E. Canon Perdido St. — have been restored, however. The chapel which served the fortress's inhabitants is now being completely rebuilt. El Cuartel is open to the public M-F 10-5 and is part of the El Presidio de Santa Barbara State Historic Park; La Caneda Adobe is a private residence. NR.

Outside the "Red Tile Tour" area are several other historic properties which will deepen one's appreciation of Santa Barbara's cultural heritage.

FERNALD HOUSE (1862, 1877) and TRUSSELL-WINCHESTER ADOBE (1854), 412 W. Montecito St. Back to back, these two historic houses are now owned and maintained by the Santa Barbara Historical Society. The former is a delightfully eclectic Gothic Revival-Eastlake-Queen Anne-mansion that was enlarged in 1877; containing fourteen rooms, each handsomely furnished. The adobe is more Anglo in style than Spanish, with clapboarding covering some sections. The Fernald House was built for Judge Charles Fernald, a Maine native; the Trussell-Winchester for Captain Horatio Gates Trussell, also a down-Easter. Timbers from the shipwrecked *Winfield Scott* were used in the Trussell-Winchester Adobe along with sun-dried bricks. Like the Fernald House, it, too, is well furnished with period antiques. Both houses are open to the public, Su 2-4. Free. (805) 966-1601.

FOX ARLINGTON THEATER, 1317 State St., 1929-30. Like the county courthouse, this is considered one of the major landmarks of the Spanish Colonial Revival style. Imagine if you can an auditorium which presents a panorama of a Spanish peasant village at each side of the screen, and a star-crossed ceiling upon which moving clouds could be projected. Such were the days when going to the movies was a great event and a theater was meant to dazzle the eye as much as the images that passed over its screen. Fortunately the theater has been restored and is being used as a movie theater and a community performing arts center. (805) 965-5362.

Santa Barbara vicinity

STOW HOUSE, 304 Los Carneros Rd., Goleta, 1872. The Goleta Valley Historical Society maintains this frame Gothic Revival ranch house as a museum. It has been handsomely restored and furnished. Open Sa-Su 2-4. Donations accepted. (805) 964-4407.

While you are in the **Goleta-Hope Ranch** area, a drive through some of the older residential areas should prove pleasurable. It is not always easy to see just what is there beyond the lush landscaping, but, even when a residence is hidden away, there are the beautiful grounds to enjoy. Of particular interest are a number of large well-maintained estates off Las Palmas Dr. in Hope Ranch.

Montecito, located on the other side of Santa Barbara from Goleta, is an older retreat for the fashionable. There are private homes here designed by such master architects as George Washington Smith, Frank Lloyd Wright, Carleton Winslow, Bertram Goodhue, and Bernard Maybeck. Like the Hope Ranch area, many of the homes are enclosed within a green barrier, and, in this climate where vegetation is more or less permanent, an opportunity to see through the leaves may not often present itself. For anyone wishing to know more about the houses in this remarkable neighborhood, a reading of David Gebhard and Robert Winter's *Guide to Architecture in Los Angeles & Southern California* (Peregrine Smith, Inc., 1977) is highly recommended.

Santa Paula

CALIFORNIA OIL MUSUEM, 1003 Main St., 1888-89. Santa Paula's money has been made in oil, and the town lies at the center of an area that has produced the precious liquid since the 1880s. The museum is housed in the Union Oil Company Building, previously known as the Santa Paula Hardware Co. Block. It is a wonderful Queen Anne style commercial building with a side tower and second-story bay windows which extend out from the brick building. Inside there is old drilling equipment and pictures and papers which relate to the golden age of oil production in the area. Open W-Su 10-4. Free. (805) 525-6672.

Simi

R. P. STRATHEARN HISTORICAL PARK, 137 Strathearn Pl. The park includes several historic properties: **Colony House** (1889), **Strathearn Home** (1890s), **Victorian House** (1890s), and **Simi Adobe** (c. 1800). Rancho Simi was one of the original California land grants, and, like the ranches of the nearby San Fernando Valley area, most of the land has gone the way of subdivisions. The Simi Valley Historical Society and the Rancho Simi Recreation and Parks District jointly administer this historical park. A **museum** is located in the oldest building, the adobe. Here one finds antique furniture, household items, ranch tools—all the paraphernalia of a well-furnished ranch house. Of the other buildings which have found a home on this spread, the Colony House is the most interesting. It is one of two buildings that remain of a settlement of twelve, created in 1888-89 by settlers from Chicago who came to the area for their health. They had purchased building lots in what was then only a townsite called Simiopolis and which eventually became Simi Valley. The materials for the houses were prefabricated in the Chicago area and shipped to California about the time the settlers departed the Midwestern city. Although each two-story building was basically alike in floor plan, placement of partitions and porches allowed the individual homeowner to personalize the building. The colony did not last for very long, but the inexpensive buildings served well for many years. The park is open for tours, Su 1-4. 🚶 (805) 526-6453.

Solvang

MISSION SANTA INES (Santa Ynez), 1760 Mission Dr., 1804, 1812-17. Santa Ines was the 19th of 21 Franciscan missions founded but was one of the best situated. Parts of the complex have been reconstructed; the bell tower is an anomaly, however, and doesn't fit in at all. The original Indian frescoes and an old painted wooden altar in the church have miraculously survived. The Franciscans returned to the mission in 1924. It is open during the winter, M-Sa 9:30-4:30, Su 12-4:30; summer, M-Sa 9:30-5, Su 12-4:30. 50¢ adults, no charge for children under 16. (805) 688-4815.

While in the Solvang area you may wish to go on into town. It is a Danish community, founded in 1911, and almost everywhere the Scandanavian heritage is celebrated—some say a bit too commercially. *Chacun à son gout.*

Ventura

MISSION SAN BUENAVENTURA, 225 E. Main St., 1782, 1809. The mission was

founded by Father Junipero Serra in 1782, and the adobe church completed in 1809. It has since been rocked badly in earthquakes (1815 and 1857) and sadly neglected. It was first extensively renovated in the 1890s and then was restored to much of its early 19th-century form in 1957. Some important details were glossed over at that time, but the thick walls remain original as do the bell tower and the buttresses. Also left standing in the complex is an adobe barrel-vaulted water filtration house, or settling tank, which was at one time linked to an extensive water system. A large variety of religious and historical artifacts are on view in the museum. The site of the mission was an early Chumash Indian settlement, and archaeological digs have uncovered important Indian artifacts which are also exhibited here. NR. Open M-Sa 10-5, Su 10-4. 50¢ adults, special group rates. (805) 643-4318.

OLIVAS ADOBE, 4200 Olivas Park Dr., 1837, 1849. The first home built by Raimundo Olivas in 1837 was a one-story adobe. He became so wealthy as a result of his cattle ranching that he was able to build a two-story addition in 1849 to help house his family of 21 children. The newer building was designed in the style of the classic Monterey adobe with a second-story porch. A courtyard lies at the center, enclosed by the two buildings. The adobe was extensively restored in the 1970s by the California Division of Parks and

Olivas Adobe, Ventura

Recreation. It stands as a museum in the midst of landscaped grounds in Olivas Park. A small museum building has been built nearby. NR. Open Sa-Su 10-4. No charge. (805) 644-7421. 👫

VENTURA CITY HALL, Poli St., between Chestnut and Oak, 1911-12. The former county courthouse, a neo-classical lesson in good taste, has been sensibly recycled for continued public use. The building is beautifully situated and sits well with its neighbor, the former courthouse annex dating from 1939.

San Luis Obispo, Monterey, San Benito, Santa Clara, and Santa Cruz Counties

The five counties which extend from San Luis Obispo in the south to Santa Clara in the north represent what is traditional Hispanic California for many people. Lo-cated within the region are the remains of nine of the historic Franciscan missions and the only surviving presidio chapel at Monterey. Around most of these mission communities were established pueblos or cities which became in the second half of the 19th century centers of American culture. Monterey, Carmel, Santa Clara, Santa Cruz, San Juan Bautista, San Miguel, San Luis Obispo—the names themselves express the richness of the Old World culture on which the new society was built. El Camino Real, the King's Highway, was the first connecting link between the mission towns, and, with new forms of transportation, the distances were gradually rendered less important. Today a freeway, US 101, connects the inland cities, and CA 1 winds up and down the scenic shore. Either route will take you deep into the colorful past of the mission country.

Carmel

Is there any town in America that can be considered more romantic? The setting along the Pacific coast has been popular with artists and tourists since the late 19th century. Visitor Robert Louis Stevenson termed the cypresses of the famed Monterey peninsula "ghosts fleeing before the wind." They are haunting and beautiful reminders of scenic America before the age of fast food emporiums. Edward Weston, Robinson Jeffers, Jo Moara, Ambrose Bierce, and many other writers and artists found Carmel a very congenial place in which to create original works. It is still a pleasantly uncommercial place where privacy is respected. Most Carmel properties do not even have street numbers. The two major sights—the Robinson Jeffers House and the Mission San Carlos Borromeo—are well labeled, however, and easy to find.

ROBINSON JEFFERS HOUSE, 26304 Ocean View Ave., 1919-62. The renowned poet lived and wrote in this house for 43 years. It was built with his own hands out of stone rubble and includes a 40-foot medieval-inspired tower. The building is maintained as a private residence, but is viewable from the public way. NR.

MISSION SAN CARLOS BORROMEO, 3080 Rio Rd., 1793-97. The Carmel mission is distinguished in many ways. It was not founded here, but in Monterey in 1770, and is the second mission to have been established in California. The present site is such a lovely one, overlooking Carmel Bay, that it is perhaps no surprise that Fray Junipero Serra moved the mission here. It was Serra's home until his death in 1784, and his body lies buried in a simple tomb inside the present mission church which was built ten years later.

Fermin Francisco de Lasuen, Serra's successor as director of the Franciscan missions, was responsible for the building of the present church of San Carlos. Like many other mission buildings up and down the coast, it quickly fell to ruins in the mid-19th century after the lands were seized by the Mexican provincial government. By the 1880s restoration was called for, but the work was not done very correctly. Many of the mistakes made at this time were corrected between 1936 and 1940 when restoration work was again undertaken. Unlike many of the mission churches, San Carlos is built of sandstone blocks—five feet thick—rather than adobe. The building has a baroque magnificence about it which sets it apart from all other mission churches with the exception of Santa Barbara. The quality of the craftsmanship which went into carvings, paintings, and the stone work is of a high order. NR, NHL. ♦

The mission is open M-Sa 9:30-4:30, Su 10:30-4:30. Free. Donations accepted. (408) 624-3600.

Cupertino

PICCHETTI BROTHERS WINERY, 13100 Montebello Rd., 1880-1920. Much of this northwest corner of Santa Clara County has already been bulldozed for single-family dwellings laid out one on top of another. It is refreshing, then, to come across a large expanse of open land which is being kept free of development. The grounds and buildings of the Picchetti Winery, which began operations in the 1890s and lasted until the 1960s, constitute a park for all of the people. It is a happy mixture of history and ecology. Undoubtedly the Picchetti brothers, who started with a 160-acre ranch and increased it in size to 200 acres, would drink to the future as well. The firm was just one of over 100 wineries located in the Santa Clara Valley around the turn of the century, a number greater than that reached in Napa County.

Grapes are still cultivated on five acres of the tract, and the wine is bottled under the label "Ridge/Picchetti" by the nearby Ridge Vineyards. The red brick winery still contains redwood wine-storage tanks in its great rough stone cellar. NR.

LE PETIT TRIANON, De Anza College campus, 21250 Stevens Creek Blvd., 1892. Charles A. Baldwin was also a successful wine producer, but his estate, Beaulieu, was not a mere ranch like that of the Picchetti brothers. One of the most whimsical buildings on the grounds is one fashioned after the Petit Trianon at Versailles. Whether Mrs. Baldwin played house here as did Marie Antoinette at the original is unknown, but it would have been a good place for summer tea parties. The copy is built of redwood and is stuccoed over to imitate plaster. The little building also has a monumental wood facade with Ionic columns. The Baldwin estate is now the home of a coeducational junior college, and the Petit Trianon can be viewed while strolling on the campus. NR.

Felton

FELTON COVERED BRIDGE, Covered Bridge Rd., 1892. It will perhaps come as a surprise to learn that there are covered bridges, a form usually associated with New England, in California. The Felton bridge is one of eleven remaining in the state and the only one in this reagion. Typically, it was constructed of redwood. At 140 feet long and 34 feet high, it is one of the tallest covered spans in America. An adjacent iron bridge replaced it in use in 1938. NR. ♿

Jolon vicinity

MISSION SAN ANTONIO DE PADUA, Monterey County G14, NW of Jolon,

1810-13. The third oldest mission, founded in 1771, in the chain of Franciscan settlements is now the best restored of them all. The buildings were repaired once or twice in the 19th and early 20th centuries, but not until 1948-49 did extensive restoration take place. The area is isolated, and it perhaps did not seem wise earlier to spend quite so much time and effort on such restoration work. The excellence of the work can be seen now in the church, gristmill, soldiers' barracks, tannery, and patio garden. The concept of a mission community of soldiers, Indians, priests, and settlers is successfully presented here within the context of the restored buildings. There is no need to have these roles played by actors or mannequins.

A museum houses Indian relics and a colonial-period wine press. The mission is affiliated with the Franciscan Friars of California. There are special guided tours. NR. Open M-Sa and holidays 9-4:30, Su 11-5. Free. (408) 385-4478.

When in search of San Antonio Mission, you may come across **Las Milpitas,** headquarters building of the Hunter-Liggett Military Reservation, also on Monterey County G14. While San Antonio is pure and original "Mission" in style, La Milpitas is pure "Mission Revival," built early in this century and designed by Julia Morgan, who also designed William Randolph Hearst's palatial mansion in San Simeon. Hearst used Las Milpitas as the headquarters for one of his ranches. The 43,000-acre Ranch Milpitas had been previously owned by the wealthy Atherton family of the San Francisco area.

Monterey

Monterey is history and vice versa. By 1775 the city had succeeded San Diego as the capital of Spanish Alta California and as the center of religious administration. It continued as the capital city when the Mexican republic was established in 1822 and was still the center of government when American forces took over the territory in 1846. Only when the capital was moved in 1849 did Monterey begin to fade into obscurity. It is probably just as well that this happened, for much more of the past was preserved here than in other historic California cities. The Monterey area was rediscovered in the early 1900s, and its splendid Spanish-style architecture was appreciated anew. John Steinbeck's image of the town, enshrined in *Cannery Row* and other novels with a Monterey setting, is of a sleepy fishing town. Monterey has awakened a great deal since the 1930s; but except for a brief fling with urban renewal in the 1960s, the citizens of Monterey have appeared content with the culture given to them.

Excellent tours of Monterey are available. A self-guided "Path of History" tour includes buildings in the State Historic Park as well as other landmarks. A map can be obtained at the Monterey USO Building, El Estero Webster St. An orange-red line has been painted down the center of all the streets which lead to historic buildings. There are also Gray Line sightseeing tours which depart from Fisherman's Wharf and the Double Tree Inn.

ROYAL PRESIDIO CHAPEL, 550 Church St. 1789. Originally called the Church of San Carlos, the chapel was part of the mission community of the same name founded in 1770. The chapel is the only surviving building of the Presidio complex and the only presidio chapel left in California. It was here that the Spanish royal governors worshipped. A wing, transept, and new altar were added in the 19th century. The chapel is open daily 8-6. Free. (408) 373-2628.

PRESIDIO OF MONTEREY MUSEUM, Pacific St., N of Decatur. The U.S. Army museum is located in an area known as Presidio Hill and in a 1909 ordnance building. Here can be found exhibits which interpret the Indian, Spanish, and Mexican periods of Monterey history. Open Th-M 9-12:30 and 1:30-4. Free. (408) 242-8547.

MONTEREY STATE HISTORIC PARK, from the shore to Madison St., and from Washington to Pacific Sts., 19th century. Eight buildings have been preserved, seven of which can be visited. The hours are the same for all, 9-5, but the days differ and

these are noted in the individual listings that follow. Admission is the same for each building: 50¢ adults, 25¢ children and senior citizens, free for children under 6. (408) 649-2836.

The Custom House, Custom House Plaza, 1827, is an adobe building and a fine example of a Monterey-style house with a second-floor balcony. The building was enlarged in 1841 and 1846 to include a one-story center section and two two-story wings. Monterey's Custom House was the only such governmental structure in Mexican California and continued until 1867 to serve as a U.S. custom house where duties were collected on foreign goods. It was here on July 7, 1846, that the American flag was first raised over California. NR, NHL. Open daily.

The Pacific House, Custom House Plaza, 1847. This handsome building facing the open plaza was one of several properties originally owned by Thomas O. Larkin, Monterey's most prominent merchant and U. S. consul to Mexico in Monterey from 1843-46. Pacific House was first used as a government storehouse and after 1850 became a tavern and a place for county offices. From the 1880s on, after Monterey had declined as an economic and political center, the building returned to use as a storehouse. Pacific House is now a museum of California history and houses the Holman collection of Indian artifacts; the grounds include a beautiful garden. NR. Open daily.

Casa del Oro, corner of Scott and Olivier Sts., 1845. There is no evidence that this building ever served as a gold depository, but the name has persisted in use to this day. Behind the Pacific House, it was first used as a general store—the Boston Store. Today it includes displays of trade items that would have been common in the early days of Monterey. NR. Open daily.

Casa Soberanes, 336 Pacific, 1830. Although given to the State of California, the house is still maintained as a private residence and can only be viewed from the street. It is a lovely two-storty adobe dwelling and was built by Jose Rafael Papias

Estrada. A cousin, Ezequiel Soberanes, became the owner in the mid-1800s. NR.

Larkin House, corner of Jefferson St. and Calle Principal, 1835, was built and designed by Monterey's most prominent citizen, Thomas O. Larkin. Its wraparound two-story porch (a porch formed from a first-floor veranda and a second-floor balcony) has a balustrade across the upper level. The framework of the house, including the porch, was built of redwood. Larkin House is beautifully furnished with many family possessions which date to the 1830s and '40s. It can be seen only on guided tours which take approximately 35 minutes. Tours are conducted W-M at the regular park hours. NR.

Casa Gutierrez, Calle Principal, near Madison St., 1841. Joaquin Gutierrez built this modest two-story adobe when he was 25 and newly married. It is quite typical of the kind of residence that was home for the average citizen of the time. The building is now rented to a Mexican restaurant. NR.

First Theater, corner of Scott and Pacific Sts., 1846-47. An English sailor, Jack Swan, built what was to be a lodging house (adobe section) with an attached barroom (frame section). The sections of the long adobe portion are clearly delineated by the four entrance doors and windows on the street side. There were, however, only easily removable partitions between the various sections, and, when it was suggested in the late 1840s that the building be used as a theater, Swan was glad to oblige. Nineteenth-century plays are presented here each week. Open W-Su.

Stevenson House (Gonzales House), 530 Houston St., 1835. Because Robert Louis Stevenson spent the Fall of 1879 in this house as a roomer, it has been named after him in modern times. The two-story adobe was built by Don Rafael Gonzales, a customs administrator, and sold in the 1850s to Juan Girardin, a Swiss emigré, and his wife, Manuela Perez. After the death of her husband, Mrs. Girardin was forced to take in roomers and called the building the French Hotel. Stevenson had come to stay

Larkin House, Monterey

and to court another Monterey widow, Fannie Osbourne, who eventually became his wife. None of Stevenson's major works were penned while he was a resident here, but the writer did understand and appreciate Monterey's colorful history; it was reflected in a series of articles that he wrote for the local newspaper.

The Stevenson House is very accurately and effectively furnished with period antiques—from kitchen implements to bedroom furniture. There are several rooms devoted to Stevenson memorabilia. The house is open daily for 45-minute guided tours. NR.

CASA AMESTI, 510 Polk St., 1834, 1846. An exceptionally elegant example of the Monterey style of Spanish Colonial architecture, Casa Amesti combines exterior and interior details characteristic of buildings in the East with early California forms and materials. The house is of adobe construction with the distinctive Monterey two-story wraparound porch. Don Jose Amesti first built a one-story building and in 1853 extended the building and added a second floor. The interior rooms are marked by handsome moldings, door frames, and other types of elegant wood-

work. The house remained in the Amesti family until about 1914 and then briefly served as a boarding house. It was rescued from decay by Mr. and Mrs. Felton Elkins in 1918, and they restored the mansion and beautifully furnished its rooms with antique objects. Mrs. Elkins bequeathed Casa Amesti to the National Trust for Historic Preservation. It is now used by the Old Capitol Club, a private men's luncheon group. The house is open to the public Sa-Su 2-4, and other times by appointment. 50¢ adults, 25¢ students. NR.

COLTON HALL, Civic Center, Pacific St., 1849. This is Monterey's former town hall and public school. More importantly, it was the place where delegates from California gathered to write the state's first constitution in 1849. Two two-story stone buildings, designed in the Greek Revival style, now serve as a museum of local history and as a genealogical research facility. The former town hall was named after the Rev. Walter Colton, mayor of Monterey at the time the building was built. NR. Open Tu-Su 10-12 and 1-5. Free. (408) 646-3851.

Just south of Colton Hall is the **Old Monterey Jail,** Dutra St., 1854. It is main-

Casa Amesti, Monterey

tained as a branch museum of Colton Hall. A suitably sturdy one-story sandstone building, it has housed any number of 19th-century desperadoes, including Anastacia Garciá, a killer who is said to have performed his murderous acts with a smile. The jail is open for inspection Tu-Su 10-5. Free. (408) 375-9944. 🏃

CASA SERRANO, 550 Calle Principal, c. 1845. Thomas Larkin was the builder of this very modest one-story adobe residence, and Florencio Serrano bought it in 1845 for his new wife and himself. The Serrano family occupied the house for nearly a century. One of its unique features is a sleeping loft for children reached by an outside staircase. The building is now owned by the Monterey History and Art Association and is used as its headquarters. It has been restored and enlarged. Open Sa-Su 1-4. Free.
(408) 372-2608.

New Almaden

NEW ALMADEN MERCURY MINING MUSEUM, 21570 Almaden Rd., 1845. At one time the most important mine in California, New Almaden was one of only four 19th-century sources in the world for mercury. The mines are now inactive, but they were worked from around 1845 until well into the 20th century. Because there was a great need for quicksilver in the gold mining processes, flasks of the metal were shipped to the gold fields. Remaining on the mining village site is a collection of wood and adobe buildings, including **Casa Grande,** the mine superintendent's mansion (1854), and the **Wells Fargo building** which houses a museum. The museum's collections are, of course, strong in mineralogy, but they also include Indian artifacts and other archaeological materials. Visiting families will be delighted to know that there is also a children's museum. Open Feb-Nov, M, Th-F 1-4, Sa-Su, holidays 10-4. $2 adults, $1.75 senior citizens, 75¢ children. 🏃

Pacific Grove

GOSBY HOUSE INN, 643 Lighthouse Ave., 1887. A pleasant Queen Anne style boarding house, Gosby House is typical of the type of accommodation which existed to serve those who came to Pacific Grove—the "Chautauqua of the West." The town was founded in 1875 as a Methodist summer camp and was formally laid out along Monterey Bay in 1883. J. F. Gosbey (the *e* was dropped in the inn name) built his boarding house right across the street from the First Methodist Church. The house was built originally in a simple version of the Stick Style and was revamped in the Queen Anne style in the 1890s. For information regarding accommodations at the completely restored inn, see its listing under Lodging and Dining. NR. (408) 375-1287.

POINT PINOS LIGHTHOUSE, off Asilomar and Lighthouse Aves., 1853. An early stone lighthouse, Point Pinos is now the property of the Pacific Grove Museum of Natural History. NR. It can be toured on Sa-Su 1-4. Free. (408) 372-4212.

Palo Alto and Stanford

Although its influence extends everywhere in the Palo Alto area, Stanford University is a political subdivision of its own and an older one than the community it is usually identified with. Palo Alto was founded in 1889, four years after Leland Stanford and his wife gave $30 million to establish a university in memory of their only son. The communities adjoin each other, and today there is little or no difference between them.

Stanford, a New York State native, was California's greatest 19th-century citizen. He served as governor of the state during the Civil War and later as U.S. senator. His fortune was made in mining and in railroading. The Central Pacific Railroad was almost completely owned by Stanford, and the Southern Pacific was also closely held by Stanford and his friends. The university was built on his 9,000-acre stock farm where thoroughbred horses were bred. For a time the campus was called "The Farm."

Considering the size of the Stanfords' gift, worth at least ten times as much today, it may not be surprising to learn that it was invested so handsomely in buildings and grounds. Frederick Law Olmstead, America's most famous 19th-century land-

scaper, was commissioned to produce the site plan, and he is credited with the quadrangle concept. Shepley, Rutan, and Coolidge, the Boston firm that designed so many late 19th-century landmarks, was responsible for the first major buildings. Since that time Stanford has been the site of many other innovative experiments in design and architecture.

The Stanford campus, near CA 82, can be toured M-F (11 and 2:15) with a guide. Tours leave from the **Information Center,** Quadrangle main entrance. A map and folder outlining a self-guided tour is also available from the Information Center which is open M-Sa 10-4 and Su 1-4. (415) 497-2560.

QUADRANGLE, Serra St. at the end of Palm Dr., 1891. The group of 27 yellow sandstone buildings with red tile roofs has a dignified but inviting quality about it. In the best Richardsonian architectural tradition followed by Shepley, Rutan and Coolidge, the buildings appear always to have stood in this spot, their mass distributed in the flowing horizontal lines of the colonnades which link one section of the quadrangle to the next. Romanesque forms are mixed with those of the Spanish Colonial tradition in an appealing manner.

Standing at the center of the Quadrangle is the **Memorial Church,** 1903, 1913, the

design of which is specifically identified with Charles Allerton Coolidge of the architectural firm. It was built in memory of Leland Stanford by his wife and is noted for its fine mosaics and stained-glass windows. NR. Open M-F 7:30 am-9 pm, Sa-Su 9-9. Free.

HANNA-HONEYCOMB HOUSE, 737 Frenchman's Rd., 1937-61. Given to Stanford University in 1974, this residence is one of Frank Lloyd Wright's most important. It was the first of his houses to be built in a hexagonal form with the kitchen and bathrooms located in the center of the building where they are lighted by clerestory windows. The Hanna family had the house built in four phases over a 25-year period. A hobby shop, guest house, and storage room were added in 1950. In 1957 the original study and four small bedrooms no longer needed for children were converted into a library, master bedroom suite, and small guest bedroom. Finally, in 1961, a garden house and two pools were added. All of these changes and additions were provided for in Wright's original plan. The American Institute of Architects has designated the building "one of seventeen buildings designed by Frank Lloyd Wright to be retained as an example of his architectural contribution to American culture." NR.

LOU HENRY HOOVER HOUSE, Cabrillo Ave., 1919. The home of President and Mrs. Hoover was named for the first lady because of the direct hand she took in its design. Arthur B. Clark and Birge Clark worked out the architectural plans. Al-

though basically Mission Revival in style, the interpretation was very modern and reminiscent of the work of Irving Gill in the Los Angeles area. The home is owned by the university and has served as the residence of the president. NR. Private but viewable from the public way.

San Jose

San Jose began life as San Jose de Guadalupe in 1777, and is recognized as being the first secular town established in California. In 1849 it succeeded Monterey as the capital of the state only to lose this honor several years later to Sacramento. Since at least the mid-19th century, however, San Jose has been the undisputed capital of the rich Santa Clara County agricultural area. Now the wealth is primarily concentrated in industry. There have been unfortunate attempts to rebuild the center city by demolishing it, but some important buildings have survived the bulldozing.

HISTORIC SAN JOSE, 635 Pehlan Ave. The San Jose Historical Museum has established an outdoor exhibit area in which the area's Indian, Spanish, Mexican, and American history is explained. Among the objects displayed are Indian baskets, farm wagons and implements, bicycles, motorcycles, mining artifacts—including items from the New Almaden mercury mine (see previous listing)—and dolls. Open M-F 10-4:30, Sa-Su and holidays 12-4:30. $1 adults, 50¢ for children under 15. 🏃 (408) 287-2290.

LUIS MARIA PERALTA ADOBE, 184 W. St. John St., 1804. The Historical Museum is responsible for preserving the last surviving building of the downtown Pueblo de San Jose de Guadalupe area. The adobe is a rare example of a pioneer California dwelling. NR. The building is open from 9 til dusk each weekday. Free. (408) 287-2290.

SAN JOSE MUSEUM OF ART, 110 S. Market St., 1892. When first the post office and then the public library abandoned the old building for a new, the civic art gallery moved in. A monumental Richardsonian Romanesque sandstone building, it provides just the right kind of interior space for the display of art. At one corner of the two-story building is a dramatic four-story block tower with balconies and a parapet. NR. Open Tu-Sa 10-4:30, Su 12-4. Free. (408) 294-2787.

WINCHESTER MYSTERY HOUSE, 525 S. Winchester Blvd., 1884-1922. One of the strangest homes in all of America, the Mystery House grew from an 8-room farmhouse to monstrous proportions—160 rooms—because of one bizarre reason: Sarah L. Winchester believed that if she kept building she would never die. The work came to an end 38 years later when she, naturally enough, died like anyone else. ✠

The cost of all the additions is estimated at more than $5 million. There are thousands of doors and windows, 40 stairways, dozens of fancy gabled dormers, blank walls, secret passageways, trapdoors, etc. Mrs. Winchester moved to the San Jose area from the East in the 1880s and closely followed the advice of a spiritual medium. As the widow of the son of the famed rifle manufacturer, she had sufficient funds at her disposal for pursuing such a wild race with death. NR.

Guided tours of the house are held on the hour, daily 9-6 in the summer, 9-4:30 in the winter. $5.95 adults, $3.75 children 5-12, free for children under 5. A house and grounds tour which includes a museum devoted to Winchester rifles and other arms costs $6.95 for adults, $4.75 for children 5-12, free for children under 5. (408) 247-2000 or 2101.

San Juan Bautista

Until the 1870s and the coming of the railroad, San Juan Bautista was an important stop on the north-south stagecoach routes which traveled El Camino Real or The King's Highway; earlier the town was the center of a major mission community. Today, San Juan Bautista—bypassed by US 101—is a living museum of 19th-century California history.

SAN JUAN BAUTISTA STATE HISTORIC PARK, bounded by the streets sur-

rounding the plaza, 19th century. The San Juan Bautista mission was founded in 1797, the fifteenth Franciscan community to have been established in California. The park includes the restored church and monastery as well as four other buildings dating from 1803-1874. NR, NHL. Open daily 9-4:30. 50¢ adults, 25¢ children 6-17 and senior citizens. (408) 623-4881. All five properties within the park are worth visiting:

Mission San Juan Bautista's church, the largest of its kind in the state, and *convento* or monastery have survived in part since 1813. Work commenced on these buildings in 1803 but was not completed until ten years later. The community was secularized along with the other Franciscan missions by the Mexican territorial government in 1835, and the condition of the buildings gradually declined. Since that time they have been badly damaged several times by earthquakes. Not until the early 20th century was much attention paid to the mission, and by this time reconstruction of the complex was required.

Mission San Juan Bautista, although part of the state park, is still owned by the Church. Parts of the complex can be toured, for which there is a nominal charge. Of special interest is the altar wall painted by an American sailor, Thomas Doak; other walls hold original Indian decorations. In the monastery wing relics of the Spanish colonial period—chairs, candelabra, figures of saints, baptismal fonts—are exhibited.

The mission is open Mar 1-Oct 31, daily 9:30-5:30; Nov 1-Feb 28, daily 10-4:30. 50¢ adults, $1 family. (408) 623-4528.

The Castro House, facing the plaza, was built by the Castro family in 1840-41 and was intended to be the administrative headquarters of the northern area of Mexican California. After the mission property was secularized in 1835, and until California was annexed in 1846 by the United States, Jose Tiburcio Castro and his son, Jose Maria Castro, governed the community. It was even renamed San Juan de Castro in the 1830s. Castro House, an eight-room adobe, has been restored and appears now as it might have in the 1840s. It has been furnished in the style of the 1870s.

The Plaza Hotel (1858) adjoins Castro House and was built from the remains of an 1813-14 adobe barracks for soldiers stationed at the mission. Their parade grounds were right across the street in the plaza. The hotel, like Castro House, has furnishings dating from the 1870s.

The Plaza Stable was associated with the hotel and is catty-cornered from Castro House. Built c. 1861, it now houses an assortment of carriages and wagons and other 19th-century items. A furnished blacksmith's shop is found behind the stable and houses the kind of tools commonly used by a wagonwright. ♔

In 1868 the owner of the hotel, Angelo Zanetta, built a second two-story building known as the **Zanetta House** or **Plaza Hall** on the same block as the stable, using the adobe bricks of an earlier building on the site. Zanetta hoped that his new building would be chosen as the courthouse of newly founded San Benito County, but Hollister was selected as the county seat. Subsequently, the first floor was converted for use as the Zanetta family residence, and the second was used as a dance hall and meeting room.

San Luis Obispo

The site of California's fifth Franciscan mission, San Luis Obispo is today much more a Victorian town than a Spanish Colonial settlement like Monterey or San Juan Bautista. During the last decades of the 1800s, San Luis Obispo became an important stopover between Los Angeles and San Francisco. It has continued to draw travelers in the 20th century who are traveling for business or pleasure along either the coastal CA 1 or the mid-county 101 freeway. The city, however, has managed to hold on to some of its principal historic buildings from the Spanish, Mexican, and early American periods.

DANA ADOBE, southern end of Oak Glen Ave., c. 1839. Captain William G. Dana was responsible for the construction of this 1½-story, thirteen-room adobe. He provided goods (soap, candles, and cloth) and services such as carpentry and blacksmithing to the surrounding ranchos and the missions of La Purisma Concepcion and Santa Ynez. The adobe was significant as one of the major resting places along the San Luis Obispo-Santa Barbara road, or El Camino Real. Here mail riders from the northern and southern sections of the state exchanged pouches and spent the night. The building is maintained by the San Luis Obispo County Historical Society. Open May-Oct, Su 1-4:30. Free. (805) 543-0638.

Also maintained by the society are the **Dallidet Adobe**, 1185 Pacific St., 1853; and the San Luis Obispo County Historical Museum, 696 Monterey St., 1904. The museum is located in the former **Carnegie City Library** and features exhibits of pioneer and Indian artifacts. There is also a separate children's museum. Open W-Su 10-4. Free. (805) 543-0638.

MISSION SAN LUIS OBISPO DE TOLOSA, 782 Monterey St., 1772. The fifth mission, San Luis was founded by Fray Junipero Serra. Named for the son of King Charles II of Naples and the nephew of Louis IX of France who joined the Franciscan order in 1294, the mission still functions as a parish church. Like the other California mission buildings, San Luis suffered significant damage in the 19th century; the church and adjoining one-story adobe buildings were extensively restored in the 1930s. One of the important elements pieced back together was the red tile roof of the church which had been replaced with wooden shingles. It was here at San Luis that roofing tiles were first made and used instead of the traditional roof covering—grass tule or thatch.

An eight-room museum is now housed in what was the original priests' residence or *convento*. Here may be found a collection of Chumash Indian artifacts and such religious articles as the church's original stations of the cross, altar pieces, and robes. Open June 14-Sept 15, daily 9-5; Sept 16-June 14, daily 9-4. 50¢ adults and children, $1 per family. (805) 543-6850.

San Miguel

MISSION SAN MIGUEL ARCANGEL, Mission St. (off CA 101), 1816-18. Located in the Salinas Valley midway between San Francisco and Los Angeles, Mission San Miguel was founded as the sixteenth mission in 1797. The original buildings were destroyed by fire in 1806 and the present church, larger than its predecessors, was erected as a replacement. The exterior is unpretentious except for the unique arcade which features arched openings of various sizes. The church is noted chiefly for its interior mural decorations. The frescoes were executed in 1821 by Esteban Munras of Monterey with the assistance of the mission Indians. Fortunately, these fine examples of religious art have never been retouched, a rarity in the turbulent history of the California mission chain. Restoration was begun as early as the 1880s, although the task of preserving this relic did not begin in earnest until the Franciscans regained control of the mission in 1928. NR. Daily 10-5. Donations welcome. (408) 467-3256.

CALEDONIA ADOBE, S. of 10th St., 1850s. This two-story adobe, located just south of the Mission San Miguel Arcangel, was a hotel and stage stop for many years but was originally built as a private residence. NR.

San Simeon

HEARST SAN SIMEON STATE HISTORICAL MONUMENT, off CA 1 at the village of San Simeon, 1919-51. Publishing magnate William Randolph Hearst called his palatial retreat La Cuesta Encantada—The Enchanted Hill. Until 1958 sightseers along the coastal highway had to be satisfied with just a glimpse of the mansion's twin ivory-colored towers through a coin-in-the-slot telescope. Today, visitors can actually enter the stately Hispano-Mooresque mansion, La Casa Grande, as well as stroll through the grounds, and their elaborate gardens, pools, terraces, and regal guest houses. Principally designed by Julia Morgan, a distinguished Berkeley architect, the grand estate posed numerous construction problems, and building continued past Hearst's death.

Blended into this exotic setting are dozens of valuable art objects, including a profusion of marble statuary, sarcophagi, fountains, and ornate stairways. The marble-faced Neptune Pool surrounded by an Etruscan-styled colonnade is a highlight for visitors, but the 100-room La Casa Grande, the pride of the owner, is indescribable. Each visitor will have to decide for himself whether the place is a millionaire's palace of art or an incomparably vulgar collection of expensive kitsch. The Refectory features a hand-carved ceiling and life-size saints, while the Assembly room displays a priceless collection of Gothic and Renaissance tapestries. The entire house is a tasteless but dazzling showcase of antique silver, Persian rugs, Roman mosaics, and wood, marble, and stone statuary. NR. Tours daily 8:20-3:20. $7.80 adults, $3.80 children 6-12. Reservations may be made through Ticketron up to 60 days in advance. (805) 927-4621.

Santa Clara

MISSION SANTA CLARA DE ASIS, on the Almeda, University of Santa Clara campus. Only the bell, given to the Santa Clara mission by Charles IV of Spain in 1798, and the original mission statues remain from the church founded in 1777. The present building is a modern one and not a reconstruction. Open daily all year. (408) 984-4256.

Santa Cruz

At the head of Monterey Bay, Santa Cruz is one of the best situated towns on the coast. It has been a popular resort town since the late 19th century and is primarily a mixture of Victorian and modern buildings, although some evidence remains of the city's founding in the 1790s. Santa Cruz was the site of a Franciscan mission established in 1791.

GOLDEN GATE VILLA (McLaughlin House), 924 3rd St. Built for Maj. Frank W. McLaughlin, a protégé of Thomas

Edison and a promoter of the area's gold mining interests, this is the town's best remaining Queen Anne residence. It has the assymetrical shape and side tower characteristic of the style. The interior appointments include an elephant-hide wall covering donated to the major by President Theodore Roosevelt and an onyx fireplace. NR. Private, but viewable from the street.

MISSION SANTA CRUZ, Emmit and School Sts., 1931. What is now standing close to the original mission site is a half-size replica of the first church. The building had been weakened by an earthquake in 1840 and then fell completely to the ground in a second major quake in 1857. Open daily 9-5. Free. Donations accepted. (408) 426-5686.

Nearby is the **Santa Cruz Mission State Historical Monument** and the only building remaining from the mission, the **Neary-Hopcroft** (also known as Neary-Rodriguez) **Adobe,** 130-134 School St., c. 1810. It is a one-story building and probably served as the mission's barracks. The complex is not yet open to the public. For further information, call the California Dept. of Parks and Recreation, (916) 445-4209.

SANTA CRUZ HISTORICAL MUSEUM (Records Building, County of Santa Clara), 118 Cooper St., 1882. The octagonal-shaped building was a novelty form favored by 19th-century American architects ever since Orson Squire Fowler popularized the idea in the 1840s and '50s. A one-story brick building, the former county hall of records is said to have been modeled after the 1855-56 U.S. gold piece. Today it serves as the headquarters and museum of the Santa Cruz County Historical Society. NR. Open M-Sa 12-5. Free. (408) 425-2540.

Saratoga

VILLA MONTALVO (Senator James D. Phelan Mansion), Montalvo Rd., off Saratoga-Los Gatos Rd., 1912. Many of the great Santa Clara and San Mateo country estates of the late 19th and early 20th centuries have been broken up or otherwise dismembered. Montalvo has been saved for the enjoyment of the public and now serves as a park, aboretum, and art center. The villa is built in the Spanish Renaissance style and is surrounded by such amenities as a guest house, carriage house (now used as a theater), amphitheater, and formal gardens. A fountain was dedicated by Senator Phelan, the original owner of the estate, to Ordanez de Montalvo, the first man to use the name *California* (in 1620). The grounds were landscaped by John McLaren, the landscape architect of the Golden Gate Park grounds in San Francisco. NR. The grounds are open daily 8-5. Free. The galleries are open Tu-Su 1-4. 25¢ adults on Sa-Su only, free for children. (408) 867-3421 or 3586.

Soledad vicinity

MISSION DE NUESTRA SENORA DE LA SOLEDAD, west of town and of US 101, 1777. The mission's name, roughly translated as "Our Lady of Solitude," could not be more fitting. The thirteenth of the missions to be founded, it was one that never achieved any degree of prosperity or stability. It is said that the priest-in-charge refused to leave after the mission was secularized in 1835 and died of starvation on the altar. Most of the buildings have been in ruins for many years. Recently, the adobe chapel has been restored. Open daily, except Tu, 10-4. Free. Donations accepted. (408) 678-2586.

Merced, Mariposa, Madera, Fresno, Kings, Tulare, and Kern Counties

The immense seven-county south central area of California is a land of extraordin-ary contrasts in topography and history. From the traveler's viewpoint, most of the interest is concentrated in the eastern section, in Yosemite National Park and in the two national parks of Sequoia/Kings Canyon. The flat middle ground of the San Joaquin Valley is rich in agricultural resources but not in history. If you are on your way to one of the parks, however, there are refreshing oases of culture to be visited.

Allensworth

ALLENSWORTH HISTORIC DISTRICT, principally along Palmer and Stowe Aves., 20th century. This small rural farming community is unique among California's towns as the only community which was founded, financed, and governed by black Americans. In 1908 Colonel Allensworth, himself a former slave, organized the California Colony and Home Promotion Association for the purpose of establishing a community where blacks might live and work apart from the debilitating influences of racial prejudice. Originally comprised of 8 public buildings and 31 residential dwellings, the town never really prospered because of the arid soil and an overdependence on an agricultural economy, and was almost abandoned.

The **Allensworth School** (1912) on Douglas Ave. is still used for educational purposes and, along with the Colonel's house nearby, remains in good condition. Those involved in the town's school system were at the forefront of defending the right of black children to a quality education in the state of California. Both the school and the Allensworth house are part of the **Colonel Allensworth State Historic Park,** with headquarters and an interpretive center at 4099 Douglas Ave. The park has been created to encourage the restoration of other town buildings and to continue the legacy begun by Allensworth. Operated by the California Department of Parks and Recreation. NR. Open all year, daily 1-5. Free. Groups by reservation. (805) 765-5004.

Bakersfield

PIONEER VILLAGE (Kern County Museum), 3801 Chester Ave., 1868-1910. This unique outdoor museum village contains nearly 60 structures on fourteen acres and provides the visitor with an opportunity to experience a typical frontier community in central California. As with other museums of this type, many of the buildings have been relocated to the village from other sites. Several houses are of particular interest. The **W.A. Howell House** (1891) is a Victorian mansion which was moved from its original location on the corner of 17th and H Sts. in 1969. Most of the furnishings are a gift of the Howell family. The **Barnes Log House** (1868) is located on San Emigdio St. and was originally built by Thomas Barnes on the Canfield Ranch. It, too, is furnished with objects typical of the period. Also on San Emigdio St. is the **Sheepherder's Cabin,** built in 1906 by Tom Quinn and originally located east of Delano. Beginning at the corner of San Emigdio and Claraville is a group of buildings known as the **Weller Ranch Ensemble,** consisting of a ranch residence, barn, windmill, tankhouse, and cook wagon. The village is open M-F 8-3:30, Sa-Su and holidays 10-3:30. $1 adults, 75¢ senior citizens and children. (805) 861-2132. ⛪

Bakersfield vicinity

WALKER PASS, 60 miles NE of Bakersfield on CA 178, 1834. This 5,248-foot-high pass through the Sierra Nevada mountains remains largely unaltered except for the paved road which follows the original grade. The pass was discovered by pioneer Joseph Reddeford Walker, who led the first emigrant wagon train through the Sierras in 1843. NR.

Delano

DELANO HERITAGE PARK, Lexington and Garces, 1890-1912. Located along the main valley line of the Southern Pacific Railroad, the city of Delano emerged as a packing and shipping center for the surrounding orchards. A grouping of historic properties administered by the city's Parks and Recreation Department in affiliation with the Delano Historical Society includes the 1890 **Heritage House,** the 1916

Jasmine School, a replica of the **Jasmine School Stable,** the 1876 **Delano Jail,** and the 1912 **Orcier Famosa Store.** Open by appointment only; guided tours for groups. Free. (805) 725-2937.

Fresno

Fresno dates from the 1870s when the Central Pacific Railroad came through the San Joaquin Valley. It must have been difficult then to visualize any kind of settlement in such an arid, flat, and bleak area. With the development of modern irrigation techniques, however, Fresno and the surrounding farmland began to blossom. By the early 1900s the land was providing a handsome dividend for fruit farmers. Fresno was the natural economic center, the place to exchange agricultural products for services and manufactured goods. Industry is now as well ensconced in the city of Fresno as the raising of raisins and cotton is in the countryside. As in some of the large Midwestern towns which developed out of farming communities, there isn't a great deal left of the past to enjoy. It is as if land were considered too valuable not to be "replanted" with new buildings every generation or so. But even here in Fresno, there have been the individualists, some call them eccentrics, who have defied the accepted gospel and preserved the heritage of the past.

FORESTIERE UNDERGROUND GARDENS, 5021 West Shaw Ave., 1906-45. Baldasare Forestiere, a Sicilian immigrant, designed and created this bizarre complex of underground caverns, grottoes, patios, and garden courts to encircle his underground home of some fifty rooms. Designed as a retreat from the arid heat of the San Joaquin Valley, the subterranean world was carved out of approximately ten acres (since reduced to five). Stone arches and domed ceilings took 40 years to carve; other supports were made of reinforced concrete. The underground spaces, lighted by means of skylights, are connected by passageways and promenades, including an 800-foot automobile tunnel. Forestiere delighted in growing citrus fruit and grapes in an almost climate-controlled environment. He died in 1946 at age 67. His extraordinary work had been accomplished using only such tools as a pick, shovel, and wheelbarrow. NR. Open June 15-Sept 15, daily 10-4, weather permitting. Tours available. $5 adults, $2 children and senior citizens. (209) 485-3281.

KEARNEY PARK AND MANSION, 7160 Kearney Blvd., 1892. M. Theo Kearney, a wealthy landowner and first president of the California Raisin Growers Association, decided to lay out his estate — Fruit Vale — in the late 1880s. He began by constructing the broad, seven-mile-long Kearney Blvd. to connect the property with the town. In addition, a 160-acre park was designed by landscape architect Rudolph Ulrich as a proper setting for a mansion. A San Francisco firm was commissioned to design a sumptuous residence in the Chateau style. Kearney's death in 1905, however, put a halt to construction. Only the estate superintendent's house was completed. But what a house it is! It featues an elaborate hipped roof and an open wraparound porch. The style is somewhat French in appearance. The Fresno City and County Historical Society is now located here. Its collections include antique clothing, furniture, and domestic and farm objects. NR. Open Mar-Dec, Th-Su 1-4; Jan-Feb, Sa-Su 1-4. $1 adults, 25¢ children. (209) 441-0862.

MEUX HOUSE, 1007 R St., 1889-90. This 2½-story frame, clapboard, and shingle house is the oldest substantial residence in Fresno. It was lived in by the same

Hanford

TAOIST TEMPLE, No. 12 China Alley, 1893. Hanford once had the nation's second-largest Chinese population, the first being in San Francisco. China Alley, a 200-foot-long avenue, lies at the center of Hanford's Chinatown. Oriental workers were originally drawn to the area to work at railroad construction and in the production of fruits and vegetables on nearby San Joaquin Valley farms. Most of the Chinese immigrated from the Far-yuen region. They brought their religion with them, and the temple was the most important building on China Alley. It has changed very little since it was built. NR. Privately owned, but visible from the street.

family until 1970 and was never remodeled or greatly redecorated. For this reason, anyone who is interested in authentic Victorian design should not pass the Meux House by. Thomas Richard Meux, a prominent physician, had the house built in a mixture of Queen Anne and Eastlake styles, an eclectic approach common at the time. The exterior features an off-center entrance porch which also wraps around three sides of the house, and a two-story polygonal side tower with carved panels. The interior is typically late-Victorian, with handsome papers used for walls and ceilings. The woodwork is richly stained and varnished throughout the house. All of the lighting fixtures are excellent examples of gas units. The house is maintained as a museum. NR. Open Tu-Su 12-4. $1.50 adults, 50¢ children. (209) 233-8007.

SANTA FE PASSENGER DEPOT, 2650 Tulare St., 1899. Around the turn of the century the Santa Fe Railroad constructed a number of stations which remain today as fine examples of Mission Revival architecture. Fresno is fortunate to have one of them, even if its interior has been ruinously "modernized." The brick and plaster station was constructed under the direction of W.B. Storey, Jr., who later became the president of the line, and features the characteristic arches and tiled roof of the Mission Revival style. NR.

Inyokern vicinity

BANDIT ROCK (Robber's Roost), SW of Inyokern near jct. of CA 14 and 178, c. 1871-75. Easily seen from CA 14, this promontory of jagged rocks and deep crevices marks the hide-out of Kern County's most notorious bandit gang. Rising 4,000 feet above the desert floor, the rock outcropping afforded Tiburico Vasquez, the notorious leader of the gang, an excellent view across the arid landscape, as well as protection from the severe desert weather. From this base amid the craggy peaks, Vasquez plundered weary travelers until he was caught in Los Angeles and hanged in San Jose on March 19, 1875. The secluded hide-out has remained largely unaltered through the years. NR.

Bandit Rock, Hanford

Lebec vicinity

FORT TEJON STATE HISTORIC PARK, 35251 Fort Tejon Rd., 1854-64. The United States Army established Fort Tejon (Indian for "badger") on June 24, 1854. Visitors to the fort in the early days described its scenic location as "an oasis in the desert where all is freshness and life." The Army, however, chose the spot for its proximity to a nearby pass which stock rustlers often traversed. The fort also functioned as a place from which to safeguard the Indians of the San Joaquin Valley. In 1857 an experimental "Camel Corps" was implemented at the fort for transporting supplies to isolated posts throughout the arid Southwest. Abandoned by the Army in 1864, the settlement contained over twenty buildings at the peak of its activity. Today the barracks building and the orderlies' quarters have been restored, and the foundations of several other buildings remain. Operated by the State Department of Parks. NR. Daily 10-5, 50¢ adults, 25¢ children 6-17 and senior citizens. (805) 765-5004.

Rosamond

BURTON'S TROPICO GOLD MINE (Kern-Antelope Historical Society), Star Rte. 1. The small village of Rosamond has been known as a shopping center for ranchers and miners in the region for some time. A mine and mill are the principal attractions of an historical nature and these are affiliated with the area's historical society. The mine is open Th-Su 10-4. $2.50 adults, $1.50 children. For information regarding hours at the mill, call the society. The organization also operates a museum which features early photos of the area and Indian and Antelope Valley artifacts. (805) 256-2644. 🏃

Sequoia/Kings Canyon National Park

The parks are accessible only from the west via Visalia (CA 198), Fresno (CA 180), and Bakersfield (CA 178). While they are two distinct parks, they blend into each other geographically and are managed by the National Park Service as one unit. Though not as familiar, perhaps, as Yosemite to the north, these two parks lie flush across the heart of the Sierra Nevada in east central California and include 1,300 square miles of the most spectacular scenery to be found anywhere. The variety is astounding—towering granite peaks, deep canyons, and hundreds of alpine lakes—and of course the giant sequoias. The largest living things on earth, these trees are so popular among tourists and campers that the Park Service quips, "you might well miss the forest for the trees." Mount Whitney, the highest point in the continental United States, can also be found here, leaving one with the impression that nearly everything grows to extremes in this land of giants. The park is maintained by the National Park Service. Jan-May, Oct-Dec, daily 9-5; June-Sept, daily 8-5. Free. (209) 565-3341.

Several historic lodges and campsites related to the development of these park areas can be found along the winding trails:

Giant Forest Lodge Historic District (Camp Sierra). One of the first sites within the park to be developed for tourist accommodations (1900), the area began as a tent camp called Camp Sierra. Construction of the Giant Forest Hotel—actually just a simple hall designed for cooking and dining—took place in 1914. Eventually, the area developed into a village of rustic cabins using sequoia bark or redwood shake materials which harmonize well with the natural environment. NR.

Giant Forest Village (Camp Kaweah). The Camp Kaweah portion of this historic area stands on a forested slope just north of the Giant Forest Village and consists of an office/warehouse and 41 wooden cabins which were erected between 1926 and 1940. Developed in response to the building of the General's Highway through the Giant Forest section of Sequoia National Park, these early cabins remain in good condition. NR.

Tharp's Log. A fallen, fire-hollowed redwood large enough to use for a cabin, the log is found on the northern edge of Log Meadow in the Giant Forest section of Sequoia National Park. In 1858 Hale Tharp made the first recorded entrance of a non-native American into Giant Forest and carved his name and the year on the side of the log. Shortly after 1860 Tharp began using the meadows of Giant Forest as a summer range for his cattle and subsequently adapted the huge hollow log for use as a cabin. The cabin can still be seen and entered along the trail. NR.

The **Squatter's Cabin.** Located in a beautiful grove of giant sequoias at the north end of Huckleberry Meadow in the Giant Forest, the cabin was built with walls of horizontal peeled logs. It was erected in 1886 by John Vest, a member of a unique socialist organization intending to develop a utopian community based on logging. Vest was forced to abandon his cabin and claim when it became known that the land had already been sold to Hale Tharp. NR.

Shorty Lovelace Historic District. Joseph Walter "Shorty" Lovelace, a fur trapper who spent much of his life in the Sierras, developed a system of as many as 36 shelters along the watershed of the South Fork in Kings Canyon National Park between 1910 and 1940. These consisted of either single-room log structures or shelters constructed among natural boulders. Of these, nine sites have been specifically

Tharp's Log

identified, and two of the cabins, at Vidette Meadow and Cloud Canyon, remain in fair condition. NR.

Taft

THE FORT, SW corner of Ash and Lincoln Sts., 1938-40. Undertaken as one of the largest WPA projects in the San Joaquin Valley and certainly one of the most unusual in the United States, the Fort was built for use as a community center. The adobe brick reconstruction approximates the form and plan of John Sutter's original 1839-44 fort in Sacramento. Inside there are individual buildings which today house county, state, and federal offices. Only a central building, the auditorium, has had to be rebuilt in succeeding years because of earthquake damage. NR.

Visalia

TULARE COUNTY MUSEUM, 27000 Mooney Blvd. Ten buildings are set in this beautiful 150-acre oak grove and feature historical exhibits such as Indian artifacts, early farm equipment, antique guns, clocks, and dolls. Also included on the grounds is a statue by sculptor James Earl Frazier entitled *End of the Trail*. Among the historic buildings are an 1854 log cabin, an 1872 jail, and a farmhouse, library, blacksmith shop, school, and print shop, all c. 1890. Since some of these buildings may be closed as various times, it is wise to call ahead. Generally open Th-M 10-4. 50¢ per person, 25¢ school group tours. (209) 733-6613.

Yosemite

YOSEMITE NATIONAL PARK, 58 miles NE of Fresno on CA 41. In 1864 this magnificent valley became one of California's first state parks, and, soon after the surrounding area was designated a federal park in 1906, the state ceded its section to the federal government. John Muir, the naturalist who was largely instrumental in obtaining national status for the region, wrote that here are "the most songful streams in the world . . . the noblest forests, the loftiest granite domes, the deepest

ice sculptured canyons." Indeed, most of the park's 2½-million yearly visitors would agree that Yosemite's high wilderness country, Alpine meadows, and towering waterfalls are unsurpassed in this country, or anywhere. The popularity of Yosemite as a haven for campers also results in monumental traffic problems as visitors must often wait in line for campsites. Reservations are available through Ticketron during the peak spring and fall season by calling (213) 372-4605. The park is operated by the National Park Service and admission is $3 by the carload.

Visitors who wish to explore the park's history while savoring its natural beauty should concentrate their efforts on the Yosemite Valley area off CA 140 and the Wawona section in the south off CA 41. The Valley section of the park is the location of the **Valley Visitor Center,** where an orientation slide program and publications are available. The Center is open daily 9-5 and can be reached by phone at (209) 372-4461.

The Ahwahnee Hotel is located in the general vicinity of the Valley Visitor Center. The largest building in Yosemite, it was built in 1925 and designed by architect Gilbert Stanley Underwood. Ahwahnee, an Indian word meaning "deep, grassy meadow," fittingly describes the pastoral setting of this rustic lodging at the base of the north valley wall. Although the primary building material is reinforced concrete, the visual appearance suggests the rustic style of timber and granite. Decorative geometric patterns created by California Indian tribes abound in the interior — from the lobby floors and bath tiling to the interior of elevators. The roar of nearby Yosemite Falls still lulls visitors to sleep. NR. See Lodging and Dining for details regarding accommodations.

While in the vicinity of the Yosemite Valley Visitor Center, be sure to stop by the **Indian Cultural Museum and Village** directly behind the Center, a reminder of the Native Americans who inhabited the region long before a park was necessary to protect it. 🚹

Also located just off CA 140 is the oldest building in Yosemite, the **Yosemite Valley Chapel,** a small board-and-batten struc-

Ahwahnee Hotel, Yosemite National Park

ture designed in 1879 by Charles Geddes and moved to its present site in 1901.

David and Jennie Curry established their innovative **Camp Curry** (1899-1924) at the base of Glacier Point at a time when a hotel was the only other site available to the Yosemite Valley visitor who wished to sleep somewhere other than a public campground. Begun with seven tents, the complex eventually included cabins, bungalows, and a registration office — all of which feature the familiar peeled-bark rustic exteriors. NR. Camp Curry is accessible via park trails. See Lodging and Dining for details regarding accommodations.

Wawona Hotel and Pavilion, located off CA 41 in the southern section of Yosemite National Park. In 1856 Galen Clark discovered that his homestead ranch, conveniently located only a day's journey from both Yosemite Valley and the tall trees at Mariposa, was an ideal location for wayfarers who wished to spend the night. Clark soon added a partner to his venture, but failing business forced him to sell the property to the Washburn brothers, owners of a Yosemite concession, in 1870. The Washburns are responsible for the hotel as it is today — constructing the main hotel building in 1879, another building in 1885, and the annex in 1915. Finally, in 1934 the land and hotel were sold to the National Park Service and have been run by the Yosemite Park and the Curry Company ever since. The hotel's white hacienda-style exterior features wide verandas shaded by tall cedars, while the interior is

highlighted by the Sun Room, decorated with rattan furniture and inlaid wood paneling. NR. See Lodging and Dining for details regarding accommodations.

Also in the Wawona section of the park, just a few miles from the Mariposa Grove, is the **Pioneer Yosemite History Center**

which includes a covered bridge, several historic buildings, horse-drawn wagons, and exhibits. A living history program is offered during the summer; guided tours in the spring and fall. Check with Park Information at (209) 372-4461 for hours and program details. Free. 👥

Calaveras, Alpine, Tuolumne, Mono, and Inyo Counties

The counties of east-central California have been somewhat isolated from the great surge of post-World War II economic expansion and population growth that have transformed so many rural parts of the state into suburban tracts. The areas to the north of this region along CA 49 may be crowded with sightseers during at least the summer months, however, since this is gold-mining country. Every other town seems to be a "ghost town" of the Wild West, and the traveler has to be aware of fool's gold, the merely flashy and not at all authentic in lodgings, restaurants, and even "historic" sights. There are, nonetheless, some wonderful places to explore—Bodie, Sonora, and Columbia, among others. Further south is the great expanse of Death Valley and its strange and wonderful sights, many of which predate recorded history.

Angels Camp

ANGELS HOTEL, Main St. at Birds Way, 1855. The original hotel was a huge canvas structure which was soon replaced by a one-story wooden building where local miners danced with each other in the absence of women. The present stone structure was erected in 1855 from volcanic material quarried nearby. It was during these early days that Mark Twain, then living with a friend at nearby Jackson Hill, was a frequent visitor to the hotel. It is believed that the bartender here was the first to tell the story of the famous frog who hopped his way down Main St. and into Twain's famed story "The Celebrated Jumping Frog of Calaveras County." Today the up-

stairs has been converted into apartments and the first floor is commercial, but an annual frog jumping competition in May commemorates the hotel's celebrated past. NR. Open during regular business hours.

Bishop vicinity

LAWS RAILROAD MUSEUM AND HISTORICAL SITE, E on Silver Canyon Rd. off US 6, 1883. The Laws Railroad Depot is the highlight of this narrow gauge railroad complex which was once the northern terminus of the Laws-Keeler Branch of the Southern Pacific Railroad. Railroad enthusiasts, both young and old, will enjoy browsing through the restored station agent's five-room home and examining the hand-operated gallows-type turntable, as well as the water tower, pumphouse, and loading bunkers which saw daily service nearly a century ago. Twenty-one buildings and structures with original equipment scattered throughout eleven acres, make this a railroad buff's paradise. The complex is affiliated with the Bishop Museum and Historical Society. NR. Dec-Mar, Sa-Su 10-4; Apr-Nov, daily 10-4. Free. Donations accepted. 👥 (714) 873-5950.

Bridgeport

MONO COUNTY COURTHOUSE, Main St., 1880. Stops at Bridgeport and nearby Bodie are well worth a detour for those interested in the architectural heritage of California during the 19th century. Bridgeport came to be the county seat in a rather unusual manner. As early as 1861 Aurora had been the site of the county government, but a new survey that year revealed the embarrassing fact that Aurora was actually located in Nevada. The Italianate courthouse, with a delightful miniature cupola, is readily visible from the street, although public access to the interior is restricted. NR.

Bridgeport vicinity

BODIE HISTORIC DISTRICT, Bodie Rd., 13 miles E of junction with CA 395 and 6 miles S of Bridgeport, 1859. Bodie was named after Waterman S. Body (the change in spelling has been attributed to an illiterate sign painter) who discovered gold here in 1859. With the discovery of the Comstock Lode at Virginia City in 1858, miners began to cross the Sierras and the wild rush to the desert high country had begun.

By 1879 Bodie boasted a population of more than 10,000 and the town's 65 saloons no doubt contributed to an epidemic of lawlessness, a "sea of sin, lashed by the tempests of lust and passion" as the Rev.

Warrington commented in 1881. Such catch-all phrases as "Badman from Bodie" and "Goodbye God, I'm going to Bodie" were common during the town's restless boom years, but as so often was the case in western mining towns, the mineral deposits were eventually depleted and the miners sought their fortunes elsewhere.

Today, more than 100 buildings are maintained in an arrested state of decay as part of the **Bodie State Historic Park**. The largely unrestored town is best visited during the summer when the weather is more predictable. A self-guided tour will take you and your family through the main part of town which includes a c. 1879 church, jail, two-room schoolhouse, miners' union hall, and a hillside cemetery where younger family members may enthusiastically search for the marker of Bodie's famed "Badman." The village buildings are usually accessible seven days a week from 9 until sunset. Because the park is in such an isolated location, however, it would be wise to check ahead if the weather is inclement. The Department of Parks and Recreation

Bodie bank vault

Bodie jail, Bodie State Historic Park

should be able to provide you with information. NR, NHL. (916) 525-7232. 🛉

Death Valley

DEATH VALLEY NATIONAL MONUMENT, 70 miles E of Lone Pine via CA 136 and 190. To many, Death Valley is the epitome of desolation, an almost surreal landscape of rugged desert, salt flats, and towering peaks—a geologist's paradise. The valley is believed to have been an inland sea millions of years ago, before radical movements beneath the earth altered the surface and the blazing sun evaporated the water. The site of the lowest point on the continent, this arid region receives less than two inches of rainfall annually and is known for the harshness of its extreme temperature fluctuations. Death Valley is said to have received its morbidly appropriate name in 1849 when gold-seekers in search of a shortcut through the mountains became stranded on the salt flats. The famed 20-mule teams hauled borax from the valley after 1881, and soon the area developed as a tourist attraction. Because of the vastness of the region, it is wise to begin one's tour of Death Valley at the **Visitor Center** located off CA 190 at Furnace Creek. The Center is open mid-Apr-

Oct, daily 8-5; Nov-mid-Apr 8-9. Free. Guided tours are also available. 🛉 (714) 786-2331.

In the vicinity of the Visitors Center are two museums which will prove useful and informative to any traveler unfamiliar with the area's history. The **Death Valley Museum** (open daily 9-5) offers a good general introduction to the valley, while the nearby **Borax Museum** (open daily 8:30-5) traces the role of this mineral in Death Valley's history and development. The Visitor Center area also provides a good starting point for courageous backcountry enthusiasts who wish to stray from the beaten path in search of several well-marked mining ruins. It is also a fine place to begin one's trek to two of Death Valley's featured attractions: **Scotty's Castle** to the north, and **Death Valley Junction** to the southeast.

Harmony Borax Works, located just north of Furnace Creek and the Visitor Center, features the remains of a plant complex which includes adobe ruins, part of the furnace and boiler, and the dissolving tanks where the raw mineral was boiled before becoming crystallized borax. It is believed that the idea for a 20-mule team originated here when a plant superintendent decided to see how much borax could be hauled when two teams of mules were hitched together. The teams later became the trademark of the operation and were eventually incorporated as the company symbol. NR.

Not as well-known as the Harmony works, the **Eagle Borax Works** to the south of the Visitor Center are accessible only via a dirt road.

The remnants of the old gold mining town of **Skidoo** are located directly west of the Visitor Center, but are only accessible by turning off CA 190 at Emigrant and proceeding through Emigrant Canyon to a trail entrance designed for four-wheel-drive travel only. Mine shafts and test pits are scattered over the countryside as reminders of this once prosperous boom town, but these ruins are only worth the trip for hardy would-be prospectors. NR.

A detour off the main road from the Visitor Center to Scotty's Castle in the north leads one through Titus Canyon to the old prospecting town of **Leadfield**. Remarkably good remains of dugouts and tin structures, as well as the main mine shaft, can still be seen.

Death Valley Scotty Historic District (**Scotty's Castle**) off CA 72, 1922. In 1904, publicity hound and prospector Walter Scott convinced a Midwestern insurance magnate named Albert Johnson to construct this desert mansion which employs stucco and a red roof intended to imitate the popular Spanish Colonial adobe style. The fact that materials had to be transported miles over rough terrain was inconsequential to the eccentric Scott, who gained notoriety in 1906 when he staged a fake skirmish to frighten other "grubstakers" from pursuing the location of his alleged gold mines. NR. Guided tours of the ranch and mansion begin every hour on the hour, 9-5, and cost $4. 🕴

Death Valley Junction Historic District, CA 127 and 190, 1923-26. The town of Death Valley Junction first appeared on the map in 1907 upon the completion of the Tonah & Tidewater Railroad by the Pacific Coast Borax Company. The construction of a mill at the Junction and a sixteen-mile narrow gauge spur which connected the company town to the main line led to the formation of a substantial village population. Two groups of low

Death Valley Junction Historic District

adobe buildings built around a plaza provide evidence of this expansion. Exhibiting a skillful manipulation of traditional Spanish Colonial elements, these town buildings from the '20s create a civilized environment in the midst of the harsh desert. As the historic entrance to Death Valley itself, the Junction plays host to nearly a half-million visitors each year. The old recreation hall has been converted into the internationally-known **Amargosa Opera House,** whose owners, in addition to having saved the town for posterity, are responsible for one of the most unbelievable theater-interiors in modern history: an "audience" of 266 16th-century Spanish characters painted on the walls! Tours by appointment only. Free. (209) 296-4519.

Independence

EASTERN CALIFORNIA MUSEUM, 155 Grant St. This natural history museum exhibits Paiute and Shoshone Indian baskets, as well as pioneer artifacts and memorabilia related to mining, railroading, and ranching in the area. Open M, Th-F 9-12, 1-5; Su 12-5. Free. (714) 878-2411.

The museum also has jurisdiction over two historic houses in Independence. The Queen Anne-style **Commander's House** (1872) at Main St. and CA 395 is open Mar-Oct, Su 1-4:45. The **Edwards House** (1865) is located at 124 Market St. and is open intermittently—believe it or not—whenever a woman is seen weaving in the front room of the house. If you don't feel up to peeking in windows, you might call the museum for the current hours.

Independence vicinity

MANZANAR WAR RELOCATION CENTER, 6 miles S of Independence off CA 395, 1942-45. This is the site of the first detention camp for Japanese-Americans during World War II. The remains of the camp stand as a painful reminder of a shameful moment in American history. The camp was established in March, 1942, one month after President Franklin Roosevelt signed executive order 9066 authorizing the secretary of war to

designate areas for the proscription of Japanese-Americans. Relocation became a polite word for "internment," since many of the nearly 10,000 inhabitants were American citizens held against their wills simply because of their Japanese ancestry. Manzanar was closed in November, 1945, and the desert quickly reclaimed many of the campsite's structures. An auditorium, cement foundations, stone steps, and two sentry posts remain. Recently the State Parks Department has studied the feasibility of incorporating the camp into the state park system. NR.

Mokelumne Hill

HOTEL LEGER, CA 49 and 26, 1851. Over 100 years ago George Leger came from Europe to establish this unique hotel in the Gold-Rush boom town of Mokelumne Hill. It soon became famous throughout the West for its service and hospitality. Originally known as the Hotel l'Europe, the Leger has been renovated but still contains its original stone facade and windows, black walnut bar, and balustraded staircase. NR. See Lodging and Dining for details regarding accommodations.

Murphys

MURPHYS HOTEL, Main and Algiers

Sts., 1860. Originally constructed as a stagecoach stop to serve traffic on the road to Calaveras Grove of the Big Trees, the original building was thought to be fireproof until a conflagration in 1859 proved otherwise. The walls of the new hotel which opened the following spring were constructed of stone, which saved the building in the fire of 1874 and the great explosion and fire of 1893. The hotel houses a saloon, and furnishings date to before the turn of the century when many notable guests stayed at the hotel, including Mark Twain, Horatio Alger, U.S. Grant, and John Jacob Astor. NR. See Lodging and Dining for details regarding accommodations.

Located off CA 4, the picturesque village of Murphys features many other buildings which are old and quaint. The best is the much-photographed Classical Revival **Murphys Grammar School** on Jones St. (1860), which was the first public school in the state. NR. Private, but visible from the public way.

San Andreas

CALAVERAS COUNTY COURT-HOUSE, Main St., 1867. Since the construction of the new government center on the east edge of town, the courthouse has served as the **Calaveras County Museum and Archives** housing Indian artifacts and mining and pioneer memorabilia. Two stories high, this brick building contained the jail, courtroom, and sheriff's office. The county jail, located on the first floor in the rear, features wooden cells, although the original solid plank cell doors were replaced with iron grilles in 1900. The elusive Charles Bolton, known throughout the West as "Black Bart," was held here during his trial for robbing stagecoaches. Between 1875 and 1883 the legendary bandit plundered 27 stages in the surrounding hills, but was eventually convicted and sent to San Quentin following his short stay here. Little wonder that even "Black Bart" never ventured a breakout through the stone rubble walls of the jailyard—twelve feet in height and eighteen inches thick. NR. Tu-Su 10-4. 50¢ adults, 25¢ children. (209) 754-4203.

While in the area, visit the **Thorn House,** 87 E. St. Charles, c. 1857. A California variation on the traditional Gothic style, this residence was built by Benjamin

K. Thorn, who served as deputy sheriff of the county for nearly 50 years. The roof is steeply pitched and has ornamental bargeboards which provide a distinctly Gothic effect. NR. Privately owned, but visible from the street.

Sonora

TUOLUMNE COUNTY JAIL, 156 W. Bradford St., 1866. While the first "jail" in town consisted of a substantial chain attached to a sturdy tree to which prisoners were attached "like pendants on a necklace," the present jailhouse held prisoners until the 1960s when the building was designated as the **Tuolumne County Museum** (weekdays 9-4:30).

The mining town of Sonora was not exempt from the problems of maintaining law and order which plagued many towns during the lawless Gold Rush years. In 1851 a Vigilance Committee was formed in response to the record 30 murders which had occurred the previous year. The immediate hanging of three men produced temporary results. As the official report stated, "Many who strutted insolently about the streets with pistols and knives in their belts have quietly laid them aside, and walk about like decent people . . ." The construction of the county jail would assure that the sidewalks of Sonora remained peaceful. NR.

While in town, take the time to pass by the **Tuolumne County Courthouse** on West Yaney Ave., a Classical Revival structure whose clock tower rises 88 feet above the street. NR.

Sonora vicinity

COLUMBIA STATE HISTORIC PARK, 4 miles NW of Sonora on CA 49, 1850s. Gold was discovered in Columbia in March of 1850. A month later the population had blossomed to 6,000 and would reach a peak of 15,000. The early years of the town witnessed a slow development as the water necessary for mining gold and sustaining the population was scarce. The town did prosper, however, and came to be known as the "Gem of the Southern

Mines" until productivity decreased about 1860. Today Columbia has been faithfully restored, and, as a state historic park, it is one of the best preserved of the old mining towns, with many buildings in excellent condition. Though still in the process of restoration, most of the buildings are open and accessible. Operated by a branch of the Department of Parks and Recreation. NR. Daily 8-5. Free. (209) 532-4301. Several of Columbia's historic structures are particularly noteworthy: ♦♦

The **City Hotel,** begun in 1857, and once known as the "What Cheer House," was one of the largest buildings in Columbia. The furniture and fixtures are owned by the state, but the restored 20-room inn is operated by resort management students at nearby Columbia College. See Lodging and Dining for details regarding accommodations.

Columbia Firehouse, also located on Main St., has played a crucial role in a town which has witnessed several devastating fires throughout its history. Also on view here is *Papeete,* a two-cylinder fire engine built in Boston in 1852. Still in fine working condition, it was originally headed for Tahiti, but ended up in Columbia instead.

The **Schoolhouse** on State St. was built in 1860 for $5,000. The two-story brick structure was closed in 1937 and was later restored through the fund-raising efforts of a group of California schoolchildren.

The **Fallon House Theater** on Washington St. was built in the early 1860s by Jim Fallon and later became the candle-glittering social center during Columbia's gold mining era. Plays are presented during the summer season by students from the University of the Pacific. For information and/or reservations, write to the university in Stockton at 3601 Pacific Ave. (209) 946-2311.

The **Wells Fargo Building** at the end of Main St. was the first building in town to undergo restoration (1953). The one-time depository of the town's $87 million gold fortune, it dates to the town's early years and has become the visual focus of the restored village.

Yosemite National Park

GREAT SIERRA MINE HISTORIC SITE (Dana Village), W of Lee Vining in the park, 1881-84. The Great Sierra Mining Company established Dana Village as a support facility for the operations of the Sheepherder Lode, a silver vein high in the Sierras which was allegedly discovered by a young sheepherder in 1874. The vein proved less than prosperous, however, and the remains of five stone cabins, a wooden blacksmith shop, and a small stone powder house can be seen today. The original mine equipment has been removed for preservation purposes and is displayed at the History Center in the Wawona section of Yosemite National Park. (See also previous listing for Yosemite National Park.) NR.

Northern California

NORTHERN California offers a way of life as distinctive as southern California's, but in its own way quite different. El Camino Real fades away when it reaches beyond San Francisco Bay, thus signaling the end of Spanish and Mexican cultural influence. In climate and historic origins northern California is Yankee land when compared with the south. The old Anglo-Saxon stock, however, has been enriched by the welcome addition of the French, Italians, Germans, Portuguese, Irish, Chinese, and Japanese, among others. San Francisco, for example, would not be San Francisco without its distinct ethnic neighborhoods and traditions.

The term used to describe the life style of Marin County—"laid-back New England"—might well be applied to all of northern California. The temperate climate has always been extremely attractive to settlers from New England and other parts of the world where people enjoy more than the sun. While everyone hustles in this part of California—as elsewhere in the country—there is a bit more style to daily life. Part of northern California is wine country, and every resident of the counties north of San Francisco knows that a good vintage cannot be enjoyed on the run.

The resources of the northern counties—lumber, fish, minerals, fertile farm land—have drawn fortune hunters since the early 1800s. The population of the region exploded in the 1840s and '50s during the peak of the Gold Rush. Centered in the eastern Sacramento Valley and the Sierra Nevada mountains, the mining activity had a ripple effect on the economy of the whole region. Settlements grew into towns overnight, and some almost as quickly shrank to nothing again when it was discovered that a few nuggets did not lead to many.

Life in other parts of northern California has never been quite so exciting as in the gold country. But the redwoods have created many fortunes as great as those made in gold, and the naturally irrigated lands lying between the Sierra Nevadas and the coastal range bring forth splendid harvests every season. Today there are great mansions to tour in the farming and lumbering communities; picturesque wineries to visit in Napa and Sonoma counties; and seemingly endless miles of natural beauty to enjoy in state and national parks.

The principal cities of the Bay area—San Francisco, Oakland, and Berkeley—are a world unto themselves and always have been exceptional places. It sometimes appears that nearly every neighborhood is historic in some way. San Francisco symbolizes northern California's sophisticated and relaxed way of life. Possibly America's most beautiful city, it has the charm of a much smaller town. It is perhaps the respect for the past and a love for its old-shoe comforts which have endowed this city—and much of the region it serves as a cultural capital—with such attractive qualities.

In the pages that follow northern California is divided into seven sections, starting with the Bay area to the south, proceeding north along the coast and then east to the gold country, and ending finally in the central Sacramento Valley.

Stadtmuller House, San Francisco

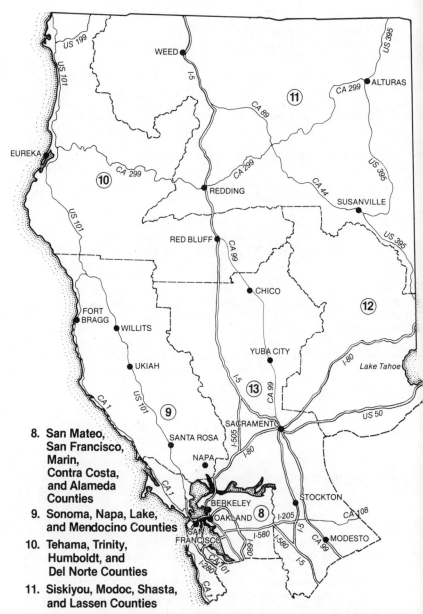

8. San Mateo,
   San Francisco,
   Marin,
   Contra Costa,
   and Alameda
   Counties

9. Sonoma, Napa, Lake,
   and Mendocino Counties

10. Tehama, Trinity,
    Humboldt, and
    Del Norte Counties

11. Siskiyou, Modoc, Shasta,
    and Lassen Counties

12. Plumas, Sierra, Nevada, Placer, El Dorado, and Amador Counties

13. Glenn, Butte, Colusa, Yuba, Sutter, Yolo, Solano, Sacramento,
    San Joaquin, and Stanislaus Counties

San Mateo, San Francisco, Marin, Contra Costa, and Alameda Counties

The counties of San Mateo, San Francisco, Alameda, Contra Costa and Marin surround beautiful San Francisco and San Pablo bays — actually a single body of water running for nearly 50 miles, roughly north to south. The single outlet to the Pacific is through the Golden Gate, so named by Colonel John C. Fremont when he caught sight of the narrow passage to the ocean more than a century ago.

There is no doubt that most of the bay area's historic attractions lie within the city of San Francisco itself, but the outlying areas have a lot to offer. From Oakland's fine museum, to the sophisticated Berkeley campus of the University of California, to the windswept wilderness of Point Reyes National Seashore, claimed for England by Sir Francis Drake hundreds of years ago, the Bay area combines magnificent natural settings with superb architecture and fascinating lore in a way that is certain to appeal to every taste.

Belmont

GEORGE CENTER MANSION (Twin Pines Manor), 1219 Ralston Ave., 1906. The San Mateo County Arts Council is housed in this early 20th-century landmark, once a luxurious private home. Contemporary works of local artists are featured. Open all year, M-F 9-5, Su 12-4. No charge. (415) 593-1816.

WILLIAM C. RALSTON HOME, College of Notre Dame campus, 1864-68. Ralston was an eminent San Francisco financier who played a major role in the exploitation of the Comstock Lode mines in Nevada and in developing industry and railroads in California. In its heyday, his ornate Victorian mansion, expanded several times, could acccommodate more than 100 guests for a weekend. The interior, lavishly decorated with fine woodwork and featuring columned doorways, skylit foyers, and cavernous living space,

has been carefully maintained by the college which now occupies it. NR. (415) 574-6161.

Berkeley

Berkeley developed in the 19th century around two areas: the flatlands of Ocean View near Oakland and the Bay, and the gentle hills where the University of California was founded (as College of California) in 1859. The original plan for the school, of which only University Avenue remains today, was drawn up by Frederick Law Olmstead. Bernard Maybeck, one of California's preeminent architects, contributed enormously to the ambience one finds in Berkeley today. Over his career, from the late 1800s until the 1920s, Maybeck, who served for a time as a professor at the University, was responsible for designing nearly 150 buildings in the state, many of which are in the Berkeley area. It is fitting that today the University owns and occupies many of Maybeck's most striking landmark buildings, both on the central campus and in the surrounding areas to which it has spread.

ANNA HEAD SCHOOL FOR GIRLS, 2538 Channing Way, 1892-1927. A complex of one-, two-, and three-story redwood-shingled buildings grouped around a central quadrangle and connected by a covered arbor, the Anna Head School, although developed over a period of 35 years, is uniform in style, resembling English medieval country house design with distinct western touches. The unfinished redwood exteriors, whose rustic simplicity blends well with the surrounding hills, were chosen because of the cheap, plentiful supply of that lumber available to the architects.

For seventy two years the complex was home to Miss Anna Head's School for Girls, one of the two oldest private schools in California. In 1964 the school was moved to Oakland and its buildings sold to

First Church of Christ, Scientist, Berkeley

the University, which uses them to house various campus services. NR.

Just to the southeast stands Bernard Maybeck's **First Church of Christ Scientist,** Dwight Way and Bowditch St., 1910, considered to be the architect's masterpiece. Maybeck combined the simplest and most basic of building materials — steel, concrete and redwood — to great effect. At first glance the church appears to be oriental in style, but elements of Gothic and Romanesque were used as well. All of the design and construction, both interior and exterior, was done to his specifications. NR, NHL. Open by appointment. (415) 845-7199.

ST. JOHN'S PRESBYTERIAN CHURCH, 2640 College Ave., 1910. Designed by Julia Morgan, who achieved great fame as architect for William Randolph Hearst's estate in San Simeon, St. John's is a sophisticated redwood example of the Craftsman style so popular in northern California. NR. Open for Sunday worship.

SENIOR HALL, University of California

campus, 1905-06. This one-story log building was designed by John Howard, who founded the University's School of Architecture. It was used as a meeting place for seniors involved in the growth of student government. NR. (415) 642-5215.

WILLIAM R. THORSEN HOUSE, 2307 Piedmont Ave., 1908. The Pasadena architectural firm of Greene and Greene designed this rambling shingled landmark, which is now the home of Sigma Phi Fraternity. Stained glass is used as decoration on the front door and side panels; the large glass windows were unusual for a time when small casements were the rule. NR.

Berkeley vicinity

HERSHELL-SPILLMAN MERRY-GO-ROUND, Tilden Regional Park, 1911. Still operated by the same 7½-horsepower Westinghouse electric motor installed originally, and with two vintage band-organs providing lively accompaniment, the merry-go-round has been bringing enjoyment to children and their parents for more than 70 years. Horses, giraffes, roosters, zebras, frogs, and many other ornately carved and painted wooden animals twirl here, protected by a wooden domed pavilion. NR. (415) 845-1212. 👫

Byron vicinity

JOHN MARSH HOUSE, six miles west via Marsh Creek Road, 1853-56. A cross between a Victorian Gothic cottage and an Italian villa, the John Marsh House was one of the first permanent structures in Contra Costa County. The three-story stone and brick landmark was the residence of one of California's earliest physicians. His letters extolling the wonders of California to friends in Missouri had a considerable influence on emigration: the first overland emigrant party to the Sierra Nevadas made Marsh's ranch their destination. NR. Privately-owned.

Fremont

MISSION SAN JOSE, Mission Blvd. at Washington, c. 1809-10. Fermin Francisco de Lasuen founded Mission San Jose in 1799; temporary frame buildings were hastily erected and later replaced by more permanent adobe structures. The only remaining building here was part of the living quarters: a long, low, one-story brick residence roofed in tile. At its height, Mission San Jose accommodated nearly 2,000 people. NR. Open all year, daily 9-5. Donations accepted. (415) 656-9125.

At Niles Blvd. and Nursery Ave. is **Jose de Jesus Vallejo Adobe** (c. 1850), now used as a guest house for the California Nursery Company. Once part of the Rancho Arroyo de la Alameda, an enormous spread of nearly 18,000 acres, the simple one-story adobe was the first of several built by Jose de Jesus Vallejo in the vicinity. Vallejo was administrator at the Mission San Jose from 1836-1840 and military commander at the Pueblo de San Jose for a brief period. In 1850 he was appointed postmaster of the mission. NR.

Hayward

MEEK MANSION AND CARRIAGE HOUSE, 240 Hampton Rd., 1869. William Meek, considered one of the state's pioneers in the science of fruit growing, brought the first grafted trees to the Pacific Coast in 1847 and farmed over 2,200 acres. The interior of his handsome mansion features oak floors embellished with inlaid mahogany parquet. Ceilings and walls have cast plaster medallions of acanthus leaves, nuts and fruit. NR. For information call (415) 881-6700.

Livermore

RAVENSWOOD, Arroyo Rd., 1893.

This rural estate was constructed in 1893 for San Francisco politcal boss Christopher Buckley. The original 100 acres included a main house, carriage house, bedroom house (the main house was used only for entertaining), and outbuildings. Outlying lands were planted in wine grapes, and the grounds surrounding the residence were landscaped with rose gardens, palm trees, and other species of trees and plants, many of which still exist. Ravenswood was designed for the entertainment of Buckley's associates. The main building was devoted to that function, with only a single bedroom in the large structure for a servant. An adjacent building, known as the Bedroom House, served as living quarters for the Buckley family and guests. Buckley became known as the Blind Boss of San Francisco in the 1880s. At age 30 he lost his sight, but nothing stopped his continued rise to power. He dispersed political patronage as it suited him, recognizing his visitors by the way they shook hands. Assistants, nicknamed "lambs," would read newspapers and necessary documents for him. Buckley's experimental farm has been subdivided in recent years; 30 acres, including the residences, are now owned by the Livermore Area Regional Park District. The main house is used for social events, while the bedroom house is being converted to a museum. NR.
(415) 447-1606.

Martinez

JOHN MUIR NATIONAL HISTORIC SITE, 4440 Alhambra Ave., 1882. Through his many published writings, John Muir established himself as an authority on the glaciers and mountains of the West and made a major contribution to the conservation movement in the United States. He voiced his concern for the necessity of preservation at a time when few understood his vision—or the need for ecological caution: after all, in the latter half of the 19th century, the West was still primarily undeveloped. Muir made his home on an 800-acre ranch in Martinez where his two children were raised, most

of his writing was done, and from which he traveled both to the nearby Sierras and to other wilderness spots around the globe, studying the landscape and making notes for future works. The frame Victorian house where he lived is now a museum; the adjacent **Martinez Adobe**, constructed in the 1840s, was home to one of Muir's daughters and his son-in-law for a time.

NR. Open all year, daily 8:30-4:30. 50¢ adults. (415) 228-8860.

A side trip to **Muir Woods National Monument,** named for the naturalist during his lifetime, will give the visitor an excellent idea of Muir's vision: acres of massive redwoods, some stretching more than 200 feet into the air, have been preserved for generations to enjoy. Six miles of trails wind throughout the forest, both paved gradients and rocky dirt paths. Everywhere are towering, graceful trees, some of which have stood sentinel for hundreds of years. Muir Woods, located about 17 miles north of San Francisco via I-101 and CA 1, is open all year, daily 8-sunset. Small admission fee. (415) 388-2595.

Menlo Park

CHURCH OF THE NATIVITY, 210 Oak Grove Ave., 1872. This was the first Catholic church built in Menlo Park. Lovingly cared for, it remains a superb example of the Victorian Gothic Revival style as translated by western architects. NR. (415) 323-7914.

MENLO PARK RAILROAD STATION, 1100 Merrill St., c. 1880. This diminutive shingled Eastlake-style railroad depot is now home to the Chamber of Commerce, which has taken great care to preserve it as it appeared 100 years ago. NR. (415) 325-2818.

Mill Valley

OUTDOOR ART CLUB, 1 West Blithedale Ave., 1904. The Outdoor Art Club was formed in 1902 by concerned Mill Valley residents who banded together to preserve the natural surroundings endangered by the ever-increasing population and weekend hikers and campers. Bernard Maybeck, the dean of San Francisco area architecture, was commissioned to design the organization's clubhouse, a shingled redwood building consisting of two wings at right angles to each other, with the main entrance at the apex of the angles. Situated in the midst of the downtown commercial area, the Club remains today a staunch supporter of preservation activities. NR. (415) 388-9886.

Novata vicinity

MARIN MUSEUM OF THE AMERI-CAN INDIAN, 2200 Novato Blvd. This site was first settled in the 15th century when the California Coast Miwok Indians established it as a major village. Evidence of habitation is visible in the form of two aboriginal house pits and a petroglyph. Also on the site are the ruins of an adobe structure built c. 1830 for Camilion Wunitia, the last headman of the Olompali tribe. Stone retaining walls in the creek near the adobe and a stone reservoir built on the ranch in the 1860s and '70s still function today. The museum interprets the history of ancient tribes, ranging from Alaskan to Peruvian and features photographs, artifacts, and archaeological materials. NR. Open all year, Tu-Sa 10-4, Su 12-4. 50¢ adults, 25¢ children. 🚻 (415) 897-4064.

Oakland

The city of Oakland, dwarfed by its famous neighbor across San Francisco Bay, tends to get short shrift on the vacationer's itinerary, except for the obligatory baseball or football game when the As or the Raiders are in town. The Bay Bridge and major highways offer views at 55 miles per hour which are hardly inspiring. There is much to see here, however, and the city is easily reached either by car or by BART —the Bay Area Rapid Transit System—a modern, convenient, and fast subway line.

Oakland was settled in the mid-19th century and grew rapidly because of its fine port and its location as western terminus for the Western Pacific Railroad. By the mid 1880s it was among the most successful manufacturing cities on the coast. Although many of the fine stands of oak which gave the city its name have been sacrificed to the needs of land developers, there are a number of city parks, including many preserved acres around Lake Merritt, where nature does not take a back seat to progress.

THE ABBEY, Joaquin Miller Park, 1886. Miller, known as the "poet of the Sierra," was the first major literateur of the Far West. His *Songs of the Sierras, Songs of the Sunlands,* and numerous plays, novels, essays, and autobiographical writings deal for the most part with the exploits of pioneers, outlaws, Indians, and with the scenic marvels of the land he loved. The Abbey, which was Miller's home until his death in 1913, consists of three interconnected one-story, one-room frame buildings. Nearby is the Fremont Monument, where, according to Miller, General John C. Fremont first caught sight of the Bay in 1864 and dubbed it the "Golden Gate." NR. Open all year, daily 9 a.m.-11 p.m. No charge.

JACK LONDON SQUARE, foot of Broadway at the waterfront, 19th-20th centuries. Named for the famous western writer, the square's major claim to fame is the **Last Chance Saloon,** a favorite haunt of London, which still quenches thirst while acting as a museum for bits and pieces of London lore. A boardwalk along the Bay's edge provides an uninterrupted view of the harbor and the many ships sailing to and from this large working port. A cabin where London once lived has been relocated here, and characters and artifacts from his life and work are recreated. Open all year, daily. (415) 444-3188. 🚻

CAMERON-STANFORD HOUSE, 1426 Lakeside Dr., 1871. Located near the center of downtown Oakland, this two-story Italianate structure was built by Will W. Cameron, who later sold it to Josiah Stanford, brother of Leland, Sr., founder of Stanford University. Purchased in 1907 by the city, the building was altered when it was converted into a museum. A lecture hall was added in 1913 and the carriage house incorporated into the building. The Oakland Musuem was located here until 1967, when its new complex was completed. (see following) NR. The building now functions as a house museum. Open all year, W 11-4, Su 1-5. No charge. (405) 836-1976.

DUNSMUIR HOUSE AND GARDENS, Paralta Oaks Ct., 1899. This large three-story Victorian landmark has a facade decorated with galleries and porches which give it a totally asymmetrical look. The interior second story is designed around a mezzanine which surrounds and overlooks the staircase, and which is lighted by a square central opening decorated with Tiffany glass. NR. Open Su 12-4; $1 admisson (50¢ gardens only). (415) 562-7588.

On the grounds is the 1920s **Dinkelspiel House,** now home to **Patti McClain's Museum of Vintage Fashion** — a collection of late 18th- to 20th-century clothing, with emphasis on the Victorian period. Open Su 1-4, M-F 10-2 (group tours only). $3 adults, $1.50 children, group rates. (415) 638-1896.

OAKLAND HOTEL, 260 13th St., 1912. This massive U-shaped building occupies an entire city block in the center of Oakland. Constructed after the 1906 earthquake and fire which decimated most of San Francisco, the hotel was planned to attract new business and industry to Oakland, hardly touched by the disaster. From opening day until the Depression, this was one of the most lavish and elegant hostelries on the West Coast. Guests included Presidents Wilson, Coolidge, and Hoover, Charles Lindbergh, Amelia Earhardt, Sara Bernhardt, and Jean Harlow. Mary Pickford sold Liberty Bonds here in 1916. The hard years of the '30s, followed by World War II, combined to signal disaster: in 1943 the hotel was taken over by the Army for use as a regional hospital and later served as a VA hospital. From 1963 until recently, it remained vacant and was in danger of being torn down in the name of progress. Now, happily, wiser heads have prevailed, and it has been restored and renovated to accommodate rent-stabilized senior citizen's housing. NR.

OAKLAND MUSEUM, Oak between 10th and 12th Sts. A modern concrete building beautifully integrated with its natural environment, in a park-like setting on the shores of Lake Merritt, the Oakland Museum is, in fact, three museums: Art, Natural History, and History, housed in one four-block complex. This is certainly an essential stop for travelers who wish to familiarize themselves with the history of the Bay area. Open all year, Tu-Sa 10-5, Su 12-7. No charge. (415) 273-3402.

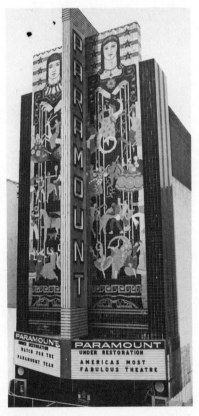

PARAMOUNT THEATRE, 2025 Broadway, 1931. This black stone building is considered one of the finest examples of the Art Deco style in the nation. Two terracotta panels on the facade are decorated with mosaics depicting human figures. Interior lobbies, balconies, lounges, and the auditorium itself are elaborately decorated with rugs, draperies, grillwork, and carved paneling. Truly a feast for the eyes, the former movie palace is now home to the Oakland Symphony. Try to catch a concert while you're in town. NR. Open for tours the first and third Saturday of each month, 10 a.m. $1 admission. (415) 893-2300.

PARDEE HOUSE, 672 11th St., 1869. Home of George Pardee, governor of California during the San Francisco earthquake of 1906, this elegant Italianate residence was built by an early Oakland resident who became a successful doctor and mayor of the city. Though the house is privately owned, it's well worth a detour to have a look at it from the street. NR.

Pacifica

SANCHEZ ADOBE HISTORIC SITE, 1000 Linda Mar Blvd., 18th-19th centuries. This five-acre park includes the site of an aboriginal Costanoan Indian village, the remains of a mission outpost established in 1786 by Mission Dolores of San Francisco, and an adobe built in 1842 with materials from the outpost's ruins by Don Francisco Sanchez, mayor of San Francisco and commandant of the Presidio. Operated by the San Mateo County Historical Museum. NR. Open all year, Tu-Su 1-5. No charge. (415) 359-1462.

Point Reyes

POINT REYES NATIONAL SEASHORE, 1870. Located about 30 miles north of San Francisco via CA 1, Point Reyes offers a combination of historic lore and natural beauty certain to appeal to even the most jaded palate. For centuries before Europeans arrived, the Coast Miwok Indians inhabited these shores. In the summer of 1579, they greeted Francis Drake as he beached his ship, the *Golden Hinde,* on the coast to make repairs. After staying for about five weeks, Drake left behind a brass plaque claiming the land for Queen Elizabeth I. The English never returned, however; it was the Spanish, and later the Mexicans, who colonized the area nearly 200

years later, followed by ranchers, the descendants of whose herds can still be seen roaming the brushy flatlands.

The **Visitor Center** at the Bear Valley entrance, the **Kenneth C. Patrick Visitor Center** on Drakes Bay, and the **Point Reyes Light Visitor Center** have exhibits detailing the history and culture of the various peoples who have lived in the area. The **Point Reyes Light,** situated on a breathtaking promontory overlooking the Pacific, is accessible only on foot, 300 steps down the peninsula. Built in 1870, the light still signals its warning to ships at sea. Open Th-M 10-4:30, no charge. (415) 663-8522. The park itself is open daily all year without charge. 🚻

Portola Valley

OUR LADY OF THE WAYSIDE, 930 Portola Rd., c. 1920. This lovely little Mission Revival church has been welcoming travelers and residents alike for more than half a century. NR.

Redwood City

LATHROP HOUSE, 627 Hamilton St., 1863. A simple shingled house, but with elaborate Gothic detail that is unusual for its place and time, Lathrop House was moved to its current location in 1905 and has been restored to its original condition. Maintained by the county. NR. Open all year, Tu-F 11:30-3. No charge. (415) 365-5564.

Richmond

POINT RICHMOND HISTORIC DIS-
TRICT, bounded by Washington and
West Richmond Aves. and Park Pl., early
20th century. Most of the homes in this
small residential area were constructed between 1900 and 1920 to house residents
drawn to the area to work at the Pacific Oil
Company refinery (later Standard Oil) just
north of the community. From 1902,
when the first oil was produced, until
1940, Standard Oil was the single largest
employer in the Richmond area. Hotels,
shops, and tavern were built within a fairly
short time. The oil executives had luxurious suites in the **Hotel Mac** or at the
New Todd Hotel, both of which can be
seen today; while the workers stopped by
the **Baltic Tavern** to relax and perhaps to
chat with Jack London, who was a regular
patron. The Baltic has been carefully
restored and is still open for business.
Most of the buildings in the district, however, are private homes—and primarily
modest ones. Various styles are common:
Queen Anne, San Francisco Stick, Neo-
classic, and variations on the bungalow
contribute to the relaxed, welcoming
character of the neighborhood. NR.

San Francisco

The city by the Bay has long been one of
the most popular vacation spots in
America, for perhaps in no other American
city does even the first-time visitor feel so
instantly at home. San Francisco is quite
small—certainly as compared to the urban
sprawl of Los Angeles or New York—and
it's easy to find one's way around. Star-
tlingly beautiful views wait around unex-
pected corners, flowers bloom everywhere, and overall is a sense of community
pride evident in the spanking fresh paint,
trim gardens, and well-kept residential
streets, many of them lined with multicolored Victorian houses—San Francisco's
famous "painted ladies."

It's difficult to imagine the San Francisco
of 200 years ago: a series of barren, treeless
hills shunned both by the Indians who had
long been residents of the West Coast, and

by the Spaniards and Mexicans who
moved north to colonize other areas of
California. (If you drive north across the
Golden Gate Bridge and look up to the
bluffs on your left, you'll get some idea of
the San Francisco that was.)

A group of Spaniards led by Juan Bautista de Anza chose an easily-defensible spot
just south of what is now the Golden Gate
Bridge for their Presidio in 1776, and thus
the first settlement was born. By the
mid-1800s, however, the population was
still hovering at about 500 souls: and
although an enterprising resident, Jasper
O'Farrell, had laid out a small town plan,
it was the discovery of gold that created a
city, almost overnight. Through the latter
half of the century, aided both by fortune
hunters and by the development of the
transcontinental railroad which termina-
ted across the bay in Oakland, San Francisco grew and prospered. While the devastating earthquake and fire of 1906 destroyed
much of the burgeoning city, Bay area residents were quick to rebuild, and there do
remain a number of earlier structures that
escaped the holocaust.

A major part of San Francisco's charm is
her historic cable cars. Catch one at Union
Square, Fisherman's Wharf, or anywhere
en route and go where it takes you just for
the fun of it. When you tire of land, hop a
ferry to Tiburon (Red and White Fleet,
bottom of Powell St.) or Sausalito (Golden
Gate Ferry, bottom of Mission St.). If
you're lucky, the famous San Francisco fog
will be rolling in by the Golden Gate
Bridge. For the less spontaneous, and
because the cable cars and ferries don't run
everywhere, San Francisco's attractions
have been divided into five geographical
areas: **South,** including the Civic Center
area and environs; **Central,** including
Union Square, Nob Hill, Russian Hill, and
the Financial district; **East and Northeast,**
including the Embarcadero, Fisherman's
Wharf, and the islands of the Bay; **Northwest,** including historic Presidio and
Pacific Heights; and the beautiful Golden
Gate and Lincoln Parks of the **West.**

SAN FRANCISCO CONVENTION
AND VISITORS BUREAU, 1390 Market
St., (415) 626-5500, offers a good, clear

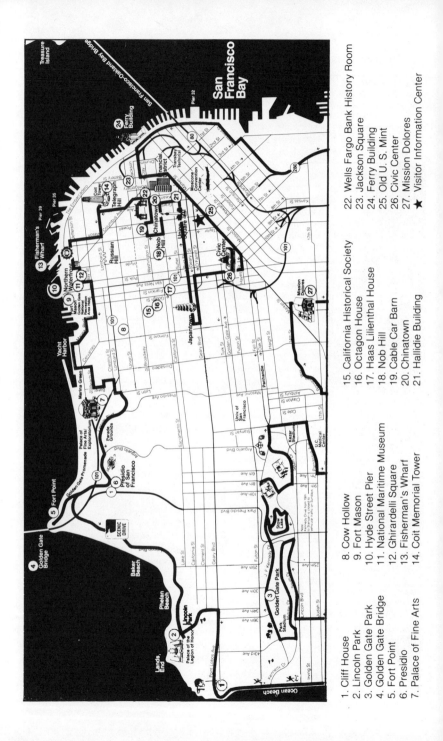

1. Cliff House
2. Lincoln Park
3. Golden Gate Park
4. Golden Gate Bridge
5. Fort Point
6. Presidio
7. Palace of Fine Arts

8. Cow Hollow
9. Fort Mason
10. Hyde Street Pier
11. National Maritime Museum
12. Ghirardelli Square
13. Fisherman's Wharf
14. Coit Memorial Tower

15. California Historical Society
16. Octagon House
17. Haas Lilienthal House
18. Nob Hill
19. Cable Car Barn
20. Chinatown
21. Hallidie Building

22. Wells Fargo Bank History Room
23. Jackson Square
24. Ferry Building
25. Old U. S. Mint
26. Civic Center
27. Mission Dolores
★ Visitor Information Center

San Francisco

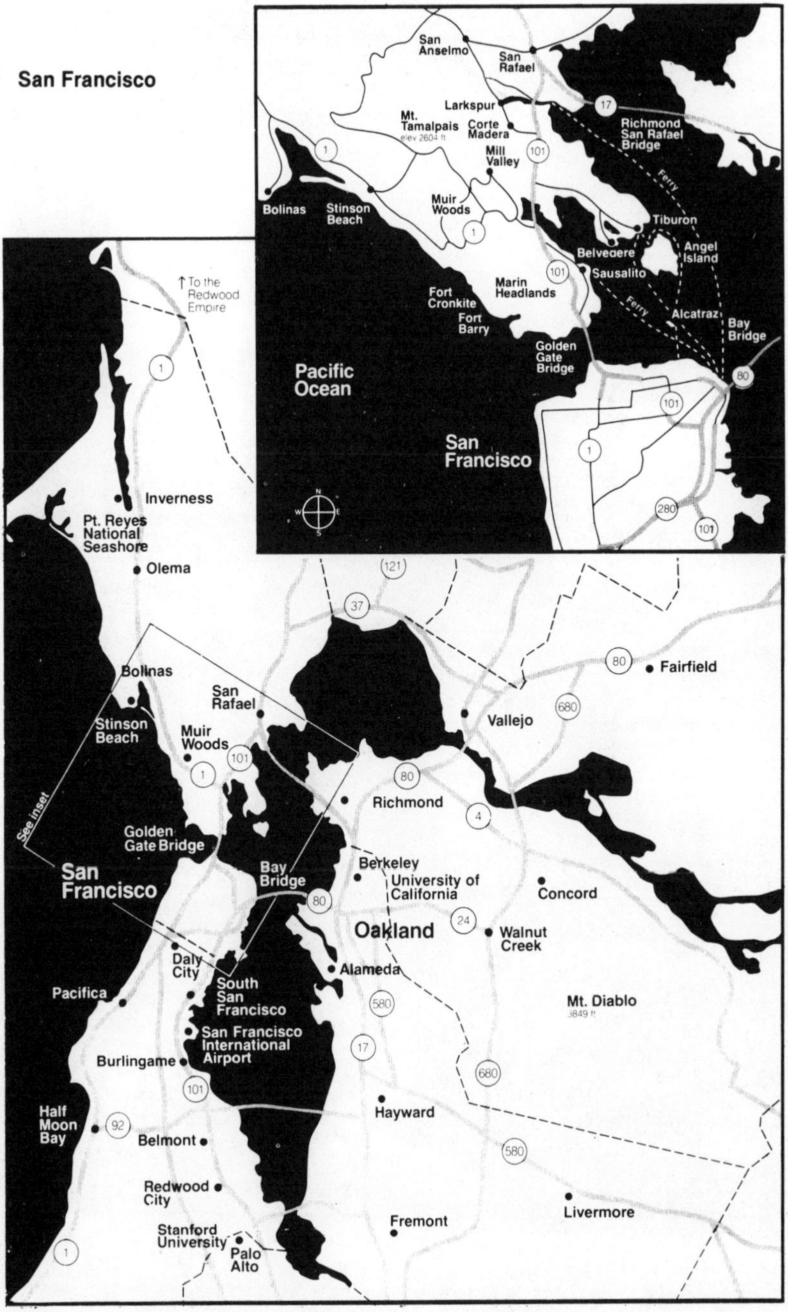

San Anselmo
San Rafael
Larkspur
Mt. Tamalpais elev 2604 ft
Corte Madera
17
Richmond San Rafael Bridge
Ferry
Mill Valley
101
Bolinas
Stinson Beach
Muir Woods
1
Tiburon
Angel Island
Belvedere
Sausalito
101
Marin Headlands
Fort Cronkite
Fort Barry
Ferry
Alcatraz
Bay Bridge
Golden Gate Bridge
80
Pacific Ocean
101
San Francisco
1
280
101

↑ To the Redwood Empire
1
Inverness
Pt. Reyes National Seashore
Olema
121
37
80 Fairfield
Bolinas
San Rafael
Stinson Beach
Muir Woods
1
101
Vallejo
680
Golden Gate Bridge
80
Richmond
4
Bay Bridge
Berkeley
University of California
Concord
San Francisco
See inset
80
24
Oakland
Walnut Creek
Daly City
Alameda
Mt. Diablo 3849 ft
Pacifica
South San Francisco
580
San Francisco International Airport
17
Burlingame
680
101
Hayward
Half Moon Bay
92
580
Belmont
Redwood City
Stanford University
Palo Alto
Fremont
Livermore
1

visitors map which includes many of the city's most famous attractions, among them the 49-mile scenic drive that winds through the city and down the peninsula along the Great Highway. As you head south, stop at **Cliff House** for a drink or lunch or just for the remarkable view of the roaring Pacific Ocean. The building itself is noteworthy—a Victorian extravagance originally constructed in the 1860s, which twice burned to the ground before the present structure was erected in 1908.

South San Francisco

LOTTA CRABTREE FOUNTAIN, Market, Geary, and Kearny Sts., 1875. If you're lucky enough to be in San Francisco on September 9th of any year, you can come by to see the ceremonies held here at this cast-iron statue and fountain, which was donated to the city by one of the most famous entertainers of the late 19th century. NR.

MISSION DOLORES, 320 Dolores St., 1782-91. Constructed by mission Indians under the direction of the Franciscan Fathers, Mission Dolores has four-foot-thick walls of sun-dried adobe brick, redwood roof beams, and a sloping tile roof. No nails were used in its construction: rather, the building was secured by means of wooden pegs and rawhide. The mission was established as San Francisco de Asis and gave the city its name. The adjacent cemetery contains the graves of many California pioneers. NR. Open all year; May-Oct 9-4:30; otherwise 9-3:30. 50¢ adults. (415) 621-8203.

OLD UNITED STATES MINT, 5th and Mission Sts., 1869-74. The Old Mint was established as a subsidiary of the Philadelphia Mint as a result of the enormous gold production of the California Mother Lode. Placed on an independent basis, it soon became the principal mint in the United States and the chief Federal deposit for gold and silver produced in the West. This 19th-century Federal building is one of the few in downtown San Francisco that survived the 1906 earthquake and fire. Now a museum, the Old Mint displays gold bars, gold nuggets, a gold coin collection worth $3 million, and such miscellany as an 1860 stage coach, a turn-of-the-century phonograph exhibit, and an authentic miners' cabin. NR, NHL. Open all year, Tu-Sa 9-4. No charge. (415) 556-3630.

SAN FRANCISCO CIVIC CENTER HISTORIC DISTRICT, bounded by Golden Gate Ave., Franklin, Hayes, and Market Sts., early 20th century. A series of monumental buildings surrounding a large open plaza, the Civic Center was the result of the City Beautiful Movement which spread throughout the United States following the 1893 World's Columbian Exposition in Chicago. The great white classical buildings constructed for that exposition, a startling change from the unplanned urban sprawl which surrounded them, captivated the American public and served as an inspiration to planning and design for nearly 40 years. **City Hall,** the crown jewel of the Civic Center, is distinguished by its massive dome and was constructed on the site of the original city hall which had been completely destroyed by the 1906 earthquake. The impressive **San Francisco Public Library** is diagonally across the plaza from City Hall. NR. Open all year, Tu-Th 9-9; M, F, Sa 9-6. No charge. (415) 558-5034.

The Opera House/War Memorial,

City Hall

completed in 1932, was the site of the historic meeting which established the United Nations in 1945; the conference which resulted in the Japanese Peace Treaty was held here in 1951. Open for seasonal events, the **Society of California Pioneers Museum and Library** at 456 McAllister St. is noted for its comprehensive displays of state history. Many paintings by California artists are hung here. Open all year, M-F 10-4. No charge. (415) 861-5278.

Central San Francisco

CABLE CAR BARN/MUSEUM. 1201 Mason St., 1887. Built to house machinery powering the original Ferries and Cliff House Railway, the barn was virtually destroyed in 1906 and rebuilt the following year. Today, restored to its general turn-of-the-century appearance, it provides power for moving 10½ miles of 1¼-inch cable beneath some of the city's sharpest hills at a steady 9½ miles per hour. The system's equipment is basically the same as that Andrew Smith Hallidie tested for the first time on August 1, 1873. He had begun working on a mechanical system in 1869, spurred by his concern for the horses then used to pull heavy passenger cars up the steep hills. The first cable car in service is now on display in the barn, along with photos and other artifacts commemorating what is surely San Francisco's most famous and beloved attraction. NR, NHL. The museum is open all year, daily Apr-Oct, 10-6; otherwise 10-5. No charge. (415) 474-1887.

CHINATOWN. Grant Ave. is the main street of this colorful area, where more than 65,000 people—the largest Asian community outside the Far East—live. Countless restaurants and shops are located here; it would be easy to spend at least a day just wandering from shop to shop, sampling exotic delicacies and looking at the beautiful crafts on display. Stop in at the **Chinese Culture Center Gallery**, 750 Kearny St., for a look at its exhibits of Chinese art and folk arts, crafts, and early photographs. Open all year, Tu-Sa 10-5. No charge. (415) 986-1822.

JAMES C. FLOOD MANSION (Union

Club), California and Mason Sts., 1886. James Flood was one of the bonanza kings of the Nevada Comstock Lode. In 1873 he and his partners obtained control of the Consolidated Virginia Mine, probably the richest body of gold and silver ore found up to that time. His brownstone mansion, the only Nob Hill town house to survive the 1906 disaster, is now the property of the exclusive (and private, alas) Union Club. NR, NHL.

HAAS-LILIENTHAL HOUSE, 2007 Franklin St., 1886. This bold Victorian mansion exhibits 19th- and early-20th-century furniture, accessories, and paintings. Guided tours are offered of both the interior (furnished in period antiques) and the historic exterior. NR. Open all year, W 12-4, Su 11-4:30. $2 adults. $1 children. (415) 441-3004.

HALLIDIE BUILDING, 130 Sutter St., 1918. Named in honor of Andrew S. Hallidie, an early regent of the University of California and inventor of the cable car in 1872, this eight-story landmark is notable for its imaginative Victorian Gothic ironwork used for cornices and stair balconies to mask fire escapes. NR.

JACKSON SQUARE HISTORIC DISTRICT, roughly bounded by Sansome, Washington, and Kearny Sts., Columbus Ave., and Broadway, 19th-20th centuries. The Jackson Square Historic District contains the sole surviving buildings from the Gold Rush period in San Francisco. Originally located on the waterfront, the area contained offices and stores and was the commercial and financial heart of the boom town. Land uses varied greatly, from buildings housing facilities for the production and sale of liquor, cigars, glassware, and books to the offices of the infant newspaper publishing business, foreign consulates, and large banking institutions. Of the nearly 100 buildings within the area, about 25 percent predate 1890, and more than half were constructed between that date and 1912. Theatres, businesses and a wide variety of restaurants are now housed in these San Francisco landmarks. NR.

WELLS FARGO BANK HISTORY ROOM, 420 Montgomery St. A Concord stagecoach is exhibited here, along with gold ore, early banking implements and documents, photographs, Gold Rush relics, antique guns, and Pony Express memorabilia—all recalling the rowdy days of San Francisco's early history. Open all year, M-F 10-3. No charge. ♦♦ (415) 396-2619.

The most elegant and historic of San Francisco's hotels can be found on Nob Hill: California St. boasts the **Stanford Court,** **Mark Hopkins,** and **Fairmont,** all constructed between 1906 and 1927. From atop the latter two can be seen some of the most spectacular views of this picturesque city. Be sure to stop by either for a drink. Twilight is an ideal time. Off Union Square (at Stockton and Geary) is the recently refurbished **City of Paris** store (1900) whose elegant interior was modeled on French department stores of the period.

East and Northeast: The Embarcadero and the Bay

ALCATRAZ ISLAND. *Alcatraz,* an English adaptation of the Spanish word for *pelican,* is a large rock in San Francisco Bay, originally barren and covered with white pelican droppings. Subsequent to American acquisition in 1848, it was turned into a fortress. Throughout the 19th century its buildings were mostly of masonry and brick, including a lighthouse built in 1853, and served to guard the entrance to the bay. First used as a prison during the Civil War, Alcatraz's facilities were expanded thereafter, and it became

one of America's most famous penal institutions, housing some of the country's most dangerous criminals, including Al Capone and "Machine Gun" Kelly. After the prison was closed in the 1960s, the island stood vacant for a decade, serving only as the site of various demonstrations by Indian tribes, who at one point occupied the premises for more than a year. The National Park Service now operates Alcatraz as a museum. NR. Tours leave from Pier 43 near Fisherman's Wharf. Advance reservations are necessary. (415) 546-2805.

ANGEL ISLAND STATE PARK, San Francisco Bay, 18th-20th centuries. Angel Island is really a part of Marin County, north of San Francisco. It is included here, however, since ferries to the island leave from the San Francisco waterfront on a regular basis.

This lovely tree-covered island, so different from its forbidding neighbor, Alcatraz, was first visited in 1775 by Juan Manuel de Ayala, who used it as a base while exploring and charting San Francisco Bay. From then until 1850, ships of several nations called at the island. Its strategic location attracted military attention on the part of the U.S., and in 1850 President Millard Fillmore designated it a military reserve; it was returned to the state for park use in 1954.

The remains of hundreds of years of history can be seen here: Indian dwelling sites, numerous military buildings dating from the 19th and 20th centuries, and such government related structures as a quarantine station, detention facilities, and navigation aids. (After World War I, the island served as the immigration station for thousands of Orientals beginning new lives on the West Coast.)

The ferry ride alone is reason enough to come to Angel Island: pick a nice day, pack a picnic lunch, and spend some time wandering the paths. The views of San Francisco, Marin County, and the surrounding hills are matchless. NR. Ferries leave San Francisco (Pier 40) and Tiburon for the island daily from late May-early Sept, weekends and holidays the rest of the year. For information and schedules call Harbor Carriers, Inc. (415) 398-1141. ⁜

FERRY BUILDING, Embarcadero at Market, 1903. Originally known as the Union Ferry Depot, this is a San Francisco landmark—an enormous structure, designed in the Beaux Arts style, with a 235-foot tower. Until the Golden Gate and Bay bridges opened in the late 1930s, the depot served 50 million bay commuters a year—more than 100,000 per day. Eight ferry slips accommodated 170 bay crossings per day—at 10¢ a ride. In room 2022 is the **California Division of Mines and Geology Mineral Museum,** with exhibits on paleontology, rocks and minerals, mine models, gold and gold facsimiles, and gems. Open all year, M-F 8-4:30. No charge. (416) 557-0634.

Moored at Pier 3, near the Ferry Building, is the **Santa Rosa Ferryboat,** the first steel-hulled diesel-electric ferry to operate in San Francisco Bay, which was placed in service between the city and Sausalito in 1927. Recently restored, the *Santa Rosa* was kept in service—part of the time in Seattle—until 1968. NR.

COIT MEMORIAL TOWER, Telegraph Hill, 1934. WPA murals around the base of the tower depict San Francisco life and scenes. From the top, splendid views of the Bay, Fisherman's Wharf, and the entire city make this a "must" on the visitor's itinerary. Donated by Lillie Coit in memory of her late husband, the tower serves to commemorate volunteer firemen of the 19th century. Open all year, daily 10-4:30. Admission 75¢. ⁜

FISHERMAN'S WHARF, Taylor and Embarcadero. Stroll past the old crab-fishing boats that still tie up here—and perhaps stop for a sample at one of the sidewalk stands. If you're in the mood for a more formal meal, there are a number of fine restaurants to choose from. Lots of curious little shops, the ever-present seagulls, and a variety of colorful sights and sounds make this among San Francisco's most famous and popular attractions. ⁜

GHIRARDELLI SQUARE, North Point, Beach and Larkin Sts., 1860-1916. The old Ghirardelli Chocolate Company factory buildings have been cleverly transformed into a series of shops and restaurants, with the addition of some recent buildings which complement the whole. This was the first such renewal project in the nation and has served as the model for many more, including Boston's famous Fanueil Hall complex. Nearby on Leavenworth Street, between Beach and Larkin, is **The Cannery,** a 1909 building that has been similarly recycled.

NATIONAL MARITIME MUSEUM, Beach St. west of Polk. This is the place to come if you're a sailor at heart: 100,000 photographs of ships and shipping, ship models, 12,000 books and periodicals devoted to maritime lore, artifacts from historic vessels, small craft, and more are displayed here. The museum administers and maintains a number of early ships which are berthed nearby and available for tours. Among them is the **Balclutha,** an old square-rigger located at Pier 43, which was launched in 1886. It carried general cargo and grain between Europe and San Francisco via Cape Horn, was later sold into the lumber trade, and finally, renamed *Star of Alaska,* carried Alaskan salmon before being retired in the early 1930s. NR.

At **Hyde Street Pier,** two blocks east of the museum, are the schooners **Alma** (1891) and **Wapama** (1915), used to haul agricultural products and lumber respectively throughout many years of service. NR. Several other ships are berthed here. The **C.A. Thayer,** last surviving example of 122 sailing schooners designed especially for use in the 19th-century Pacific coast lumber trade, was built in 1895, and retired only in 1950. NR, NHL. The **Eureka,** a large ferry boat originally employed in passenger and freight service between San Francisco, Oakland and Sausalito, was launched in 1890. NR. The tug **Hercules** (1906) towed canal locks fabricated here down to the Panama Canal. NR. The mu-

seum and Hyde Street Pier are open all year, Labor Day-Memorial Day, daily 10-5, otherwise 10-6. No charge. The *Balclutha* is open all year, daily 10-10. $2 adults, $1 children. (415) 556-8177.

THE WINE MUSEUM OF SAN FRANCISCO, 633 Beach St. The California wine industry is vital to the state's economic prosperity, and its history is a fascinating one, involving entrepreneurs from many countries and hard work over many years. Art, rare books and ancient glasses are among the exhibits displayed here for oenologists, professional and amateur. Open all year, Tu-Sa 11-5, Su 12-5. No charge. (415) 673-6990.

Northwest: The Presidio and Pacific Heights

CALIFORNIA HISTORICAL SOCIETY, 2090 Jackson St. The 1894 **Whittier Mansion,** an impressive stone edifice which served as the German Consulate shortly before World War II, and for a while housed Mortimer Adler's Institute of Philosophical Research, is now home to the

historical society's fine collection. Paintings, drawings, watercolors, sculpture, decorative arts, and other memorabilia of California's long and colorful history are displayed here. NR. Open all year, W, Sa, Su 1-5. $2 adults, 50¢ children. (415) 567-1848.

COW HOLLOW, Union St. between Van Ness and Fillmore. This colorful area is part of what gives San Francisco its unique charm. The bucolic name stems from the fact that this was once a dairy farming region. Later, elaborate Victorian mansions sprang up along the street, and they are now home to a succession of quaint shops and restaurants. Spend some time ambling along—and be prepared for many happy surprises.

FORT MASON HISTORIC DISTRICT, north and east of Franklin St. and McArthur Ave., 18th-19th centuries. Because of its strategic location on San Francisco Bay, this site was fortified by the Spanish in 1797. The fortification was neglected shortly thereafter and reverted to sand dunes until 1850, when an executive order reserved the point for public use. Settlers, unaware that the property belonged to the government, began to buy the land and erect houses on it. With the outbreak of the Civil War and the threat of Confederate privateers in the Pacific, the army occupied and fortified the point in 1863, converting the private residences into quarters. Four of these houses comprise the historic district today, all but one dating from 1855. The headquarters of **Golden Gate National Area,** an enormous federal park which includes a good part of San Francisco's waterfront, is located here, as are such disparate areas as Muir Woods and the National Maritime Museum, both previously described. NR. Call (415) 556-0560 for further information.

FORT POINT NATIONAL HISTORIC SITE, Lincoln Blvd. at Funston Ave., 1854. Located in the shadow of the Golden Gate Bridge, Fort Point was at one time a high white cliff, where in 1776 Spanish Colonel Juan Bautista de Anza raised his country's flag, choosing the site as the location for a presidio. In 1794 an adobe brick fort, no longer extant, was built on the cliff to protect the Presidio of San Francisco, which

was subsequently built in a sheltered valley about 1½ miles southeast. When the area passed to United States control in 1847, a permanent fort was constructed by the Army. Fort Point is the most massive brick fortification (150 x 250 feet) erected on the West Coast. It was never attacked and has long been obsolete, though it was occupied during World Wars I and II and during construction of the Golden Gate Bridge. It is now operated by the National Park Service. Civil War artifacts are displayed at the **museum** here. NR. Open all year, daily 9-5. No charge. (415) 561-3837. 👫

GOLDEN GATE BRIDGE, CA 101, 1937. There are now longer bridges in the world, but probably there is no more beautiful one than this. Leading from San Francisco north to Marin County and the wine country, the Golden Gate, designed by Joseph B. Strauss, spans the cliffs on either side of the inlet to San Francisco and San Pablo bays. A drive or a walk across it is not to be missed. Bring your camera. 👫

McELROY HOUSE (The Octagon), 2645 Gough St., 1861. Built by William McElroy, a miller, this octagonal house has details reminiscent of an Italian villa. Now operated by the National Society of the Colonial Dames. NR. Open first Sunday and second and fourth Thursdays each month. (415) 885-9796.

PALACE OF FINE ARTS, 3601 Lyon St., 1915. Designed by Bernard Maybeck, this monumental Greco-Roman colonnaded rotunda was built for the Panama-Pacific Exposition. Restored in 1962, it now houses the **Exploratorium,** a participatory museum with 500 exhibits illustrating man's sensory mechanisms. This is a good place to bring the children. Open all year, W 1-5, 7-9:30; Th-F 1-5; Sa-Su 12-5. $2.50 adults (six month admittance), seniors and groups $1.25. No charge on W. (415) 563-7337. 👫

ABNER PHELPS HOUSE, 329 Divisadero St., 1850. The Gothic Revival Phelps House is considered to be the oldest unaltered residence in San Francisco. Set upon a high foundation, the house has a steep gable roof and a one-story veranda across

the main facade. NR. Privately owned, but visible from the street.

THE PRESIDIO, Van Ness and Lombard Sts., 1776. First established by Spanish authority to guard the entrance to San Francisco Harbor, the Presidio passed to United States control in 1847, and six years later the Federal Government built a fort on the site. Though militarily inactive since 1914, the fort is still standing. The **Presidio Army Museum** in Building 2 covers the history of the military on the Pacific Coast from the Spanish period to the present. NR, NHL. Open all year, Tu-Su 10-4. No charge. (415) 561-3319.

SAN FRANCISCO FIRE DEPARTMENT MUSEUM, Presidio Ave. and Bush St.

Engine 15 Firehouse

Tours of old San Francisco firehouses can be arranged here. The museum's collection includes artifacts, memorabilia, and apparatus relating to the firefighting history of the city. Open all year, Th-Su 1-4. No charge. (415) 861-8000.

Presidio Army Museum

West: Golden Gate and Lincoln Parks

GOLDEN GATE PARK, bounded by the Pacific Ocean, Fulton and Stanyan Sts., and Lincoln Blvd., late 19th century. It's hard to believe that this breathtaking public park, covering more than a thousand acres of pleasant lawns, trees, and winding drives, was once a barren wasteland full of nothing but shifting sand. Frederick Law

Olmstead had advocated setting aside parts of the city for public recreation; the genius of John McLaren, park supervisor from 1887 until the mid 1940s, is responsible for much of the pleasure to be derived from the park today.

A number of museums are located here: the **Asian Art Museum** (Avery Brundage Collection); the **California Academy of Sciences,** including the Alexander F. Morrison Planetarium, which will be sure to captivate the children; and the **Fine Arts Museum** (M.H. de Young Museum), one of the most extensive collections of painting, sculpture, and the decorative arts in the country.

Stop by the beautiful **Japanese Tea Garden,** built in 1893 as part of the 1894 California Midwinter International Exposition. The 1875 Conservatory, shipped around Cape Horn in prefabricated pieces, is an enormous Victorian glass structure which has miraculously survived even the 1906 earthquake. NR.

Take the children for a ride on the **Children's Quarters Carousel,** built in 1912. Plan to spend a day in the park: there are ball fields, picnic areas, bicycle trails, and other attractions certain to please — and it's a refreshing change from the bustle of the central city. 🕴

LINCOLN PARK, Lincoln Blvd. and Point Lobos Ave. **The Palace of the Legion of Honor,** a replica of its namesake in France, displays French art of three centuries. Open all year, W-Su 10-5. No charge.

SAN FRANCISCO ZOO, Zoo Rd. and Skyline Blvd. When the children get cranky and you need a break from things human, visit this beautiful zoo, where more than a thousand animals are on parade. There's even a children's zoo for the little ones to enjoy. Open daily, 10-5. $2 adults, no charge for children if accompanied by an adult.

Just south of the zoo is beautiful **Lake Merced,** a fine recreation area where you might enjoy a swim or a sail. 🕴

San Francisco vicinity

TREASURE ISLAND, Oakland Bay Bridge exit. The largest military museum in the western part of the United States, the **Navy and Marine Corps Museum,** is located here. Exhibits explain the history of both branches of the service from 1813 onward; there are also displays of California history, with special emphasis on San Francisco. Open all year, daily 10-3:30. No charge. 🕴

San Rafael

BOYD HOUSE, 1125 B St., 1879. This early frame house with decorative balustrades is now a museum of Marin County history and artifacts operated by the County Historical Society. Early newspapers and photographs, books, brochures, and maps are displayed. NR. Open all year, W-Su 1-4. No charge. (415) 454-8538.

CHINA CAMP STATE PARK, 247 N. San Pedro Dr., 19th century. Chinese fishermen began taking shrimp in California waters as early as the mid-1860s. Numerous villages were established on the shores of San Francisco and San Pablo bays in the following decades. China Camp was one of the largest settlements of this type, and it remains the last vestige of the Chinese shrimp fishery in the state. When immigrants arrived from China, they generally intended to remain for the shortest time possible. Thus few western tools or methods were employed: what remains today are vestiges of the Chinese lifestyle transported to a new land. Four wooden buildings in the village date from the earliest days of the settlement; several others were constructed at about the turn of the century. NR. Open all year, daily, sunup to sundown. No charge. (415) 456-0766.

FALKIRK (Robert Dollar Estate), 1408 Mission Ave., 1879. Captain Robert Dollar, a San Francisco shipping magnate, bought this fine Eastlake-Queen Anne mansion in 1906 and named it after his birthplace in Scotland. The interior features a fine collection of Victorian stained-glass windows, carved woodwork, and decorated bronze fittings and hardware. Antique furnishings are exhibited here by the Falkirk Community Cultural Center, which now maintains the building. Open all year, M-F 9-5, Sa 10-12. No charge. (415) 457-6888.

MISSION SAN RAFAEL ARCANGEL, 1104 5th Ave. at A St. The original mission on this site was built in 1817 as an *asistencia* (outpost) of San Francisco's Mission Dolores. The current chapel was rebuilt in 1949, and is open daily 11-4. No charge. (415) 456-3016.

Sausalito

The picturesque town of Sausalito serves as a suburb of San Francisco — and also as a very popular tourist attraction. Many fine restaurants, most with wonderful views of the Bay and the city beyond, are located here, along with fashionable shops and the historic **Casa Madrona Hotel**. Situated on one of Sausalito's many hills, the hotel was originally built as an elaborate Victorian residence by William G. Barrett, a wealthy, Vermont-born lumber baron, in 1885. Marble fireplaces, stained-glass windows, brass chandeliers, and elaborate wrought-iron grillwork decorate the interior. The mansion was a private home only until 1902, when it was converted into a guest house. From then until the present owners took over the property in 1976, it had a long, colorful, and not always happy history, variously serving as a hostelry, boarding house, and, rumor has it, bordello. Casa Madrona has finally been restored to its former Victorian elegance; furnished with antiques, and boasting a fine restaurant and lovely grounds, it's an ideal place to wile away a few days. NR. See Lodging and Dining for information about accommodations.

Tiburon

Just a few miles (via CA 101) from its more famous neighbor, Sausalito, Tiburon has so far been left largely untouched by the tourist invasion that threatens to spoil the communities north and east of the Golden Gate. There are many shops and restaurants in the downtown area, some with water views; but the town is less pretentious, quieter, and generally more relaxed in feeling than Sausalito.

OLD ST. HILARY'S IN THE WILD-FLOWERS CHURCH, a small, simple Carpenter-Gothic building dating from 1888, is now the Landmarks Society Museum. Located above the intersection of Alemany and Esperanza Sts., it is surrounded by fields of wildflowers and commands an impressive spot on a hillside. Social and architectural history, artifacts of early California domesticity, and botanical specimens are displayed. NR. Open Apr-Sept W, Su 1-4 and by appointment. No charge. (415) 435-1853.

Walnut Creek

OLD BORGES RANCH, 1035 Castlerock Road, early 20th century. Originally part of an old Spanish land grant purchased by Juan Pacheco in 1843, this active working cattle ranch remained in the Borges family for four generations after it first settled here in 1899. Francisco Borges, a Portuguese immigrant, was one of the original pioneers to settle Walnut Creek. He and his family constructed barns and other outbuildings, raised cattle — and children — and developed a successful ranch which is still worked today by his descendants, though the land itself now belongs to Contra Costa County. The original farmhouse, horse and cow barns, wagonshed, milkhouse, woodshed, and corrals — all constructed in the early 20th century — remain in use today. The complex looks much as it did more than 80 years ago: even some of the original farm machinery is still in operation. NR. Open year round on Sa only at present. No charge. 👫 (415) 934-6990.

Woodside

WOODSIDE STORE, 471 Kings Mountain Rd., c. 1854. For more than a generation this simple general store was the gossip, cultural, and entertainment center of the small logging community of Woodside. Now operated as a museum, the store retains much of its original equipment and furnishings. NR. Open all year, M, W, Su 12-5. No charge. (415) 851-7615.

Woodside vicinity

FILOLI (Bourn-Roth Estate), Canada Rd., about 4 miles northwest of Woodside, 1917. William B. Bourn II, a financial and civic leader, had this 2½-story Georgian Revival brick mansion built on a roomy estate surrounded by formal landscaping. The seventeen acres of gardens are well maintained, and the whole reminds one more of a Tidewater Virginia plantation than of a northern California millionaire's playground. Owned by the National Trust for Historic Preservation. NR. Open mid-Feb-Nov., Tu-Sa 10-1 by appointment only. $5 adults, $2 students. (415) 364-2880.

Sonoma, Napa, Lake, and Mendocino Counties

The four-county region to the north of the San Francisco Bay area offers more beautiful scenery and interesting historical lore than just about any other part of the state. Tourism is a big business both along the rocky Pacific coast and inland among the pines and lakes. This bucolic country is devoted to the cultivation of wine and fruit and the protection of great stands of redwoods. There has been tremendous population growth in the southern part of the region since World War II, but somehow a measured pace of life has been maintained. Nature helps. This is a cool climate, and in the summer it may get rather foggy, at least near the ocean. On the other hand, it never gets so terribly cold that one needs to escape to a "southern" clime. A temperate climate such as this fosters an economy based on agriculture and tourism. Perhaps because the outdoors is still so accessible, there has been little development of theme parks. People come here for the real thing. This they will find at Fort Ross, at Petaluma Adobe, at Jack London's ranch near Glen Ellen, by riding the rails between Fort Bragg and Willits. There are many more pleasures to be discovered.

could reach Calistoga by taking a steamboat as far as Napa and then boarding the train. In the first year of the Napa Valley Railroad's operation—1868—3,000 tourists were reputed to have made the trip in a single month.

Napa Valley Railroad Depot before restoration

NAPA VALLEY RAILROAD DEPOT, Lincoln Ave. and Fair Way, 1868. The trains haven't run to Calistoga for many years, but the station—one of the oldest in the state—is still standing. It has been completely restored and is in use as a complex of fashionable shops. NR. The building is open every day except Tu from 10-6.

Calistoga

Calistoga was founded in 1866 by promoter Samuel Brannan as a fashionable spa. The town was given its curious name by Brannan. It is a combination of *Cali*, for California, and *stoga*, meant to conjure up the image of America's then most famous spa, Saratoga, New York. San Franciscans

Fort Bragg

Fort Bragg and the neighboring coastal towns of central Mendocino County will remind some travelers of the northern Maine coast. This has been lumber country almost from the time in the mid-19th century when a fort named after Mexican War hero Gen. Braxton Bragg was established here. Little is left of this fortress worth viewing today, but the town is pleasant to stroll through. A logging museum is particularly interesting for the family as is a wonderful excursion railroad line offering a 40-mile trip.

CALIFORNIA WESTERN RAILROAD, Laurel St. This is an old logging line and not a ride-around-the-block novelty attraction. The railroad was established in 1885, and steam passenger service began in 1904. The trip to Willits, 40 miles to the east, was first available in 1911. The nickname of the railroad—"The Route of the Skunk"—comes from the stinky gas-powered yellow cars that replaced steam service in 1925. Today both steam-powered and diesel-powered trains ride the rails.

A number of different trips can be made on the line. The trip between Fort Bragg and Willits takes a bit over 3 hours, and the round trip roughly 7½ hours including rest stops. The alternative is to take the train only approximately half-way across the territory—to Northspur. This trip, departing Fort Bragg, requires 1½ hours; from Willits, about 2 hours.

The countryside through which the train passes follows the Noyo River and the redwood-covered hills. Two tunnels and some hairpin curves are encountered when entering and leaving Willits.

The railroad, owned by the Georgia-Pacific Corporation, operates throughout the year but with reduced passenger service in the winter. The summer schedule gets underway the third Saturday in June and extends until the first Sunday in September. Fares are: Fort Bragg to Northspur and Willits to Northspur round trips, $6.90 adults, $3.90 children; Fort Bragg to Willits and Willits to Fort Bragg round trips, $9.90 adults and $4.95 children; Fort Bragg to Willits and Willits to Fort Bragg one-way, $7 adults, $3.50 children.

For more information regarding schedules, fees, and equipment available for trips, call (707) 964-6371 or write the railroad at Box 907, Fort Bragg, CA 95437.

FORT BRAGG REDWOOD MUSEUM, 90 W. Redwood Ave. In addition to its railroad, Georgia-Pacific sponsors this collection of historic artifacts and materials on the redwood industry. The exhibits deal primarily with the past, and emphasis is given to the equipment used by the logger. The museum building was part of the town's original fort complex at one time. Open W-Su 8:30-4:30. Free. (707) 964-5651.

WELLER HOUSE, 524 Stewart Ave., 1886, 1897. Fort Bragg's oldest house, the Weller mansion, has to be its most impressive. It started life as a 1½-story Victorian and was enlarged to three full stories in 1897. Horace Weller, associated with the redwood lumber business, made sure that only the best woods were used in the ten first-floor rooms, the four master bedrooms on the second level, and the 40-foot square ballroom on the third. The wood used for paneling and moldings is clear grained heartwood logged from old growth redwoods. It can never be duplicated. Weller House, a private residence, is open for private tours by small groups. NR. For information regarding a tour, for which a nominal fee is charged, call (707) 964-3061, or write to Mrs. Arlene A. Schade, 524 Stewart St., Fort Bragg, CA 95437.

Glen Ellen vicinity

JACK LONDON STATE HISTORIC PARK, end of London Ranch Rd., 1913, 1919. There are few literary landmarks quite as romantic as writer Jack London's ranch in the area known as the Valley of the Moon. It is hard to say which of the two sites on the 49-acre property (of the original 1,500 acres) is more interesting— the ruins of the Wolf House which burned in August, 1913, just before the Londons were to take possession, or The House of Happy Walls which Charmian Kittredge London built in 1919, three years after her husband's death at age 40. This was Charmian's home until she died at 84 in 1955, and, as expected, is full of London memorabilia. The author of such well-recognized classics as *Call of the Wild* and *White Fang,* London traveled throughout the world before settling down on the ranch.

The entrance to the park is near The House of Happy Walls. The house is built of fieldstone gathered on the property and is furnished with the London furniture intended for the Wolf House. After visiting here, one can follow either a hiking trail or the fire road to Jack London's grave, marked by a huge lava boulder. Nearby are the Wolf House ruins; the once magnificent house was built of redwood, stone, and glass and had 25 rooms, 9 fireplaces, a courtyard reflection pool, and a fireproof manuscript vault. Why did it burn? No one has ever been able to say for sure. NR, NHL.

The House of Happy Walls museum is open daily 10-5; the park, daily 8-sunset. Admission is $2 a car, $1 senior citizens, and 50¢ dogs (yes, dogs). (707) 938-1519.

Gualala

OLD MILANO HOTEL, 38300 CA 1, 1905. Located in an unspoiled part of the California coast as charming as the name of the settlement, the inn has been serving travelers for many years. Gualala, meaning the "meeting place of waters," is at the mouth of a river of the same name. In the old days visitors could arrive at the hotel either by motor car or by train (the Garcia Railroad), which, alas, no longer runs. See Lodging and Dining for information concerning accommodations. NR.

Jenner vicinity

FORT ROSS STATE HISTORIC PARK, N of Jenner on CA 1, 1812. In the early 19th century Russia wished to profit from the rich fur trade on the California coast and to be able to supply her Alaski territory with fresh agricultural products. What better place to establish a colony than northern California? And this the Russians proceeded to do in 1812 before the Spanish marched any further north. The site chosen, 87 miles north of San Francisco, is picturesque and was designed to be easily protected. For approximately 30 years the Russian colony existed at Fort Ross. It was not a great economic success, but neither did it come to a sad end. It was simply sold to John Sutter, the wealthy trader from Sacramento, in 1842 when it seemed wise to return to the north.

The principal buildings which existed within a stockade high up on a bluff overlooking the Pacific have been reconstructed or restored in our time by the state of California. In the 1830s, however, there were also 40 to 50 houses located outside the stockade. Some of them were occupied by Russian members of the community and by Aleut Indians from Alaska.

The only original building which has survived the years is a **Commandant's House** constructed in the 1830s. It is

Fort Ross Commander's House

Russian Chapel, Fort Ross, before fire

thought that it was probably built for Alexander Rotchev, the last commandant. Two blockhouses and a chapel, however, have been reconstructed in recent years. The original church was destroyed by fire in 1970; even the Russian bells were completely melted by the fire. The chapel has been rebuilt and one of the bells recast. The stockade has been reconstructed with some original materials being used. NR.

Fort Ross is open daily 10-5. Free. (707) 847-3286.

Lakeport

LAKE COUNTY MUSEUM, 255 N. Forbes St., 1870. Rather than being torn down—the usual fate of "obsolete" public buildings—the historic Lake County courthouse now serves as a cultural center featuring exhibits on pioneer life, antique guns, and old currency. Indian artifacts on display include Pomo baskets and arrowheads. Open May-Sept, Tu-Su 11-4; Oct-Apr, Th-Sa 10-4. Free. (707) 263-2276.

Mendocino

MENDOCINO AND HEADLANDS HISTORIC DISTRICT, bound by the ocean on the W and S, Little Lake St. on the N, and CA 1 on the E, 19th century. There is a good reason why Mendocino is so reminiscent of a northern New England village—it was settled by natives of Maine who came to log the redwoods after the town's founding in 1851. Wonderful false-front commercial buildings line Main St., and along

Masonic Temple in Mendocino and Headlands Historic District

the side streets are rows of clapboard and board-and-batten homes.

The one truly exceptional landmark in town, however, owes nothing to the New England tradition. This is the 1854 **Chinese Joss House** at 45160 Albion St., on a small rise overlooking the Pacific. The tiny temple is a simple redwood building without much in the way of ornamentation. Inside are almost all of the original furnishings. From all available evidence, it would appear that this is the oldest Chinese religious building in the state. Privately owned. NR.

Napa

First settled in the 1830s, Napa became a prosperous mining center in the mid-century and in the 1860s began its development as the capital of the wine country. It is superbly situated at the head of the navigable Napa River, an important link with San Pablo and San Francisco bays. Among the most interesting of downtown buildings are the Italianate *Napa County Court House,* between 2nd and 3rd Sts. on Brown St., 1878; the **Napa Opera House,** 1018-1030 Main St., 1879, designed by the imaginative Victorian architectural firm of Samuel and Joseph Newsom; and the stone **Sam Kee Laundry Building,** 1245 Main St., 1875, which was once part of a brewery and the home of the Old Stone Saloon, NR.

One of the most impressive and interesting buildings in town is associated with the wine trade. Although there were once a half-dozen wineries operating in the city, only a single winery building remains:

LISBON WINERY, 1720 Brown St., 1880. The building is used for storage now, and what a handsome landmark it is! J.A. Mathews, a native of Lisbon, Portugal, founded the winery and was responsible for the stonework of the building. An accomplished mason, he formed the decorative arches of the doorways and dressed the stones for the facade. After a lengthy interruption during the Prohibition era, winemaking continued from 1933 until 1976. NR.

Lisbon Winery

Napa vicinity

MONT LA SALLE VINEYARDS, 4411 Redwood Rd., 7 miles NW of CA 29. The Christian Brothers' winery is now one of the most popular attractions in the Napa Valley. It is said that the first vineyards in the area were planted by settlers who received cuttings from the padres at the Sonoma and San Rafael missions. Winemaking was a major activity at almost every one of the Spanish religious communities. In addition to the winery, a Christian Brothers novitiate is located here. The winery is open for 30-minute guided tours daily, 10:30-4. (707) 226-5566.

Oakville vicinity

FAR NIENTE WINERY, S of Oakville at 1577 Oakville Grade, 1885-86. Like other California wineries not under the spiritual wing of the Church, Far Niente was a victim of Prohibition. It is a handsome example of a stone "gravity-flow" winery built on three levels in the side of a hill. Hamden W. McIntyre, an architect and engineer, refined the "gravity-flow" system in the 1880s and was responsible for Far Niente's design. Wagons carried the grapes to the top floor for crushing. Gravity flow moved the liquid to the second floor for fermenting, and finally to ground level for aging and storage. NR. Private, but visible from the road.

Petaluma vicinity

PETALUMA ADOBE STATE HISTORIC PARK, 4 miles E of Petaluma on Casa Grande Rd., 1836-46. Mariano Guadalupe Vallejo was the most important citizen of northern California during the first half of the 19th century. Named Military Commandant and Director of Colonialization of the Northern Frontier in 1834, he was responsible for developing a number of towns and enterprises in the region. His own rancho, Petaluma, was the area's largest; Vallejo claimed some 175,000 acres. The adobe headquarters that he built in the center of the immense property took ten years to complete.

What the visitor sees today is a reconstruction—and a very good one—of approximately one-half of the original buildings. There were originally four sections surrounding a courtyard. Just how many rooms existed in the 1840s is difficult to determine. Each of the wings had two floors and was surrounded by verandas that protected the adobe walls. The headquarters was much more than a residence; it was a village and built almost like a fortress. There were store rooms; places for making blankets, clothing, and rugs; and shops for the blacksmith and toolmaker, among other craftsmen.

Petaluma Adobe suffered extensive damage in the 19th century. After the annexation of California by the United States, the fortunes of such Mexican-American figures as Vallejo slowly declined. The great adobe and some of the land around it was sold off as early as 1857. The Native Sons of the Golden West helped to save what remained of the old adobe in 1910, and finally in 1951 the state came to the rescue. Many of the rooms are now furnished with antiques and equipment from the rancho period. In addition there are exhibits which enable the visitor to visualize how the building was used and laid out in the early days.

NR, NHL. Open daily 10-5. 50¢ adults, 25¢ children 6-17 and senior citizens. (707) 762-4871. 🚹

St. Helena

The history of St. Helena is largely the history of winemaking in California. It is a very attractive town, and even those who prefer a soft drink or hard liquor will have to agree that there is much to see and enjoy in this Napa Valley community.

BALE MILL, 3 miles NW of St. Helena off CA 128, 1846-47. One of the area's most scenic attractions, Bale Mill is also one of the few that has nothing to do with wine culture. The grist mill is built on a hillside on three levels. The great overshot waterwheel rises almost the full height of the building. NR. The mill is maintained by Napa County as a museum. 50¢ admission. For hours and additional information call (707) 942-4575.

CHRISTIAN BROTHERS WINERY (Greystone Cellars), 2555 Main St., 1889. The largest stone wine cellar in California and possibly the world, this facility, now owned by Christian Brothers, is also an architectural landmark. The massive building was designed in the Richardsonian Romanesque style and was constructed of a light gray volcanic stone with trimming in a similar kind of red stone. William J. Bourn, a San Francisco financier and civic leader, had the building designed by the firm of Percy and Hamilton. Such a storage facility was badly needed at the time. By the 1890s the facility had come under the control of the California Wine Institute which used "Greystone Cellars" as its label. Christian Brothers acquired the site during the 1950s. The cellars are used today for the aging of wine and for the storage of champagne. The tasting room has been admired for its handsome appointments for many years. NR. Tours of the cellars are held daily, 10:30-4:30. Free. (707) 963-2719.

CHARLES KRUG WINERY, St. Helena Hwy., 2800 Main St., 1861. Oldest operating winery in the Napa Valley, this facility was built for pioneer winemaker

Charles Krug, the first commercial wine-maker in America. The winery building was partially destroyed by fire and was added on to in 1874. Like many of the other area wineries, it is built of stone and has arched windows and doors. A huge stable is now used as an aging cellar. C. Mondavi & Sons acquired the business in 1943 and continue to label their wines "Charles Krug." NR. Open for tours daily 10-4. Free. (707) 963-2761.

BERINGER HOUSE (Rhine House), 2000 Main St., 1883. Winemaker Frederick Beringer built a replica of his house in Mainz, Germany, and it now serves as the wine tasting and sales center for the winery he founded. It is a high-Victorian extravaganza and must have cost a fortune in its day. The leaded windows, oak lumber, and marble were imported from Germany. Beyond the house on the hill are 1,000 feet of cellars. 2,000 acres of vineyards surround the property. NR. Open for tours daily 9:30-3:45. Free. (707) 963-2334.

NICHELINI WINERY, 2950 Sage Canyon Rd., E of St. Helena, 1890. A small, family-owned business, the winery was established by Anton Nichelini, an Italian Swiss. The 19th-century equipment is still on the site and includes a primitive lever press. The second and third floors of the stone main house were once used as the family residence. NR. Open Sa-Su 10-6. Free. (707) 963-3357.

SILVERADO MUSEUM, 1490 Library Lane. The life and works of novelist Robert Louis Stevenson are studied here at the museum named after the community described in his novel *The Silverado Squatters* (1883). In it Stevenson told of life in the desolate California mining camp that had been his home in 1880. In addition to first editions, letters, and manuscripts, the visitor can enjoy paintings, prints, and sculpture relating to Stevenson and his family. Open Tu-Su 12-4. Free. (707) 963-3757.

Santa Rosa

Santa Rosa has grown to be one of the largest cities north of San Francisco. In the pro-

cess it has somehow managed to retain some of the charm of a smaller town. The county seat and commercial center of Sonoma County, Santa Rosa lies at the heart of very rich farm land. It was no accident that the famous American horticulturist Luther Burbank moved here from Massachusetts in 1875 to develop his experimental garden.

LUTHER BURBANK HOUSE AND GARDEN, 200 block of Santa Rosa Ave., 1883. A three-acre lot in the middle of town was the place where the man often called the "Plant Wizard" performed his many experiments. The gardens, arranged around a large inner circle of grass with planting beds along both sides of the paths, are now included in a town park. Among the plants exhibited are an ornamental blackleaf plum tree and a rare type of walnut, two of the many strains and varieties of plants introduced by Burbank during his fifty-year career.

The plant wizard's house, greenhouse, and stable occupy the rest of the three-acre property. Burbank, who died in 1926, is buried under the 188-foot cedar of Lebanon tree planted in front of the house. Mrs. Burbank occupied the house until her death in 1977. NR, NHL. Its original furnishings intact, the house is now open for tours Tu and Sa 10 and 3:30. 50¢ adults, 10¢ for children 9-17, free for children under 9. The gardens are open daily 8-4. Free.

McDONALD MANSION, 1015 McDonald Ave., 1876. This extraordinary Victorian mansion was built for Col. Mark L. McDonald, a financier and community leader. As one admirer has recounted, the house recalls the long-ago days "of the iron fountain and fancy urn in which flowers were planted; the time when cast-iron pigeons were to be seen perched on the ridge of a barn, when every stable had its weather vane . . ." Victorian elegance of the highest order marks the frame house inside and out. A carriage house and a gazebo also stand on the five-acre grounds which were once formally landscaped. The house and grounds were the setting of the Walt Disney movie *Pollyana*. NR. Private, but may be viewed from the avenue.

RAILROAD SQUARE DISTRICT, bounded by Third, Davis, Wilson and Sixth Sts., and Santa Rosa Creek, 1888-1923. Santa Rosa became an important railroad center in the 1870s, and this area, centering on Railroad Square, developed in the following years. The most important buildings were built of cut stone by Italian craftsmen. These include the **Northwestern Pacific Railroad Depot**, 1904; the **Western Hotel**, 1903; the **La Rose Hotel**, 1907; and the **REA Express Building**, c. 1915. All are located around Railroad Sq. Nearby along 4th St. are other brick commercial buildings which date from the early 20th century. NR.

Sonoma

Settled first by Franciscan missionaries in the 1820s, Sonoma emerged in the 1830s and '40s as the administrative center of northern California under the direction of General Mariano Guadalupe Vallejo. The mission was reduced to mere parish status, but the rest of the community grew into a settlement of strategic and economic importance. Today this heritage is visible in the restored buildings of Sonoma State Historic Park and the home of General Vallejo. His ranch, in nearby Petaluma (see listing under that town), should be visited in association with the Sonoma landmarks. Later in the 19th century, Sonoma lost much of its position of power and slipped back into the comforting sleep of a small town. The business of making wine,

however, prevented the name Sonoma from disappearing completely.

SONOMA STATE HISTORIC PARK is divided into two sections: the first is the area around the town Plaza bounded by Spain, Napa, and E. and W. 1st Sts.; the second is the Vallejo Home property at the end of W. 3rd St. All of the historic buildings date from the period 1820-50. NR, NHL. The park is open daily 10-5. 50¢ adults, 25¢ for senior citizens over 61 and children 6-17, free for children under 6. (707) 938-1578. Among the most interesting sights in the historic park are the following:

Mission San Francisco Solano, NE corner of W. Spain St. and E. 1st St., 1823. The Sonoma mission was the last to be founded by the Church and the most short-lived. The mission's chapel was built around 1840-41 and was restored in the 20th century. The only surviving part of the original mission is a residential wing east of the chapel.

Blue Wing Inn, on E. Spain St. across from the mission, 1820s and later. Now a two-story adobe building, the Blue Wing Inn probably began life as a much smaller one-story dormitory for Mexican soldiers stationed at the mission. Blue Wing Inn was the name of the enlarged Gold Rush-era tavern and gambling room that replaced the barracks. The building now houses several gift shops.

Toscano Hotel (1850s) and **Barracks,** (1830s and '40s), corner of Spain St. and E. 1st, facing the Plaza. These two adobe buildings adjoin each other. The Toscano was first used as a retail store and rental library but soon became a hotel, originally known as the Eureka. With the arrival of Italian immigrants in the area around 1890, the name was changed to what it is today. The Toscano is furnished with turn-of-the-century furniture. The Barracks were built for troops brought to Sonoma by General Vallejo in the mid-1830s. After the Americans took over the town in June, 1846, U.S. troops were stationed here.

La Casa Grande, Spain St. between E. 1st and W. 1st, facing the Plaza, 1836-40. On-

Barracks, Sonoma State Historic Park, 1960

ly the servant's wing of General Vallejo's mansion is now standing. The main wing burned in 1867.

Vallejo Home ("Lachryma Montis") W. 3rd St., 1851-52. Vallejo's other estate was named after the spring which flowed on the property. The Indians called the location "crying mountain" and "Lachryma Montis" ("mountain tear") was an appropriate translation. The main house was built beside the spring and its pool. It is a two-story wood-frame Carpenter Gothic residence that was prefabricated in Boston and then shipped to California on a clipper ship around Cape Horn. The inside appointments are very fine, each room having its own white marble fireplace. Also on the grounds are a kitchen, a small cabin, and an enclosed summer house. A building constructed originally as a warehouse was converted in the 19th century to residential use and came to be called the "Swiss Chalet." It is now a museum and interpretive center for the Vallejo property. General Vallejo lived in this home until his death in 1890 at age 82.

BUENA VISTA WINERY (Haraszthy Cellars), 18000 Old Winery Rd., 1857. Colonel Agaston Haraszthy, a Hungarian nobleman, was only slightly less important to the history of the Sonoma area than General Vallejo. The pioneer winemaker arrived in town in 1856 and two years later had 85,556 vines in cultivation. His stone cellars were built at the same time, and visitors can tour these and the cool man-made limestone storage caves dug deep into the rock. Of the several wineries in the immediate Sonoma vicinity, Buena Vista is the most important to the history of winemaking in America. A visit is strongly recommended. Open daily 10-5. Free. (707) 938-1266.

Ukiah

THE SUN HOUSE, 431 S. Main St., 1911-12. The home of John and Grace Hudson was a center of considerable culture in the Ukiah area. Mrs. Hudson's paintings brought her national renown; Mr. Hudson's ethnographic work won him professional respect. Together they collected Indian baskets and other priceless artifacts documenting the life and times of a vanishing race. Their home was designed in the Craftsman style and utilizes massive redwood timbers. Indian designs are incorporated in the woodwork. It is now owned and maintained by the city of Ukiah. Open W-Sa 12-3. $1 adults, 75¢ students, no charge for children. (707) 462-3370.

Tehama, Trinity, Humboldt, and Del Norte Counties

The counties of northwest California will always be identified with the redwoods—the most historic of all the natural resources in California. Fortunes in lumber were made and spent in the coastal towns of Humboldt and Del Norte counties and in the back country of Trinity and Tehama. There was gold, too, in the hills, especially around Weaverville; a man could also grow rich from ranching in the upper reaches of the Sacramento River Valley around Red Bluff. But the redwoods then and now are what have drawn most men to the region. Today, with so much of th valuable timber protected by the state and federal governments, the trees earn tourist dollars. The Redwood Highway, US 101, which winds through Redwood National Park, quickly fills up with cars during the summer months. Save time, as you should, for the historic towns and villages which are not as scenic as the woods but which may be more restful throughout the year.

Eureka

Eureka was meant to be a boom town, and there is no question but that it was and is a prosperous and energetic place. Long ago it outstripped Arcata and Humboldt City to become the county seat and the home of many lumber barons. No one is building new houses quite as beautiful or as large as the famous Carson Mansion which overlooks Eureka Harbor, but the town has seen a great deal of old house restoration, with thoughtful attention devoted to the central business district in particular. There is much to be saved and to be enjoyed in this small city of 25,000 people.

CARSON MANSION, 143 M St., 1884-86. This is one of a number of houses which Samuel and Joseph C. Newsom, San Francisco architects, built for Eureka families who had made their money in the lumber trade. The mansion is so handsomely elaborate that it is almost impossible to detail all of the decorative elements and motifs which are found in the gables, center tower, windows, doors, and extraordinary wraparound veranda. The house has come to represent everything about the Victorian period which is elaborate, colorful, fanciful, and slightly wacky. Unfortunately, the house is not one that can be toured. The city of Eureka had an opportunity to buy the house but passed it up. The mansion is now the home of the Ingomar Club, a private men's group. It has done a superb job in preserving the building. In any case, the Carson Mansion is not a place that can be hidden away from view. Positioned on a rise, it can be enjoyed from a number of vantage points.

CLARKE MEMORIAL MUSEUM, 240 E St., 1912. The former Bank of Eureka building, a Beaux Arts palace, makes a fine home for the local historical museum. Pioneer and Indian relics are among the objects displayed. The visitor will also be able to see Victorian period costumes and furniture, china, and glassware. Open Tu-Sa 10-4. Free. (707) 443-1947.

FORT HUMBOLDT STATE HISTORIC PARK, 3431 Fort Ave., 1850s. Federal troops were stationed at this site from 1853 to 1865 to protect the area from the Indians. Ulysses S. Grant was the most famous of the figures who served here. Most of the original buildings are now gone, but exhibits which interpret the military history of the fort make a visit to the park particularly worthwhile. Open daily 8-5. Free. (707) 443-7952.

HUMBOLDT CULTURAL CENTER, 422 1st St., 1875. First St. lies along the waterfront and is at the heart of Eureka's original business district. Through a combination of governmental support and private initiative, the Victorian neighborhood has been successfully renewed. The cultural center is located in the E. Janssen Building, a brick, commercial structure with a glass and cast-iron facade. With high ceilings and an interior bathed with natural light, it is a perfect place for the display of artwork.

NR. Open Tu-Su 12-5. Free.
(707) 442-2611.

The area from 1st to 3rd and from C to G Sts. is now known as **"Old Town."** It is a pleasant and interesting area in which to stroll. Nearly all of the buildings date from the 1870s to World War I, and many house a variety of specialty shops to visit. One of the most delightful buildings to be encountered is the **French Empire Mansard Build-**

ing, 123 F St., 1883. It was built as the Odd Fellows Hall. NR.

Red Bluff

A pleasant and picturesque town in the upper Sacramento Valley, Red Bluff was founded in 1850. It is the county seat of Tehama County. As in many other small centers of northern California industry and agriculture, the idea of preserving landmark buildings was not a popular one until recently. Consequently, some of the town's most important 19th-century buildings have been lost. Many interesting places, however, remain to be explored by the visitor to Red Bluff. For 25¢ a "Map Tour of Victorian Red Bluff" can be picked up at the Kelly-Griggs House Museum (see following listing) or at the Chamber of Commerce, 100 Main St.

KELLY-GRIGGS HOUSE MUSEUM, 311 Washington St., 1880. This Victorian house in the Italianate style houses a colorful collection of antique furniture and furnishings. The museum is also quite strong in Indian and pioneer artifacts and Victorian-era costumes. Open Th-Su 2-5. Free. Donations accepted.
(916) 527-1129.

ODD FELLOWS BUILDING, 342 Oak St., 1883. This is one of the delights of Red Bluff. The appearance of the building has hardly changed at all in the past century. Built of brick which has been stuccoed, the lodge was erected for the Independent Order of Odd Fellows which still owns it. The building has handsome cast-iron details and an unusual ground floor loggia.

Odd Fellows Building

Retail stores are on the first floor and the lodge hall on the second. NR.

Red Bluff vicinity

WILLIAM B. IDE ADOBE STATE HISTORY PARK, 2 miles NE of Red Bluff on Adobe Rd., c. 1850. William B. Ide was the only president of the California Republic. The state restored his home in 1958, and exhibited there are antique household furnishings and artifacts of pioneer life. Open 8-5. Free.
(916) 527-5927 or 895-4303.

Redwood National Park

Redwood National Park begins north of Eureka and continues up the coast for more than 50 miles. It includes within its boundaries **Jedediah Smith, Del Norte Coast,** and **Prairie Creek state parks.** The traveler can enjoy much of the area by following the **Redwood Highway, US 101,** one of the few highways in the country to be included on the National Register of Historic Places. The road that one follows through the preserves of the ancient redwoods — the world's oldest living things — is itself an historic attraction.

Information on park facilities can be obtained from Redwood National Park, 1111 2nd St., Crescent City, CA 95531. (707) 464-6101.

OLD REQUA (Rekwoi), Redwood National Park, north bank of Klamath River, 0.7 miles W of Requa. The largest Yurok Indian village on the California coast was located here. It is known from archaeological digs to have had 23 houses and other special buildings. There are now more than 20 house pits, an historic cemetery, and a reconstructed Yurok dwelling on the site. It is on land owned by the Del Norte County Historical Society, Crescent City. NR. For information regarding access to the site, call (707) 464-3828.

Scotia

THE PACIFIC LUMBER CO. MUSEUM, US 101, 1920. Scotia is one of the last completely company-owned towns in California. The Pacific Lumber Co.'s first plant was opened in 1886. The former **First National Bank of Scotia** building

Old Requa

(1920), assembled totally of redwood, serves as a museum, featuring displays of old logging equipment and the history of the company interpreted through pictures. Next to the museum is the **Winema Theatre,** also dating from 1920. On both this building and the museum, redwood trunks serve as neo-classical columns. The museum is open June-Sept, M-F 7:30-12 and 1-4:30. Free. The Pacific Lumber Co.'s plant can be toured year-round, M-F 7:30-12 and 1-4, excepting the first week of July and Christmas week. ♦♦
(707) 764-2222.

Trinidad

HOLY TRINITY CHURCH, Parker and Hector Sts., 1873. This Roman Catholic church is a reminder of the days when Trinidad was an important town on the northwest coast. The name Trinidad (Trinity) was given to the community because explorers took possession of the region for the Spanish crown on the day after the feast of the Holy Trinity in June, 1775. The population of Trinidad included many thousands in the mid-19th century, but the town has not known more than several hundred inhabitants since then. The church overlooks Trinidad Harbor and is a very picturesque wood frame building with a small bell tower. NR.

Trinidad vicinity

TSAHPEK, Dry Lagoon State Park, N of Trinidad on US 101. Smaller than the Yurok village near Requa (see listing for Old Requa), Tsahpek once had as many as ten or eleven houses. Settlement probably began as early as the 14th century, ceased for several centuries, and then commenced again in the mid-1800s, lasting until the 1940s. Evidence of five houses from this more recent period of settlement can be seen, and two of the buildings are still standing. NR. For information, call (707) 443-4588.

Weaverville

The tourist looking for the Old West need go no further than Weaverville, the county seat of Trinity County. It is not a reconstructed museum village or a tourist trap located in the "Mother Lode" country of central California, but an honest-to-goodness well-preserved town. Its population was once about half-Chinese, and one of the most important of the historic sites is the **Joss House,** a Taoist temple which is now maintained by the state as part of an historic park. Weaverville has 25 buildings within its historic district which date from the gold-mining era.

WEAVERVILLE HISTORIC DISTRICT, principally both sides of Main St., mid-and late-19th century. Main Street is lined with one and two-story buildings, some with false fronts or parapeted roofs, and a number with verandas. Several of the buildings had the first floor owned by one individual and the second by another. To accommodate the upper story proprietor, an outside spiral cast-iron staircase was provided. Aside from the **Trinity County Courthouse** (1856), the most important town institutions are the county museum and the Chinese temple. NR.

J.J. Jackson Memorial Museum, 508 Main St., is housed in a new building. Exhibits are devoted to the history of Trinity County and to the town's unique mixture of Chinese, Indian, and pioneer cultures. Open May-Nov, daily 10-5. Free. Donations accepted. (916) 623-5211. ♦♦

Weaverville Joss House State Historic Park, Main and Oregon Sts., 1874. The first temple dated from the early 1850s, and the furnishings from this building were incorporated in the 1870s replacement. The altar is said to be more than 3,000 years old. Other materials which were brought from China by the immigrant workers include valuable hand-painted tapestries. Exhibits on Chinese life, early history, and contributions to California's development are located in a separate museum building. NR. Guided tours are available daily in the summer every half hour from 10-4:30, and in other seasons daily every hour from 10-4. 50¢ adults, 25¢ for senior citizens over 61 and children 6-16, free for children under 6.
(916) 623-5284.

Siskiyou, Modoc, Shasta, and Lassen Counties

California's heavily-forested northeast counties feature some of the most breathtaking scenic vistas in the state — equal perhaps to the glacial canyons of Yosemite or the seacoast view from Big Sur. Two national parks — Lassen Volcano National Park and Lava Beds National Monument — attest to the volcanic activity which once formed the region.

The beauties wrought by nature, however, took second place to the furious scramble for gold during the 1850s, as fortune-seeking prospectors ripped and clawed into the hillsides. Towns sprang up over night, and many folded just as quickly. Towns like Whiskeytown, and Yreka — as their names imply — will forever be associated with their rowdier pasts. Many have weathered their turbulent histories and survive today in part as communities catering to hikers and other tourists. Several of the towns in this forgotten corner of the state have remained virtually unscathed by the 20th century, and a drive down Main Street will often reveal quaint old homes with Victorian verandas — pleasant reminders of a bygone era.

Alturas

MODOC COUNTY HISTORICAL MU-SEUM, 600 S. Main St. Alturas is right in the middle of a region where the classic struggle between the Indian and the white man was waged. The historical museum serving the area has artifacts which relate to the Modoc Indian Wars as well as a collection of more than 4,000 Indian arrowheads and spear points. A fine antique gun collection is also housed here. Open May-Oct, M-F 9-4, Sa-Su and holidays 10-4:30. Free. Donations accepted. (916) 233-2944.

While in Alturas, stop by the **Nevada-California-Oregon Railway Company General Office Building** at 619 W. Main St. Built in 1917-18, the building reflects both the Mission and Spanish Colonial styles. The bell tower is particularly handsome, although few realize that only one of the bells is made of metal; the others are actually wooden dummies. Now owned by the local Elks lodge, the building can be admired from the street.

Cottonwood

COTTONWOOD HISTORIC DISTRICT, both sides of Front St., 19th century. Cottonwood started as a creekside store and ferry crossing for early miners and settlers. A place where one could buy

N.C.O. Building

132

"a plug of tobacco and get a bite to eat," Cottonwood was essentially a miners' trade center. Named for the profusion of cottonwood trees in the area, the town eventually moved to its present location in 1872 to meet the northern extension of the Southern Pacific Railway. A significant number of 19th-century brick buildings are still standing along the main thoroughfare, and hitching rings can still be seen on the high curbs along Front St. NR.

If you follow Main St. east from the center of Cottonwood, you'll notice that the roads turn distinctly rural as they meander through cattle country. About five miles from town is the **Reading Adobe,** a one-story structure of reddish adobe brick topped with a shingled roof. In 1845 Pierson Barton Reading acquired the 26,000-acre Rancho Buena Ventura which stretched along the Sacramento River and was the northernmost Mexican land grant. A smokehouse, barn, and Reading's mansion were eventually built on the site. The simple adobe was constructed in 1846 and served as the bunkhouse of Reading's cowhands. Although fallen into a state of disrepair, the adobe and Reading's grave nearby are all that remain of this once grand estate. NR.

Fall River Mills

FORT CROOK HISTORICAL MUSEUM, Fort Crook Ave., CA 299. This general history museum features collections related to the history of northeastern California. Among the subjects treated in interesting displays are agriculture, industry, transportation, Indian culture, and pioneer homemaking. Open Apr-Oct, daily 1-4; other times by appointment. Free. (916) 336-5110.

Fort Jones

FORT JONES HOUSE (Louis Heller Studio), Main St., c. 1851. Attributed to architect James E. Thomas, this frame house was originally built as a stage stop and hotel on the California-to-Oregon stage route. The house received its name from the fort which stood only 1½ miles away.

Soldiers were frequent visitors here—at least until a barracks was built for them—and several of the young recruits who frequented the Fort Jones House went on to distinguish themselves in the military, George Pickett and Philip Sheridan among them. Later the house was adapted as a studio for Louis Heller, a prominent 19th-century photographer well known for his work during the Modoc Indian War, and even served as the post office during Heller's stay. Today the house is a private residence, but can be readily seen from the public way. NR.

French Gulch

FRENCH GULCH HISTORIC DISTRICT, 5 mi. off CA 299, 19th century. This small town of less than 300 inhabitants, with a picturesque main street and large tree-shaded lawns bordered with white picket fences, has changed little since the town was founded in the 19th century. One does not have to venture outside town to view the scars of the old placer mines to get a sense of the town's past. The 19th century is evident everywhere, especially in the false fronts and verandas which grace the main thoroughfare. One of the most notable buildings in the district is **Franck's Store,** a stone structure constructed in 1867 and long operated by descendants of the founder. On Main St. opposite the store is the **French Gulch Hotel** (formerly the Feeny Hotel). Built in 1887 and still in operation, it features a covered portico with turned wood columns. Perhaps the most striking building in town is the Gothic Revival **St. Anne's Catholic Church** (c. 1900) on the east side of Main St. This single-story frame place of worship is graced with a handsome bell tower and steeple. NR.

Lassen Volcano National Park

LASSEN VOLCANO NATIONAL PARK, accessible via the town of Mineral on CA 36. Although Lassen Peak, a 10,457-foot plug volcano, was last active between 1914 and 1921, the eerie remains of the lava flows, as well as the forests,

Main St., French Gulch

lakes, and meadows which have survived the eruptions, provide the visitor with some of the most spectacular scenery in California. Lassen Park Rd. surrounds three sides of the Peak (named for a Danish pioneer, Peter Lassen) and affords many beautiful views of the lava beds and the surrounding natural wonders. The road also provides accessibility to two visitor information centers, at **Sulphur Works** (south entrance) — where boiling mud pots and escaping sulphurous gases can still be witnessed — and the **Loomis Visitor Center** at Manzanita Lake (northeast entrance). Besides providing would-be geologists and curious visitors with valuable information about the park, the Loomis Center has an interesting history of its own. Benjamin Franklin Loomis, for whom the center is named, was born in Illinois but moved to the Lassen Peak vicinity in 1874. An amateur photographer, Loomis was witness to the volcanic eruption of 1914, and many of his photographs of the once-in-a-lifetime event are displayed in the present center. The original museum on the site was dedicated to his only child. Constructed in 1927, the building was deeded to the National Park Service, along with the adjoining seismograph building. NR. The visitor centers are open mid-June-late Sept, daily 8-8. Guided walks are offered during the summer. Camping is available in seven campgrounds located throughout the park. (916) 595-4444.

Redding

Although it would be nice to believe, as many do, that the town of Redding owes its name to Pierson B. Reading, on whose Rancho Buena Ventura the town was built (see Cottonwood), Redding was actually named for the far less colorful B.B. Redding, a land agent for the Central Pacific Railroad. Redding, consequently, was a railroad shipping point for local farmers, fruit-growers, and miners.

REDDING MUSEUM AND ART CENTER, 1911 Rio Dr. Shasta County history is celebrated in this local institution. The emphasis is on Indian and pre-Columbian art and artifacts. Open June-Aug, daily except M 10-5; Sept-May, Tu-F and Su 12-5, Sa 10-5. Free. (916) 243-4994.

After visiting the museum, take a look at the **Old Pine Street School** (1922) at 1135 Pine St., a simple Mediterranean Revival structure that reminds one once again of how California architecture turned to its Spanish colonial heritage in the early years of the 20th century. The school was abandoned in 1967 and successfully "recycled" as a shopping complex that retains the building's architectural integrity. NR.

A right turn out of Redding leads to a back road to the mining camps of **Igo** and **Ono**. If you've ever wondered how miners invented names for their overnight boom towns, here's one story that will tax your credulity. It seems that a local miner was met at his departure each morning with his small son's demand, "I go." "Oh, no," was the inevitable response. Perhaps a camp named after his second son, Hugo, exists somewhere.

Sawyers Bar

ST. JOSEPH'S CATHOLIC CHURCH, located in Klamath National Forest, 1855. In 1853 Father Florian Schwenninger, a Benedictine monk, began administering the sacraments to the local miners along the Salmon River. A church was finally constructed in the small miner's town of Bestville, but when gold was discovered a quarter of a mile to the east in Sawyers Bar, the population moved, but the church remained. Later, the area surrounding the church was hydraulically mined, leaving the tiny church and cemetery alone on the knoll as it sits today. The modest exterior features a gabled roof of hand-split shakes, while the interior is surprisingly ornate. The altar is in excellent condition — perhaps the best-preserved part of the church — and is believed to be the handwork of the original priest. A painting of the Crucifixion, 7-feet high by 6-feet wide, is hung above the altar, and is believed to have been brought over from Austria by the same priest. This simple place of worship remains a valuable relic of the pioneer missionary era of the Catholic Church in northern California. NR. Open for worship.

Sawyers Bar vicinity

WHITE'S GULCH ARRASTRA, E of Sawyers Bar on Forest Rd., 19th century. The Mexicans originated the "arrastra," a simple mining contrivance which is nothing more than a stone-lined hole in the ground into which pieces of quartz were added to be ground by two stones rotated with the assistance of mules. When gold-bearing quartz was discovered along the Salmon River in 1860, this primitive, but effective, means of extracting the ore was modified slightly, substituting water power for mule power. The arrastra at White's Gulch is the only such contrivance in the county which remains largely unaltered. NR.

Shasta

SHASTA STATE HISTORIC PARK, CA 299 W of Redding, 19th century. Once known as the Queen City of California's northern mining district, Shasta began its rise to fame and fortune after Pierson B. Reading discovered gold in the area during the summer of 1848. An abundant supply of wood and natural spring water provided early gold seekers with all the essentials for the making of a boom town. Following the opening of a whipsaw mill in the spring of 1850, wood frame buildings began to spring up along Main St., and within two years Shasta boasted a substantial population. Shasta's prosperity continued, largely because of its advantageous location as the northern terminus for the major supply roads from Sacramento and San Francisco. Of course, with the extension of these roads and the arrival of the railroads, Shasta's decline was imminent by the 1860s.

Today, many of Shasta's old buildings remain, including the 1854 **Brick Row Ruins**, the 1856 **Litsch Store**, the 1855 **Whaley Brewery**, the 1859 **Foster Barn**, and the 1855 **Shasta County Courthouse** which has become the central feature of the historic park. The old brick building has been restored to its appearance in 1861, the year it was converted from commercial usage, and it currently features historical exhibits, a collection of paintings, and other artifacts. Operated by the State Department of Parks. NR. Daily 10-5. 50¢ adults, 25¢ children and seniors. ⚐ (916) 243-8194.

Susanville

ROOP'S FORT (Roop's Trading Post), N. Weatherlow St., 1854. This 1½-story log fort was the first building erected by white men in Lassen County. It was also the first

trading post encountered by emigrants on their way west after Fort Hall in Idaho. Known for a time as Roop House, it later became Fort Defiance during the county border dispute known as the Sagebrush War. The builder, Isaac Roop, was the area's first settler and the first elected governor of the unofficial Nevada Territory (1859-61). NR. Open May-Sept, F-Tu 10-4. Free. (916) 257-5721.

Before traveling to Susanville, think about stopping by the **William H. Pratt Memorial Museum,** located at 105 N. Weatherlow St. This regional museum contains historical items related to Lassen County, but is open by appointment only. Free. (916) 257-2757.

Tulelake vicinity

LAVA BEDS NATIONAL MONUMENT, SE of Tulelake, off CA 139. The rugged landscape of this national park was formed by volcanic eruptions centuries ago. The resulting lava has long since cooled and hardened, and today the area consists largely of grassland, chaparral, and pine forests teeming with wildlife. A unique feature of the region is the formation of lava-tube caves caused by the unusual flow patterns of molten lava. Nineteen caves are open for public exploration.

The lava beds were also the site of the Modoc War, an Indian conflict which was the only one fought in California. In 1872 the Indian leader "Captain Jack" led the Modocs into the rugged lava country, where they managed to hold out against Federal and volunteer troops for nearly six months. Two important battle sites are lo-

cated in the northern section of the park within access of CA 139, the main road through the park. **Hospital Rock,** located near the northeast entrance to the park, features the remains of small fortifications used to shelter U.S. troops. West of Hospital Rock off CA 139 is the area known as **Captain Jack's Stronghold,** where a small band of 70 Modocs met with heavy resistance. Further within the park at Hardin Butte is the **Thomas-Wright Battlefield,** the site where nearly 70 soldiers, 5 officers, and 20 enlisted men were killed. Information concerning all of the natural and historical points of interest within the park can be obtained at the **Park Headquarters** off CA 139 at the southern end of the park. Operated by the National Park Service. Open daily 8-5. Free. (916) 667-2282. 🏃

Whiskeytown

TOWER HOUSE DISTRICT, off CA 299 in the Whiskeytown National Recreation Area, 19th century. Many of the structures which once supported this farming and mining community still remain. Though efforts to preserve the Western character of the town have not reached the scale of towns like Columbia in Sonora County, the somewhat down-at-the-heels look of this district offers a true "Old West" flavor, nonetheless. The **Tower House,** built by Levi Tower in the early 1850s, served travelers on the road between Shasta and Yreka for many years before being destroyed by fire. The other major structure in the district is still standing, though in a state of deterioration. The **Camden House,** built around the same time as the Tower House, is a two-story wooden building with several remaining outbuildings. The remains of the nearby gold mining complex at **Bickford Mine** can also be seen. NR.

Parts of the old settlement of Whiskeytown were submerged during the formation of Whiskeytown Lake. The reservoir was created several years ago by the construction of the Whiskeytown Dam, and the entire area has become a National Recreation Area known as the Whiskeytown Unit. A **visitors reception center** is located off CA 299. For further information, contact the park superintendent at Box 188, Whiskeytown, CA 96095, or call (916) 246-1225.

Yreka

WEST MINER STREET-THIRD STREET HISTORIC DISTRICT, 19th century. The town of Yreka sprang up in 1851 when gold was discovered on the flats west of town. With the decline of gold mining, the town became increasingly important as a commercial and political center, but the real beauty of this district can be found not in its history, but in its architecture. A row of brick buildings along Miner St. dates from 1854-1900 and features several fine examples of Italianate styling. Of particular interest is the former **Franco-American Hotel** at 306-312 W. Miner. This painted brick structure was built in 1855 and was later enlarged in 1867.

Third St. contains more old houses than any thoroughfare in town, most of them Victorian structures from the 1890s. The **Judge Rosborough House** at 301 Third St. was built in the early 1860s and is the best example of Victorian Gothic in Yreka. The houses within this district are largely private, but are visible from the public way.

For more information about Yreka's past, be sure to stop by the **Siskiyou County Museum** at 910 S. Main St. This local history museum features exhibits covering a wide range of subjects and also maintains several historic buildings in town, including an 1895 log cabin, an 1870 miner's cabin, a blacksmith shop, schoolhouse, country store, and milliner's shop. The museum is open June 1-Sept 1, M-Sa 9-5; Sept 2-May 31, Tu-Sa 9-5; Mar 1-Nov 1, Su 1-5. Free. (916) 842-3836. 🚻

Plumas, Sierra, Nevada, Placer, El Dorado, and Amador Counties

The gold country of California, centered around the Sierra Nevada mountains, includes some fo the most beautiful—and forbidding—terrain in the Western United States. Towering mountain peaks, turbulent rivers, and bottomless lakes abound. Today the region's economy is bolstered in large measure by the thousands who enjoy both summer and winter sports in and around the mountains. Little more than a hundred years ago, however, the hardy pioneers who settled the area found hardship, rather than recreation, to be their normal lot.

The famous Donner party, marooned in the high Sierras when winter paid them an unexpectedly early visit, was nearly destroyed en route to milder climes. The more fortunate early arrivals, even when successful in their search for gold deposits, had to contend with rugged, wild country, harsh living conditions, and unscrupulous claim jumpers—or worse. One of the early mining settlements is popularly called Hangtown to this day because of the number of thieves and murderers who met justice at the end of a rope in the central square.

It is in large part because of the perseverance and enthusiasm of the early gold seekers that California developed as a major Western center. Once the first yellow specks were accidentally discovered in 1848, there was no stopping the rush. Thousands came overland, and thousands more by ship around Cape Horn. Many found gold; many failed; and still more succeeded at other pursuits. The result was to change the course of history in the Western United States.

Auburn

OLD AUBURN HISTORIC DISTRICT, bounded by I-80, Maple St., Hamilton Ln., and High St., late 19th century. Claude Chana, a Frenchman who came over the Sierras in 1846, is credited with finding the first gold near Auburn. Other settlers followed and soon began a mining camp known as North Fork Dry Diggings because of its proximity to the north fork of the American River. According to some reports, men were bringing out an average of $800 to $1500 a day from their claims. In late 1849, the town's name was changed to Auburn, allegedly because so many of the miners hailed from a community by that name in New York State. Two years later, Auburn became the Placer County seat.

Today, aside from the paving of streets and the laying of sidewalks, old Auburn remains largely unchanged from its appearance in the late 1800s. A fire ravaged the town in 1855, and most structures date from the post-fire rebuilding. As you walk through the district, look for the following landmarks:

The **Placer County Courthouse,** a three-story brick and masonry structure, was erected in 1894 and still serves its original purpose. The first meeting of the Court of Sessions was held here in 1898. The **American Hotel,** now the Shanghai Restaurant, was Auburn's premiere hotel for many years. At one point it also housed offices of the California Stage Company. Located on Washington St., it was built just after the 1855 fire.

The **storefronts** on Commercial St. appear unchanged from the early 1850s; interiors have been altered somewhat to accommodate various businesses, but they are furnished in the style of the Gold Rush era they sprang from.

An early Chinese settlement in Auburn was largely centered on hilly Sacramento St. Few of the original buildings, with the exception of the c. 1856 **Joss House,** used as a house of worship, remain. Also on Sacramento St. is the first permanent **post office,** constructed in 1857—and still in use today.

Placer County Museum, 1273 High St. Located at the turn-of-the-century Gold Country Fair Ground, the museum collection includes, as one would expect, extensive displays of early mining equipment. But there's lots more: Indian and Chinese artifacts, rooms decorated in 19th-century style, farm tools, and a collection of winery and agricultural equipment. (Placer County, after the Gold Rush days, became the major plum-producing area in the country during the early 1900s.) NR. Open all year, M-F 10-4, Sa-Su, 10-5. No charge. (916) 885-9570. ♿

Blairsden vicinity

PLUMAS-EUREKA STATE PARK, 310 Johnsville Rd. (west, off alt. I-40), 19th century. High on the east slopes of the Sierra Nevadas, Plumas-Eureka State Park sits amid spectacular mountain scenery in the headwaters country of the Yuba and Feather Rivers. Within the park, the historic mining town of **Johnsville** and the partially-restored **Plumas-Eureka stamp mill** (NR) vividly recall the time when hard-rock gold mining was the primary activity in the region and an important part of the California economy.

In 1872, the Sierra Buttes Mining Company, a heavily capitalized English company, moved in and bought most of the operating mines. The company consolidated the miscellaneous activities of the earlier operators and launched a highly efficient mining program that was to return handsome profits for about twenty years before the mines were abandoned, sold off, or leased to subcontractors. Under the direction of the local superintendent, William Johns, the company established a new town (Johnsville). Tramways were built to bring ore down to a central mill near Johnsville, and the records indicate that at one time there were as many as 400 men working in the company's mines and stamp mills.

Today 70 miles of long-inactive sealed-off mine shafts and tunnels remain. The wood and stone stamp mill, tram station, stable, and some residences are extant. A **museum**, exhibiting Indian artifacts and displays of geology and natural history, is housed in a former bunkhouse. Open all year, daily 8-4:30. No charge. (916) 836-2380.

Downieville

SIERRA COUNTY MUSEUM, originally an 1852 residence constructed of shist (shale rock), is home to a fine collection of early Sierra County history and artifacts. Here you can see such oddities as horse snowshoes, as well as Indian and Chinese artifacts and a replica of an early gold stamp mill. Open May-Oct, daily 10-5. No charge. (916) 289-3566.

Colfax vicinity

DUTCH FLAT, 15 miles northeast of Colfax, via graded road, 19th century. If you've ever wanted to visit a town so well preserved that it looked like a western movie set, then Dutch Flat is the place. The entire town is lined with typical Gold Rush architecture: one- and two-story wooden frame buildings, constructed with utility, rather than beauty, in mind. Dutch Flat was noted as the site of rich hydraulic mining from 1854 to 1882. In 1860, it had the largest voting population in Placer County and was the key point on the Dutch Flat-Donner Lake freight route linking the silver mines of Nevada to California. It was in Dutch Flat that the most practical route for the railroad through the Sierras was determined; the first document drawn up to form the Central Pacific railroad and the first money pledged to build it were organized here by Theodore Judah and Dr. D.W. Strong. During its heyday, the town numbered 2,000 Chinese among its residents, but an adobe building, the **China Store**, is all that remains of Dutch Flat's original Chinatown. Both Bret Harte and Mark Twain found inspiration for their lively stories in the town. A number of buildings dating frm the 1850s are still in use, among them the **General Store, Clay Lodge Masonic Hall,** and the **Dutch Flat Methodist-Episcopal Church.** The **Dutch Flat Schoolhouse,** a two-story frame building completed in 1898, now serves as a community center. NR.

Emerald Bay (Lake Tahoe)

VIKINGSHOLM, Emerald Bay State Park, 1929. In 1928 Mrs. Lora J. Knight, a

Main St., Dutch Flat

wealthy resident of both Santa Barbara and Chicago, purchased an isolated site at the head of Emerald Bay and instructed Lennart Palme, a Swedish-born architect who had married into her family, to design a home without disturbing a single one of the area's magnificent trees. After a trip to Scandinavia, they decided to reproduce a Norse fortress of about 800 A.D. in full detail. Vikingsholm, considered the finest example of Scandinavian architecture in the Western Hemisphere, was Mrs. Knight's summer home from its completion until her death in 1945. Guest houses and a tea-house on Fannette Island were constructed to complement the 38-room stone mansion. Turrets, towers, intricate carvings— even hand-hewn timbers—were used in the mansion itself. The sod roof, with its living grass, is like those sometimes used in Scandinavia to feed livestock during the winter months. Many of the furnishings that Mrs. Knight specified for Vikingsholm were so historically significant that their export was forbidden by the Norwegian and Swedish governments; consequently, she had them copied in detail, down to the measurements, colorations, and aging of the wood. Vikingsholm, set in a spectacular natural setting which offers numerous recreation activities, is open daily from July 1-Labor Day. No charge. (916) 525-7277.

Fiddletown

FIDDLETOWN, E of CA 49, 19th century. Fortunately bypassed by CA 49, Fiddletown is a colorful reminder of the Gold Rush era. The unusual name is reputedly a gift of the Missouri settlers of the town who were fond of fiddling. Changed to "Oleta" by the state legislature in 1878, the name was restored in 1932. In the early 1850s and '60s, Fiddletown became a trading center for a number of local placer mines. The town was also the site of a steam-powered sawmill, which after 1853 provided the lumber for the construction of many local houses.

Fiddletown remains a quiet rural community in the foothills of the Sierra Nevadas. As in many California towns, this sleepy village features a substantial Chi-

nese settlement, here located at the lower end of Main St. Today the contents of the **Chew Kee Store** comprise the holdings of a **Chinese Museum.** The collection of Chinese artifacts has been described by at least one expert as perhaps the most outstanding expression of Chinese-American culture in the United States. The museum is maintained by the Fiddletown Preservation Society, which also oversees the upkeep of the 1850 **Joss House,** the 1863 **Shellhorn Building,** the 1868 **Cooper Residence,** and the 1853 **Farnham House,** farm, and outbuildings. The buildings are open for tours by appointment only. Donations accepted. (209) 296-4519.

Grass Valley

EMPIRE MINE (Empire Mine State Historic Park), 338 E. Empire St., late 19th century. When an enterprising young man named George D. Roberts came to the Grass Valley area in 1850, it was lumber, rather than gold, that he expected to harvest. He had plans to cut timber and split out lumber to sell to the placer miners working just north of the hill to which he had acquired rights. But on his first day of work, he found a rock outcropping streaked with gold: he was standing atop what would become known as the Empire Mine. Roberts quickly staked his claim: within days, neighboring hills were claimed and overrun with miners. After working the claim for only one season, however, Roberts sold out to Woodbury, Park and Company, which already owned several adjacent mines. Over the next few decades the mine changed hands several times; it is estimated that, all told, more than $100 million in gold was extracted from the one site.

In 1867 William B. Bourn II, a wealthy California entrepreneur, took control of the Empire Mine. His **mansion,** located on the grounds, is one of several monumental stone and brick structures built for him in California, all of which were designed by prominent architect Willis Polk. Other buildings still standing near the mine which date, as does the mansion, from the late 19th century, are the **mine office and refinery,** the **machine shop,** a conserva-

Empire Cottage, Empire Mine, Grass Valley

tory, and several small **residences** now occupied by park employees. The old buildings are in various stages of disrepair, and plans call for renovation and reconstruction where necessary. NR. Open all year, daily 10-5. 50¢ adults, 25¢ children. ♔ (916) 273-8522.

MINING MUSEUM AND PELTON WHEEL EXHIBIT, Mill St. The California Historical Society operates this museum of mining artifacts. Among the exhibits are an early 30-foot water wheel and a stamp mill. Open May-Oct, daily 11-5; Nov-Apr, Su 10-4. 50¢ adults. (916) 273-9853.

Homewood vicinity

SUGAR PINE POINT STATE PARK, Lake Tahoe, CA 89. 19th-20th centuries. Beautiful Lake Tahoe first came to the attention of the western world through the journals of John C. Fremont, who sighted it in February, 1844, while leading the Army's first official exploratory expedition across the Sierra Nevadas into California. One of the first permanent residents of the Sugar Pine Point area was an old-time frontiersman from Kentucky, "General" William Phipps, who staked out a 160-acre homestead claim in the spring of 1860 and soon afterward built himself a rough-hewn log cabin. He supported himself by fishing, hunting, and related activities, and apparently took great pleasure in his solitary existence. About 1870 he built a second cabin on his property near the lake,

and it is this **cabin** that remains today, just south of General Creek.

In 1897 and '98 Isias W. Hellman, a successful California banker, bought about a thousand acres on the point and shortly after the turn of the century built a sumptuous new summer home—a three-story Victorian "cottage"—using locally quarried granite and other native materials. Today the house, known as the **Hellman-Ehrman Estate,** serves as a visitor center, complete with interpretive exhibits describing the history of the Lake Tahoe region. NR. Open all year, daily dawn to dusk. No charge. (916) 525-7982.

Ione vicinity

PRESTON CASTLE, north on Preston Ave., 1890-94. Not really a castle at all, but a large Romanesque Revival building constructed as a reform school, this was the first building to house juvenile offenders within the complex now known as the Preston School of Industry. The building is remarkable both for its architecture —a rare example of the Romanesque Revival style in the Mother Lode region of California—and for its purpose: it represents the state's first major attempt at prison reform for young offenders. At first the entire population of the school was housed in the castle, a self contained unit which included a hospital, superintendent's quarters, dormitories, and even a swimming pool in the basement. By the end of the first year there were 234 boys in residence. In later years the facility expanded to many satellite buildings, with the main building housing the offices necessary for carrying on the business of the institution on the first floor. In 1960, the last of the staff was transferred to the present office buildings, and the large stone landmark has since been abandoned. NR.

Jackson

AMADOR COUNTY MUSEUM, 225 Church St. Jackson is the seat of Amador County and boasts some of the deepest mine shafts on the North American continent. But Jackson, unlike many of the other early mining communities, is far from being a ghost town. Its county museum is housed in an 1859 house and, of course, features gold mining artifacts, as well as general exhibitions related to Western history and the Indian and Chinese settlements in the region. Open all year, M, W-Su 10-4. $1 adults, 50¢ children 6-12. (209) 223-2884.

Jackson's narrow and winding **Main St.** passes between rows of iron-shuttered stone buildings with overhanging balconies. The **Amador County Courthouse** stands on Courthouse Hill, and dates to the 1850s. NR.

KENNEDY TAILING WHEELS, Jackson Gate Rd., 1914. This unique system of elevator wheels was designed to lift mine tailings (waste debris) over two hills to an impounding dam. The Kennedy Mining and Milling Company was one of the largest gold mining operations in the Jackson area during the early 1900s. Local farmers, however, complained that mining debris was contaminating their properties. Mechanical engineer James Spears was called upon by the company to study a system in Montana and create a similar transport mechanism for the Kennedy Mine. Today the tailing wheels are the only such structures found in this country. NR. Contact the Amador County Museum (see previous listing) for information and tours.

Nevada City

In 1848 James Marshall discoverd gold at Deer Creek, near what was to become the seat of Nevada County. Not satisfied with the pickings here, Marshall moved on, and his later discoveries at Coloma began the famous California Gold Rush. By 1850 there were thousands of miners working all the hills and creeks in the Deer Creek area, and Nevada City was born. Today it is one of the more picturesque and well preserved of the mining towns in the Sierras. A number of early buildings have been carefully restored and are open to the public, among them the classic **National Hotel** at 211 Broad St., a three-story brick landmark with ornamental cast-iron balconies decorating its facade, which has been welcoming guests since its construction in 1856. At the height of its popularity, more than $1,000 a day was taken in across the bar. At least stop by for a drink. NR. (See Lodging and Dining for details.) Another early building serves basically the same purpose for which it was constructed: the **Nevada City Firehouse #2**, at 420 Broad St. A fire department was only organized following a series of fires that devastated the town between 1851 and '58. The women of Nevada City took the first step toward the organization of a permanent department by raising slightly over $1,000, most at a ball given at the courthouse. Their efforts resulted in the construction of this simple Classic Revival brick building (1861) which today houses fire equipment on it main floor. The second floor is used for fire department meetings. NR.

In 1857 James J. Ott opened an assay office in Nevada City and two years later completed a report that led indirectly to a new gold rush. J. P. Stone and W. P. Morrison, two residents who had been working the Washoe deposits to the east, brought Ott samples of their ore on June 24, 1859. An article in the *Nevada Journal,* the city's first newspaper, told of Ott's report and of the fabulous ore deposits Stone and Morrison had found, precipitating the great Washoe Rush and the development of Nevada's famous Comstock Lode, which was to make fortunes for many men. Ott's original office burned to the ground during a fire several years later, and he moved into a nearby building at **130 Main St.**, a two-story brick structure that had been completed in 1855. The landmark is currently under restoration. NR. Its next-door neighbor, the **South Yuba Canal Building,** an identical brick commercial landmark, is now maintained by the Nevada County Historical Society (see following).

The **Nevada Theatre** (Cedar Theatre) at Broad and Bridge Sts. is considered by historians to be the earliest original theater extant in California. It opened in September, 1865, headlining the then famous (now forgotten) Worrell Sisters. During the late 1930s it was extensively renovated, and many of its original features, such as graceful arches and brick pilasters, were covered with plaster and stucco. It has recently been restored, however, and operates once more as a playhouse for the community, where concerts, musical and variety shows, plays, lectures and documentary films are put on. NR. Check with the Chamber of Commerce for details. (916) 265-2692. ♀

AMERICAN VICTORIAN MUSEUM, 325 Spring St. A group of century-old stone, brick, and frame buildings—once comprising a foundry where ore from the area mines was processed—now houses a museum collection. As its name implies, this museum is devoted to objects of the Victorian era. Among its most prized possessions is a Joseph Meyer pipe organ which dates from 1871. Open all year, W-Su 10:30-4. Donations accepted. (916) 265-5804.

MARTIN LUTHER MARSH HOUSE, 254 Boulder St., is operated by the American Victorian Museum. Once the home of a prominent Nevada City resident, it is a two-story Italian Villa residence topped by a cupola. A balustraded veranda extends the full length of the front facade. Virtually unaltered since its construction, Marsh House is an exceptionally well preserved example of mid-19th-century architecture, refurbished to reflect its period. NR. Open for tours by appointment with the museum.

NEVADA COUNTY HISTORICAL SOCIETY, 214 Main St. The Nevada City Firehouse #1, completed in 1861, houses the society's fine collection of objects pertaining to the county's history; mining, agriculture, railroading, communications and domestic life are among the areas covered. Open all year, daily 11-5. Donations accepted. (916) 265-9941.

Nevada City vicinity

MALAKOFF DIGGINS STATE HISTORIC PARK, 15 miles northeast of Nevada City via graded road to North Bloomfield, 19th-20th centuries. The easily-reached placer gold that could be taken from the Sierra stream banks had been deposited there over the course of centuries, brought down by the river as it wore away the gold-bearing veins along its course. As the rush of prospectors increased in the late 1840s, the easy supply began to disappear, but there were other sources—veins in the rock that might be filled with gold-bearing quartz, the river beds that might prove rich even though the gold along their banks was gone, and the "deep gravels" (ancient rivers that had long since dried up or changed course). Extricating ore from this gravel, especially when it might be buried under several hundred feet of worthless dirt, was a colossal problem. Tunneling was tried, but it took weeks or months of hard work. Ground sluicing was another method—digging a small gully down the side of the hill to be mined, then bringing water to the top by means of a flume or supply ditch, directing it down the gully, and shovelling masses of earth in with it, trusting that the gold would be trapped, while the water washed away the lighter debris. This method, unfortunately, was not terribly efficient. Finally, in 1852, a Frenchman by the name of Chabot used a hose to bring water where he needed it, eliminating the work of building a flume. When Edward Matteson added a nozzle to the hose, he became the father of hydraulic mining. Now the hillsides were simply blasted with a stream of water until the soil disintegrated. A sluice caught the heavy gold particles, as before, but the work was simplified to the point that one or two men could now process hundreds of tons of earth daily, making it economical to mine gravel that yielded only a nickel's worth of gold per cubic yard.

Hydraulic mining required vast quantities of water at high pressure—reservoirs and ditches had to be built, and drainage systems were required to reach the heaviest gold deposits. The North Bloomfield gravel company, which had already spent vast sums to build the necessary reservoirs and ditch systems, constructed an eight thousand-foot tunnel through bedrock to direct the tailings—dirt and water residue from the hydraulic operations—down to the South Yuba River. Toward the end of the '60s, as large hydraulic operations got underway, their tailings started to become

Blair House, Malakoff Diggins State Historic Park

a serious problem, especially to farmers. Their crops were overwhelmed by the waste, and the silt traveled all the way to the Golden Gate, impaired navigation of major rivers such as the Sacramento, and caused flooding in the town of Marysville. Finally, in 1884, as a result of that flood, a permanent injunction was handed down against further hydraulic mining.

What remains in the Malakoff Diggins today is a great mine pit, 7,000-feet long, 3,000-feet wide, and nearly 600 feet deep in places. This was the largest—and most profitable-of such operations. The town of North Bloomfield, whose few residents are mostly park rangers and their families, is an historic district of simple frame buildings typical of the gold regions of California. Displays in the park **museum** tell the story of the hydraulic miners and their way of life. In the **Ostrom Livery Stable,** some of the many types of wagons in use when the mine was operating are displayed. **Saint Columncille's Catholic Church** (1860) was relocated to the park from nearby French Corral. (Many North Bloomfield residents believe that Saint Columncille is the patron saint of bartenders, a breed popular among the mining folk. NR. The museum is open Tu-Su 10-5 in summer, Sa-Su in spring and fall. No charge. The park is open all year. Nominal admission. (916) 265-1740.

Placerville

EL DORADO COUNTY HISTORICAL MUSEUM, 100 Placerville Dr. Mining equipment, historical artifacts and dis-

plays, and Indian crafts explain Placerville's colorful past. Unofficially, the El Dorado county seat is still known as Hangtown because of the number of executions—or lynchings—which took place here during the Gold Rush days. Open all year, Tu-Sa 10-4. No charge.
(916) 626-2250.

While you're in town, stop by the **Episcopal Church of Our Saviour** at 2979 Coloma St., the oldest church in the county which has remained in continuous operation since its construction (1865). The first rector, Father Charles Caleb Peirce, served the community for 43 years, traveling on foot throughout the hills to minister to those who could not attend services in Placerville. The church, still open for Sunday worship, is noteworthy for its vaulted ceiling—a particular type of wooden roof support found only in the Mother Lode country of California, the result of employing former shipwrights from San Francisco. In actuality, the ceiling structure is an inverted clipper ship frame! NR. (916) 622-2441.

Placerville vicinity

MARSHALL GOLD DISCOVERY STATE HISTORIC PARK (Coloma), 7 miles northwest of Placerville via CA 49, 1848. James Wilson Marshall, a foreman for entrepreneur John Sutter, discovered gold at Coloma while inspecting a sawmill race. Two years later, the resulting gold rush of 1849-50 precipitated the establishment of California as a state. The town of Coloma, which grew up around the gold discovery site at Sutter's Mill, was the first white settlement in the foothills of the Sierra Nevada. About 70 percent of the town is now included in the state park. The original mill near which Marshall made his historic discovery has long since vanished, but a full-size replica has been carefully built on the site, and it operates on weekends and for tour groups. Throughout the park are found exhibits of Gold Rush days including mining methods, household articles, tools, and artifacts. A museum displays the story of Sutter and Marshall and of the gold discovery that so drastically altered the course of West Coast history. A well-marked trail winds past a stamp mill and other early buildings. The **Wap Hop store** displays items used by members of Coloma's once sizeable Chinese colony to sift and resift the sand and gravel in search of the precious metal. NR, NHL. Open all year, daily 10-5. $1.50 per car. (916) 622-3470. 👬

Quincy

PLUMAS COUNTY MUSEUM, 500 Jackson St. Quincy, a small valley town whose houses are set against a backdrop of high, fir-covered mountains, is the seat of rural Plumas County, an agricultural and mining area. Exhibits in the museum include costumes, historical and contemporary artifacts, Indian relics, and geological displays. Open Jan-May and Sept-Dec, M-F 8-5; June-Aug, M-F 8-5, Sa 11-4. No charge. (916) 283-1750.

Smartville vicinity

BRIDGEPORT COVERED BRIDGE, northwest of Smartville via graded road. One of the longest single-span covered bridges in the country spans the south fork of the Yuba River on the road between French Corral and Smartville. Completed in 1862, the 235-foot bridge was part of an old turnpike linking Nevada City, North San Juan, and the Malakoff mines. NR.

South Lake Tahoe

LOG CABIN MUSEUM, Star Lake Rd. An early 1930s log cabin is the setting for a museum displaying objects dealing with Lake Tahoe's history. Brochures with suggested auto tours of the area are available here. Open Memorial Day-Labor Day, daily 10-2. No charge. (916) 544-2312.

Truckee vicinity

DONNER CAMP, 2.6 miles west of Truckee via I-40, 1846. At this point in the high Sierras, a California-bound group of pioneers led by Captain George Donner was caught by two early winter snowstorms. Marooned in deep drifts, the party built rude shelters of wagon tops and brush in their efforts to survive. Seven of the fifteen who set out for help reached the California settlements, and on February 19, 1847 the first relief party arrived at the camp. Of the 89 original members of the party, only 45 survived the winter ordeal. The fate of the Donner party epitomizes the hardships and danger endured by pioneers of the overland migrations. A monument in their memory stands on the site, which is now part of **Donner Memorial State Park**. A park museum has exhibits detailing the fate of the Donner party as well as displays on the construction of the transcontinental railroad, Indian crafts, and the natural wonders of the Sierra Nevada. NR, NHL. Open all year. Museum: daily 10-4. 50¢ per person. Park: daily dawn to dusk. Nominal admission.

WESTERN AMERICA SKISPORT MUSEUM, I-80, Boreal Ridge Ski Area. If you're in the vicinity for a skiing holiday and the weather doesn't cooperate, or if you'd like a change from pioneer history, stop in at this museum of skiing memorabilia. This is certainly the terrain for it. Open in winter, Tu-F 1-4:30, Sa-Su 11-5. Off season, by appointment. No charge. (702) 322-3130.

Glenn, Butte, Colusa, Yuba, Sutter, Yolo, Solano, Sacramento, San Joaquin, and Stanislaus Counties

The fertile, broad valleys of central California have attracted settlers from every area of the world—India, China, Europe, Mexico, and the eastern United States—for more than 150 years. Since the discovery of gold in this and nearby areas to the east during the 1840s, the population has consistently increased. When the mines appeared to be worked out later in the century, there were other riches to be developed. The Sacramento and San Joaquin valleys are crisscrossed by a great number of rivers and creeks which provide that most precious of Western commodities—water—to produce superb crops. The history of the area is largely rural and agricultural, and most of the cities that have developed—Chico, Modesto, Stockton—are the product of farmland prosperity. These are towns that first grew rich on the needs of farm people and provide the facilities for the processing of foodstuffs. Only Sacramento, the center of state government, has been somewhat of an exception to this rule. Other towns—Benicia, Vallejo—tried to make their livings from government, each serving briefly as the capital city, but were rejected in preference to Sacramento. Situated at the confluence of the Sacramento and American rivers, Sacramento has been perfectly positioned as a commercial and transportation center for the entire region.

Benicia

Benicia has always wanted to be an important city and has never quite made it. Its location overlooking the Carquinez Straits between San Pablo Bay and Suisun Bay is strategically important and favorable for shipping. The Federal government, with the establishment of the Benicia Arsenal and Barracks, took advantage of this site. The city was the state capital during the years 1853-54 but lost out to Sacramento in the economic bidding for the privilege of serving as the center of government.

BENICIA ARSENAL, foot of M St., Army Point and I-680, 1850-1964. Left standing in what was one of the most important military supply and ordnance centers in the West are some handsome and important buildings. The **Clock Tower Building** (1859) is the most impressive structure in the complex, and, like most of its neighboring landmarks, is built of sandstone. The Italianate **Commandant's House** and

the **Double Officer's Houses,** all built in 1860, are also distinguished by their fine lines and solid proportions. It was from this arsenal that many of the military installations in the West were supplied with arms and ammunition. In 1964 all of the arsenal's activities were transferred to the Tooele Ordnance Depot in Tooele, Utah. The area is now the Benicia Industrial Park, and the fate of the historic buildings is uncertain. NR.

BENICIA CAPITOL-COURTHOUSE, 1st and G Sts., 1853-54. The building—which was California's capitol from February, 1853, to February, 1854—is a very handsome red brick temple with white Doric columns. The building was intended to be used as the city hall but was made available when the state legislature, meeting in nearby Vallejo, decided that the arrangements there were unsatisfactory. Benicia was, in turn, rejected by the legislators who could not resist the economic lures offered by Sacramento. From 1854 to 1858 the building served as the seat of Solano County, but that, too, was a temporary assignment which ended when the honor was awarded to Fairfield. The old Capitol is now the center of a state park. It has been restored with great care and includes exhibits and period furnishings which contribute to a better understanding of this early period in California's state government. NR. Open 10-5. (707) 745-3385.

OLD MASONIC HALL, 106 W. J St., 1850. This was the first Masonic hall built in California. It is a very simple Greek Revival clapboard building like those often found in New England or New York State. NR. Private, but visible from the street.

Chico

BIDWELL MANSION STATE HISTORIC PARK, Sowillenno Ave., 1865-66. The mansion is a striking reminder of the style of life which existed on the great agricultural ranches of 19th-century California. John Bidwell had the impressive Italian Villa residence built for his new wife, who made it into a graceful social center for the 22,000-acre Rancho Chico. The land in the upper Sacramento Valley is very fertile, and Bidwell became noted for his creative husbandry, having introduced many new crops, including the casaba melon. Agriculture, however, was only one of his pursuits. In the 1840s he served with Fremont in the military moves attendant to the takeover of California, and he gained the rank of major; during the Civil War he received the title of Brigadier General. Bidwell represented California as a congressman in the 1860s, but his later attempts to win the governorship of California were unsuccessful. Both he and his wife, Annie Ellicott Kennedy Bidwell, campaigned for many social causes, and in his last political run for office in 1892, Bidwell was the National Prohibition party candidate for President.

The Bidwells' productive life is well documented in displays which are to be found in a visitor center at the mansion. The 26-room house has been refurnished and restored to its original grand appearance. NR. It is open daily 10-5. 50¢ adults, 25¢ for children under age 18. (916) 895-6144.

Colusa vicinity

GRAND ISLAND SHRINE, 8 miles S of Colusa on CA 45, 1883. A fancy single-room Roman Catholic chapel in the picturesque Gothic Revival style stands here by the side of the road. Not at all a typical country church, Grand Island has a vaulted roof and buttresses with turrets

and crosses which support the side walls. NR.

Knight's Ferry

KNIGHT'S FERRY HISTORIC DISTRICT, on Stanislaus River 2 miles from Stanislaus-Calaveras county line off CA 108 and 120, c. 1850s-1900. Knight's Ferry is an amazingly well-preserved Victorian-era settlement lined with Greek Revival and Gothic Revival buildings. Although the mobile home has made its appearance in the Stanislaus River Valley, it hasn't been able to take over. The old general store in town dates from 1852, and the **covered bridge** just outside was erected

in 1862. The longest covered span in the state, it is still used for carrying vehicular traffic across the Stanislaus River. NR.

La Grange

LA GRANGE VILLAGE, E of Modesto on CA 132, 19th century. La Grange is one of central California's most picturesque villages; the entire town has been placed on the National Register of Historic Places. Located along the Tuolumne River, La Grange was first known as French Bar, a reference to the first settlers, French miners, who began arriving in the 1850s. The town is made up largely of adobe brick, clapboard Greek Revival, and stone buildings. On a hill overlooking the town is the **St. Louis Roman Catholic Church** (1854), the oldest church in Stanislaus County. NR.

Locke

LOCKE HISTORIC DISTRICT, bounded

by the Sacramento River, Locke Rd., and Alley and Levee Sts., 1915. During the 1870s Chinese laborers, finished with their jobs on the transcontinental railroad, found work constructing an extensive levee system in the delta area of central California formed by the confluence of the San Joaquin and Sacramento Rivers. Many of the workers first settled at Walnut Grove, but they were forced to move north in 1915 when a devastating fire ripped through their modest neighborhood. A group of ten Chinese elders from the town then founded the settlement of Locke. More than 65 years later, the main street of this small community is still largely composed of two-story commercial structures with false fronts and Carpenter Gothic touches. It has remained almost exclusively a Chinese town. NR.

Lodi

SAN JOAQUIN COUNTY HISTORICAL MUSEUM, 35251 Fort Tejon Rd. Tools and implements, Indian artifacts, textiles and costumes, and agricultural items comprise most of the objects on display at this regional museum. Considering the area's rich agricultural heritage, it is only fitting that there be a tractor and harvester collection on exhibit. In addition, the museum houses a collection of 3,000 foot-operated and hand-powered tools. The institution is the only accredited agricultural museum in California. Open W-Su 10-12 and 1-5. Free. (209) 368-9154.

Marysville

Marysville, the third largest city in the state during the mid-1800s, survived the Gold Rush days in good shape. It did not become a mere shadow of its former self—as did most of the mining towns—but continued to prosper as a commercial center and as the county seat of Yuba County. Some of the most colorful and historic Victorian buildings were destroyed in what were popularly known as urban "renewal" projects in the 1950s and '60s, but significant landmarks remain to be enjoyed by the resident and visitor.

MARY AARON MUSEUM, 704 D St., 1855. The house, with a restored kitchen and parlor furnished in the style of the Gold Rush days, is one of the most highly ornamented Gothic Revival homes left in the state. Also located on the grounds is the **County Store Museum** with a chapel, sheriff's office, and machine shop. Open Tu-Sa 1:30-4:30. Free. (916) 743-1004.

BOK KAI TEMPLE (Chinese Joss House), Yuba River levee at D St., 1880. Bok Kai is a deity worshipped by the Chinese for banishing evil spirits and controlling rains and floods of spring in time for planting. Considering the fact that Marysville is built below the level of the Yuba River, the veneration of Bok Kai seems both appropriate and prudent. The first temple was constructed in the 1860s by the large Chinese community attracted to the Marysville area by mining and railroad work. The present building is still used for worship and is the focal point of an annual celebration—Bomb Day—which takes its name from the colorful firing of fireworks to honor Bok Kai. By tradition the festival is to be held on the second day of the second month of the Chinese lunar year, but a Saturday and Sunday in March are usually chosen. The event draws thousands of tourists each year. NR. The temple will be opened for guided tours upon request, M-F 10, 12, 2, and 3. Free. Donations accepted. The contact is Joe Kim. (916) 742-5486.

JOSE MANUEL RAMIREZ HOUSE (The Castle), 220 5th St., 1851-54. One of the founders of Marysville, Ramirez, a Chilean, came to make a fortune in the mines. He made enough money to build a very fancy house said to have cost as much as $35,000, a small fortune in the 1850s. Designed in the Gothic Revival style, it features a two-story central section which projects like the prow of a ship. An 1855 Marysville directory described the house as a "splendid edifice which attracts the attention of every visitant." NR. Although still maintained as a private residence, it can be enjoyed today from the public way.

Modesto

McHENRY MUSEUM, 906 15th St., 1883. The best house in Modesto, the McHenry mansion has been superbly restored for use as a municipal museum. Robert McHenry was a successful rancher and banker; he wanted his family to live in the highest style, and this they could do in the grand Italianate home he had built for them. The ceilings in the first floor rooms are 13 feet high and feature plaster cornices and ceiling rosettes. The woodwork throughout is of the finest quality and workmanship. Visitors who appreciate the glories of Victorian splendor will enjoy the period rooms, antique furnishings, and historical exhibits. NR. Open Tu-Su 12-4. (209) 577-5366.

Modesto vicinity

MILLER HORSE AND BUGGY RANCH, 9425 Yosemite Blvd., 10 miles E on CA 132. How people traveled in the 19th century fascinates nearly everyone today, whether young or old. The Miller ranch is equipped with many different kinds of 19th-century wagons as well as fire equipment, a stagecoach, and even a 1905 horse-drawn ambulance. A variety of old-time shops, including one for a blacksmith and another for a barber, are additional amenities of this pleasant rural museum. Open daily during daylight hours. $1 adults, 50¢ for children 6-12, free for children under 6. (209) 522-1781. ♦♦

North San Juan vicinity

OREGON CREEK COVERED BRIDGE, 3 miles NE of North San Juan over Oregon Creek, c. 1860s. Most of California's eleven remaining covered bridges are still in use, and the span over Oregon Creek (in Yuba County) is one of them. It is 83-feet long and is covered with wood siding. Tom Freeman was the master builder. NR.

Oroville

OROVILLE CHINESE TEMPLE, 1500 Broderick St., 1863-1968. Three buildings comprise this Chinese temple and museum complex. The earliest is the one-story red brick **Main Temple** (1863), a simple, neoclassical structure devoid of ornamentation. The heavy outer doors lead to the principal temple room known as Lake Sing Kung ("room of many gods and goddesses"), where oriental statues abound. The two-story **Council Room and Moon Temple** was constructed later (1868-70) to accommodate the town's growing Chinese population. The **Tapestry Hall** (1968) was added in recent times, along with the courtyard, gardens, and small outbuildings.

The original temple complex was begun by the Chinese community of Oroville with funds provided by Emperor Quong She of the Ching Dynasty, and today the Center functions as a museum, community house, and place of worship. NR. Open Memorial Day-Labor Day, daily 10-11:30 and 1-4:30; Labor Day-Memorial Day, M-Tu, F-Su 10-11:30 and 1-4:30. $1 adults, free for children under 12, tours 75¢ per person. (916) 533-1496.

Sacramento

The citizens of this early trading center and mining town worked hard in the 1850s to gain the privilege of becoming the state capital. This honor was officially granted in 1855, and since that time Sacramento, like most capitals which are not the largest cities in the states they serve, has tried to be something more than a governmental center. Unlike such places as Springfield, Illinois, Albany, New York, and Jefferson City, Missouri, however, Sacramento has often succeeded in its attempt to make room for more than government offices. The home of the Pony Express and the western terminus of the first transatlantic railroad line, Sacramento also became known as a city of beautiful homes. The Crockers and Stanfords were only two of the wealthy families to have left behind a cultural legacy for all to enjoy. While a great deal of Victorian Sacramento is gone now, much attention is given to preserving the many treasures that remain.

CROCKER ART MUSEUM (E. B. Crocker Art Gallery), 216 O St., 1873. The gallery building was designed in 1873 and houses what was the Crocker family's collection of paintings; the R. A. Herold Wing was added in 1969. Seth Babson was the architect of the original building as well as the Crocker home which adjoins it. The home was built around 1853 for banker B. F. Hastings and was purchased by Crocker in 1868. A lawyer in a prominent Sacramento firm, Crocker became the counsel to the Central Pacific Railroad and was a Califronia Supreme Court justice. NR. Open Tu 2-10, W-Su 10-5. $1 adults, no charge for children under 12. (916) 446-4677.

GOVERNOR'S MANSION, SW corner of 16th and H Sts., 1877-78. The elegant Second Empire Victorian mansion was built not for a governor's use but as the home of hardware merchant Albert Gallatin. From 1887 until 1903 it was the home of the Steffens family, and here author Lincoln Steffens spent his boyhood. In 1903 the house was purchased by the state, refurbished, and a small wing added, for the use of the state's chief executive. The mansion served as home for thirteen governors, the last being Ronald Reagan. The Reagans found the mansion unsuitable for occupancy and convinced the state legislature to build a modern home. This latter extravagance, more a high-class motel than a mansion, was left empty by Reagan's successor, Jerry Brown, who refused to live in it.

The old Governor's Mansion is now maintained as a museum. It sits on one-third of an acre in the heart of town, and a carriage house is included on the property. NR. Open daily 10-5. 50¢ adults, 25¢ children 6-18, free for children under 6. (916) 445-4209.

J. NEELY JOHNSON HOUSE, 1029 F St., 1853. The Johnson House is representative of the earliest type of Sacramento dwelling—the Greek Revival temple. It is built of brick and has a two-story portico supported by octagonal columns. The house served as the official residence of the state's first and fourth governors. NR. Viewable from the street.

OLD SACRAMENTO HISTORIC AREA, bounded by I and L Sts., Front St. and I-5. While visiting Sacramento, you'll probably want to spend most of your time in this area. It is the neighborhood of the best shops and restaurants. Just about every building is historic. Some have been moved into the area from other parts of town in order to save them from destruction. The area is unfortunately cut off from the rest of the city by I-5, but this barrier—erected at great cost to the city's historic neighborhood—may now act to protect what has become a separate enclave. A **Visitor's Center** is located in the Morse Building, 1027-1031 Second St., and is operated by the Convention and Visitors Bureau. It is open daily 10-5. (916) 446-4314. Among the most important buildings and sites are:

California State Historic Railroad Museum, 125 I St. Railroad equipment and memorabilia are dramatically displayed in this new facility comprised of 21 restored locomotives and cars as well as 46 interpretative exhibits. The tour of the museum begins with a 12-minute film on riding the rails in the days of steam. After this, the visitor enters a life-size Sierra Nevada snow shed where the *Governor Stanford,* an 1862 steam locomotive is housed. The Great Hall is where most of the engines and cars are displayed. Among the most colorful are the *Gold Coast,* railroad historian Lucius Beebe's luxurious private car; the *St. Hyacinthe,* a sleeping car; and a fully-equipped diner. You can also walk through a pit beneath one of the steam locomotives to get a close-up look at the running gear. If you were not a railroad buff before starting the tour, you will have become one by the end. Open daily 10-6. $2 adults, $1 children and senior citizens. Tickets are also good for the **Central Pacific Passenger Station** next door (see next listing) if used on the same day. (916) 445-4209.

Central Pacific Passenger Station, Front and J Sts., 1869. This historic station is a reconstruction of the first California terminal for the transcontinental railroad. Waiting rooms, tickets offices, and baggage rooms can be toured. Seven pieces of antique rolling stock are also on display. Open daily 10-6. $2 adults, $1 children and senior citizens. Tickets are also good for the California State Historic Railroad Museum if used on the same day. (916) 445-4209.

Eagle Theatre, 925 Front St., 1849. Rebuilt in 1975, the Eagle is the oldest theater in the state. Plays and musicals are performed here on weekends. Open for tours daily except M 10-5. Free. (916) 445-4209 for information about tours; (916) 446-6761 for information about performances.

B. F. Hastings Museum, 2nd and J Sts., 1852. This important building in Old Sacramento has housed the Wells Fargo Co., various state offices, including the California Supreme Court from 1855-69, and a transcontinental telegraph company. The building was also the first western terminus of the Pony Express. The displays and exhibits relate to these various activities. The original State Supreme Court chambers can be toured. NR. Open daily 10-5. Free. (916) 445-4209.

Howard House, 109-111 K St., 1866. An elaborate Italianate commercial building, Howard House is used today for small shops. With its bold cornice, gigantic brackets, and fancy parapet, the decora-

tive facade is a joy to behold. An arcade is formed in front of the first-floor shops by a handsome open porch.

STANFORD-LATHROP HOUSE, 800 N St., 1857. A wonderfully ornate building originally designed by architect Seth Babson in the Italianate style, the brick mansion was made even better around 1861 with the addition of another floor and a mansard roof. The changes occurred when Leland Stanford, railroad financier and governor, bought the house. The Stanford family lived here until 1874. The residence is private but can be viewed from the street. NR.

STATE CAPITOL, between 10th and 16th and L and N Sts., 1860-74. Construction of this monumental Neoclassical Revival building designed by Miner Frederic Butler cost $2.5 million and lasted so long that the legislature almost stopped the work from proceeding. Over 100 years later the legislature decided that the building deserved careful restoration. Work began in 1976 and was completed in 1982 at a cost of $68 million after nearly every element—structural and decorative —was either strengthened or replaced. Hundreds of workers were involved in what was the most complex restoration-reconstruction project ever undertaken for a single historic building. The rotunda, inspired by that of the U.S. Capitol, rises 238 feet from street level and is 70 feet in diameter and now glows with soft colors and gold leaf. The exterior of the dome was completely refaced in copper. The Assembly and Senate chambers, badly disfigured during a 1906-08 remodeling, have been returned to their 19th-century opulence. NR. Group tours through the building are scheduled at 9:30, 10:30, 1:30, and 2:30 on weekdays. Free. (916) 445-5200.

SUTTER'S FORT STATE HISTORIC PARK, 2701 L St. and CALIFORNIA STATE INDIAN MUSEUM, 2618 K St. Sutter's Fort is primarily a reconstruction of the 1839-44 complex. Only the center building survived in one piece before the state assumed responsibility for the site in the 1890s. It is the most historic location in Sacramento, the place where the city was founded by John A. Sutter, a German who traveled throughout the world, finally settling along the American River near the center of present-day Sacramento. Daily life in such a pioneer settlement is expertly recreated. A carpenter shop, brandy distillery, blacksmith shop, saddle shop, and kitchen are all open for tours. Visitors can also view Sutter's office and private quarters. NR, NHL. Open daily 10-5. 50¢ adults, 25¢ children 6-18, free for chidren under 6. (916) 445-4209.

Located in the same park complex is the **California State Indian Museum.** It houses many exhibits on the California tribes. A Maidu Indian legend puppet show is held at 11:30 each Sa and Su. Films are shown each Sa and Su at 12:30 and 2:30. Hours, admission, and telephone number are the same as for Sutter's Fort.

Stirling City vicinity

INSKIP INN, 6 miles N of Stirling City on the Skyway, 1868. The only remnant of the small community of Inskip, the inn owes its longevity to its function first as a stage stop on the main Oroville-Susanville road and then as a convenient rest stop for motorists. The hotel has served intermittently over the years as a store and a post office. This is the second hotel on this site, the first having burned. NR. For details concerning accommodations, see Lodging and Dining.

State Capitol, Sacramento

Stockton

FOX CALIFORNIA THEATER, 242 E. Main St., 1930. Built in the days when the "talkies" were a novelty, and when five acts of vaudeville served as entertaining curtain raisers, the Fox Theater created a stir on opening night in 1930. Newspaper reports gave equal billing to the marcelled starlets in attendance and to the lavish architectural design. Detailing of the front facade and tower, little changed in more than 50 years, reflects the Spanish-Moorish interior. A two-story entrance rotunda with a circular mezzanine leads to the theater itself, whose stage, considered gigantic when constructed, was designed both for live performances and motion pictures. Curved stairs to the mezzanine were once enhanced by a bubbling fountain and pool. All that bubbles today, sadly, is the popcorn machine. But as you sit inside waiting for the lights to dim, perhaps you'll be able to hear echoes of the big bands— Dorsey's, Ellington's, and Paul Whiteman's among them—who once performed here on a regular basis. NR. (209) 941-4400.

HAGGIN MUSEUM, 1201 N. Pershing Ave. Affiliated with the San Joaquin Pioneer and Historical Society, the museum is devoted to both history and the fine arts. Antique furnishings, agricultural objects, personal effects, and replicas of local historic interiors are on display. Open Tu-Su 1:30-5. Free. (209) 462-4116.

HOLT-ATHERTON PACIFIC CENTER FOR WESTERN STUDIES, University of the Pacific. This research center is rich in the source materials of Western Americana. Included in the collections are the John Muir papers, overland maps, Spanish mission and Gold Rush territory photographs, and thousands of Indian artifacts. The center is open to the public M-F 8:30-5. Free. (209) 946-2405.

Suisun City

Deep navigable salt water marshes lead to the Pacific from this inland community, making it an easily-accessible spot. Named for the Suisune, an Indian tribe, Suisun City owed its growth in large part to the intelligence and vision of one man: Francisco Solano, chief of the Suisune and later head of all the tribes north of San Pablo and Suisun bays. Solano was given his Spanish name by the missionaries of San Francisco de Solano at Sonoma, from whom he learned to speak the language with fluency. He became a friend and ally of Spanish military leaders who held sway over the area in the early 19th century, and helped to maintain peace among the local tribes,

thus enabling the community of Suisun City to develop without interference from the Indians.

CALIFORNIA RAILWAY MUSEUM, CA 12, Star Route 283. Take the children to this museum complex, where they can watch antique railway machinery being repaired, see 80 pieces of vintage railway equipment, including trolleys, freight and work cars, Pullmans, and steam locomotives, and—best of all—take unlimited rides on some of the restored equipment at no additional charge. Open Mar-Dec, Sa-Su 11-5. $3 adults, $2 children 12-17 and senior citizens, $1 children 3-11. 👬 (707) 374-2978.

Before you leave this small town, take a look at the **Samuel Martin House** (Stonedene), at 293 Suisun Valley Rd. Constructed of hand-hewn native cut stone, in blocks a foot square or larger, the three-story residence was completed in 1861 for a prominent local farmer. NR. Privately owned.

Vacaville vicinity

PENA ADOBE, 2 miles southwest of Vacaville on I-80, c. 1840. Built of sun-dried adobe taken from nearby Lake Laguna, the Pena Adobe has exterior walls nearly two feet thick and rests on a cobblestone foundation. An 1870-80 frame addition was moved elsewhere on the grounds. Both have been restored, and the adobe, furnished with period pieces, is administered by the municipal parks department. NR. Open all year, W-Su 10-4. Donations accepted. (707) 446-6781.

Vallejo

General Mariano G. Vallejo selected the site of the town that was to bear his name while on a tour of his 99,000-acre Rancho Suscol in the late 1830s. He campaigned vigorously in later years to have his community selected as the new state capital, offering the Yankee leaders both the land and the buildings necessary to create a city of great style. His dreams proved unrealistic even though his offer was initially accepted. When the new state government officials arrived to hold their first legislative session in 1852, they quickly left again since the capitol was unfinished and there were no comfortable living quarters. The seat of government was temporarily moved to Sacramento; a year later, the legislature tried again—but only briefly. First Benicia—and, finally, Sacramento—was selected as the California capital.

In 1853, Vallejo's future was finally assured when the federal government purchased nearby Mare Island, and a naval yard was established there. Mare Island remains today as the largest naval facility on the West Coast.

VALLEJO OLD CITY HISTORIC DISTRICT, bounded by Sonoma Blvd., and Monterey, California, and York Sts., late 19th-early 20th centuries. This was the location of many of the town's first Victorian homes. Because it is on a steep hill, the area was never developed commercially, and thus the early Victorian, Mission, and Spanish Revival residences remain largely untouched by progress. If you wander through the area (and the Chamber of Commerce offers a map that will guide you), you'll see many modest landmarks, often with ornate details such as Queen Anne porches and Italianate cornices. Most of the homes are privately owned, but are easily viewed from the public way. NR. The **Chamber of Commerce** is located at 2 Florida St. (707) 644-5551.

Williams

SACRAMENTO VALLEY MUSEUM ASSOCIATION, 1491 E. Street. The little town of Williams, with a population of fewer than 1,000 people, is home to an interesting museum complex. Displays include an old general store, apothecary shop, barber shop, saddlery, as well as Indian artifacts, toys, costumes, and an outdoor exhibit of farm machinery. Open all year, M-W, F-Su 10-5. 50¢ adults, 25¢ children. (916) 473-5423.

Woodland

GIBSON HOUSE MUSEUM, 512 Gibson Rd., 1857-79. William Byas Gibson, a prominent cattleman and farmer, built this imposing brick home for his family in the mid-19th century. A curved driveway leads to the residence, through rolling lawns planted with trees and shrubs which hide the building from the street. In process of restoration, the Gibson House is open by appointment with its curator, Mr. Balch. NR. (916) 666-8265.

WOODLAND OPERA HOUSE, 320 2nd St., late 19th century. This brick landmark entertained thousands during the prime period of traveling theatre. It retains one original backdrop and the advertising curtain which hung in front of the stage. The opera house is undergoing restoration at present; plans call for it to be used as a working theatre as soon as sufficient funds can be raised. NR. Call (916) 666-9617 for information.

Yuba City

COMMUNITY MEMORIAL MUSEUM OF SUTTER COUNTY, 1333 Butte House Rd. Located on the banks of the Feather River, Yuba City was settled in the mid-19th century when John Sutter deeded the land to a group of pioneers. The history of the area is documented at this local museum, whose collection includes furniture, clothing, Indian artifacts, and local basketry. Open all year, M-F 9-5, Sa 1-4 and by appointment. No charge. (916) 674-0461.

Lodging and Dining

CALIFORNIA is blessed with many small, civilized outposts of culture and comfort where lodging is a delight and not a burden to be borne for the night. Some of the inns are like those of New England — cozy, frame and clapboard country houses expanded to take in guests. Others were built in the Spanish Colonial Revival style so popular early in the century, and are sometimes thought of as ranches. Prices tend to be somewhat higher than elsewhere in the country for inns or ranches, but they are no more expensive than most modern California motels or hotels.

As a major center of the tourist trade in the United States, urban California is bountifuly supplied with chain hotels and motels, most of which have nothing better than an anonymous flavor. You might as well be in Keokuk or Albany as in most of the places recommended for the night by the usual travel guides. Both Los Angeles and San Francisco, however, have hotel facilities with personality and period charm. These are found in both moderate and expensive categories. The concept of a bed and breakfast hostelry has also spread to the cities from the country. San Francisco is especially well equipped with such facilities.

The hotels and inns following have been broken down by region.

Imperial and San Diego Counties

Coronado

HOTEL DEL CORONADO, 1500 Orange Ave., 92118. (714) 435-6611. Carleton Lichty. Open all year. The queen of California resort hotels, the Hotel del Coronado is a National Register landmark (see listing for further details). 685 rooms. Expensive. AE, D, CB, M, V.

Julian

JULIAN GOLD RUSH HOTEL, 2032 Main St., 92036. (714) 765-0201. Mr. and Mrs. S. Ballinger. Open all year. The last of Julian's Victorian hotels has been saved for today's enjoyment. It was built in 1887 and provides easy access to the historic town. 15 rooms. Inexpensive. PC.

PINE HILLS LODGE, 2960 La Posada Way, 92036. (714) 765-1100. David and Donna Goodman. Open year-round. Less than three miles S of Julian is a true rustic lodge happily free of TV and the telephone. Built in 1912 to last for many years, Pine Hills is also the home of a dinner theater (F and Sa nights). Public restaurant. 19 rooms. Moderate. AE, D, CB, M, V, PC.

San Diego

BRITT HOUSE, 406 Maple St., 92103. (714) 234-2926. Daun Martin, Robert Hostick, and Charlene Browne. This magnificent Victorian town house is San Diego's first bed-and-breakfast guest house. The 1887 house, built by Eugene Britt and lived in by E. W. Scripps of the newspaper chain, among others, has been superbly restored. 9 rooms. Expensive. M, V, PC.

U. S. GRANT HOTEL, 326 Broadway St., 92106. (714) 232-3131. (800) 327-9157. The U.S. Grant is the San Diego area's second hotel on the National Register (see listing for further details). Public restaurant. 300 rooms. Moderate. AE, CB, DC, M, V.

Rancho Santa Fe

THE INN AT RANCHO SANTA FE, between La Gracia and Linea del Cielo at end of Paseo Delicias, 92067. (714) 756-1131. D. L. Royce. Twenty acres of woods and beautifully landscaped grounds surround the old guest house (1923) in the Spanish Colonial Revival style. There are also individual cottages of the same design with private terraces. Public restaurant. 80 rooms. Expensive. AE, M, V, PC.

Orange, Riverside, and San Bernardino Counties

Riverside

THE MISSION INN, 3649 Seventh St., 92501. (714) 784-0300. Foster Davidoff. Built in the early 1900s to recapture the flavor of the era of the Spanish missions, the inn is now justly celebrated as a National Historic Landmark property (see listing for further details). Public restaurant. 47 rooms. Expensive. AE, V, M.

Los Angeles County

Avalon, Catalina Island

ZANE GREY PUEBLO HOTEL, 199 Chimes Tower Rd., 90704. (213) 510-0966. Toby and Karen Baker. Open year-round. Author Zane Grey's home was built in 1926 and has been simply converted for the pleasure and ease of guests. 17 rooms. Expensive. M, V, PC.

Beverly Hills

BEVERLY HILLS HOTEL, 9641 Sunset Blvd., 90210. (213) 276-2251. Open year-round. The hotel is an opulent movieland palace set amidst twelve flowering acres. The original building (1911) in the Mission Revival style has had some tacky additions, but an overall air of elegance is maintained in the interior spaces. 325 rooms. Public restaurants. Expensive. AE, CB, D, M, V, PC.

BEVERLY WILSHIRE HOTEL, 9500 Wilshire Blvd., 90212. Open year-round. (213) 275-4282. Another of the Beverly Hills luxury palaces, this 1926 hybrid version of an

Italian Renaissance villa is a favorite with the Rodeo Dr. set. If this impresses you, or if you are just looking for a stylish period address, don't go any further. 445 rooms. Public restaurants. Expensive. AE, CB, D, M, V.

Los Angeles

ALEXANDRIA HOTEL, Spring at Fifth St., 90013. (213) 626-7484. Open all year. If you've grown tired of the Portman visual effects and really prefer old-fashioned elegance, try the Alexandria. It's recently been restored to a state approximating its former grandeur during World War I. 500 rooms. Moderate to expensive. AE, CB, D, M, V.

THE AMBASSADOR HOTEL, 3400 Wilshire Blvd., 90010. Open year-round. (213) 387-7011. A giant of a complex almost smack in the center of the city, the Ambassador is situated on 23 acres. It is a true resort hotel of a type first popular in the late 19th century. Today it is well suited to joggers and tennis players. 500 rooms. Public restaurants. Though more reasonable than the Beverly Hills hotels, it is still expensive. AE, CB, D, M, V.

HOTEL BEL-AIR, 701 Stone Canyon Rd., 90024. Open all year. (213) 472-1211. James H. Checkman. The hotel is the crowning glory of a hilly, beautifully landscaped area set above UCLA. The hotel began in the 1920s as a stable, was converted into an inn, and finally rebuilt as a hotel in 1945. Through it all, it has kept its basic Spanish Colonial Revival style — in pink adobe. 68 rooms. Public restaurant. Expensive. AE, D, CB, M, V.

BILTMORE, 515 S. Olive St., 90013. Open all year. (213) 624-1011. A honey of a Beaux Arts palace built in 1922-23, with further work in 1928. It overlooks Pershing Sq. in downtown LA. 1,022 rooms. Public restaurants. Expensive. AE, CB, DC, M, V.

HOTEL MAYFLOWER, 535 S. Grand, 90071. (800) 421-8851. A pleasant, moderately expensive alternative to the fancier places, the Mayflower is across the street from the Biltmore and overlooks the landmark Public Library and its park. The interior is marked with small Art Deco touches. Moderate. AE, CB, D, N, V.

Pasadena

HUNTINGTON-SHERATON, 1401 S. Oak Knoll, 91009. (213) 792-0266. The last of the great Pasadena resort hotels, the Huntington dates from 1906. It was first known as the Wentworth and was designed by Charles Whittlesey. The gardens are well maintained. 330 rooms. Public restaurants. Expensive. AE, CB, D, M, V.

Ventura and Santa Barbara Counties

Los Alamos

UNION HOTEL, 362 Bell St., 93440. (805) 344-2744. Doris U. Coen. Open F, Sa and Su year-round. An adobe building has been remodeled in recent years to recreate the style of the original Union Hotel of 1880. Lavishly furnished with period antiques. 14 rooms. Public restaurant. Expensive. PC.

Los Olivos

MATTEI'S TAVERN, CA 154, 93441. (805) 688-4820. Open seven days a week for dinner. The building has been a stagecoach stop, hotel, and saloon, and dates from 1886. Open M-F 5:30, Sa-Su 5. Moderate. AE, D, CB, M, V.

Montecito

SAN YSIDRO RANCH, 900 San Ysidro Lane, 93108. (805) 969-5046. James H. Lavenson. Open all year. A guest ranch since 1893, San Ysidro's most famous owner was screen star Ronald Colman. There are 540 acres with views of the Pacific on one side and the San Ynez mountains on the other. Some of the cottages were built at a time when the area was part of a mission complex. 38 rooms. Public restaurant. Pets welcome. Expensive. AE, M, V, PC.

Santa Barbara

COLD SPRING TAVERN, 5995 Stagecoach Rd., 93105. A restaurant serving lunch and dinner seven days a week, the Cold Spring is located in a 100-year-old stagecoach stop. Lunch, 11-4; dinner, 5-9:30. Moderate. AE, M, V.

San Luis Obispo, Monterey, San Benito, Santa Clara and Santa Cruz Counties

Carmel

HOLIDAY HOUSE, Camino Real at Seventh (P.O. Box 234), 93921. (408) 624-6267. Kenneth and Janet Weston. Open all year. This friendly, quiet guest house has met with approal from visitors since the 1920s when it was frequented by well-chaperoned Stanford coeds. The house dates to 1905 and was gradually enlarged. A no-smoking policy applies in the house. 6 rooms. Moderate. PC.

THE STONEHOUSE INN, Eighth below Monte Verde (P.O. Box 2517), 93921. (408) 624-4569. Joseph Smith. Open all year. A bed-and-breakfast establishment, the Stonehouse dates from around 1906 and was visited by such famous literary personalities as Jack London and Sinclair Lewis. The building approximates a New England inn or tavern in style. 6 rooms. Recently renovated. Expensive. PC.

Monterey

OLD MONTEREY INN, 500 Martin St., 93940. (408) 375-8284. Ann and Gene Swett. Open all year. The building dates from the 1920s, but the ambience is that of a century earlier — elegant and comfortable. 10 rooms. Expensive. PC.

Pacific Grove

THE GOSBY HOUSE INN, 643 Lighthouse Ave., 93950. (408) 375-1287. Ralph and Kit

Sotzing. Open all year. A bed-and-breakfast Victorian-style establishment, Gosby House is a National Register property (see listing for further details). 19 rooms. Expensive. PC.

THE GREEN GABLES INN, 104 Fifth St., 93950. (408) 375-2095. Roger and Sally Post. Open summers only. Green Gables is a bed-and-breakfast facility housed in an incomparable Queen Anne mansion facing the sea. It's not Brideshead Manor, but there is a private chapel. 3 rooms. Expensive. PC.

Fresno, Kern, Kings, Merced, Mariposa, Madera, and Tulare Counties

Coulterville

THE JEFFERY HOTEL, Main St. and CA 49 (P.O. Box 4). (209) 878-3400 or 3600. Bob Kingman. The last of Coulterville's eleven hotels has been in the process of restoration for two years. The once ornate building, dating from the 1840s, well merits so much loving attention. 19 rooms. Inexpensive. PC.

Sequoia National Park

GIANT FOREST LODGE, vicinity of Three Rivers, approx. 17 miles N of park entrance, CA 198. Address for reservations: Reservations Manager, Sequoia and Kings Canyon Hospitality Service, Sequoia National Park, CA 93262. (209) 565-3373. Some units open year-round. The Giant Forest Hotel, built in 1914, was stupidly torn down and replaced with a modern dining room in the 1960s. There are, however, quite a few remaining rustic cabins from the 1914 to 1936 period with redwood shake or sequoia bark paneling. They blend in very naturally with the setting—as intended. These buildings are included in a National Register historic district (see Sequoia National Park for further details). Inexpensive. MC, V.

Yosemite National Park

AHWAHNEE HOTEL, 1 mile E of Yosemite Village. (714) 372-4611. Contact for reservations: 800-692-5811. Closed first two weeks in Dec. The largest building in the park, the Ahwahnee is a great resort hotel in the rustic style. It has been designated a National Register landmark (see listing for further details). 121 rooms in hotel and cottages. Expensive. Public restaurant. AE, D, M, V.

CURRY VILLAGE, on CA 41, 1 mile E of the park headquarters, Yosemite Valley. (714) 372-4611. Contact for reservations: same as Ahwahnee Hotel. Open all year. Curry Village was originally a tent camp and still retains some of these facilities in addition to rustic-style bungalows and more modern structures. 172 cabins, 400 tents, 18 motel rooms. Cafe and snack bar. Inexpensive. AE, D, M, V.

WAWONA HOTEL AND PAVILION, on CA 41, 4 miles NE of south entrance. (714) 375-6355. Open Apr-Oct. Contact for reservations: same as Ahwahnee Hotel. There are eight buildings in the complex, and the main frame and clapboard hotel structure dates from the 1880s. This is a National Register property (see listing for further information). 63 rooms. Inexpensive. AE, D, M, V.

Alpine, Calaveras, Inyo, Mono, and Tuolumne Counties

Columbia

CITY HOTEL, Main St. (P.O. Box 1870), 95310. (209) 532-1479. Tom Bender. Open all year. City Hotel is the official State of California lodging facility in the Columbia Historic State Park village. The building dates back to 1871 and is today a training center for Columbia Junior College's hotel and restaurant management program. This, and the other park buildings, are included in a National Register historic district (see Columbia Historic District for further details). 9 rooms. Public restaurant (lunch and dinner). Expensive. M, V, PC.

Mokelumne Hill

HOTEL LEGER, CA 49 and 26. (Box 50), 95245. (209) 285-1401. Sue Clark. Open all year. George Leger's hotel looks like a Gold Rush town movie set, but he arrived from Europe well over 100 years ago; his hotel dates from 1851. The furnishings throughout are late-Victorian in style. 13 rooms. Public restaurant (dinner). Inexpensive. PC.

Sonora

GUNN HOUSE MOTOR HOTEL, 286 S. Washington St., 95370. (209) 532-3421. Peggy Schoell. Open all year. This two-story adobe building was built in 1849-51 and was restored for use as lodgings in 1963. It is furnished with Victorian antiques. 25 rooms. Moderate.

San Mateo, San Francisco, Alameda, Contra Costa, and Marin Counties

Half Moon Bay

SAN BENITO HOUSE, 356 Main St., 94019. (415) 726-3425. Carol Regan. Open all year. Eighty years ago this was the Mosconi Hotel, then Domenic's; today the San Benito (the old name for Half Moon Bay) has finally come into its prime. The building has been restored in a pleasant eclectic fashion and is overflowing with antiques. 12 rooms. Public restaurant. Moderate. AE, M, V, PC.

San Francisco

As California's #1 tourist city, San Francisco offers a greater variety of lodgings than any other locality in the state. One is not condemned to endure the banality of motel living in the Bay area—unless you want to. There are great, expensive hotels and inns, and more modestly scaled and priced accommodations available. The older grand hotels are too well known—the St. Francis, Mark Hopkins, Fairmont, Four Seasons-Clift, and Stanford Court—to need further description or recommendation. The emphasis is here given to the smaller, and sometimes less expensive, accommodations available to the traveler seeking the better than average hostelry.

THE BED AND BREAKFAST INN, 4 Charlton Court, 94123. (415) 921-9784. Robert and Marily Kavanaugh. Open all year. This charming enclave — spreading to an adjoining building — takes its form and spirit from similar London institutions. Charlton Court very much approximates a London mews. 8 rooms. Expensive. PC.

THE BEDFORD HOTEL, 761 Post St., 94109, and THE CARTWRIGHT, 524 Sutter St., 94102, are both under the same management. These are moderately-priced smaller hotels (Bedford, 150 rooms, and Cartwright, 120) with a refreshing lack of pretense but plenty of pride in good housekeeping. The Bedford has a public restaurant. Both are open all year. Both accept AE, M, V. (800) 223-9868 for reservations.

THE INN SAN FRANCISCO, 943 S. Van Ness Ave., 94110. (415) 641-0188. The 24-room mansion was once the home of John English, a city commissioner, and was built in 1878. The building has been restored to the period, but it also makes use of the most up-to-date solar heating system. Moderate. V, M.

THE MANSION HOTEL, 2220 Sacramento St., 94115. (415) 929-9444. Robert C. Pritikin. Some Victorians were not such prim and proper folk as history often recalls them. The Mansion celebrates the loonier side of the Gilded Age in its 1887 turreted Queen Anne manse. There is a music room, billiard room, and parlor among the downstairs "public" rooms. Upstairs, the curios and treasures spill over into the guest rooms. 18 rooms. Expensive. AE, D, CB, M, V, PC.

RED VICTORIAN BED AND BREAKFAST INN, 1665 Haight St., 94117. (415) 864-1978. Open year-round. Sami Sunchild. The Red Victorian is an aptly named turn-of-the-century resort hotel that has been lovingly restored. It is located near Golden Gate Park and the University of San Francisco. 15 rooms. Inexpensive. M, V.

THE SPRECKELS MANSION, 737 Buena Vista West, 94117. (415) 861-3008. Jonathan Shannan and Jeffrey Ross. Open all year. This inn consists of two buildings, the 1887 mansion and the next-door guest house built ten years later. Exceptional care has been taken to respect the character of the Colonial Revival main house. 10 rooms. Expensive. M, V, PC.

Sausalito

CASA MADRONA HOTEL, 156 Bulkley Ave., 94965. (415) 332-0502. John W. Mays. The Casa Madrona would be an extraordinary find in any location. It is perfectly suited for this hilly seaside village. A National Register property (see listing for further particulars). Restaurant open for dinner. 18 rooms. Moderate to expensive. AE, M, V, PC.

Sonoma, Mendocino, Napa, and Lake Counties

Elk

ELK COVE INN, 6300 South, CA 1 (P.O. Box 367), 95432. (707) 877-3321. Hildrun-Uta and Michael Boynoff. Open all year. The inn consists of several buildings, all pleasantly situated along the coast — the 1880s main house, a two-bedroom cabin, and the Sandpiper guest house dating from the early 1900s. A good spot for weekend hiking and biking. 8 rooms. MAF, EP (M-Th), public restaurant (dinner). Expensive. PC.

HARBOR HOUSE, 5600 South, CA 1 (P.O. Box 369), 95432. (707) 877-3203. Patricia Corcoran. Open all year. Originally the residence of a lumber company executive, the main building of Harbor House (built 1916-17) has five rooms; in addition, there are four cottages on the grounds. MAP only. Expensive. PC.

Fort Bragg

GREY WHALE INN, 615 N. Main St., 95437. (707) 964-0640. Colette and John Bailey. The Redwood Coast Hospital (1915) has been cleverly recycled for a bed-and-breakfast inn. There is a wide variety of accommodations available. 13 rooms. Moderate, EP. AE, M, V, PC.

Gualala

OLD MILANO HOTEL, 38300 CA 1, 95445. (707) 884-3256. Judith Fisher. Open Apr-Nov. This 1905 hostelry has been expertly refurbished. The property is listed in the National Register and boasts a spectacular view of the Pacific. 8 rooms. Expensive. M, V, PC.

Little River

GLENDEVEN, 8221 N. CA 1, 95456. (707) 937-0083. Jan and Janet De Vries. Open all year. A Maine settler, Isaiah Stevens, built Glendeven in 1867, and if one didn't know that the ocean outside the window was the Pacific, you might think you were in Kennebunk or Blue Hill. 7 rooms. Moderate, EP. PC.

Mendocino

JOSHUA GRINDLE INN, 44800 Little Lake Rd. (P.O. Box 647), 95460. (707) 937-4143. Bill and Gwen Jacobsen. This handsome 1879 Victorian with a delightful verandah is well situated to take advantage of the village, bay, and ocean. You can walk from here to any number of Mendocino sights. 7 rooms. Expensive, EP. PC.

THE MacCALLUM HOUSE, 740 Albion St. (Box 206), 95460. (707) 937-0289. Sue Norris. The main house (1882) is a fanciful Carpenter Gothic confection with decorative woodwork in almost every corner. The interior is similarly exuberant in style. Additional accommodations are located in various outbuildings such as a carriage house, gazebo playhouse, and greenhouse. 20 rooms. Moderate, EP. Public restaurant (dinner). Pets welcome. V, PC.

MENDOCINO HOTEL, 45080 Main St. (Box 587), 95460. (707) 937-0511. Jeff Love. A hotel since 1878, the Mendocino was fully restored in 1976. Appropriately, the rooms are furnished with Victorian antiques. 26 rooms. Inexpensive to expensive. Public restaurant. PC.

St. Helena

CHALET BERNENSIS, 225 St. Helena Hwy., 94574. (707) 963-4423. Jack and Essie Doty. Open all year. The main house, dating from 1884, was built for an early winemaker, John Thoman; it was later named The Sutter Home in honor of the winery next door. Each room has a fireplace and private bath. 9 rooms. Moderate, EP. M, V, PC.

Sonoma

SONOMA HOTEL, 110 W. Spain St., (707) 996-2996. John and Dorene Musilli. Open all year. The Sonoma Hotel, located in the midst of this historic community's cultural center, probably dates from around 1870. It was used as a bar, boarding house, meeting hall, etc., until restored and refurnished in the 1970s. 17 rooms. Moderate, EP. AE, M, V, PC.

Westport

DE HAVEN VALLEY FARM INN, N. CA 1, 95488. (707) 964-2931. Gale Fairbrother. Open year-round. A more agreeable situation is hard to imagine — an 1875 frame ranch house set amidst 40 acres along the hilly coast of northern California. The Victorian past is very tastefully stressed in furnishings and in the respect accorded the original style of the building. There are also two cottages with guest rooms. 7 rooms. Moderate, EP. Public restaurant (brunch and dinner). M, V, PC.

Yountville

BURGUNDY HOUSE COUNTRY INN, 6711 Washington St. (P.O. Box 2766), 94599. (707) 944-2855. Bob and Mary Keenan. Open all year. An 1872 brandy distillery built of fieldstone is headquarters of the inn. The building — with 22-inch thick walls — is reminiscent of those found in Europe or in the Delaware Valley of the East. 16 rooms. Moderate, EP. CB, PC.

MAGNOLIA HOTEL, 6529 Yount St. (P.O. Box M), 94599. (707) 944-2056. Bruce and Bonnie Locken. Open all year. The main building dates from 1873, and the restaurant was added in 1900. The Magnolia was always intended to be a hotel but, not unlike some others, served as a bordello for a spell. Restoration began in 1969 and continues to the present. 11 rooms. Expensive, MAP. Public restaurant F-Sa (dinner only).

THE WEBBER PLACE, 6610 Webber St., 94599. (707) 944-8384. Loren Holte. An 1850s farmhouse, the old Webber Place was moved from its original site at the end of the 19th century. It has been completely restored and refurbished after years as a family residence. 4 rooms. Expensive, EP. M, V, PC.

Amador, El Dorado, Placer, Nevada, Plumas, and Sierra Counties

Amador City

THE MINE HOUSE INN, CA 49 (P.O. Box 245), 95601. (209) 267-5900. Peter Daubenspeck III. Open all year. The building was built over 100 years ago as the Old Keystone Consolidated Mining Co. office building. This is the center of the gold mining country, and The Mine House is rich in historical lore. 8 rooms. Moderate. PC.

Grass Valley

THE HOLBROOKE, 212 W. Main, 95945. (916) 273-1353. Dick Kline. Open all year. The Holbrooke has been Grass Valley's #1 watering place since the mid-19th century.

The building dates from 1862 and was carefully restored in the 1970s. It is an official California Historic Landmark. 7 rooms. Moderate, MAP. Public restaurant (lunch and dinner Tu-Su). AE, M, V.

Jackson

NATIONAL HOTEL, 2 Water St., 95642. (209) 223-0500. Neil Stark. Open all year. The National has held forth for over 130 years, most of that time in the same three-story frame building. Will Rogers, John Wayne, Presidents Garfield, Hoover, and Reagan have been guests. Whatever your politics, you'll be in good hands. Public restaurant. 44 rooms. Inexpensive. M, V, PC. Pets welcome.

Nevada City

NATIONAL HOTEL, 211 Broad St., 95959. (916) 265-4551. Tom Coleman. Open all year. Nevada City's National is one of the town's principal historical attractions and is listed on the National Register (see listing for further details). It dates from 1856. 43 rooms. Public restaurant. Moderate. AE, M, V, PC.

RED CASTLE INN, 109 Prospect St., 95959. (916) 265-5135. Jerry Ames and Chris Dickman. Open all year. This wonderful Gothic Revival building is a delight to visit. It was built in 1859-60 and has been little altered since, except to provide modern facilities. 7 rooms. Moderate, EP. PC.

Sutter Creek

SUTTER CREEK INN, 75 Main St., 95686. (209) 267-5606. Closed only the month of Jan. California's first bed-and-breakfast hostelry is located in an 1859 residence. It will remind many of a New England inn. 16 rooms. Moderate. PC.

Volcano

ST. GEORGE HOTEL, Main St., 95689. (209) 296-4458. Marlene and Charles Inman. This out-of-the-way village settled during the Gold Rush period now has only 85 residents, excluding the guests of the St. George. The hotel was built in 1862 and an annex was added in 1961 when country weekends and extended vacations in this beautiful area became popular. 19 rooms. Public restaurant. Inexpensive. MAP available. Pets welcome in annex. PC.

Glenn, Butte, Colusa, Yuba, Sutter, Yola, Solano, Sacramento, San Joaquin, and Stanislaus Counties

Stirling City vicinity

INSKIP INN, 6 miles N of Stirling on the Skyway (Box 68, Stirling City), 95978. (916) 873-0804. A hotel that has been in continuous operation since the 1850s, the Inskip is a National Register property (see listing for further details). 10 rooms. Public restaurant. Inexpensive. M.

2. NEVADA

THE glitter and glamor of Las Vegas and Reno attract millions of vacationers each year who come in search of the sun, the stars, and the instant wealth they are sure the gaming tables will bring. When faced with the bright lights and luxury of the gambling strips, it is easy to forget how they came to be, and to overlook the many remnants of Nevada's early days which are still present throughout the state.

But there are parallels between past and present Nevada. It was wealth which attracted the first settlers more than 100 years ago, a lust for money that drew them to the gold and silver hidden in the mountains. As major strikes were made, mining towns sprang up overnight. Saloons and dance halls beckoned the miners and often took much of their new-found riches. Those fortunate—or wise—enough to parlay their earnings into large fortunes through investment in the railroads and other industry of the late-19th century prospered. Their mansions remain today, many now open as museums, refurbished to appear as they did when the magnates owned them.

Nevada is not all neon and casinos and mansions, however. Large areas of the state are left to the desert and the mountains (Nevada means "snow clad" in Spanish), with the ruins of many early mining towns dotting the slopes here and there. Nevada's scenery is often stark, but always beautiful. Major highways enable the modern traveler to cross rugged terrain in hours—not the weeks and months necessary for the pioneers who first settled here. But ignoring the back roads often means bypassing much of the state's beginnings. A word of caution: though the ghost towns and mine ruins are fascinating, they are often accessible only after traveling over miles of dirt road—some graded, some not. It is wise to plan such excursions carefully, and to make sure that you have sufficient gasoline and appropriate transportation (four-wheel drive is sometimes a necessity).

If you take the time to explore beyond the cities—and even within them—you're certain to find pieces of Nevada's past that will help you to understand her present.

The entries which follow have been divided into two geographic regions in order to facilitate easier travel: **Las Vegas and the South,** and **Carson City and the North.** Each area has great charm and many attractions, sure to stimulate even the most jaded tourist's interest.

Miner's Union Hall, Virginia City

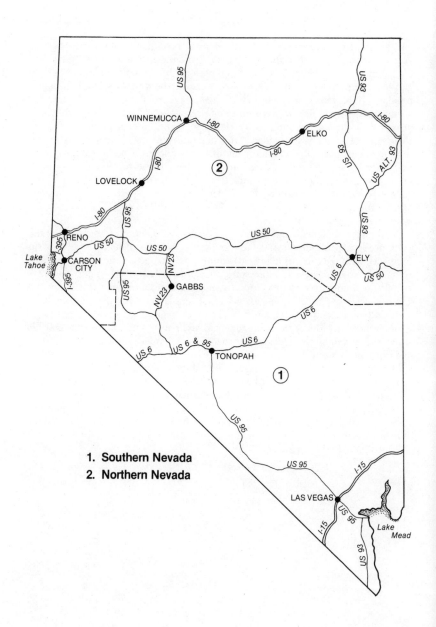

1. Southern Nevada
2. Northern Nevada

Southern Nevada

Berlin

BERLIN-ICHTHYOSAUR STATE PARK, 23 miles east of Gabbs off NV 91. This is one of the few state parks in the country where you can see both ancient fossils and the remains of an early 20th-century mining town. The fossils of giant Ichthyosaurs, or "fish lizards," are clearly visible at the site. Park rangers provide tours and explain everything you always wanted to know about these prehistoric creatures. Nearby is the **Berlin Historic District,** a mining settlement now a ghost town. Assessors' records show that the first mining activity in Berlin Canyon dates to 1869, when the Berlin mine produced four tons of ore. In its peak years of production, between 1906 and 1918, the town had about 75 frame buildings, of which 12 survive in excellent condition. NR. The park is open all year except in inclement weather, daily dawn to dusk. No charge. 885-4384. 🕇

Gabbs vicinity

GRANTSVILLE, 21 miles east of Gabbs via NV 884 and graded dirt road. Situated in a lovely canyon are the remains of this once prosperous mining town. Founded in 1863, Grantsville at one time had a population of nearly a thousand residents who supported twenty stores, a brewery, a bank, and a newspaper. The odd **jail** was a tunnel dug into a nearby hill. Today some of the sturdier brick, adobe, and frame buildings still stand amid the ruins. Stop by the local **cemetery** and have a look at the curious headings on some of the stones.

Henderson

SOUTHERN NEVADA MUSEUM, 1830 S. Boulder Hwy. Clark County operates this major museum of southern Nevada history which is located in the early 20th-century **Boulder City Depot.** Exhibits illustrate all periods of history—from prehistoric to Indian to early pioneer and later. Guided tours are available of **Beckley**

House (1912), operated by the museum. Plans call for a ghost town exhibit to be reconstructed here; buildings will be moved from their original sites to be restored and interpreted in Henderson. Open all year, daily 8-5. No charge. 565-0907.

Ione

Ione, a once thriving boom town, is located about 10 miles north of Berlin-Ichthyosaur State Park via NV 21. Silver was discovered here in 1863, and Ione became the first county seat of Nye County. There are still about a dozen sturdy residents here, who operate a small general store, a gas station, and a bar. The remains of an old rock **jailhouse,** the original county **courthouse,** and an old **barbershop** can be explored.

Lake Mead

LAKE MEAD NATIONAL RECREATION AREA, off I-93. Lake Mead, formed by **Hoover Dam** (Boulder Dam), stretches 105 miles up the old course of the Colorado River to Separation Canyon. To the south of Hoover Dam is Lake Mojave, formed in a similar way by the construction of Davis Dam. Human history here extends back more than 10,000 years to man's arrival in the Southwest. Throughout the area, ancient petroglyphs drawn on rock by the earliest Indian tribes can still be seen, although the most significant archaeological sites were inundated when the reservoirs were constructed.

Recorded history in the area began in 1826, when Jedediah Smith passed through on his first expedition in search of beaver. He was followed by such intrepid explorers as John C. Fremont, John Wesley Powell, and Joseph C. Ives. Early Mormon farm settlements and roaring mining camps sprang up along the rivers and in the mountains, and a riverboat transportation system soon developed on the Colorado. When Hoover Dam was completed in 1935, a number of the historic early com-

munities were inundated by the waters of Lake Mead.

The **Visitors Center** at 601 Nevada Hwy. operates a museum featuring archaeological exhibits, mining and historic artifacts, and guided tours. Tours through Hoover Dam are conducted daily, subject to weather conditions. Davis Dam is open every day for self-guided tours. NR. The park is open daily in summer, 8-7; winter, 8-4:30. No charge. 🏛 293-4041.

Las Vegas

The city of Las Vegas was laid out in 1905 — nearly 60 years after the first Mormon settlers had arrived in Meadow Valley (Las Vegas is Spanish for "The Meadows") and begun to plant crops and raise their livestock. Over the intervening years many of the Mormon farmers moved back to Utah or to Arizona, either because they were unable to tame the harsh desert or because of increasing friction with the "Gentiles" (non-Mormons) who were flooding into the Valley in search of gold and silver. In 1903 the farmlands at Las Vegas, either abandoned or now owned by non-Mormons, were sold to the San Pedro, Los Angeles and Salt Lake Railroad in preparation for the rail line which was to come.

The railroad, in turn, put much of the land up for sale in town lots, which were eagerly snapped up by newcomers anxious to reap the profits the rail line would bring. Although that line was completed a year later, both Mother Nature and the economy conspired to keep Las Vegas from expanding as its early residents had hoped. Floods damaged the rail lines and kept them out of service for months, and the Panic of 1907, which had a disastrous effect on the mining industry, also served to inhibit the growth of the new city. It was the imminent construction of nearby Hoover Dam that once again brought new capital — and people — to Las Vegas. By the time construction was formally begun in 1930, there were more than 10,000 residents — double the previous number.

One year later, the Nevada legislature legalized gambling. The Strip so well known today began in that year as six small gambling joints on Fremont St., near the railroad station. Las Vegas became a wide-open, rowdy gambling town, in spirit certainly not far from what it is today.

It is unfortunate that little care has been taken to preserve Las Vegas's early history. A piece of the original meadowlands included in the parcel auctioned in 1905 is now Lions Club Park; but for the most part, the rest has vanished in a sea of concrete topped by startling modern architecture and garish neon signs which beckon the unwary to the slots and the tables.

KYLE RANCH, Losee St. and Carey Ave., 1867-1910. An original adobe structure erected by Paiute Indians in the 1860s is just one of a number of ranch buildings which were for a time southern Nevada's most famous dude ranch, "Boulderado." The ranch was originally developed by Conrad Keil and his sons as a trading post for the Las Vegas Valley mining camps. Restoration is planned, but at the moment the ranch complex is not open. NR. Check with the **Las Vegas Visitors Bureau** at the Convention Center for further information. 735-3611.

LAS VEGAS ART MUSEUM, 3333 W. Washington. A display of contemporary fine art is augmented by early local paintings depicting ranching and mining activi-

Las Vegas Mormon Fort

ties of a bygone era. Open all year, M-Sa 10-5, Su 1-5. No charge. 647-4300.

LAS VEGAS MORMON FORT, 908 Las Vegas Blvd. N., 1855. The Mormons established their adobe fort in the valley as a halfway station on the Mormon trail and built eight two-story houses within it. When the Mormons returned to Utah the fort was used as a ranch headquarters, and it was the surrounding ranchlands that were sold in 1905 to create the town of Las Vegas. Only part of the original structure remains. NR. Though for a while the fort was open as a museum, it is currently closed because of insufficient funding. (So much for history in Las Vegas.) It can be seen from the street, however. 386-6510 or 386-6211.

UNIVERSITY OF NEVADA, 4505 Maryland Parkway. The University's Museum of Natural History is the most complete source in town for early archaeological and historical information about the region. Open all year, M-F 8-5 and by appointment. 739-3381.

Las Vegas vicinity

POTOSI, 9 miles south on I-15, 19 miles west on Blue Diamond Hwy. to dirt road, 1856. The Potosi lead mine was the earliest mine established in southern Nevada. Ruins of the abandoned cabins still exist, along with a nine-gauge railroad, mine shaft, and early machinery. Potosi was opened as part of the Mormon's efforts for economic self-sufficiency and was operated intermittently for over a century. NR.

SPRING MOUNTAIN RANCH (Sandstone Ranch), 20 miles west via NV 159 (West Charleston Blvd.), 1867-8. Located within the **Red Rock Canyon Recreation Lands,** at the base of the magnificent Wilson Cliffs, Spring Mountain Ranch was built on the route of the old Spanish trail and the Mormon trail, and became an important cattle ranch with its own access to the rail lines. A one-room cut-sandstone cabin, an early leveed reservoir, and a frame cabin, along with additional stone and frame support buildings remain on the site. The Nevada State Park System conducts guided tours of the ranch on weekends. The park itself is open all year. Call for hours and days open, 875-4141 or 385-6254.

TULE SPRINGS RANCH, Floyd R. Lamb State Park, 10 miles north via US 95,

Potosi lead mine

1940s. During the 1930s and '40s many ranches sprang up in the Las Vegas area which catered to would-be divorcees, who under the state law had to establish residency in Nevada for six months before their divorces could become final. Tule Springs was such a ranch, developed as a working and guest ranch which catered specifically to a temporary resident clientele. Two types of buildings remain here: those part of the working core of the ranch, primarily the stables and the cowboys' residences; and the guest houses, pleasantly arranged around a low hill, with expanses of lawn and numerous trees among them. The 680-acre park is a pleasant place to wile away an afternoon: picnic tables, grills and small lakes abound. Open all year, daily dawn to dusk. No charge.

Overton

LOST CITY MUSEUM, NV 169. The Nevada State Museum operates these exhibits of archaeology near a restored portion of **Pueblo Grande de Nevada.** Reconstructions of early Anasazi rock and adobe houses, artifacts of Indian peoples of the region, including the Paiute, and displays of objects excavated nearby are included. Open all year, daily 9-5. No charge. 🏛 397-2193.

Pioche

LINCOLN COUNTY MUSEUM, Main St. Artifacts pertaining to early Indian cultures as well as to the mining and ranching of the area are located here, along with an-

Belmont, ruins of Highbridge Mill

tique dolls, clocks, and other memorabilia. Open all year, Tu-Sa 9-5, Su 1-5. Donations accepted. 962-5207. ♦♦

While you're in Pioche, visit the recently restored **Lincoln County Courthouse** on Lacour St. Plans are underway to turn this early brick landmark (1872) into a museum. NR.

Pioche vicinity

BRISTOL WELLS TOWN SITE, 23 miles north via I93, 1870-1950. Mining claims were first staked in this area in 1870, followed two years later by the construction of a furnace to treat silver and lead ores. As new and richer deposits were found, additional ore-processing mills were built. By 1880 the business district of Bristol Wells boasted a post office, a newspaper, hotels, and many shops, and was a trading and supply center for nearby mines. After 1893 the mines were only intermittently active, the post office was closed (finally) in 1950, and today only the charcoal ovens, furnace ruins, and one original stone building — the **"Million Dollar Courthouse"** — still stand. NR.

Rhyolite

Rhyolite, four miles southwest of Beatty via NV 58, is almost a ghost town. It was established in 1905, and because of the success of its local mines became one of Nevada's major cities only two years later, with a population of 6,000. The Panic of 1907 bankrupted the mines, and by 1920 the town was empty. The **Las Vegas and Tonopah Railroad Depot** and about six other buildings still stand, including the **Porter Brothers store**, and the **Cook Bank Building.** Rhyolite's major claim to fame, however, is **Bottle House,** an odd little residence constructed of bottles, as were a number of homes in the early days, when other building materials were difficult to come by. Bottle House is presently occupied, as are several other buildings in this desolate community. ♦♦

Tonopah vicinity

BELMONT, 47 miles northeast via I-6 and NV 8-A and 82, 19th-20th centuries. Belmont was settled as a result of a silver strike in 1865. Many substantial stone and brick buildings were erected soon after its establishment to provide houses and businesses for its 2000 inhabitants. The town served as the county seat from 1867 to 1905 and became an important milling and mining area, as well as a trade center for settlements within a hundred-mile radius. Five sawmills and three stamp mills served the area until 1887, when most of the mines were shut down. Some of the best remaining structures include the 1874 **courthouse,** the **Cosmopolitan Saloon** (c. 1870), and the **smokestacks** of several mills. The courthouse is being restored, and its interior is not open at this time. NR.

Northern Nevada

Austin

AUSTIN HISTORIC DISTRICT, 19th century. Following the discovery of rich silver ore in Pony Canyon in May, 1862, a rush of prospectors and speculators created the town of Austin. Within two years Austin grew to a population of about 10,000, with many non-residents staking claims outside the town. The arrival of the Nevada Central Railroad in 1880 aided mining development and increased the town's importance as a commercial center. Before the decline of ore production in the late-19th century, more than 50 million dollars in silver ore was taken from local mines. Austin became the county seat of an area including at least 30 other mining towns. A few extant structures from the town's early days are **Gridley's Store** (1862), the **Old Engine House** of the Nevada Central Railroad, and the **Lander County Courthouse,** oldest in the state (1869). The **Bank of Austin** was built in 1861, and banking continued uninterrupted there until 1962 — a record for Nevada. The 1867 **Masonic Lodge and Odd Fellows Building** still serves its original purpose. Nevada's oldest newspaper in continuous publication was printed at the **Reese River Reveille Building** (1863) for 105 years.

Stokes Castle, built of hand-hewn granite, was constructed in 1867 for Anson Phelps Stokes, an eastern financier who built the Nevada Central Railroad. In its prominent location overlooking the Reese River Valley, it can be seen for miles around. It is privately owned but can be easily viewed as you tour this historic town.

Baker vicinity

LEHMAN CAVES NATIONAL MONUMENT, off I-50, Humboldt National Forest. Spectacular inner rooms are formed by the stalactites and stalagmites found throughout the winding caves of the Lehman monument, named for a settler who was first to realize the attraction that the caves would have for visitors. Absalom S. Lehman moved to the area in the late 1860s. Taking time off from his ranching, he explored the cave and guided parties through its underground galleries from about 1885 until his death in 1891. Remains of **Lehman Orchard** and **Aqueduct,** an innovative system of irrigation which he developed, can be seen nearby. NR. 🏕

Also nearby is **Rhodes Cabin,** a log house built as a tourist cabin for early visitors to the monument in 1928. NR. Open all year, Memorial Day-Labor Day daily 8-5; otherwise 9-4. Tours of the caves are given by rangers on duty. No charge. 289-3031.

Carson City

Disappointed goldseekers returning from the California fields decided to try their luck in this area in 1851. While they were frustrated in their attempts, a few elected to stay on and opened a trading post on the Overland route, which they named Eagle Station. The fertile valley where the new community began, fed by a winding river, was called Eagle Valley. Early settlers in the region were primarily Mormons, sent out to build new colonies by their leaders in Salt Lake City. When they were recalled in 1857, most of them sold their holdings to an entrepreneur named John Mankin, who for a brief period laid claim to the entire valley in the names of his children. Suspecting that the western part of what was then Utah Territory would be split off, surveyors mapped out lots in the townsite in 1858, giving them to anyone who would promise to build on them. The new mayor, William Ormsby, named the infant town for Kit Carson. Shortly thereafter the famous **Comstock Lode** was discovered, and the town mushroomed, as it was close to principal lines of travel. In 1861, Territorial Governor Nye declared Carson City the capital of the new territory, and it has remained so to this day. Arrival of telegraph lines from San Francisco in the early 1860s, followed by the establishment of the Virginia and Truckee Railroad connecting Carson City and Virginia City less than 10 years later, insured future growth and economic stability.

Carson City today is the smallest of our state capitals, and probably the most accessible on foot. The **Chamber of Commerce Information Bureau** at 1191 S. Carson St. has maps for suggested walking tours available, along with information on key historic sites: it should be your first stop. 882-1563. North on Carson St. is the **Carson City Post Office**, a massive red

brick building which was constructed in 1891, the first federal structure completed in the state. NR. 1217 N. Carson is the **James D. Roberts House**, said to be the oldest home in Carson City. It was completed in 1859, a wood frame structure on a sandstone foundation, and an early interpretation of the Gothic Revival style. NR. The **Abe Curry House** (c. 1871), at 406

Abe Curry House

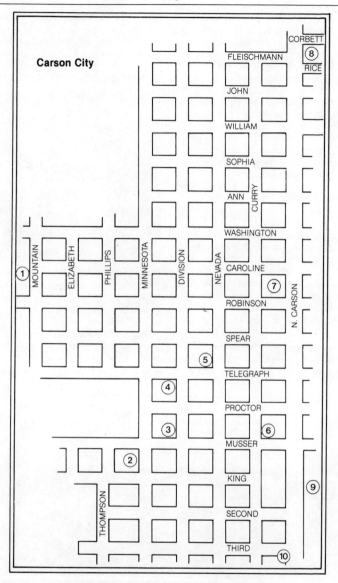

Carson City

1. Governor's Mansion
2. Governor James W. Nye Mansion
3. First United Methodist Church
4. St. Peter's Episcopal Church
5. Abe Curry House
6. Warren Engine Co. Museum
7. Nevada State Museum
8. James D. Roberts House
9. Nevada State Capitol
10. Chamber of Commerce

North Nevada, was built and lived in by the founder of Carson City, who became first Superintendent of the U.S. Mint.

To the west, at 108 N. Minnesota St., is the **Governor James W. Nye Mansion** (1860), a stone and stucco 1½-story Greek Revival residence built by William M. Stewart, a member of the state's first constitutional convention in 1863 and author of numerous constitutional provisions. It was later the residence of Territorial Governor James Nye; he and Stewart were elected the state's first two senators. NR. Further west still, at 606 Mountain St., is the current **Governor's Mansion.** Built in 1908, the two-story frame Neo-classical Revival building is distinguished by a wraparound balustraded porch. NR. The mansion is open for tours one day a week by request. 882-1563.

Two churches in Carson City date from the town's early days. The **First United Methodist Church** at 200 North Division

St. Peter's Episcopal Church

is a simple stone building completed about 1865. Known as the "cradle of Nevada Methodism," it is still open for Sunday services. NR. **St. Peter's Episcopal Church,** at 312 North Division, is a white frame structure with a pointed steeple which reminds one somewhat of early New England churches. It was built in 1868, and it, too, is still in use. NR.

As you stroll the quiet residential streets of the capital, you'll note many other early examples of Western architecture: private homes built by early entrepreneurs who made their fortunes from the mines or the railroad. Remember that these homes are privately owned for the most part, though

there are a number of museums open which will give you better insight into Carson City's often rowdy past:

NEVADA STATE CAPITOL, 101 N. Carson St., 1871. This impressive stone landmark, with an octagonal cupola and a columned portico, has been the center of Ne-

U.S. Mint

vada government since its construction. It houses portraits of past Nevada governors and features displays about the state's development. NR. Open M-F 8-5. 885-4094.

THE NEVADA STATE MUSEUM (U. S. Mint), Capitol Complex, 1869. This somewhat forbidding stone building was constructed to meet the storage and security needs created by the mineral boom on the Comstock Lode. It is now home for the state's fine museum. Collections include history, geology, Indian artifacts and much more. A replica of an early mine, illustrating the operations necessary to extract ore from the ground, is operated in the basement. NR. Open all year, daily 8:30-4:30. Donations accepted. 🚻 885-4810.

On the grounds outside the museum stands **The Glenbrook,** a wonderful old steam train engine (1875) which was one of six such workhorses used by the Carson and Tahoe Lumber and Fluming Company to haul lumber and cordwood supplies from the sawmills at Lake Tahoe to the terminus of a log flume at the head of the Carson River, where they were floated downstream to the city. NR.

Near the capitol complex is the **Nevada State Printing Office** (South Fall St. at East Second), a plain stone building constructed in 1885 as the first addition, after the capitol itself, to the cluster of state buildings which are now located here. It now contains state offices, but served for a time as the first printing plant in Nevada. NR.

VIRGINIA AND TRUCKEE RAILWAY MUSEUM, Colorado and Carson Sts. At its peak, the Virginia and Truckee Railway ran up to 45 trains a day, hauling millions of dollars in gold and silver from the mines. Dignitaries from all over the world traveled the line in its heyday. Now sight-seeing trains, powered by steam locomotives, run ten to twelve times daily along a portion of the original right of way, near ruins of some of the most famous Comstock mines. Operated by the Nevada State Museum. NR. Open May-Oct, Sa-Su 8:30-4:30. Donations accepted. 885-4810.

WARREN ENGINE COMPANY MUSEUM, Curry and Musser Sts., 1863. The oldest volunteer fire brigade in the country was established here in 1863. As long as they are not occupied in doing their jobs, members of the current Warren Engine Company Fire Department will guide you through their museum on the second floor, which has an engaging collection of early uniforms, photographs, alarm systems and other tools of their trade. Open all year, daily 1-4. No charge. 882-1663.

Carson City vicinity

BOWERS MANSION, Washoe Valley (10 miles north on I-395), 1864. Lemuel S.

Bowers made a fortune from the Comstock Lode and spent much of it to build and furnish this impressive granite landmark. In fact, he traveled throughout Europe to find antiques and furnishings which would do it justice. He and his wife spent more than $200,000 on the project: a staggering sum, especially when one translates the value of a dollar a century ago into today's terms. While many of the original furnishings have unfortunately vanished, restoration and refurbishing was done by the Washoe County Department of Parks and Recreation in the late 1960s, and the house is open as a museum. An adjacent park provides recreational facilities. NR. Open mid May-Oct 31, daily 11-4:30. $1 adults, 50¢ children. 849-0201.

If you're en route to Reno from Carson City on I-395, keep a look out for the **Old Winters Ranch,** visible from the roadway. Built in 1862, it is a two-story frame house with a veranda on all sides, designed in the Gothic Revival style. This was once the home of Theodore Winters, who helped develop horse racing in the state. He main-

Bowers Mansion

tained racing stables here and boasted two Derby winners among his thoroughbreds.

Elko

RUBY VALLEY PONY EXPRESS STATION (Northeastern Nevada Museum), 1515 Idaho St., 1860. This simple one-story log building was operated as a Pony Express station briefly after its construction. Historic exhibits include early Indian pieces, art, and a display of pioneer vehicles on the grounds. Open Sept-May, M-Sa 9-5, Su 1-5; June-Aug, M-Sa 9-7, Su 1-7. No charge. 738-3418.

Ely vicinity

WARD CHARCOAL OVENS HISTORIC STATE MONUMENT, 5 miles south via I-6, 50, 93, then 10 miles via marked dirt road. 19th-20th centuries. The Ward Mining District was organized in 1872. The residents experienced two years of prosperous gold and silver production in the late '70s, during which time the ovens were constructed. Little remains of the neighboring town today except for the six sturdy ovens which reduced timber to charcoal for use in smelting the ore. The photograph of the kilns included here hardly suggests their size: they are 30 feet tall, with floor diameters of 27 feet and walls 2 feet thick at the base. NR. Open all year, dawn to dusk. Nominal admission charge.

Eureka

EUREKA HISTORIC DISTRICT, 19th century. Eureka is one of Nevada's best preserved mining towns. It became a boom town with its first strike in 1869, and by the 1880s was second in importance only

Ward Charcoal Ovens

to Virginia City among Nevada's settlements. The main street is fronted by brick and stone commercial buildings, while the side streets are filled with the small frame, brick, and stone houses typical of a mining community. Included in the district are the log **Tannehill Cabin,** reputed to be the oldest permanent structure in town; the **opera house,** the 1879 **courthouse,** and 10 smelter sites. During the town's heyday, tunnels connected the saloons from one end of the main street to the other to protect patrons during the harsh winters. Some of the tunnel entrances are still in good condition. NR.

Fallon

CHURCHILL COUNTY MUSEUM, 1050 S. Maine St. An old grocery store in Fallon is headquarters for the museum's collection, which includes costumes, glass, quilts, Indian artifacts, and archaeological displays. Open June-Sept, M-Sa 9-5, Su 12-5; Oct-May, Tu-Sa 9-4, Su 12-4. No charge. 423-3677.

Frenchman vicinity

COLD SPRINGS PONY EXPRESS STATION, 25 miles northeast via I-50, 1860. The Edwards Creek Valley, in which the Cold Springs station is located, was an important point in three transportation and communication routes: Pony Express, Overland Stage, and Overland Telegraph. When gold was discovered in Austin in 1862, thousands of people began using the Overland Route. (I-50 follows basically the same route today.) The Pony Express was created in 1860 out of the urgent need to establish more rapid communication between the East and the gold and silver mining areas of California and Nevada. Cold Springs was one of 190 stations that operated between St. Louis and Sacramento. The remains of the station are indicative of its size: the original foundation measured 55 x 135 feet, with two-foot thick walls up to seven feet high in some places; the outlines of living quarters, corrals, windows, gunholes, and a fireplace can still be seen. NR.

Genoa

MORMON STATION STATE HISTORI-
CAL MONUMENT, 7 miles northwest of
Minden via NV 57. Colonized by the Mormons in 1850, Genoa Station served as a
trading post on the Carson branch of the
California Trail, and was the first seat of
Douglas County. The original public **trading post,** built in 1851, was reconstructed
in 1910. The 1865 **courthouse** was recently restored, and the former **Masonic
building** (1874), which also served as a
town hall, has been refurbished. A number
of other buildings from this early settlement remain, among them the **Genoa Bar**
which was constructed after the Mormons
were called back to Salt Lake City in 1857.
Examples of Queen Anne, Greek Revival,
and other more eclectic western styles remain. Genoa was the first white settlement
in the state. Operated by the Nevada Division of State Parks. NR. Mormon Staton is
open May 1-Oct 30, daily 9-5. No charge.
782-2590.

Reno

Reno advertises itself as "the biggest little
city in the world," and certainly deserves
the title. It's a wide-open gambling town
today, aping its sister city, Las Vegas, in
luxurious hotels and casinos. But Reno is
also an important center for industry, with
attractive residential areas and fine
schools, including the University of Nevada.

The first settlers came to the area in
1859, setting up a trading post in the tiny
community they called Lake's Crossing
after Myron C. Lake, one of the original
residents. When the Central Pacific Railroad arrived about ten years later, Reno
began to mushroom as a freight depot and
was renamed in honor of General Jesse Lee
Reno, a Union officer killed during the
Civil War. Lots were auctioned by the railroad company, much as they were to be in
Las Vegas in the early 20th century. By
1871 Reno had grown in importance to the
point where it was named the seat of
Washoe County, largely because of the
presence of the busy Virginia and Truckee
Railroad which allowed both the transfer

of gold and silver from the mines and
agricultural products from neighboring
farms. Major strikes at Goldfield and Tonopah in the early 20th century increased
Reno's importance as a commercial center;
the population doubled between 1900 and
1910. As the 20th century wore on,
divorce became big business in Reno:
residency requirements were decreased
from six months, to three, and then to six
weeks, as entrepreneurs—and the state
legislature—fought to retain Nevada's
eminence in this unhappy but lucrative
field. Socialites, movie queens, and other
wealthy women flocked here to shed their
husbands like last season's furs. When
gambling was legalized in the 1930s, it,
too, became a major industry. Along with
the glitter for which Reno is now best
known are to be found the remains of her
earlier, lustier time:

GLENDALE SCHOOL, South Virginia
St. and Lietzke Lane, 1864. This was the
first educational institution in Truckee
Meadows, which also served as a social
and cultural center for the community of
Glendale. The school continued to function until 1958, when it was closed because of declining registration. The wood
frame structure was moved to Reno in
1976 and sits adjacent to the **Lake Mansion** (see following). Maintained by
Washoe Landmark Preservation. NR.

LAKE MANSION, adjacent to the Cen-
tennial Coliseum on I-395, 1877. This
two-story frame Victorian house was
originally located near the site of the first
trading post in Reno and was moved to its
current location in the 1970s, where it is
being restored and refurbished as a museum by Washoe Landmark Preservation.
The original cantilever stairway, ornamental plaster ceilings, and hand-carved
paneling remain on the interior. Myron C.
Lake, one of Reno's original founders,
purchased the house in 1879 and lived here
until his death. The mansion remained in
the Lake family until recently. NR. For information call 825-9002.

NEVADA HISTORICAL SOCIETY, 1650
N. Virginia St. Here you'll find a general
collection relating to all aspects of Nevada

Lake Mansion

history—from prehistoric Indian tribes to the 20th century. Open all year, M-F 8-5, Sa-Su 9-5. No charge. 784-6397.

SIERRA NEVADA MUSEUM OF ART, 549 Court St. The lovely Georgian Revival **Hawkins House** (1911) is now home to this general art museum, whose Great Basin Permanent Collection documents the history of the region in paintings, sketches, and sculpture. NR. Open all year, Tu-Sa 10-4, Su 12-4. No charge. 329-3333.

UNIVERSITY OF NEVADA, 9th and Virginia Sts., 1874. The University was founded in Elko and moved to Reno in 1888. **Morrill Hall,** its first building, was completed in the first year of operation at the new location. The three-story brick building, topped by a central bell tower, is still in use. NR.

    Mackay School of Mines Museum is on the campus. Its collections encompass geology, mining, and metallurgy. Featured are exhibits related to the history of mining, an industry critical to Reno's growth and economic stability. Open all year, M-F 8-5, Sa 1-5. No charge. 784-6987.

Silver Spring vicinity

FORT CHURCHILL, 8 miles south of Silver Spring, off I-95, 1860. Fort Churchill was built on the central Overland Mail Route as a result of a Paiute uprising in 1860. It protected the first transcontinental telegraph lines and from 1861 to 1865 served as headquarters for Nevada military posts. After abandonment in 1870, the quadrangle of adobe structures gradually disintegrated until, by 1930, the original walls stood only two to three feet above ground. Some of the adobe buildings were reconstructed on their original foundations in the mid 1930s. The ruins of some 15 buildings remain as part of a Nevada state park. The **visitor center** has exhibits which explain the history of the fort and the surrounding area. NR. Open all year, dawn to dusk. Nominal admission.

Virginia City

VIRGINIA CITY HISTORIC DISTRICT, 1860. The Comstock Lode, richest of all the mines in Nevada, was discovered in 1859 near what is now Virginia City. One of the first prospectors named the mine camp for his home state—some say in a fit of drunken homesickness. This was the

Virginia City Historic District

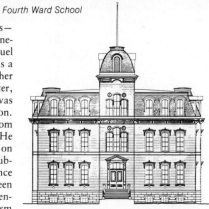

Fourth Ward School

most famous of Nevada's mining towns—and the rowdiest, attracting both fortune-seekers and chroniclers of events. Samuel Clemens (Mark Twain) worked here as a cub reporter in the 1870s. It was another reporter, nearly one hundred years later, who was responsible for saving what was left of the town from total extinction. Lucius Beebe, a society columnist from New York, arrived here in 1952. He restored one of the old Victorian houses on the outskirts of town and set about publishing the *Territorial Enterprise* once again; the local paper had long since been put to bed for the last time. Beebe's enthusiasm sparked a new wave of tourism which continues to this day, and encouraged restoration of many of the old buildings. NR, NHL. The **Visitor's Bureau** on C Street should be your first stop for information on mine tours, mansions, and other attractions. 847-0177.

As you wander the colorful streets, stop into the **U. S. Grant General Store Museum,** a reconstruction of an old-fashioned retail store as it would have appeared during the town's heyday, with original merchandise displayed on its shelves. Many Victorian homes in the outlying hills have now been restored to look as they did when constructed during the 1870s and '80s. The **Courthouse,** rebuilt in 1875 after a major fire, is still in use. At the south end of C St. is the **Fourth Ward**

School, built in 1876 to provide some semblance of gentility for the children of Virginia City's residents. At the other end of the moral spectrum, and far more noticeable, are the saloons which line the main streets. Most are open all year, and many have their original furnishings intact. Find one that appeals and stop for a cooling drink. Among other historic sites worth visiting are the following:

THE CASTLE, 70 S. B St., 1868. Robert Graves, a mine superintendent of the Empire, one of the most successful mines, built this startling home which he styled after a Normandy castle. Now open as a museum, it is furnished throughout with riches of the period. NR. Open Memorial Day-July 3 and Labor Day-Oct 31, 11-5 daily; July 4-Labor Day, 10-5 daily. $1.25 adults, 25¢ children. 847-0275.

trous fire which destroyed much of Virginia City in the early 1870s, this newspaper building has been restored to look much as it did when Mark Twain was a cub reporter here. His desk and chair, reference books, and other memorabilia are on display. Open all year, daily 9-7. Nominal admission.

PIPER'S OPERA HOUSE, Union and B Sts., late 19th century. Edwin Booth was only one of the luminaries who performed here years ago, bringing some theatrical glamor into the lives of the miners and their families. Open Memorial Day-Oct, daily 9-5. No charge.

TERRITORIAL ENTERPRISE BUILD-ING, C St., 1875. Rebuilt after a disas-

ST. MARY'S IN THE MOUNTAINS, E St., 1878. This graceful brick Victorian church is considered to be one of the most beautiful examples of western ecclesiastical architecture in America. The third building on its site, it was completed two years after a raging fire destroyed its predecessor and many of its surrounding buildings. NR. Open May-Oct, daily, and for Sunday services. Donations accepted.

Lodging and Dining

NEVADA was a relative latecomer on the tourist scene: it was not until gambling was legalized in the 1930s that vacationers began to be drawn to the area, and it was years more before the fabulous hotels of the Reno and Las Vegas "Strips" were built. In the rush to capitalize on the fortunes to be made, tradition and history more often than not took a back seat to progress. The old small hotels and boarding houses that might have been renovated to serve new visitors were shunned in favor of giant new complexes with plenty of room for restaurants, bars, casinos, and beds.

Thus the Nevada tourist in search of historic inns, hotels, and restaurants will often be disappointed, though happily a few exceptions do exist.

Carson City

JACK'S BAR, 418 S. Carson St., 89701. (702) 882-9865. J.D. and Marian Addison. The original bar on this site was a wood-frame building erected in 1859. This was torn down, and the present stone building opened as the Bank Saloon in 1899. The stone was quarried at the State Penitentiary nearby, which is still in use. Jack's Bar remained a dispenser of spirits even through Prohibition; whiskey was kept in a barrel hidden in a wall. An antique back bar imported from Germany over 100 years ago is still here. Although no food is offered, stop by for a drink and try your hand at the slots. Open all year, 8 a.m.-3 a.m. NR. Moderate.

Las Vegas

PHILIPS SUPPER HOUSE, 4545 W. Sahara Ave., 89102. (702) 873-5222. Philip Deale. The design and decor of this elegant restaurant have been carefully planned to reflect a turn-of-the-century Victorian mansion — a refreshing change from the stark modern architecture and decoration found elsewhere in Las Vegas. Open all year. Dinner served from 5-12. Expensive. AE, D, CB, MC, V, PC.

Reno

BIG YELLOW HOUSE, 4990 S. Virginia, 89509. (702) 827-3015. This Victorian restaurant is decorated with the lavish fixtures and furnishings typical of late 19th- and early 20th-century tastes. Open all year, for dinner M-Sa, brunch and dinner Su. Moderate. M, V.

EL CORTEZ HOTEL, 239 West Second St., 89501. (702) 322-9161. B. and G. Pincolini. Built in 1932, with additions two years later, the El Cortez laid claim to being the best hotel in Reno during World War II. It was renovated in 1977. Inexpensive. 116 rooms. M, V.

PRESIDENTIAL CAR, 236 N. Virginia, 89510. (702) 329-0881. This interesting restaurant has been designed to mimic a turn-of-the-century railroad car. Open daily for dinner. Moderate. AE, CB, D, MC, V.

Smith Valley

WINDYBRUSH RANCH, Box 85, 89430. (702) 465-2481. Frank and Margaret Parson. The property on which Windybrush is situated was originally an old homestead. Great care has been taken to maintain the grounds on which Piutes roamed hundreds of years ago; occasionally an arrowhead or grinding rock is found here. This is a working ranch, with goats, sheep, chickens, rabbits, turkeys, and ducks everywhere. Hiking and horseback riding are available — you can even bring your own horse. Pets welcome. 2 rooms. Open all year. AP. Inexpensive.

Tonopah

MIZPAH HOTEL, 100 Main St., 89049. (702) 482-6202. This glorious old mining hotel, built in 1907, has just been renovated by its new owners, who have successfully brought it back to its former luster. This is certainly the "grande dame" of Tonopah — and probably of all the mining towns in Nevada. NR. Open all year. 56 rooms. Moderate. AE, M, V.

Virginia City

THE SAVAGE MANSION, 146 S. D St., P.O. Box 445, 89440. (702) 847-0574. This three-story Victorian mansion was built in 1861. Originally there was a mine office on the first floor, and the mine superintendent lived on the floors above. It has been refurbished with many of its original pieces. Open all year. 4 rooms. Moderate. M, V.

SHARON HOUSE, C and Taylor Sts., 89440. (702) 847-0133. It would be sad indeed if historic Virginia City did not boast any restaurants in its landmark buildings. Happily, there is the Sharon House, where you will dine amidst authentic frontier decor. Open for dinner daily (closed W, Th in winter). Moderate. AE, M, V.

3. UTAH

UTAH is most famous because of its Mormon heritage. Members of the Church of Jesus Christ of Latter-Day Saints, under the direction of their spiritual leader, Joseph Smith, had first congregated in the Mid-west in the 1830s. When Smith and his brother were assassinated in 1844, Brigham Young and other leaders decided to abandon their settlement in Nauvoo, Illinois, and move westward, seeking freedom to practice their beliefs, and to fulfill Smith's visionary plan for a city of Zion. The exodus began in 1846. With the outbreak of the Mexican War shortly thereafter, President James Polk asked for Mormon volunteers to serve in the Army. These volunteers were among the first Mormons to see the southwest and consequently paved the way for their pioneer brethren who began arriving in Utah in mid-1847.

After the first settlement was begun at Salt Lake City, other regions were developed at the direction of church leaders. Ogden, Provo, and Manti were all established before 1850 by groups sent out from the main colony. In fact, between 1847 and 1900 more than 500 towns and outposts were begun throughout Utah Territory and adjacent areas.

Utahans are justifiably proud of the many natural wonders of their state — from the magnificent northern mountains and forests to the awesome canyons of the southeast, second only to the Grand Canyon in size and majesty. They are also enthusiastic about sharing their historic sites. As you read the pages that follow, you'll be struck by the number of early houses, museums, and parks open to the public at no charge.

Much of Utah's wilderness has been preserved in national and state parks. It is here that indications of earlier inhabitants — Fremont and Anasazi Indian tribes thought to have lived here thousands of years ago — can be seen. Facilities at most of these parks are minimal, however, and roads poor. If you plan to visit these or other rural areas of the state, be prepared. Sturdy shoes, adequate water and food, reliable transportation, and good advance planning are critical. Follow the advice of park rangers and other officials, remembering that there are often many miles of uninhabited country between rest areas or ranger stations — country that can sometimes be as inhospitable as it is beautiful.

The listings which follow have been divided into two geographic regions as a convenience for the traveler. **Southern Utah** is famed for spectacular canyonlands and natural arches formed by nature's actions over thousands of years. **Northern Utah** is home to the Great Salt Lake and to the city which bears its name, where a majority of 19th-century historic sites can be found.

Memory Grove, War Memorial, with State Capitol in background. City Creek Canyon Historic District, Salt Lake City, UT. Phillip W. Neuberg, photographer

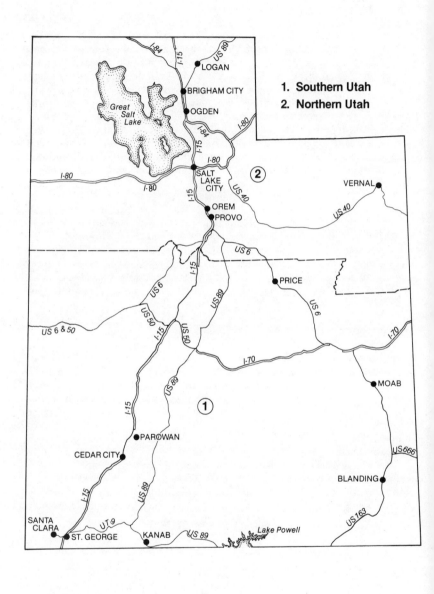

1. Southern Utah
2. Northern Utah

Southern Utah

Beaver

BEAVER COUNTY COURTHOUSE, 90 E. Center St., 1877-82. Beaver County was created by the Utah territorial legislature in 1855. Indian troubles delayed construction of the courthouse, and soon after it was finally completed, a fire partially destroyed the building. Rebuilt in the early 1890s, the courthouse, a two-story brick structure with arched windows, has been in use ever since. The courtroom occupies the front portion of the second floor. NR. Open all year, M-F 10-4. No charge.

Blanding vicinity

EDGE OF THE CEDARS STATE HISTORICAL MONUMENT, near 4th North and 4th West Sts., 800-1150. Remains of a number of ceremonial structures (*kivas*) and pit houses suggest that this was the site of a large Anasazi Indian village many hundreds of years ago, used as a regional ceremonial center by other villages of this ancient Pueblo culture. Artifacts from the Anasazi tribe, along with early relics from the Navajo, Paiute, and Ute tribes, are displayed. NR. Open all year, summer 8-7, winter 9-5. 50¢ adults. 678-2238.

HOVENWEEP NATIONAL MONUMENT, 13 miles south of Blanding via US 163, then east on UT 262. The remains of ancient towers and six separate groups of pueblos, ingenious cliff dwellings hollowed out of the forbidding local rock, can be seen here. A park ranger on duty can explain the origins of the Indian culture responsible for this primitive architecture and point out the self-guided trails which make the site more accessible. Open all year, daily 8-5. No charge.

Cedar City

Founded in the mid-19th century, Cedar City was the site of the first iron-producing blast furnace west of the Mississippi. Although iron is still mined in the area, the local furnace was not sufficiently productive, and industry was soon replaced by cattle-raising and other agricultural pursuits. **Southern Utah State College** was founded here in 1897. On its campus at 351 W. Center St. are located several fine museums: The **Museum of Southern Utah** concentrates on displays of early history and industry in the area. Open M-Sa 8-12, 1-5. No charge. The **Braithwaite Fine Arts Gallery,** with a collection of 19th- and early 20th-century American art, is housed in the **Old Administration Building** (1910). Open Sept 15-Aug 15, M-F, 10-5, 7-9; Sa-Su 1-6. No charge. 586-5432

Iron Mission State Historical Monument, located off I-15, has a large collection of early vehicles from the pioneer era and many smaller antiques—guns, butter churns, tools, even early waffle irons and other primitive kitchen appliances. Open all year, M-F 8-5, Sa-Su 9-5. 50¢ adults. 586-9290. 👫

Cedar City vicinity

CEDAR BREAKS NATIONAL MONUMENT, 23 miles east on UT 14. Nearly ten square miles of spectacular scenery is included at this superb site, nearly 10,000 feet above sea level. Lava beds and flows are in stark contrast to the lush Dixie National Forest which surrounds the area. The federal government maintains an exhibit center here, with historic interpretations and displays of flora and fauna. Open May 25-Sept 15, daily 8-6. No charge. 586-9451.

OLD IRONTOWN, 22 miles west on UT 56, 19th century. The development of Utah's iron and steel industry began in the fall of 1849, when an exploring party discovered Iron Mountain and the coal beds at nearby Cedar City. Several iron works began production in the area, and the remains of one of the early charcoal furnaces can be seen here, along with an "arrastra," a device constructed to prepare fine sand for furnace molds. Remnants of an early foundry, foundations, and walls are all that remain of a once-productive complex. NR. Open all year. Call 586-4484 for information.

Cove Fort

OLD COVE FORT, off US 91 on UT 4, 1867. Mormon immigrants named this site Cove Creek and used it as a camping place; a permanent residence was established in 1860, and the fort was erected later in the decade because of Indian attacks in the area. Of black volcanic rock, the fort had walls 18 feet tall, behind which were constructed apartments for the few hardy residents. Large hinged doors with sand between the planking—early fireproofing against flaming arrows—were hung at either end of the square defense. These and most of the walls remain, and a museum on the site displays pioneer artifacts, Indian relics, and primitive weapons. NR. Open all year, daily, dawn to dusk. 50¢ adults, 25¢ children. 438-2451.

Ephraim

EPHRAIM UNITED ORDER COOPERATIVE BUILDING, Main and 1st North Sts., 1871. In the late 1860s, Mormon communities were faced with the challenge of an ever increasing number of "gentile" (the Mormon term for people other than themselves) merchants settling in their Zion. To combat this a cooperative store was organized in Salt Lake City in 1868—

the Zions Cooperative Mercantile Institution (ZCMI), which within the next ten years directed the formation of more than 150 local cooperatives. Such cooperatives not only excluded outsiders, but enabled Mormons to purchase goods at far less cost than could others. The store at Ephraim is probably the best remaining example of the local co-op. Built of Sanpete limestone, it is now owned by the Sanpete Development Corporation. NR. Private, but viewable from the public way.

Fairview

FAIRVIEW MUSEUM OF HISTORY AND ART, 85 N. 1st East. The **Sandstone School,** erected in 1900, is home to a fine collection of pioneer relics, Indian artifacts and art, antique farm machinery and vehicles, costumes, furnishings, and tools. Open May-Oct, M-Sa 9-7, Su 2-7. No charge. 427-9916.

Fillmore

TERRITORIAL STATEHOUSE (Utah Territorial Capitol), Center St. between Main and First West Sts., 1852-55. Utah became a territory under the provisions of Henry Clay's Compromise of 1850, and a capital site was selected by a commission appointed by territorial governor Brigham Young. Fillmore got the nod because of its central location, but the impressive plans for the capitol building, designed by Truman O. Angell, were never fully realized. Only the south wing of what was to have been a large, stately building crowned by a central dome was eventually completed, and the Utah territorial legislature met here for only three years, after which the building fell into disrepair until rescued by the Daughters of Utah Pioneers in the early 20th century. Now used as a museum, the building contains an assortment of pioneer furnishings, pictures, Indian artifacts, tools, pioneer farm implements, and costumes. NR. Open all year, M-F 8:30-5. 50¢ adults. 743-6646.

Glen Canyon (see also Page, Arizona)

Territorial Statehouse

Hole-in-the-Rock

GLEN CANYON NATIONAL RECRE-ATION AREA, southeast of Escalante on UT 95. Some of the most magnificent scenery in southern Utah and northern Arizona can be found within this huge national park which surrounds Lake Powell. Also within the park are two historic sites, both of which tell fascinating stories about the development of the West. **Davis Gulch Pictograph Panel** is a sixty-foot stretch of bedrock on which can be found a number of early paintings attributed to the Anasazi tribe—primitive Pueblo Indians who inhabited the region c. 1100 A.D. The pictographs are in surprisingly excellent condition, due, in part, to their isolation, and to the fact that they are protected by a deep overhang of the sandstone alcove which permits little direct sunlight or moisture to enter. NR.

Hole-in-the-Rock was originally a natural fault in the canyon rim, 1,000 feet above the Colorado River. In November 1879, an expedition of more than 250 men, women, and children, traveling by wagon and with a thousand head of livestock in tow, reached this site en route to a new settlement decreed by Brigham Young. As they could not pass through the narrow opening, they enlarged it by blasting and drilling—an arduous job which also entailed building a log road over which the wagons could pass. In late January the entire 83-wagon caravan, with wheels braked and locked, began the downward journey through the man-made pass to the river's edge, where a ferry had been constructed to transport them across to the opposite shore. Here, also, they had to build dugout roads up Cottonwood Canyon and out onto Grey Mesa. Deep snow hampered their travel severely, and they finally camped for good at what is now Bluff City—eighteen miles from their original destination, Montezuma Creek. NR. Glen Canyon National Recreation Area is open all year. For information on access call 800-662-1754 from Utah; 800-453-1700 from other areas.

Green River vicinity

CANYONLANDS NATIONAL PARK, I-70 west to US 24 to dirt access road. Miles upon miles of rugged canyons, cut into bedrock by the surging Green and Colorado Rivers, make this one of the wildest and most spectacular of Utah's national parks. Most of the area is unpopulated—and certainly uncivilized by modern standards. Four-wheel-drive vehicles are stongly recommended here, and stout constitutions. There are no hotels, no restaurants, and only one source of water: at Needles, in the south. There are, however, several intimations of earlier civilizations: The **Harvest Scene Pictograph,** a prehistoric panel of primitive figures painted on the sandstone cliff, is thought to be the work of an early tribe which preceded the Anasazi—about 1,000 years ago. NR. The **Salt Creek Archaeological District,** estimated to date from about 1075, includes 170 sites where native Americans, possibly the Fremont tribe, lived and hunted long before white explorers. Evidence of their society remains in transient camps, storage areas, communal dwellings, and pictograph panels. The district also includes **Kirk Cabin,** a 19th-century log and stone cabin, with adjacent corrals and several pieces of early machinery remaining as the only record of an early pioneer's struggle against the wilderness. NR. The park's headquarters is in Moab. Open all year. 259-7164. ♔

Manti

MANTI TEMPLE, US 89, 1877. If you follow US 89 north through the Sanpete Valley to Manti, you will catch sight of its glorious temple long before you reach town. Situated high on a hill overlooking the community and the lush valley, the temple, of cream-colored limestone, dominates the area for miles around. Built

Manti Temple

on a site dedicated by Brigham Young, it was completed in 1888 from a design by William Folsom. As with all Mormon temples, it is not open to the public, but it is a spectacular piece of architecture, well worth a second look. NR.

While you're in Manti, drive around town. There are a number of early Mormon buildings, all privately owned, which remain as testimonials to the ingenuity and industry of their builders. The **Parry Home** at 50 North 1st West was built c. 1866 by a stonemason who worked on the Salt Lake and St. George Temples, as well as on his own Manti Temple. The **Cox Home** at 1st West and 1st North, of limestone, was constructed to house four of Frederick Walter Cox's wives. The 2½-story house, which took seven years to complete (1860-67) is divided into separate apartments, with a common room in the attic. Cox was a member of the Territorial Legislature. NR.

The influence of other religions can be seen in Manti: the **Presbyterian Church**, on US 89, was one of the earliest such buildings completed in Utah. The tall stone landmark was completed in 1881, twelve years after Presbyterianism was established in the state. Early missionaries tried to attract converts from the Mormon faith by offering superior educational facilities to the populace at large. The Rev. Duncan McMillan, first pastor of the church, attained early success with this policy, but only until the Mormons upgraded their own schools in a successful attempt to dilute the influence of the "gentiles." Today the church is operated as a lodge hall. NR.

Mexican Hat vicinity

PONCHO HOUSE, near Monument Valley. This is not a house at all, as evident from the accompanying photograph, but a superb cliff dwelling containing an estimated 200 separate units, built on the cliffs of which it is an integral part. It is estimated that the cliff dwelling was constructed c. 100-1300 A.D. by the Anasazi tribes. Much remains to be learned about

Poncho House

the site and the peoples who inhabited it, since there has been little study of the area to date, and no archaeological excavation. NR. Accessible by dirt road.

Moab

MOAB MUSEUM, 111 E. Center. As Moab is centrally located between several national parks, the museum, along with the park service office listed below, is a good place to stop for information. Museum displays include exhibits on local history, archaeology, and geology. The staff will suggest walking tours of the area. Open May 15-Sept 15, daily 1-5, 7-9; otherwise, 3-5, 7-9. Donations accepted. 259-7430.

Arthur Taylor House (see Lodging and Dining, Moab)

NATIONAL PARK SERVICE, 466 S. Main St. Both Arches National Park and Canyonlands National Park are within a short drive of Moab. Park officials can provide brochures, topographical maps, and suggestions for various tours of the areas under their jurisdiction. (See individual listing under Green River for Canyonlands National Park). Arches National Park, whose entrance is one mile north of Moab, contains the greatest number of natural stone arches to be found anywhere in the world. These giant formations have been caused by erosion, eruption, and the action of running water on stone over millions of years. Spectacular towers, mammoth shapes resembling figures of

men and animals, balancing rocks, and other odd forms abound.

Within the park are the Courthouse Wash Pictographs, whose primitive designs represent several different cultures. The sheep, deer, and snake figures are typically prehistoric, with figures on horseback later Navajo or Ute additions. NR.

Wolfe Ranch, a log cabin, corral, and dugout cellar built by early settler John Wesley Wolfe in 1888, is also located in the park. Because of harsh terrain and scarcity of building materials, logs were hauled six miles from the banks of the Colorado River, attesting to the struggle for existence in early Utah. NR. The park is open all year; fall and winter, daily 8-4:30; spring, 8-5; summer, 8-6. $1 per car. 259-7164.

Monticello

MONTICELLO MUSEUM (Public Library building), Main St. Visit this museum for some background information on the history and prehistory of the area. Its collection includes geological specimens, Indian artifacts, and pioneer relics. Open June-Sept, daily 9-9 and by appointment. 587-2281.

Then drive 14 miles north of town to Indian Creek State Park, where you'll find a large petroglyph panel under an overhang at the base of the canyon wall. Evidence of two different cultures can be found here: the oldest group, which anthropologists believe dates back nearly 2,000 years, includes birds, stick men, and wavy lines attributed to the Fremont era. The second group, including horned anthropomorphs, mountain sheep, deer, horses, and many geometric designs, is attributed to the historic Utes of the 18th century. Also in the area are the remains of early pioneer campsites. NR.

Pine Valley

PINE VALLEY CHAPEL AND TITHING OFFICE, Main and Grass Valley Sts., 19th century. Pine Valley Chapel and its adjacent Tithing Office are representative

Petroglyph panel, Indian Creek State Park

of early Mormon Church regulations which have lasted to this day. The "law of tithing" began in 1830. Church members were instructed to donate ten percent of their incomes to the church, and tithing offices were generally built near the churches. Tithes of hay, grain, potatoes, vegetables, and other goods were brought to the office and receipts issued for them. The stored goods were then passed out to the needy for worthy projects as the bishop directed. Pine Valley Chapel was designed and built in 1868 by Ebenezer Bryce, a former shipbuilder from Australia, who used his talents to assemble the frame walls on the ground. They were then raised into position and joined by wooden pegs and rawhide. Inner walls and partitions were "hung" on the basic structure of ponderosa pine. The small red-brick tithing office was constructed in the 1880s. NR. The chapel is open for Sunday services.

Price

PREHISTORIC MUSEUM OF THE COLLEGE OF EASTERN UTAH, City Hall, Main and Second East Sts. Bring the children here to see the dinosaur and fossil displays, certain to be a hit even with the most cranky. And then have a look at the archaeological exhibits which do so much to explain the development of Utah civilization over thousands of years. Operated by the state. Open all year, M-Sa 9-5; summer 10-6. No charge. 637-5060.

PRICE MUNICIPAL BUILDING, 200 East and Main Sts., 1938. This plain two-story concrete and brick building is easy to miss, for its facade is unassuming. But enter the foyer, and you will be surrounded by a superb mural painted by Utah artist Lynn Fausett in 1938 as part of a WPA project. The mural depicts, in figures basically half life-size, significant events and themes in the history of Carbon County. The artist worked from photographs, tintypes, and personal recollections in recreating the characters portrayed. The Price Mural is an important historical document which preserves and portrays much of the color and flavor of the region's history. It has been a source of great local pride, and city officials are dedicated to its preservation. NR. Open during office hours. 637-2788.

Brigham Young's Winter Home

St. George

BRIGHAM YOUNG'S WINTER HOME, 67 West 2nd North, 1874. As early as 1856 missionaries had been sent to the Virgin River area to experiment with cotton production, and within five years the town of St. George was founded. Brigham Young spent his winters here from 1873 until his death in 1877. The dwelling is T-shaped and built of adobe. A one-story balustraded veranda occupies two sides of the facade. Much of the original interior wood remains, and the house is now a museum, with household furnishings and articles typical of the 19th-century western condition, including some of Young's belongings. His one-room office next door is also adobe with a stone foundation. NR. Open all year, daily 9-9. No charge. 673-2517.

TEMPLE VISITOR CENTER, 444 S. 300 East. Operated by the Mormon Church, the Temple Visitor Center is staffed by knowledgeable guides who can explain St. George's early history and development by pioneers sent by Brigham Young. Access to the **St. George Tabernacle** is by appointment from the center. The Tabernacle, at the intersection of Tabernacle and

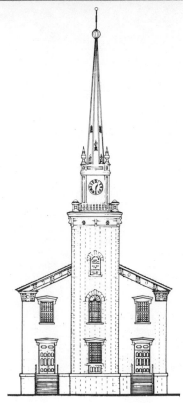

Main Sts., is reminiscent of a New England church of the colonial period. Its walls are of red sandstone, and a tower on the east end rises 140 feet. The interior is equally suggestive of eastern houses of worship; a gallery extends around three sides, supported by solid turned columns, and reached by one of two circular staircases. NR. The Temple Visitor Center is open all year, daily 9-9. 673-5181.

While you're in St. George, have a look at the **Old Washington County Courthouse** at 85 E. 100 North. Built in 1876, it is the only major public building in the county erected when Utah was still a territory. The two-story brick landmark was erected on a foundation of basalt rock, with a cupola topping the whole. NR. Open all year, M-F 9-4, Sa 9-12. 673-3671.

Santa Clara

JACOB HAMBLIN HOUSE, UT 91, 1863. Hamblin, a Mormon missionary to the Indians of southern Utah, may have come to the Santa Clara area as early as 1854. Three years later he was appointed president of all the southern Indian missions by Brigham Young. Hamblin's fellow missionaries built this two-story sandrock home for him, and he lived here until 1871, when he was called to work in nearby Kanab. The house was built into a hillside, with two porches running its full length. It is now operated by the state and is furnished with period pieces, some belonging to the Hamblin family. NR. Open all year, daily 9-9. Free. 673-2161. ♦♦

Silver Reef

WELLS FARGO AND COMPANY EXPRESS BUILDING, Main St., 1877. Silver Reef, now a ghost town, was once the largest community in southern Utah. Prosperity, which lasted from 1877 to 1888, came as a result of the discovery of rarely-found commercial quality silver-bearing ore in sandstone formations. The population soared at one point to 1,500, and there were five major mining companies operating in the area. When the mines were played out, Silver City was left to die. The one-story red sandstone **Wells Fargo Building** is one of the few remaining structures in town, as most of the rest were of frame construction. Only it and the nearby **Rice Bank** remain as reminders of a more prosperous time. NR.

Spring City

SPRING CITY HISTORIC DISTRICT, 19th century. Spring City was settled in 1852 as part of the colonization of the Great Basin planned and directed by members of the Mormon church, who envisioned a line of settlements stretching the length of the valley to ensure effective control of the area. In town plan and distribution of farm land, Spring City, like other Mormon communities throughout the state, adhered to a "farm village" system: houses, barns, vegetable gardens and orchards were contained within the village boundaries, and farmers commuted daily to their outlying fields. In the intervening years since the town was settled, there has been little intrusion of modern industry to interrupt the rural ambience of this Mormon agricultural community.

Various types of "folk houses" from the 1865-1890 period comprise over a third of the extant total, and range from primitive one-room cabins to two-story hall-and-parlor houses. Adobe and stone have been the most common building materials, though log, frame, and brick are also in evidence. As you drive along the wide tree-lined streets you'll notice two creeks, Canal and Oak, which supply water to the residents, as well as the plentiful spring which gave the town its name. There are no major museums or landmark homes here: just a quiet, private little community which has been largely spared the ravages of modern industrial development. In its own quiet way, Spring City presents a pleasant, low profile to the visitor interested in Utah's early rural development. NR.

Torrey

CAPITOL REEF NATIONAL PARK, UT 24. The desert environment of this rugged part of Utah is less than hospitable to man: sculptured rock and stubborn cactus stretch on for miles. In the 1880s, however, there was an attempt made by the Mormons to establish a settlement in what is now the national park. The Mormons called their community Fruita, and all that remains of it today is the old **Fruita School-house,** a one-room log building constructed in the 1890s. The shingle roof replaced the original sod roof after World War I. The schoolhouse is now used as the **Visitor Center** for the park and displays historic artifacts pertinent to the region. NR. Open all year; summer, daily 8-7; winter, daily 8-4:30. No charge. 425-3871.

Northern Utah

Brigham City

BRIGHAM CITY MORMON TABER-NACLE (Box Elder Stake Tabernacle), Main St. at 200 South, c. 1876, 1896. The original tabernacle on this site was built of fieldstone with a tower at each corner. Rebuilt in brick and stone after a fire gutted the interior, the tabernacle acquired sixteen brick buttresses, each one topped by a steeple. A three-stage tower with a domed mansard roof was constructed above the main entrance. Windows and doors have pointed arched openings. NR. Open June-Aug, daily 9-9. Free. 734-2158.

BRIGHAM CITY MUSEUM/GAL-LERY, 24 N. Third West. The community of Brigham City was settled in the 1850s and renamed for Brigham Young after he last addressed its population in 1877. The museum collection includes early furnishings, books, photographs, and documents which relate to the development of the area since its inception. Open all year, M-Sa 11-7. Free. 823-6769.

Brigham City vicinity (Promontory)

GOLDEN SPIKE NATIONAL HISTOR-IC SITE, northeast of Great Salt Lake, 1869. Here the last spike was driven in May 1869 to complete the nation's first transcontinental railroad. The ceremony celebrated the completion of 1,800 miles of railway in less than seven years, forming a junction of the Union Pacific from the east and the Central Pacific from the west, and marked the beginning of a new era in trade, development, and political communication between the two coasts. Photographs, manuscripts, letters, and memorabilia commemorating the lives and struggles of the many persons connected with the railroad's development are displayed here. During the summer months there are costumed reenactments of the driving of the golden spike. Administered by the federal government. NR. Open all year, summer 8-8, winter 8-4:30. Free. 🕌 471-2209.

Corinne

CORINNE METHODIST EPISCOPAL CHURCH, Colorado and S. 6th Sts., 1870. Corinne, the northernmost town on the first transcontinental rail line, was settled not by Mormons, but by Catholics and Protestants. The small brick Methodist church is thought to be the first one organized in the new community. NR.

Nearby the Sons of Utah Pioneers operate a **Railroad Museum**, displaying a train of two engines, three passenger cars, mail car, open-air cars, and caboose—all much as they were in the days before Corinne's importance was overshadowed by the construction of alternate rail routes and the development of Ogden, Utah's second largest city. Also at the museum are a reconstructed blacksmith shop, early farm machinery, Indian relics, and a Chinese laundry—a reminder of the importance of the Oriental workers to the completion of the railroad. Open all year, M-F 9-5, Su 2-5. Free. 744-2626. 🕌

Fairfield

STAGE COACH INN, c. 1858. In the middle of the 19th century, John Carson settled in the Cedar Valley in what was to become the little town of Fairfield. The Stage Coach Inn was originally the Carson family dwelling, which was converted to house travelers. As Carson was an elder in the Mormon Church, he would not allow liquor to be served in his two-story adobe hostelry; the inn continued to welcome tee-totaling guests until the late 1940s. Some of the original pine floors and glass windows remain amid the displays of pioneer relics, furniture, and military memorabilia which are now housed within. Operated by the state. NR. Open Mar 15-Nov 15, daily 9-5. 50¢ admission. 768-9888.

About half a mile from the Inn, across a small creek, is the **Camp Floyd Historical Monument.** This was the site chosen by Colonel Albert Sidney Johnston for an army camp from which to maintain surveillance over the Mormon settlements of Salt Lake City and Provo in 1858. The original army commissary building has been restored, and an old cemetery survives. Operated by the state. NR. Open Mar 15-Nov 15, M-Sa 9-5. Free. 533-6011.

Farmington

PIONEER VILLAGE (Lagoon Amusement Park), Connor St. Lagoon Amusement Park, one of the largest such complexes in the west, will keep the children captivated for hours. Within the park is a recreated village of the mid-19th century made up of 25 log and stone buildings of the period of Utah's settlement, including both stores and homes. The display features guns, Indian and pioneer relics, furnishings, and carriages, all maintained by the Society of Utah Pioneers. Open Apr-May, Sept-Oct, Sa-Su 10-7; June-Aug, daily 10-8. $2 admission. 292-0466.

Heber City

HEBER AMUSEMENT HALL, 1st West and 1st North, 1906. Used now as a supply center for regional schools, this T-shaped sandstone building originally served as a center for social and recreational functions. Its most unusual feature is a spring-mounted dance floor. NR.

WASATCH STAKE TABERNACLE, Main St., 1887-89. This trim sandstone building with a central bell tower and pointed-arch Gothic windows is reminiscent of the sort of religious landmark one might find in New England. Located on Heber City's distinctive town square, it once played an important role in the cultural, religious, and social life of the community. Now owned by the town, it is open for summer stock productions. NR. 654-3666.

If you happen to be lucky enough to catch a play here, stroll around the town before curtain time. Particularly worth notice is the **Abram Hatch House** at 81 E. Center St., a quaint little sandstone dwelling owned during the late 19th century by the Mormon bishop of Wasatch County, who was a territorial legislator, merchant, and rancher as well. The house is privately owned, but visible from the street. NR.

Logan

Nestled in the beautiful, fertile Cache Valley, Logan was settled in 1859 by a group of rather independent-minded Mormons who, not content to wait for the direction of their spiritual leader, Brigham Young, requested permission to emigrate to the site in order to take advantage of the rich soil and ample water supply. Their first homes—built in the fort style along what is now Center Street, close to the Logan River—were of sturdy log construction to guard against attack from the Shoshoni Indians who considered the valley their private hunting preserve. Once the threat of Indian attack had been eliminated, and at the direction of Young who gave his blessing to the settlement, Logan residents began to construct permanent homes and fences of native stone and adobe. They also built their tabernacle and concentrated on nourishing their crops and their children. Logan's dependence on farming lessened with the industry made possible by completion of a railroad line to the community, and today the town's economy is bolstered by various forms of manufacturing as well as by its role as host to the prominent Utah State University.

DAUGHTERS OF THE UTAH PIONEERS MUSEUM, 52 W. 2nd North, Civic Center. As in so many communities throughout the state, the Daughters of Utah Pioneers is at the very center of local historic pride. Its museum maintains exhibits depicting Logan's beginnings and interprets the city's most important historic sites. Open June-Aug, M-F 1-5 and by appointment. No charge. 752-2161.

LOGAN TABERNACLE, Main and Center Sts., 1864-91. This two-story stone building was the primary meeting hall for members of the Latter-Day Saints in Cache Valley. The nearby **Logan Temple,** a massive stone building, was one of the earliest built in Utah (1877). The grounds of both are open to all, but these landmarks are, unfortunately, closed to visitors. NR.

As you leave the grounds, have a look at the exotic **Lyric Theatre** on West Center St.—an early 20th-century building

worlds away from its spiritual neighbors in feeling and purpose. NR.

OLD MAIN, Utah State University campus, 1889-1902. The state's oldest continually-used building at an institution of higher learning, Old Main was constructed in the first year after the university was chartered. With its peaked towers and pyramidal roof, this 3½-story brick landmark remains dominant even among the modern buildings which now surround it.

Five miles south of the campus, on US 89-91, the university maintains the **Man and Bread Museum,** an extensive complex whose purpose is to preserve the methods, materials, and buildings of 19th-century western farm life. **The Ronald V. Jensen Living Historical Farm** is a part of the museum, with early farm implements as well as later steam and gas tractors which are still used to till the soil and harvest the crops. Open all year, M-F 10-4. 50¢ adults, 25¢ children. 245-4064.

Ogden

Several decades before the first Mormon pioneers arrived in the Great Basin, trappers wintered at the site of what is now Ogden; the first permanent settler—not a Mormon—was Miles Goodyear, who in the 1840s built a cabin and trading post here (see listing following). He held it for only a couple of years, however, before selling out to incoming Mormons in 1847. Ogden was laid out on the "City of Zion" plan according to Mormon teaching, with large squares bounded by generously broad streets, and the central tabernacle reminiscent of others found throughout the state. For more than 30 years this was primarily a farming community, until the arrival of the railroad heralded a new age of industrial development. Today this second largest of Utah cities is a pleasant mix of the old and new, of rural and urban characteristics.

FORT BUENAVENTURA STATE HISTORICAL MONUMENT, 2450 A Ave. This replica of the original 1848 fort has been constructed as a memorial to the first white settlement in the Great Basin and features displays of early items of trade, traps, guns, furs and pelts, furnishings, and railroad artifacts. Administered by the state. Open all year, daily 8-6. $2 per car. 621-4808.

MILES GOODYEAR CABIN, Tabernacle Sq., 1845. This simple log cabin is the oldest pioneer dwelling in Utah. Built of cottonwood logs, it became a regular stopping place for travelers en route to California. It has been moved from its original site and is maintained by the Daughters of Utah Pioneers. NR. The organization also administers adjacent **Relic Hall,** a museum of early handicrafts, costumes, and household items. Both museum and cabin are open June-Aug, M-Sa 10-5 and by appointment. Free. 782-8023.

OGDEN UNION STATION MUSEUM, 25th and Wall Ave., 1924. The original 1889 depot on this site burned in the early 1920s and was replaced by this irregular brick landmark, which is decorated with blue mosaic tiles and ornamental brickwork. NR. The rail station is now a repository for both a museum of railroadiana and a fine exhibit of early Browning firearms, as well as inventors' models, early machinery and tools, and classic cars. Open all year, M-Sa 12-6. $1 adults, 50¢ children. 392-1776.

The traveler who takes time to wander off along the pleasant streets of the downtown area will find a number of historic buildings worthy of attention: the **Bertha Eccles**

Community Art Center, at 2580 Jefferson Ave. is housed in an impressive Romanesque Revival mansion with round-arched windows and cylindrical towers. The work of local artists is displayed here. NR. Open all year, M-F 9-5, Sa 10-4. Free. 392-6935. At 2439 Washington Blvd. is **Peery's Egyptian Theatre,** where movies are still shown regularly. Built in 1924, the fantastic Egyptian Revival structure, the only one of its kind left in the state, was designed to produce shows in the grand tradition of the times. While the elaborate decorative scenes which once graced the interior walls have been painted over in recent years, there remain, both inside and out, enough exotic touches to suggest the glories wrought by designers almost sixty years ago. NR.

Park City

MAIN STREET HISTORIC DISTRICT, Main St. and Heber Ave., 20th century. This primarily commercial district represents the best remaining mining town business district in the state. The Park City silver mines, the first of which opened in 1869, were immediately recognized as bonanzas, and the district at their center boomed, aided by the completion of the transcontinental railroad. A severe fire in 1898 destroyed most of the early buildings, but the city was quickly rejuvenated. With the silver bust of the 1920s came a long period of deterioration, halted finally by a new type of boom in the early 1960s.

The area's magnificent western scenery and its superb skiing have made Park City a four-season resort, bolstering a badly flagging economy and a community which had been in danger of total extinction. The **Chamber of Commerce**, located in the Holiday Inn, has maps available which suggest walking tours of the historic area. 649-8899.

Outside of the district is **St. Mary's of the Assumption Catholic Church**, 121 Park Ave. Built in 1883, this oldest of the Catholic churches in Utah managed to escape the devastating fires of the latter part of the century unscathed, and is still open each Sunday for services.

Provo

BRIGHAM YOUNG UNIVERSITY, University Ave., 1875. A group of six brick buildings, each three stories tall and trimmed with stone embellishments in a variety of styles, forms the core of this university, which is today the largest in the nation. NR. On the large campus are located two museums of special interest to the traveler interested in Utah traditions. The **Harris Fine Arts Center** houses a collection of American art, emphasizing the works of

Indian and Mormon craftsmen. Open all year, M-F 8-5, Sa 8-10. No charge. 378-2881. The **Museum of Peoples and Cultures** in Allen Hall concentrates on Indian artifacts and archaeology. Open all year, M-F 8-5. No charge. 378-6111.

PROVO TABERNACLE, 50 S. University Ave., one of the largest of the Mormon houses of worship, has been the site of major religious meetings since its construction. It is formed of brick, in the shape of a cross, with arched entrances and pointed-arched windows. NR. Open June-Oct, M-F 6-10, Sa 10-6. No charge.

Salt Lake City

A small band of Mormons sent ahead by their leader Brigham Young, selected this valley a few miles east of the Great Salt Lake as a potential location for their new settlement in 1847. Seeking relief from religious persecution, they created a haven in the new town which they called Deseret —a barren, desert wilderness tamed by their determination and hard work. Young gave his blessing to their choice and selected the important central location which was to become Temple Square—the heart of the city—where the Tabernacle, Temple, and Assembly Hall of the Church of Jesus Christ of Latter-Day Saints were erected.

The city was laid out around the square according to a plan established by church founder Joseph Smith in 1833 for the "City of Zion": the basic scheme incorporated large squares bounded by wide avenues running directly north to south or east to west. Crops were planted and irrigation systems developed, adobe or log houses built, schools begun.

Situated in a picturesque valley at the foot of the high Wasatch Mountains, Salt Lake City today is an important business and industrial center, surrounded by rich farmlands and productive copper, gold, and silver mines. It remains, as it began, the headquarters of the Mormon Church.

AVENUES HISTORIC DISTRICT, roughly bounded by 1st and 9th Aves., State and Virginia Sts., 19th-20th centuries. Loca-

ted just east of the State Capitol is this huge residential area, where examples of every architectural style popular in the city from the 1860s to the 1920s can be found. This was the first developed section of Salt Lake City to deviate from the original city plan of ten-acre blocks—probably because the hilly terrain could not afford such generous regularity. It was here that a middle-class suburb for the downtown commercial district developed, where church officials, artisans, merchants, mining entrepreneurs, educators, and laborers alike built their homes. If you drive through the district you'll notice Queen Anne, Shingle Style, Classical Revival, and Colonial Revival homes, ranging from the ornate mansions of wealthy industrialists to the simpler homes of teachers and office workers. **Brigham Young's grave** is included within the district at 140 First Ave. The only family plot cemetery in the neighborhood, it is situated on a portion of the land owned by Young, close to his residence on South Temple St. NR.

BEEHIVE HOUSE, 67 E. South Temple, 1854. Brigham Young, second president of the Church of Jesus Christ of Latter-Day Saints and first governor of the state of Deseret—later Utah Territory—built and lived in the Beehive House until his death

Beehive House

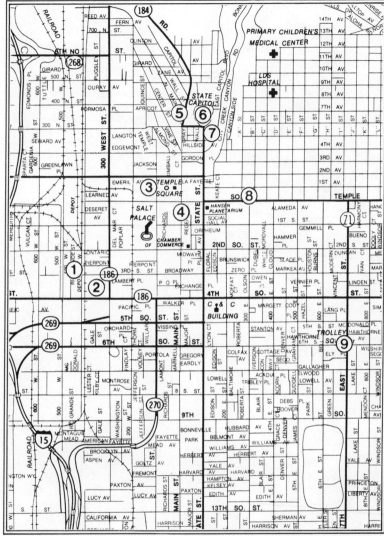

Courtesy of The Salt Lake Area Chamber of Commerce

Salt Lake City

1. Utah State Historical Society
2. Old Pioneer Fort Site
3. Temple Square
4. Z.C.M.I. Cast Iron Front
5. Council Hall
6. Utah State Capitol
7. Pioneer Memorial Museum
8. Beehive House
9. Trolley Square

in 1877. For a short time it served as the official presidential residence before being restored by the church in the late 1950s. The house is two stories high, surmounted by a cupola topped with a beehive, the traditional Mormon symbol of industry. The interior has been refurbished with many of the original pieces and artifacts, including a commissary where Young's family ordered supplies. NR. Open all year, M-Sa 9:30-4:30, Su 10-2:30. No charge. 531-2672.

Next door is **Lion House,** once part of Young's home, which now serves as a private social center and is closed to public tours. The lion over the doorway is a tribute to its owner, who was referred to by some as the "lion of the Lord" because of his inspired leadership of the church. NR, NHL.

CATHEDRAL OF THE MADELEINE, 331 E. South Temple St., 1900-1909. Built through the efforts of Roman Catholic miners under the direction of Bishop Lawrence Scanlon, this grand, soaring cathedral with projecting five-story corner towers and pointed arched windows dominates the area surrounding it. Its beautiful rose window is modeled after one in the cathedral in Toledo, Spain. NR. Open all year, daily 8:30-5:30.

CITY CREEK CANYON HISTORIC DISTRICT, bounded by Capitol Blvd., A

City Creek Canyon Historic District; Thomas W. Hanchett, photographer

St., 4th Ave., and Canyon Rd., 19th-20th centuries. The area which today encompasses two city parks, Memory Grove, and Canyon Road, with a small residential area at its south end, was part of the terrain where the Mormons briefly camped when they came to the valley in 1847. City Creek, which runs through the district, provided a good source of water for drinking and irrigating. In the 1860s and '70s Brigham Young started to divide his property in the area. Much of it went to his children, who later sold it to Salt Lake residents. The first homes were built here in the 1880s, most by influential church members who could afford elaborate mansions. In the early 20th century a number of smaller bungalows were constructed. Of particular interest is **Ottinger Hall**, 233 Canyon Rd., a two-story brick building constructed at the turn of the century. Salt Lake City had established its first paid fire department in 1883 with George M. Ottinger as chief. Under his leadership the Veterans-Volunteer Firemen's Association was organized in 1890, and ten years later the hall was constructed as a meeting and social hall for the firemen. Today it houses pioneer fire fighting equipment, including Utah's first fire engine, and is still used by relatives of the original builders. Open occasionally, so write ahead for information. NR. ♠

COUNCIL HALL (Old City Hall), Capitol Hill, 1864-66. This red sandstone building served as Salt Lake's city hall and the meeting place for the territorial legislature until 1894. Afterwards it housed the police court and offices. In the early 1960s the entire structure was dismantled, moved to its present site, and rebuilt with a minimum of modifications. It now contains the offices of the Utah Travel Council, an excellent source for brochures and other information about the state. NR. Open all year, M-F 8:30-5; summer also Sa, Su 9-5. No charge. 328-5681.

FORT DOUGLAS MUSEUM, Fort Douglas Military Reservation, 1862. The first military encampment was made on this site in October, 1862, with the construction of temporary quarters for officers and men,

in addition to an adobe commandant's residence, guardhouse, bakehouse, commissary, quartermaster tents, hospital, and stables. A year later these makeshift quarters were replaced with more permanent buildings. The camp received its permanent name, Fort Douglas, during the 1874-76 rebuilding when the present officers' circle was constructed. In addition to the Victorian infantry barracks (1875) in which the museum is housed, two other structures remain from the 19th century—the chapel (1883) and the camp theater (1864). The museum's collection includes military uniforms and memorabilia explaining the fort's prominent role in early Utah history. Operated by the federal government. NR, NHL. Open Tu, Th, Sa 10-4. No charge. 524-4154.

THOMAS KEARNS MANSION AND CARRIAGE HOUSE, 603 E. South Temple St., 1902. A millionaire who had made his fortune as a partner in the Silver King Mining Company, Kearns had this elaborate marble Victorian home built while he was serving in the U.S. Senate. His widow donated it to the state for use as the governor's official residence in 1937, a capacity which it once again serves today, having been extensively restored and renovated by the Utah State Historical Society, which used it as temporary headquarters from 1957 until early 1980. NR.

Just across the street is the **Keith-Brown Mansion and Carriage House**, 1900. The mansion, a three-story limestone residence highlighted by four massive Tuscan columns, was built by David Keith, a Nova Scotian who established the Silver King Mining Company in partnership with Thomas Kearns. Now owned by the Terracor Land Development Corporation, the elegant residence has been carefully adapted to serve as offices. NR.

LIBERTY PARK, 1000 South and 600 East Sts. This 100-acre recreational area offers many amusements for Salt Lake citizens, including tennis courts, a swimming pool, an outdoor theatre, and playgrounds. Also located here are two historic landmarks of relevance to the city's past:

Thomas Kearn Mansion

Isaac Chase Mill, believed to be the only gristmill built by early Utah pioneers still standing on its original site, was completed in 1852 and purchased by Brigham Young in 1860. The mill was constructed of adobe blocks cemented with clay mortar. Much original machinery from the mill, which ceased operating in the 1880s, remains. NR. Open all year. Tu-Su 10-7. No charge. 555-7771.

Grant Steam Locomotive No. 223 stands nearby. Built in 1881 for the Denver and Rio Grande Railroad, it is the last of the

narrow gauge engines constructed by the Grant Locomotive Works. In operation for more than 60 years, it hauled freight in both Utah and Colorado. The Utah State Historical Society plans to move the locomotive to a more appropriate place several blocks west — the organization's home at the Denver and Rio Grande Railroad Depot. (See listing for the Utah State Historical Society.) NR. 🏃

MARMALADE DISTRICT, bounded by North, Center and Quince Sts., 19th-20th centuries. The whimsical name for this small residential area relates to those of its streets which reflect the fruit trees and plants established here by early neighbors.

The **John Platts House,** 364 Quince St., is an excellent surviving example of the small, unpretentious Mormon pioneer home. Built of local fieldstone in the 1850s, with later brick additions, the house is indicative of its owner's occupation: he was a fruit grower and made use of his harvest in building — apricot pits are used for binding in the mortar! The house is privately owned, but may be viewed from the public way.

As you stroll through this lovely, modest neighborhood you'll be struck by the amount of careful restoration which has been done by current owners of these private homes, and by the houses' location—so close to the bustling, modern downtown area, but a world away in feeling. NR.

ALFRED McCUNE HOME, 200 North Main St., 1901. Situated on a commanding hillside site, this large, turreted brick residence was built by a prominent industrialist whose loyalty to the Mormon Church prompted him to donate the house to it in the 1920s. It has since served as the McCune School of Music, part of Brigham Young University, and is currently headquarters for the Sweetwater Corporation. NR.

OLD PIONEER FORT SITE, Pioneer Park between 3rd and 4th South, 2nd and 3rd West, 1847. A week after the arrival of the first Mormon emigrant group to Salt Lake Valley, a general assembly was called in which it was voted to unite the various camps into one location and construct a corral, houses, and a fort for protection against Indian attack. The site, now Pioneer Park, was the settlers' home until they began to move to their town lots in 1848 and 1849. It was here that a meeting was held late in 1848 at the home of Heber C. Kimball to organize the provincial State of Deseret. While none of the early adobe and log buildings remain, this was the site of the first permanent settlement in the Great Basin. NR.

PIONEER CRAFT HOUSE, 3271 South 5th East, 1890. The **Scott School,** a simple two-room building, was constructed in the late 19th century to replace two more rudimentary structures of logs and adobe. Exhibits of Utah history and art are now housed here. Open all year, M-F 9-4, Sa 9-12. No charge. 467-6611.

PIONEER MEMORIAL MUSEUM, 300 N. Main St. The wagon in which Brigham Young rode into the Salt Lake Valley in 1847 is but one of scores of relics from

Utah's early days which are housed in this imposing columned building and the adjacent carriage house. Furnishings, farm tools, other pioneer vehicles, crafts, and manuscripts from the 19th century form the most complete record available of the city's development. Several rooms have been authentically reconstructed to represent those of early dwellings. Operated by the Daughters of Utah Pioneers. Open all year, M-Sa 9-5; also Su 1-5 Apr-Oct. No charge. 533-5759.

PIONEER TRAIL STATE PARK, 2601 Sunnyside Ave. **Emigration Canyon,** where the park is located, forms the passage through the Wasatch Mountains to Salt Lake Valley traversed by Brigham Young and his followers in their journey from the Missouri Valley. From this site, now marked by an enormous monument, Young allegedly stated that this valley was the place he had seen in a vision as the destined home for his people. The monument also pays tribute to earlier trappers and explorers who had passed through the area prior to its settlement.

Relocated to the park from its original site at Ashton Ave. is the **Brigham Young Forest Farmhouse,** established in the 1850s by Young as part of an experimental farm on which the first alfalfa in the valley was grown, mulberry trees planted, and registered cattle imported and bred. The frame residence which replaced an earlier adobe structure in the 1860s was built on a stone foundation in the shape of a double cross. It has been restored, with many of its original furnishings, and presents a clear picture of the early, quite comfortable lifestyle of the more prosperous Mormon pioneer. NR. The farmhouse is open from Apr-Oct, Tu-Sa 9:30-4:30; Su 1:30-4:30. The park is open all year, daily 9-5. Both are free. 582-2853.

ST. MARK'S CATHEDRAL, 231 East First South, 1871. St. Mark's Episcopal is the oldest non-Mormon cathedral in Utah. Built of sandstone, cutstone, and rubble, it was designed by noted architect Richard Upjohn in the massive, soaring Gothic Revival style. NR. Open all year, M-F 9-4.

SALT LAKE CITY AND COUNTY BUILDING, 451 Washington Sq., 1891-94. This massive, many-turreted landmark served as the first state capitol of Utah and is located on an original site set aside as a public square by the city's planners. County offices occupy one half of the Romanesque Revival structure, and city offices the other. NR. Open all year, M-F 8:30-5.

TEMPLE SQUARE, 19th century. Monumentally impressive Temple Square, the heart of Salt Lake City, best captures the essence of the Mormon achievement in building a "kingdom of Zion" in the Utah desert. The walled square symbolizes the strong cultural and religious individuality of the Mormons. **The Temple** itself, which dominates the complex, is an enormous granite Gothic Revival landmark designed by Truman O. Angell, which was begun in 1853 and completed 40 years later. The statue of the Angel Moroni, who appeared to Brigham Young in the vision which prompted the settlement in Salt Lake City, sits atop the highest spire. The Temple, as is the case with all Mormon ceremonial buildings, is open only to those of the faith.

The **Tabernacle**, however, is open to all. The unsupported domed roof, one of the largest in the world, the magnificent organ, and the building's acoustical qualities are among its outstanding features. Designed by Henry Grow, the Tabernacle was begun in 1863 and completed in 1875. The world-famous Mormon Tabernacle Choir practices and performs here; rehearsals, Th, 8 p.m.; concerts, Su 9:30-10 a.m. Organ recitals are also given, M-F 12, Sa-Su 4. Other special programs are offered from time to time.

Assembly Hall, completed in 1882, is the Mormon house of worship, devoted to nonsectarian religious, social, and intellectual uses. It was constructed of materials remaining after the Temple was completed and is also in the Gothic Revival style.

There are **visitor centers** at South Temple and Main Sts., which include complete information on these important Mormon landmarks, along with exhibits and guided tour schedules. Open all year, daily 8 a.m.-10 p.m. No charge. The gates of Temple Square are open all year, daily from 7 a.m. to 10:30 p.m. NR, NHL.

If the feet wear out or the children start to fuss, relief is only a block away. The **Hansen Planetarium,** in the old **Salt Lake City Public Library building** at 15 S. State St., offers hour-long armchair tours of the galaxies that may prove a welcome diversion. The building itself is an impressive classical landmark which dates from the turn of the century. NR. Open all year, M-Sa 9-5 and 7-10:30, Su 1-5. $2.50 adults, $1.50 children. 535-7007. ⛪

UNIVERSITY OF UTAH CIRCLE, University of Utah, early 20th century. The University of Deseret, now the University of Utah, was established in 1850, only 2½ years after the first group of Mormon pioneers arrived in the Salt Lake valley, and was the first land grant college west of the Mississippi. For nearly 50 years the university's classes were shunted from one building to another; it was not until 1894 that Congress granted the 60 acres from Fort Douglas military reservation which became the university's permanent home, and it was seven years later before the first buildings were completed on what is now the Circle. **The Library, Normal,** and **Physical Science** buildings were designed by Richard K.A. Kletting, the architect of the Utah State Capitol. The **Park Building,** designed by S.C. Dallas, is an excellent example of Neo-Classical architecture. While the Circle remains the heart of the campus, take time to stroll through the rest. Several fine museums are located here, including the **Utah Museum of Fine**

Arts at the Art and Architecture Center. The collection includes 19th-century paintings, furniture, and graphics. Open all year, M-F 10-5, Sa, Su 2-5. No charge. 581-7049.

The **Utah Museum of Natural History** offers anthropological displays in its Hall of Man. Open daily 9:30-5:30, except major holidays. $1 adults, and 50¢ children. 581-6927.

UTAH STATE CAPITOL, Third North, Columbus, and East Capitol Sts., 1915. This imposing native granite building, with stately columns and large copper dome, stands on a hill just north of Temple Square. It was designed by Richard K.A. Kletting. **Exhibition Hall** within contains displays of state products, natural attractions, and native art. The soaring interior rotunda is of Georgian marble, its ceiling painted with seagulls in flight—a rather odd choice until one considers that the birds are said to have saved the first Mormon crop from a plague of locusts. Not surprisingly, the gull has been designated the state bird in gratitude. The **Gold Room** is so named because its chandeliers and some furnishings are adorned with gold leaf from Utah mines. NR. Guided tours

are conducted daily, M-F 8:30-5; Sa-Su 9:30-6. Free. Call the Chamber of Commerce for more information. 364-3631.

UTAH STATE FAIR GROUNDS, 10th West and North Temple Sts., 20th century. Seventy acres on the west side of the city have been home to the Utah State Fair since 1902. A number of historic buildings stand here, among them the 1902 **Horticulture Building** and 1905 **Exhibition Hall**. The fair itself has been a Utah institution since 1856. It began as a major instrument for implementing the policies of the Mormon church, which insisted on total self-sufficiency in agriculture and industry. Since shortly before the fair moved to this location at the beginning of the century, however, its purpose has paralleled that of other state fairs: to promote good feeling and fellowship while advancing pride in the country's agricultural heritage. NR. The fair is held each September. Call the Utah Travel Council for specific dates. 328-5681. 🏃

UTAH STATE HISTORICAL SOCIETY, Denver and Rio Grande Railroad Depot, 300 Rio Grande St. The huge brick and terra-cotta station, constructed in 1910,

Horticulture Building; John McCormick, photographer

has been home to the society only since 1980. Prior to that, its museum was contained in the Kearns Museum, an equally historic Utah landmark. The depot, with its cavernous waiting room, is an especially apt repository for the society's collection of Utah artifacts and memorabilia, as the tumultuous history surrounding its construction is significant not only to Utah's development, but to the emergence of the great transcontinental rail lines in the late 19th and 20th centuries which did so much to change the face of the West. George Gould, son of famous financier Jay Gould, established a transcontinental route to compete with the Union Pacific line under the control of Edward H. Harriman. Two connecting lines, the Western Pacific from San Francisco, and the Denver and Rio Grande from Denver, met in Salt Lake City. The Rio Grande station was constructed to provide facilities for district offices as well as to present a modern, impressive station to lure travelers away from the competing Union Pacific. It stands today as a reminder of the financial struggles for control of the nation's transportation system by the great railroad barons of yesterday. NR. Open all year, M-F 8-5. No charge. 533-5755. 🏃

Nearby on South Temple (at 400 West) is the rival **Union Pacific Depot,** completed in 1909, which still houses offices of the line in addition to Amtrak ticket offices. Recently cleaned and restored, the elegant station boasts a domed waiting room with marble floors and stained-glass windows. NR.

WHEELER HISTORIC FARM, 6351 S. 900 East, 1898. This 75-acre farm complex, preserved in excellent condition, includes a 2½-story brick and adobe farmhouse, adobe granary, woodhouse and workshed, and wood icehouse and chickenhouse. Livestock, crops, horse-drawn farming equipment and early irrigation techniques are employed to portray the rural life of the late 19th and early 20th centuries. NR. Open all year, M-Sa 8-6 and by appointment. Free. 468-9384. 🏃

Z.C.M.I. CAST IRON FRONT, 15 S. Main St., 1878. All that remains of the original Zions Cooperative Mercantile Institute building is the impressive three-story facade of cast iron and stamped sheet metal, which was saved when the original structure was razed. The institute itself was formed in 1868 by the Mormon Church, and by 1880 it had 156 branch stores in 24 counties. The main building was one of the first true department stores in the country. Today a modern shopping mall hides behind the historic facade. NR. Open all year, M-Sa 10-6.

Salt Lake City vicinity

BINGHAM CANYON OPEN PIT COPPER MINE, 16 miles SW on UT 48, 1904. This immense open pit, some 1½ miles wide and nearly half a mile deep, was the first mine of its kind in the world, and one of the three largest. The output from the works, established in a region where copper deposits had been largely ignored in favor of the 19th-century fever for gold, silver, and lead, lifted Utah from a minor copper-producing state to fourth by 1919. The mine still yields a high percentage of all American copper production. NR. NHL. Viewing facilities are provided for visitors on the west rim of the pit.

Willard

WILLARD HISTORIC DISTRICT, roughly bounded by 200 W., 200 N., 100 E. and 200 S. Sts., 19th-20th centuries. Settled in 1851, and planned in the usual north-south, east-west grid pattern typical of Mormon towns, Willard developed as a closely-knit agricultural village. The twelve-block historic district is comprised of numerous 1½- and 2-story stone,

frame, and brick-gabled dwellings; barns, granaries, corrals, sheds, fences, and pleasing open spaces punctuate the whole.

The superb rock construction of a majority of the homes within the district demonstrates the efficacy of the Mormon settlement system: as pioneers were sent forth to begin new communities, the church members who went along were carefully selected according to their talents so that men and women with the necessary basic skills—in construction, education, medicine, farming—were always included. Each colonizing group could therefore develop a totally self-sufficient community. The ingenuity of these pioneers in making use of available natural building materials, while striving for pleasing architectural designs, is perhaps nowhere better demonstrated than in this rustic town, where time has virtually stood still for more than a century. Although the landmark homes are still privately owned, a stroll or drive through the neighborhood can be both instructive and pleasurable. NR.

Lodging and Dining

BECAUSE the Utah territory was not settled until the middle of the 19th century, and because its early pioneers were predominantly of the Mormon faith, for whom food and drink (non-alcoholic) were merely a part of everyday life rather than a cause for celebration, there are few historic restaurants in the state. Home and family were all important, and travel was not encouraged, so few early hotels remain. Most of the ones that do exist did not begin life as lodgings, but as churches or private homes, converted and restored by entrepreneurs who wanted to mix hospitality with an atmosphere reminiscent of pioneer times.

Utah invites the adventuresome and energetic: scattered throughout the state are scores of campgrounds, some located within the glorious and historic national parks, some at state facilities. But everywhere the mountains, canyons, and valleys of this scenic state provide superb accompaniment to a meal or a good night's sleep.

Cedar City vicinity

CHATEAU MEADEAU VIEW LODGE, Mirror Lake, Dixie National Forest, UT 14, (P.O. Box 356), 84720. (801) 648-2495. Harry and Gaby Moyer. Open May 20-April 10. This is a rustic mountain retreat, not old in years but certainly historic in feeling. It is located in the center of one of Utah's earliest developed areas, as well as one of its most scenic. 9 rooms. MAP or EP. Moderate. PC.

Kanab

PARRY LODGE, 89 East Center St., 84741. (801) 644-2601. Kenneth G. Broadhead. Open all year. The property upon which the lodge stands was once owned by Jacob Hamblin, an important figure in Utah history. Part of the office and lobby was once a private home, built in the 1920s. The restaurant was established in 1929, and cabins were added several years later. 89 rooms. Moderate.

Moab

GRAND OLD RANCH HOUSE RESTAURANT, U.S. 63, 84532. (801) 259-5753. The Taylor Farmstead, now a lovely restaurant, remains as an essentially intact late 19th-century farm complex. Begun in 1894, the farmhouse is similar in form to others of the period: it is a two-story brick structure with a porch and balcony in the Eastlake style. NR. Moderate, AE, CB, D, M, V, PC. Open daily, 5-10.

Monument Valley

GOULDING'S LODGE, UT 47, (Box 1), 84536. (801) 727-3231. Gerald LaFont. A stone trading post, built in 1924, serves today as the hotel office and as a shop for arts and crafts. NR. The hotel itself is modern, but the history of the area's development and the

215

sheer beauty of the valley warrant the lodge's inclusion here. The lodge is now part of a Navajo Indian reservation. 19 rooms. Pets welcome. EP. Moderate. M, V.

Provo

HOTEL ROBERTS, 192 South University Ave., 84601. (801) 373-3400. Mark Anderson, Jr. Open all year. The oldest operating hotel in Provo began life in 1882 as a boarding house. A three-story wing with a kitchen on the main floor was added in 1890, and another three-story wing in the early 1900s, followed by the addition of another floor to the main building in 1926. NR. Inexpensive.

Salt Lake City

HOTEL UTAH, Main and South Temple, 84110. (801) 531-1000. Open all year. This is Utah's most famous old luxury hotel, an imposing white terra-cotta and marble structure, completed in 1911, with a magnificent lobby. NR. It is ideally located in the center of the city, just opposite historic Temple Square. Pets welcome. 500 rooms. Moderate to expensive. AE, D, CB, M, V, PC.

RISTORANTE DELLA FONTANA, 336 South 4th East, 84111. (801) 328-4243. An early Salt Lake church, built in 1892, now houses this Continental restaurant. The original stained-glass windows remain, as do the wooden pews and pulpit. One exotic note: a waterfall descends from the ceiling. Open for lunch and dinner. Moderate. M, V, PC.

THE ROYAL PALACE, 249 South 400 East, 84111. (801) 359-5000. This wonderfully eclectic building, with stained-glass windows and Moorish dome, began life as the B'nai

Israel Temple. Completed in 1891, the temple was an elegant statement of the wealth and power of Jewish settlers in a predominantly Mormon enclave. NR. The elegant restaurant now housed here is open daily for lunch and dinner. Expensive. AE, CB, D, M, V.

TROLLEY SQUARE, 5th South and 7th East. Early trolley car barns, dating from the late 19th century, have been converted into an ingenious complex of shops and restaurants. Among the many offerings to please the palate are those of **The 47 Samurai** at #299. (801) 363-8334. A Japanese menu is offered. Open for lunch and dinner. Moderate. A, MC, V. **Giuseppe's,** at #23, offers hearty Italian fare. (801) 328-2377. Open for lunch and dinner. Moderate. AE, MC, V.

4. ARIZONA

ARIZONA is probably best known for the breathtaking Grand Canyon in the north and for its progressive southern cities, most notably Tucson and Phoenix, which each year attract thousands of sunworshippers to vacation or to live. There is, however, much more than sun and scenery here.

By the time the white man (or Anglo, as he was sometimes known) arrived, he was very much the latecomer. Before the first American colonists settled in the territory in the early 1800s, there had been human habitation in the state for thousands of years. Arizona, "the Apache State," is home to more Indian tribes than any other state in the Union, and its development is inextricably linked to those tribes. Evidence of the early colonies is everywhere in the state—from monumental cliff dwellings fashioned out of unyielding limestone to ancient Indian art painted on canyon walls.

Spanish and Mexican explorers moved into Arizona hundreds of years ago to found the first missions and forts, following the conquistador Coronado's entry into the area in search of gold in the 1500s. The stark white adobe mission buildings, some now only ruins, some still very much whole and actively used, are evidence of the influence of the Spanish culture.

Eastern pioneers were attracted to areas such as Tucson, Phoenix, and Tombstone because of rich ore deposits in the nearby hills. They often stayed for other reasons, drawn by the climate and the beauty of the surrounding deserts and mountains.

A major source of early Arizona wealth was cattle ranching. Many of the early ranches established in the 1820s and '30s are still active today. The ingenuity of the prehistoric Indian tribes played an important role here: their clever systems of irrigation were copied or taken over by the Anglos as essential sources of water for fodder.

During the Civil War, development of the territory was severely curtailed, and it was the railroad's arrival later in the century that brought new economic growth commensurate with the advances of 19th-century industry. The transcontinental rail lines also made Arizona accessible to tourists: early hotels in the Grand Canyon area date as early as the late 1800s.

In some ways, Arizona is still very much a primitive part of America. It was 1912 before statehood was granted, and even today the population centers are miles apart. Three geographic areas have been delineated in the pages that follow: **Tucson and the South; Phoenix and the West;** and the **Northeast Canyon Country.** In traveling through Arizona, you should remember, however, that as in other parts of the West, distances are vast, and ample travel time should be allowed. It is also wise to insure that your car is in good working order for long road trips and that you bring ample supplies of water when traveling to desert or wilderness areas. The summer months, especially, can be brutally hot, and facilities are often scarce, even at the national parks.

With all that in mind, the vacationer interested in exploring the heritage of a state as much Mexican and Spanish as it is American will find much to enjoy in Arizona.

Arizona State Capitol Building

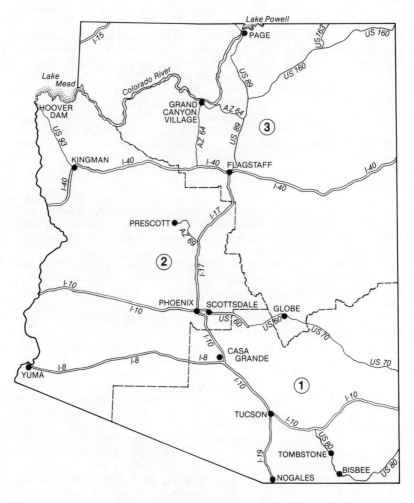

1. **Tucson and the South**
2. **Phoenix and the West**
3. **Northeast Canyon Country**

Tucson and the South

Ajo vicinity

ORGAN PIPE CACTUS NATIONAL MONUMENT, 16 miles south on AZ 85. The rare, 20-foot-high organ pipe cactus, which resembles the instrument for which it was named, blooms brilliantly on spring nights in this 560-square mile desert area. Organ Pipe is Arizona's largest national monument, a wilderness preserve for animals, natural terrain, and multicolored plants with names like owlclover and creosote bush. Prehistoric cultures as old as 12,000 years are hinted at by excavated stone implements, pottery fragments, and remnants of campgrounds. Ruins of the **Gahado Well and Line Camp** and the **Victoria Mine** are located here. During the winter months, and irregularly at other times of year, illustrated talks on the history of the area are given at the **visitor center**. Two graded, self-guided scenic drives, **Ajo Mountain** and **Puerto Blanco**, follow the historic routes of early desert travelers and wind through impressive stands of cactus. Camping facilities are available. NR. Open all year, daily 8-4:30. No charge. 387-7050.

Bisbee

BISBEE HISTORIC DISTRICT, Main St. and Copper Queen Plaza, late 19th and early 20th centuries. A former copper and silver mining town, Bisbee retains some of the rowdy spirit that ruled in its heyday at the turn of the century, when forty saloons along **Brewery Gulch** did a booming business. Although many of Bisbee's early structures were devastated by fire and floods, the historic district contains a number of early buildings, among them the **Copper Queen Library and Post Office** and the **Woolworth Store**, both constructed in 1906. The Post Office, Arizona's second oldest, houses models and displays of Bisbee history. Stop by to mail a letter, and have a look. One of the finest hotels in the West is here—the 1904 **Copper Queen** has been restored to its original turn-of-the-century elegance (see Lodging and Dining). Several of the early landmarks now house museums:

Bisbee Civic Center and Mining and Historical Museum, Main St., 1880. Housed in the **Old General Office Building** of the Phelps Dodge Corporation, this is a repository for articles and artifacts from Bisbee's past, including much information about early mining activities, and curiosities from those turbulent days. NR. Open all year, M-Sa 10-4, Su 1-4. Donations accepted. 432-7071.

Bisbee Restoration and Historical Society, 37 Main St., 1915. The Restoration Association is dedicated to preserving the pioneer past, and it has done so admirably in this collection, housed in the old **Fair Store** building in the heart of the historic district. The hand-stitched dresses and accessories of pioneer women are displayed here, as is an old bar and blackjack table from infamous Brewery Gulch. Open all year, M-Sa 10-3. Donations accepted. 432-3006.

Bisbee vicinity

CORONADO NATIONAL MEMORIAL, 30 miles west of Bisbee via AZ 92 and Montezuma Canyon Rd., 1540-42. A glorious scenic area is the site of Francisco Vasquez de Coronado's expedition to the Southwest in the 16th century. From Coronado Peak, view the route by which the Spanish entered the United States from El Fuerte, Mexico. At the park **museum and visitor center** is a collection of costumes, weapons, and documents from the exploration period. There are foot trails, picnic sites, and guided tours of the area. NR. Open all year, daily 8-5. No charge. 366-5515 or 458-9333.

FORT BOWIE NATIONAL HISTORIC SITE, 12 miles south of Bisbee via graded dirt road, 1862-94. Established during the Civil War and abandoned by the Army in 1894, this was a crucial outpost in the white man's numerous altercations with the native Chiricahua Apache tribe, led at various times by Geronimo and Cochise. Ruins of the fort are accessible only via a 1½-mile foot trail through the Apache Pass, a strategic crossing point of the Chiricahua Mountains. In addition to the stabilized adobe fort walls, there are ruins of the **Apache Pass Stage Station.** Summer hikers to the fort should carry water. Artifacts, photographs, and military records are exhibited. NR. Open all year, daily 8:30-4:30. No charge. 847-2500.

Coolidge

CASA GRANDE RUINS NATIONAL MONUMENT, AZ 87, c. 1000-1450. The purpose of the "Big House" in this partially-excavated group of prehistoric Indian villages is unknown; it may have been an astronomical observatory or a ceremonial building. It is a four-story tower with unreinforced packed-clay walls, built by the agrarian Hohokam 600 years ago. Ball courts, pottery vessels, platform mounds, and decorative items uncovered in excavations from 1891 to the present are the highlights in this 18-village cluster of ruins. NR. Open all year, daily 7 am-6 pm. $1 per car, 50¢ adults. 723-3172.

Florence

McFARLAND HISTORIC STATE PARK, 5th and Main St., 1878. This old section of downtown Florence, the seat of Pinal County and one of the oldest desert settlements in Arizona estabished by white men, contains original adobe buildings that are among the finest of their type in the state. The first **Pinal County Courthouse,** which was built in 1877, is now a law and history musuem, displaying some personal belongings of former Governor Ernest McFarland, who was also a U.S. senator and state Supreme Court justice. NR. Open all year, daily 8-5. Modest admission. 868-5216.

PINAL COUNTY HISTORICAL SOCIETY MUSEUM, 2201 Main St. Depictions of early life in this town set dramatically between the desert and the mountains may be viewed here: agriculture, mining, and the artifacts of Indian, Spanish, Mexican and Anglo cultures are documented. Open all year, W-Su 1-5. No charge. 868-4382.

An unusually large number of 19th-century buildings still stand in town, making Florence a required stop on the traveler's itinerary. The **Pinal County Visitors Center,** located in the restored **Jacob Sutter House** (1880) offers additional information. Open Mar-Nov, M-F 9-5; Dec-Feb, M-F 9-5, Sa 10-2. No charge. 868-4473.

Nogales

PIMERIA ALTA HISTORICAL SOCIETY MUSEUM, 223 Grand Ave. Housed in the former **Nogales City Hall,** this is a distinguished collection of prehistoric and historic Indian relics, as well as mining artifacts and items which illuminate the history of the 19th- and 20th-century settlement of South Arizona and North Sonora, Mexico. Open all year, M-F 10-4, Sa 10-1, Su 1-4. No charge. 287-5402.

Nogales vicinity

TUMACACORI NATIONAL MONUMENT, 18 miles north on I-19, 1691-1828. The mission of San Jose de Tumacacori was a northern outpost of the Sonora mission chain founded by Jesuit priests in the 17th century. Ruins of the extraordinary church built in the early 19th century to replace the original mission still stand: you can see the extra-thick (Apache proof) adobe, and the semicircular facade. The faded colors originally applied by Indian workmen are still visible, as is the unfinished, burned-brick bell tower. The mission was abandoned in 1828. A **park office and museum** are located in a Sonora Mission-style building, where early life in the mission is convincingly recreated. NR. Open all year, daily 8-5. $1 per car. 398-2341.

Patagonia

STRADLING MUSEUM OF THE HORSE, 1317 McKeown St. It's only fitting that there should be a museum dedicated to this creature without which the West could not have been won. This world-famous collection, the most complete of its kind in the country, celebrates everything equine from ancient Greece to the present: vehicles, saddles, harnesses, books, paintings, bits, and spurs. Indian artifacts are displayed, as is period furniture. Open all year, daily 9-5. $1 adults. 394-2264. ♦♦

Pima

EASTERN ARIZONA MUSEUM AND HISTORICAL SOCIETY OF GRAHAM COUNTY, 2 N. Main St. The museum's permanent collection includes an accurate reproduction of a pioneer home and an assortment of Indian and pioneer artifacts. The 1880 **Old Cluff Hall** is also administered by the museum. Open all year, M-F 9-12 and 1-5. No charge. 485-2761.

Sierra Vista

FORT HUACHUCA HISTORICAL MUSEUM, Boyd and Grierson Sts., 1877. Today, this adobe fort dating from the days of the Indian wars serves as a training center for military intelligence; it's the command center for the army's worldwide communications network. The **Old Post** area, which dates to 1885, looks almost unchanged from that time: it is a typical western frontier post, with three frame barracks and numerous adobe structures. There is an **historical military museum** on the post. A special display documents the history of black American soldiers. Other displays include Kachina dolls and a gallery highlighting famous military expeditions and the men who made them. The B Troop of Fort Huachuca (the word means "place of thunder or wind or rain") is a special commemorative group which charges across the parade grounds, dressed in cavalry uniforms, for a 20-minute show on the middle Wednesday of each month. On the last workday of the month, B Troop and the modern divisions participate in a military review starting at 8:30 a.m. ♦♦

   Close by at the Fort are the **Garden Canyon Petroglyphs,** carvings of birds, human faces, spirals, and dots in a small limestone cave, whose origins are unknown. NR.

The fort is open all year, M-F 9-4, Sa, Su 1-4. No charge. 538-5736.

Superior

BOYCE THOMPSON SOUTHWESTERN ARBORETUM, 2 miles west on U.S. 60, 1923. Western businessman William Boyce Thompson established this 1,221-acre arboretum in 1923 to study plant life in sub-arid regions: it was the first such privately-endowed establishment in the world. The permanent structures include research, educational, and visitor facilities, and an early 20th-century home, the **Clevenger Homestead,** built into the north wall of Queen Creek Canyon. Old tools are displayed here. Then there are trails, walkways, roads, and several unexcavated Indian archaeological sites to wander through. In the arboretum itself are varieties of soil, plants, and animals, and topography exhibits. NR. Open all year, daily 8-5:30. $1 adults. 689-2811.

Tombstone

Tombstone's halcyon days, full of gunfights, loose women, and barroom brawls between drunken silver miners, have been immortalized in countless movies about Doc Holliday, Wyatt Earp, and Bat Masterson. Its motto is "The Town Too Tough to Die," a reference to the catastrophic fires and floods that would have destroyed a less feisty community than Tombstone. The entire town was designated a Registered National Landmark in 1962, forever legitimizing the history of this present-day health and winter resort. As is unfortunately the case with other popular tourist attractions, many specialty and souvenir shops have sprung up as well — some offering the ultimate in kitsch. The whole, however, remains an important and well-documented complex in which to delve into Arizona's lusty past.

TOMBSTONE COURTHOUSE STATE HISTORIC PARK, 219 Toughnut St., 1882. The courthouse itself is a two-story brick building with stone trim. It has an interior iron spiral staircase to the courtroom, and a square central cupola. Arizona's oldest extant courthouse, it was designed by Frank Walker. An addition to the rear was made in 1904. Dolls, guns, silver and china, and medical equipment are displayed; there are collections dealing with minerology, anthropology, archaeology, government, industry, and cattle ranching. NR. Open all year, daily 8-5:30. 50¢ adults. 457-3311.

TOMBSTONE HISTORIC DISTRICT, late 19th century. The boom town that sprang up around prospector Edward Scheiffelin's silver mining claim is well preserved. Many of the old buildings are open as museums, and you won't want to miss the famous **Boothill Graveyard,** to the northwest of town, which contains about 250 early graves, some of them unmarked, and some with unusual epitaphs. If you're a movie Western fan, you'll recognize some of the names on the stones. Open all year, daily 8-6. Donations accepted. 457-3972.

Wet your whistle at the restored **Crystal Palace Saloon** (5th and Allen) which is open M-Sa 10 a.m. to 1 a.m., Su 12 noon to 1 a.m. 457-3611. The **Silver Nugget Museum** nearby at 6th and Allen is the place in which to see relics of Tombstone's mining history, along with various reconstructed room settings, gambling equipment, pioneer and ranching items, and other curiosities. Open all year, daily 9-6. $1 adults, 50¢ seniors. 457-3394.

The **Bird Cage Theatre,** with cages dangling from its ceiling which were once filled with feathered saloon girls whose job it was to entice the patrons to tarry a while longer, is a lusty frontier cabaret decorated with many of its original furnishings and fixtures. Open all year, daily 8-6. $1 adults, 50¢ children. 457-3421.

The dangerous history of **Wells Fargo** is recalled in a museum by that name at 511 Allen St. Over 75,000 items are displayed in four early buildings. Open all year, M-Sa 8-5:30. $1 adults, 50¢ children. 457-2254.

April is the best time to visit the **Rose Tree Inn Museum,** Toughnut and 4th Sts., for that is when the 7,500-square-foot rose bush, said to be the world's largest, bursts

into bloom. In a nearby 1880 house, decorated with original furniture, is the museum, whose collection will transport you back to a time in frontier history long since vanished. Open all year, daily 9-5. $1 adults. 457-3326.

Tombstone's most popular historic site is undoubtedly the **O.K. Corral** on Allen St., the scene of a legendary 1881 gun battle between the Earp and Clanton factions. The stagecoach, office, and stables have been restored. Open all year, daily 8:30-5. $1 adults, 50¢ children. 457-3456.

As you walk through town among the other historic landmarks, you'll notice the **City Hall** (1882), which because of its size

and detailing is a prominent feature of the district hard to miss. It still serves as city hall today. **St. Paul's Episcopal Church,** at Safford and 3rd Sts., was also completed in 1882; it is a Gothic Revival landmark of adobe brick, with its eight original stained-glass windows still intact.

The **Chamber of Commerce** (457-3552) can supply additional information on this most famous of Western towns. Be sure to allow plenty of time to see it all.

Tubac

TUBAC PRESIDIO STATE HISTORIC PARK, Broadway and River Rd., c. 1760. The Tubac Presidio is the oldest of three Spanish military outposts built in the state. Tubac itself was the first Anglo settlement in Arizona; it also had the state's first state park and first newspaper. The Presidio was founded in response to a Pima Indian uprising in 1751. It was constructed of unfired adobe bricks, closely-spaced cottonwood or pine poles, grass, willow wands, and packed dirt. Today only low mounds mark the outline of the outpost, along with remains of the foundation.

The 1885 one-room **Old Tubac Schoolhouse**, also of adobe brick, has been restored. A **museum**, opened in 1954, displays material from Indian, Spanish, Mexican, and American cultures to relate their significance to the Presidio and Tubac, along with costumes, reproductions of Arizona's first newspaper, hand presses, and other artifacts. NR. Open daily 8-5:30. 50¢ adults. 398-2252.

Tucson

The Presidio that was originally founded at Tubac in the early 18th century was moved to Tucson in 1776 and was laid out as a military post for the Spanish approximately in the area now bounded by Washington, Pennington, and Church Sts., and Main Ave. The compound enclosed more than ten acres, covering twice the area of most such encampments—an indication of its importance. By 1820 nearly 400 people lived within the Presidio's walls, repeatedly defending themselves against Apache attack. Little by little, Mexicans ventured out of the Presidio to build houses nearby, using bricks from the fortress walls. Thus the walls began to disappear. With Mexico's independence from Spain in 1821, Spanish funding for the encampment ceased. But shortly thereafter adventurers began to arrive, some on their way to California. Attracted by the possibilities of this lively settlement along the lush banks of the Santa Cruz River, many stayed, or returned to Tucson after finding fortunes—or losing them—in the western gold fields. The cultural and historic influences on

Tucson's development—both Spanish and Anglo, Indian and Mexican—can be seen in its museums and historic districts, which are described in the pages following. Residents are proud of their colorful heritage and find many reasons to celebrate it. Parades, fiestas, and a wide variety of festivals are held annually—most in the cooler, more temperate winter and spring months. **The Tucson Convention and Visitor Bureau,** 120 West Broadway, 85726 (791-4768), can supply details about time and place.

Tucson is a sophisticated city, blessed with a hot, dry climate, the beauties of the surrounding desert, healthy modern industry, and fine resorts. Because of the attractions, it is growing at an alarming rate (as are other cities of the Southwest.) Vacationers and retirees are flocking to the area in ever-increasing numbers. One can only hope that the history which has been part of the area's attraction for newcomers in the first place will be vigorously preserved.

ARABIAN HORSE MUSEUM, 4633 E. Broadway. While the Stradling Museum of the Horse in Patagonia celebrates all horseflesh, Tucson's equine museum is devoted to one elegant breed. You'll find history, paintings, sculpture, saddles, trophies, photographs, and more—all about the beautiful and noble Arabian. Open all year, M-F 9-5. No charge. 326-1515. 🛉

ARIZONA HERITAGE CENTER (Arizona Historical Society), 949 E. 2nd St. A wealth of items describing and illustrating Tucson's past is exhibited here, including ranching equipment, clothing, American military weapons, and mining equipment. The Spanish Colonial and Mexican cultures, which strongly influenced Tucson's development, are explored. Historic houses under the Society's jurisdiction include the **Charles O. Brown House** (see following), the 1859 **American Flag Ranch House and Post Office,** and the 1890 **Oro Belle Mining Camp.** Open all year, M-Sa 9-5, Su 1-5. No charge. 628-5774.

ARIZONA STATE MUSEUM, University of Arizona. Indian cultures of Arizona and the Southwest from 10,000 years ago to the present are traced in great detail in this

Courtesy of Arizona Department of Transportation

Tucson

1. San Xavier del Bac
2. Tucson Museum of Art
3. Arizona Heritage Center
4. Arizona State Museum, University of Arizona

5. Fort Lowell
6. Pima Air Museum

Old Main, University of Arizona

museum located on the beautifully-land-scaped grounds of the university. While you're here, take a look at the first building on campus, **Old Main,** which dates from 1887. It's a one-story brick structure designed by James M. Creighton, a rare example of indigenous, eclectic building design. NR. The museum is open all year, M-Sa 9-5, Su 2-5. No charge. 626-1180.

ARMORY PARK HISTORIC DISTRICT, bounded by East 12th, 19th, and 2nd Streets and Stone Ave., 1880-1900. This was considered Tucson's most fashionable neighborhood in the latter part of the 19th century; it was then mainly inhabited by Southern Pacific Railroad employees whose new-found wealth gave them access to details of architectural styles which were new to Tucson: Queen Anne and Neo-Classical Revival. The historic district includes 90 such buildings south of the city's central business area. Most are still privately owned, including the 1908 Queen Anne-style **Weinzapfel Brammeier** House on Fourth Ave., which is worthy of special

mention. The **Tucson Public Library,** on South Sixth Ave., was built in 1900 with a grant from Andrew Carnegie and was designed by Henry Trost in the graceful Neo-Classical Revival style. If you stroll through the district, and then visit both the Barrio Libre and El Presidio districts, described following, you'll be immediately struck by the contrast of Spanish and Anglo architecture.

BARRIO LIBRE, bounded roughly by 14th and 19th Sts. and Stone and Osborne Aves., 19th century. This is one of only a few Southwestern neighborhoods which retain the 19th-century traditions of Hispanic architecture and culture. Although some examples of Anglo architecture sneak in here and there, the flavor is definitely Spanish—with adobe brick walls, roofs of vigas (beams) and saguaro ribs, and packed-earth floors. These are mostly one-story dwellings, since the brick walls lacked the structural strength necessary to support higher floors. One of the most interesting sights in Barrio Libre is **El**

El Tiradito (Wishing Shrine)

Tiradito, 221 S. Main St., the wishing shrine of adobe brick constructed in 1871. It was built near the spot where Juan Oliveras, a local outcast ("el tiradito") was murdered; he is reputed to grant wishes to those who pray at the site of his death before the statue of the Virgin Mary and the wrought-iron cross.

CHARLES O. BROWN HOUSE (The Old Adobe Patio), 40 West Broadway, 1850s-88. One of Tucson's oldest territorial homes, this was the residence of an early entrepreneur, who, on his arrival in the town at the age of 28, had already spent many successful months in the California gold fields. The house is in excellent condition and represents two distinct styles of adobe architecture, both Mexican-inspired territorial and a more elaborate Anglo. Brown took excellent care of his home, adding to it over the years with no expense spared in the process. NR. A restaurant and specialty shops are now located here, along with exhibits of early furnishings and memorabilia. Operated by the Arizona Historical Society. Open all year, Tu-Sa 10-4. No charge for museum. 628-5774.

EL PRESIDIO HISTORIC DISTRICT, bounded by North Court, North Meyer, North Main and Granada and by West Franklin, Council, West Washington and Alameda, 19th century. Resting upon a prehistoric Hohokam archaeological site,

Owl's Club, 378 N. Main Ave.

Steinfeld House, 300 N. Main Ave., El Presidio Historic District

El Presidio is comprised of approximately 90 buildings which trace Tucson's development from an 18th-century walled enclave, to the territorial years during which it expanded significantly, to the 19th century which heralded the arrival of the railroad and the Anglos who ran it. The building styles differ greatly, as one would expect: they run the gamut from traditional adobes with pyramidal roofs to the creations of Tucson's brilliant first-generation architects. One sight within the district not to be missed is:

The **Tucson Museum of Art,** 140 N. Main Ave. The museum operates several historically noteworthy buildings as part of its complex. **La Casa Cordova** (c. 1750) is possibly the oldest surviving structure in all of Tucson. It's a primitive L-shaped, single-story adobe house, built when the area was part of Mexico. By contrast, the **Edward Nye Fish House** (1868) was the city's social hub. A handsome Victorian with Brussels carpets, it was the home of a wealthy merchant and politician from Massachusetts. Still another contrast is provided by the ruins of the prehistoric **Hohokam pithouse,** dating between 700 and 900 A.D. The museum is open all

year, Tu-Sa 10-5, Su 1-5. No charge. 624-2333.

The **Pima County Courthouse,** a massive three-story landmark with a great dome highlighting its central section, dominates an entire block at 115 North Church Street. NR. Open during business hours. 792-8041.

Just north of El Presidio is **Levi Manning House,** 9 Paseo Redondo, which although not currently open to the public is well worth a look. This impressive house, on 10 acres of gardens and trees, was built in 1907 by a prominent local civic leader and entrepreneur. Of stuccoed brick on a rock

Levi Manning House

Pima County Courthouse

foundation, the mansion has wonderful details: three towers, and two porches floored with decorative tiles. The ceiling of one porch is painted with birds and flowers. Manning was reputed to have thrown wonderful parties at his showplace. NR.

FORT LOWELL MUSEUM, 2900 North Craycroft Rd., 1873-91. Located in Fort Lowell County Park, this museum recalls the Arizona Apache wars in great detail. Uniforms and military weapons are displayed, along with period furnishings. Fort Lowell, originally called the Post of Tucson, was an important supply depot for southern Arizona and a center for escort duties.

The 1875 **Commanding Officers Quarters** served as the home of Army Colonel Kautz and his family, among others. Kautz was commandant of the fort in 1886. Refurbished to depict life in an army outpost in the late 19th century, it is operated by the Arizona Historical Society. NR. Open

Oct-May, W-Sa 10-4; June-Sept, W-Sa 9-1. No charge. 885-3832.

FREMONT HOUSE, 949 East 2nd St., 1858. The once-common "Zaguan" plan of this adobe dwelling incorporates two separate living areas joined by a drive leading to an interior courtyard. John C. Fremont, 5th territorial governor of the state, is reputed to have lived here with his family. The walls are adobe covered with stucco; the wooden detailing over the two west doors is a special highlight. Collections of 19th-century furniture and decorative arts are housed within. NR. Open all year, W-Sa 10-4. No charge. 622-0956.

OLD TUCSON, 201 S. Kinney Rd. Built as a set for the movie *Arizona*, Old Tucson is a replica of the city as it is thought to have appeared in the 1860s. It is still the setting for both films and television shows, but has been expanded to include a Western amusement park with shops, an old jail and other buildings, and restaurant facilities. This is "history" with a large grain of salt, but take the kids here when they have had enough of museums and artifacts to see the staged daily gunfights and to ride in a narrow-gauge train or on a stagecoach. Open all year, daily 9-5:30. $5.95 adults, $3.45 children. 883-0100. 🏃

PIMA AIR MUSEUM, 6400 S. Wilmot Rd. This is another good place to bring petulant children and weary daddies, not to mention bona-fide aviation buffs, for there are more than 100 vintage aircraft displayed here, along with a unique collection of aviation lore and memorabilia, housed in a World War II wooden barracks. Open in winter, daily 9-5; in summer, daily 8-5. $2.50 adults, $1 children. 889-0462. 🏃

Tucson vicinity

MISSION SAN XAVIER DEL BAC, AZ 11, 9 miles south of Tucson, 1783-97. The celebrated Jesuit missionary and explorer Father Kino established the first church here in 1700. The present building, illustrated on the cover of this book, is widely considered the finest example of mission architecture in the country and exhibits Moorish, Byzantine, and late Mexico Rennaisance overtones. It is made of stucco and brick in a series of domes and arches, with all its surfaces decoratively painted. The central main facade is ornately carved and molded; the elaborate interior is Baroque. The place is enormously photogenic. It is now an active parish on the San Xavier Indian Reservation, with a **museum** of missionary and Spanish colonial artifacts nearby. NR, NHL. Open all year, daily. Museum: 9-6. Masses: M-F 8:30 a.m., Sa 7 p.m., Su 8, 10:30, 12:30. No charge. 294-2624.

Phoenix and the West

Camp Verde

FORT VERDE STATE HISTORIC PARK, off I-17, 1872-73. This 10-acre site is the best preserved military post from the time of General George Crook's campaign against the northern Apaches, who raided the Verde Valley for corn after the white man encroached on Indian hunting and gathering grounds. In addition to three officers' quarters, adjutants' buildings, and parade grounds, the area contains the **State Park General Museum**, with photographs from 1872-90, local military and domestic hardware, Indian artifacts, and furniture. NR. Open all year, daily 8-5:30. Adults 50¢. 567-3275. 🏃

Camp Verde vicinity

CLEAR CREEK PUEBLO AND CAVES, 4 miles SE of Fort Verde, 1100-1400. Excavated in 1890 by Dr. Edgar Mearns, who was stationed at Fort Verde, this is one of the largest prehistoric structures in Arizona, situated in what is now **Coconino**

National Forest. Comprised of over 50 rooms, 200-250 caves, a plaza, and, arguably, a ceremonial kiva, the highly-visible complex is situated on a terraced mesa overlooking West Clear Creek, a tributary of the Verde River. NR.

A half mile up the road is **Clear Creek Church**, (1890-1903), the first church built in the Verde Valley. Of hand-hewn limestone blocks quarried from a nearby site, the church, which has since been a school and a cannery, has a high gabled roof of cedar shingles. NR. Private, but visible from the public way.

For more information about the National Forest and pueblos, call 779-3311.

MONTEZUMA CASTLE NATIONAL MONUMENT, off I-17, 900-1425. This five-story, 20-room pueblo is one of the best preserved cliff dwellings in the United States. Although Montezuma himself never visited it, the site was named by white settlers who mistakenly believed it had been built by the Aztecs. The "castle" and a similar structure, **Castle A,** nearby,

Commanding Officer's House, Fort Verde

Officers' Quarters, Fort Verde

were erected by an Indian tribe known as the Sinagua, who worked the flat farmlands of the Verde River terrace, four miles away. These impressive house clusters were built of river boulders and limestone laid in adobe mortar, and were occupied for two centuries until overpopulation and drought caused the community's demise.

Montezuma Well, 9½ miles northeast of the castle, is a limestone sink 470 feet in diameter and 55 feet deep. The Sinagua and later Hohokam Indians diverted its water into irrigation ditches that flowed down into their farmland. Because of preservative qualities of the lime in the water, the ditches are still visible today. Make the **visitor center** your first stop for a look at exhibits which help explain this historic architecture and the people responsible for it. NR. Open Labor Day-May 31, daily 8-5; June 1-Labor Day, daily 7-7. $1 per car. 576-3322.

Clarkdale

TUZIGOOT NATIONAL MONUMENT, 2 miles east of Clarkdale, 1000-1400. 120 feet above the Verde Valley stands this ancient remnant of a prehistoric pueblo, two stories high, which its inhabitants entered first via ladders to the roof, then through narrow hatchways leading directly into the 110 rooms. The Tuzigoot Indians (the name means "crooked water") were joined in 1125 by the Sinagua, and the two tribes lived together peacefully until the legendary 13th-century Southwestern drought, which lasted 84 years, decimated the area. There is a **museum** with collections of ancient grave offerings, tur-

quoise mosaics, and jewelry made of shells traded from California Gulf Indians, recovered by two University of Arizona professors during the 1930s. Nearby are the similarly intriguing **Hatalacva Ruins,** which existed at the same time as the Tuzigoot settlement. These ruins constitute an authentic Sinagua "culture site," complete with pueblo ruins and trash mounds. NR. Open daily in winter 8-5, daily in summer 7-7. $1 per car. 634-5564.

Fredonia vicinity

PIPE SPRING NATIONAL MONUMENT, AZ 389, 15 miles southwest of Fredonia. So-called because of the free-flowing water that attracted thirsty wayfarers in the arid Arizona Strip, the monument honors the memory of Mormons who found, settled, and developed this area of the Southwest. Because the prairies were unsuited to farming, early settlers raised horses and the fierce breed of cattle known as Texas longhorns. A fort on the premises, once called **Winsor Castle,** was built in the early 1870s of native red sandstone, ponderosa pine, and earth—a relic of the days when Navajo raids made life in the new territory difficult for these pioneers. Many of them, being Mormons, were polygamous. A trail alongside the fort was dubbed the "Honeymoon Trail" because so many young couples traveled it on returning from weddings at a nearby temple. Tours of the fort and the monument area, which includes a harness room, telegraph room, spring room, blacksmith shop, cheese-making room and a corral of juniper logs, are available. NR. Open June 1-Sept 1, daily 7:30-6; Sept 2-May 31, daily 7:30-5. 50¢ adults. 643-5505.

Jerome

JEROME STATE HISTORIC PARK, U.S. 89A, 1883. Like Bisbee to the south, Jerome was once a swaggering, wide-open mine town. The former copper center of the world, it was named for the cousin of Winston Churchill's mother. Eugene Jerome was a New York financier for United Verde Copper Company, which flourished here to the tune of nearly two million pounds of copper a year. Jerome's narrow streets wind dizzily up the Mingus Mountains; old frame houses on stilts cling to the sides of cliffs. The precarious look of the place has some validity, for Jerome has been gradually slipping downhill since a powerful dynamite blast in 1925. One of the original homes, the **James H. Douglass Mansion,** is now a museum displaying objects related to mining history in the Black Hills. Across the street is a water-jacket blast furnace dating to 1883. NR, NHL. Open all year, daily 8-5:30. 50¢ adults. 634-5381.

Kingman

MOHAVE MUSEUM OF HISTORY AND ARTS, 400 W. Beale. Artifacts revealing the history of Mohave County are on display here — local history books and manuscripts; Indian items; archaeological, anthropological, and military exhibits; a blacksmith shop. Local Indian souvenirs and goods are offered for sale, and lectures and tours may be arranged. Open all year, M-F 10-5, Sa-Su 1-5. No charge. 753-3195.

Kingman vicinity

OATMAN, 24 miles southwest of Kingman via AZ 66, 1906. Oatman, affectionately called the "Heart of the Gold Mines," was born during the boom years of the early 20th century and was once a city of thousands. Millions of dollars in gold were mined in the area from the first strikes until the 1930s. Fox Fire, starring Jeff Chandler and Jane Russell as a mining executive and his socialite wife, was filmed here, as were several other westerns whose producers were attracted to the beautiful countryside and the rustic town buildings. Now mock shootouts are occasionally staged in the main street, where wild burros roam freely, and weekend swap-meet stands do a brisk trade. Old mine sites, a hotel, and several antique shops lodged in the early buildings are worth a visit, and the Black Mountains are a rock-hound's paradise. 735-6106.

Parker

COLORADO RIVER INDIAN TRIBES MUSEUM, Second Ave. at Mojave Rd. Founded in 1953, the museum has excellent archaeological and anthropological exhibits: Mojave, Hopi, and Navajo histories are well-documented, as are those of less-familiar tribes such as the Chemhuevi, Patayan, and Mogollon. Open all year, M-F 8-5, Sa 10-3. No charge. 669-9211, ext. 213.

The **Old Presbyterian Church,** southwest of Parker on Second Ave., is administered by the museum. A crude building of mud and sticks was erected on the site in 1910 by Presbyterian missionaries who had come to convert the Mojave Indians. Seven years later the original timbers were recycled into this adobe brick structure with an open square wooden belfry and gable roof. The rectangular, one-room mission measures a mere 43 by 24 feet. Since the church's construction it has served as a religious and community center for the area tribes. NR.

Phoenix

Named for the fabled bird of ancient Egypt which was supposed to have arisen from the ashes of its own funeral pyre, Phoenix was settled in the early 1870s by pioneers who made their first encampment on the grounds of an ancient Indian ruin (see Pueblo Grande Museum, following). Arizona's largest city and state capital has grown alarmingly in recent years, as thousands are drawn to its dry, temperate climate to vacation or to live permanently. Because of its rapid development, history has to some extent been sacrificed. Few early buildings remain, but many museums harbor the relics of pioneer times. The **Convention and Visitors Bureau** at 2701 E. Camelback Road (957-0070) can help the visitor to ferret out remnants of the past, as can the museum staffs at the various facilities listed here.

ARIZONA CAPITOL MUSEUM, 1700 W. Washington, 1900. Housed in the Neo-classical Revival granite **Capitol Building,** the museum's collection displays

Courtesy of Arizona Department of Transportation

Phoenix and vicinity

1. Pioneer Arizona
2. Arizona Capitol Museum
3. Arizona Museum
4. Heritage Square
5. Arizona Historical Society
6. Heard Museum
7. Pueblo Grande Museum
8. Hall of Flame

vintage newspapers, including a 1912 edition recounting a murder and suicide that took place there. There is a piano believed to be one of the first in America, and the flag with 45 stars carried by Teddy Roosevelt and his Rough Riders up San Juan Hill in 1898. The office of Arizona's first state governor, George Wylie Paul Hunt, has been preserved; he was reelected seven times! The Arizona Mining Association contributed 30,000 pounds of copper for the roof and dome. NR. Open all year, M-F 8-5. Tours at 10 and 2:30 daily. 255-4675.

ARIZONA HISTORICAL SOCIETY (Central Arizona Museum of History), 1242 N. Central Ave., 1917. Housed in the old **Ellis-Shackelford** mansion, displays include a costume gallery, early 1900s drugstore, a mine tunnel, and a hands-on museum for children. Built of "tapestry brick" — wire-cut brick made in Colorado — the mansion was designed by a Swiss architect named Thoma who supervised the installation of electrical wiring and outlets long before such things were common. The house was indeed unique: it had solar hot-water heat, a central vacuum system, and automatic flush toilets. Open all year, Tu-Sa 10-4. No charge. 253-4479.

ARIZONA HISTORY ROOM, FIRST NATIONAL BANK OF ARIZONA, First Ave. and Washington St., 1877. This reconstruction of the **Territorial Bank,** the first chartered bank in the Arizona territory, has pine floors, pressed tin ceilings, brass-grille tellers' cages and spittoons, and an old tear-gas device intended for use on robbers. It recalls the days of "rough" banking, when nervous tellers hid gold under crumpled paper in a wastebasket because the vaults were easy prey to holdup men. Bank records from pre-statehood Arizona are on display, as is original furniture from the old bank, including chair seats bearing marks worn in by the rivets of ranchers' jeans. Open all year, M-F 10-3. No charge. 271-6879.

THE ARIZONA MUSEUM, 1002 Van Buren St. Established in 1923, the museum has an eclectic assortment of Arizona artifacts, ranging from pioneer relics and clothing to Kachina dolls and the first motorcycle engine. Also on display are paintings, minerals, prehistoric and Indian artifacts, and two steam locomotives. Open Sept-May, W-Su 10-4; June-July, W-Su 9-12. No charge. 253-2734.

HALL OF FLAME, 6101 E. Van Buren St. Its whimsical name notwithstanding, this is a unique collection of fire-fighting equipment, featuring steam engines, hand- and horse-drawn vehicles, and motor-powered fire engines from around the world. The history of the Fire Service is well-documented in the 4,000-volume library, where old manuals are available for use on the premises. Guided tours. Open all year, M-Sa 9-5. $1.50 adults, 50¢ students. 275-3473.

THE HEARD MUSEUM, 22 E. Monte Vista Rd. The cultural history of the American Southwest is a long and fascinating one, and there is no better place in Phoenix to get an overview of the early tribes that inhabited the plains, mesas, and hills of the state. Temporary and permanent exhibits display the arts and crafts of native Americans and other non-Western cultures. Open all year, M-Sa 10-5, Su 1-5. $1.50 adults, 50¢ children. 252-8848.

HERITAGE SQUARE, 6th St. and Monroe, c. 1890s. This area of restored early homes, specialty shops, and restaurants includes a rare example of Victorian architecture in Phoenix, **Rosson House,** a handsome edifice designed in the Eastlake style, which was the home of Dr. Ronald Rosson, an army physician stationed at nearby Fort McDowell. It features a wraparound veranda, a shingled roof with a hexagonal turret, and an elaborate old lightning rod. The house has been furnished to the period, and tours are available. NR. Open W-Sa 10-4, Su 12-4. $1 adults, 50¢ children.

The **Information Center** just south of Rosson House is the place for tickets to tour the mansion and for information about other historic homes around the square, including the 1900 **Teeter House.** 262-6711.

PIONEER ARIZONA, Black Canyon Stage, I-17 at Pioneer Rd., 19th century. This outdoor living history museum of Arizona in the late 19th century has 26 historic exhibits, including a jail, bank, lumberyard and carpenter shop, miners' camp, blacksmith, and original buildings from the Mogollon Rim. The livestock, garden, and orchard that would have served a typical ranch family are available for perusal, and amenities such as a restaurant, shops, craft demonstrations, and a horse-drawn wagon tour make this a pleasant all-day history lesson. Open Oct-May, Tu-Su 9-5; June-Sept, Tu-Su 8-4. $3.50 adults, $3 senior citizens, $2.50 students, $1.25 children. 993-0210. ⛪

PUEBLO GRANDE MUSEUM, 4619 E. Washington. Excavated by a Smithsonian Institution team in the 1930s and '40s, the ruins here date from 200 B.C. to the final phase of occupation, 1150-1450 A.D. This is one of the few remaining large Hohokam village sites in the Southwest, with a recreation ball court and platform mounds 20 feet above the desert floor. Nearby is the **Park of Four Waters,** four prehistoric irrigation canals that served the inhabitants. The museum has collections of Hohokam artifacts, as well as archaeological and historic exhibits. NR. NHL. Museum open all year, M-Sa 9-4:45, Su 1-4:45. Admission 50¢. Ruins open all year, M-F 9-5, Su 1-5. 275-3452.

Prescott

Set in a pine valley between the desert and the mountains, Prescott was settled in 1863 after the Walker Party discovered gold in the central Arizona highlands. The settlement was almost immediately named the territorial capital, as its new residents, removed from the strife of the Civil War and concerned mainly with working their claims, were thought to have no political axe to grind for either the south or the north. Tucson, a far more settled community, was felt to harbor strong southern sentiment, and was therefore bypassed in Prescott's favor. Because of its new importance, and the success of the mines, the town grew quickly, and was the scene of many Arizona firsts. The year 1864 saw the opening of the first school in the territory, along with the first sawmill. While the capital was moved only three years later to rival Tucson, causing economic hardship for a time, Prescott remained as the county seat of Yavapai, largest of the four counties into which the territory had been divided, and one blessed with rich mineral resources.

Most of the town is included in the **Territorial Buildings Multiple Resource Area,** a National Register designation given because of its many remaining early buildings, which together make up one of the oldest and finest preserved collections of American architecture in the Southwest,

Courthouse Plaza fountain, Prescott

Courthouse Plaza bandstand, Prescott

Governor's Mansion

with styles ranging from Mission and Bungalow to Queen Anne, Renaissance Revival, and Eastlake.

The **Courthouse Plaza Historic District**, within the multiple resource area, is bounded by Gurley, Montezuma, Goodwin, and Cortex Streets, and is home to the impressive **Yavapai County Courthouse** and also to the more suspect **Whiskey Row**, so named because of the many saloons and gambling halls which once lined the street. The **Palace Bar**, a well-preserved saloon from the turn of the century, now houses a popular art gallery.

SHARLOT HALL MUSEUM COMPLEX, 415 West Gurley St., 19th century. This group of historic buildings is named for Sharlot Hall, once Arizona's state historian and a well-known poet. The building which bears her name was constructed

of native rock and pine logs during the Depression. It features a gallery of clothing, photographs, and American Indian artifacts such as Yavapai/Western Apache baskets. Behind it is the **Iron Turbine Windmill**, an early 20th-century structure still in production. NR.

The **Governor's Mansion** is a two-story log house built for Arizona's first territorial governor, John N. Goodwin, in 1864. It has been restored and furnished with period items. NR. The **William C. Bashford House** is an elegantly furnished 1877 Victorian full of territorial antiques. Threatened with demolition in 1973, it was saved by citizens of Prescott, who raised $25,000, donated materials for restoration, and volunteered labor to move it to its present site.

Old Fort Misery (1876) is a two-room log cabin, the home of Arizona's first lawyer, John Howard. The 1877 **John C. Fremont House,** a frame building furnished to the period, was home to Arizona's fifth territorial governor. In a **Memorial Rose Garden** on the complex grounds grow more than 350 different varieties of roses, honoring that number of exceptional women in Arizona history. Periodically there are demonstrations at one or another of the historic houses where costumed volunteers reenact spinning, wool carding, quilting, blacksmithing, butter churning and other crafts little practiced today. Open all year, Tu-Sa 9-5, Su 1-5. Donations accepted. 445-3122.

Scottsdale

TALIESIN WEST, 106th St. and East Shea Blvd., 1938. One of Frank Lloyd Wright's most important works, this complex of interacting buildings served as his winter-spring headquarters. Designed in "kinship" with its desert setting, the complex has what has been called the most sumptuous masonry of the 20th century—horizontally striated walls recalling the Mayan stonework which Wright admired. Taliesin, named for a 6th-century Welsh bard (Wright was of Welsh descent) echoes all the architect's major principles; it is geometric, multi-leveled, and emulates the spaciousness of the desert mesa. Glass, plastic, wood, and rock are the materials Wright used in creating this spectacular environment with low ceilings, garden walls, pools, and terraces. The angular drafting room and the theater, which burned in 1964 but which have been completely restored, are of particular note—they are roofed in translucent plastic (originally, canvas) to filter and direct the desert's intense, enveloping light. Taliesin West is now a living and working facility for architects. NR. Open all year, daily 10-4, with tours on the half hour. $3.00 adults, $1.00 children under 12. 948-6670.

Tempe

TEMPE HISTORICAL MUSEUM, 3500 S. Rural Rd., 19th and 20th centuries. Exhibits include documents, photographs, and objects relevant to the early history of Tempe. Farm and ranch tools and vehicles (an old chuck wagon, for instance), toys, clothing, furniture, and domestic implements give clues to what life was like in this town close to Phoenix. Historic houses on the grounds are the 1888 **Tempe Bakery,** 1892 **Hackett House,** and 1892 **Niels Peterson House.** Tours may be arranged. Open all year, Tu-Sa 9-5. No charge. 966-7902.

Wickenburg

DESERT CABALLEROS WESTERN MUSEUM, 20 N. Frontier St. The history of this once-lusty gold mining town is explained through Indian and late pioneer artifacts, as well as mineral, art, and mining displays. The Maricopa County town is extremely well-preserved, although the settlement near the **Vulture Gold Mine** (see following) has the starkness of a typical southwestern ghost town. Open all year, Tu-Sa 10-4, Su 1-4. $1 adults. 684-2272.

Wickenburg vicinity

VULTURE GOLD MINE, Vulture Mine Rd., 13 miles west of Wickenburg, 1863. Henry Wickenburg, an Austrian originally named Heinrich Heintzel, came to America in 1862 and joined the stream of expectant gold prospectors headed west. He discovered the gold deposit that became Vulture Mine a year later. A self-guided tour of the area reveals remnants of a millsite community called Vulture City; an original mine shaft, assay office, and other buildings are worth a stop. Ironically, although his mine produced millions of dollars worth of ore, Wickenburg was penniless when he ended his life with a Colt revolver. Today, Vulture City is a ghost town, where you may wander at will. The mine is open mid-Sept to mid-May, daily 9-5. No charge. 259-9785.

Yuma

CENTURY HOUSE MUSEUM AND GARDENS, 240 S. Madison Ave., 1870. One of Yuma's early merchants, Eugene A. Sanguinetti, had this impressive adobe house built in 1870; it was enlarged after

1885. Photographs, documents, and objects chronicle the history of Yuma County's social and economic development. The building, now furnished as an Arizona Territory home, is operated by the Arizona Historical Society. Open all year, Tu-Sa 10-4. No charge. 783-8020.

YUMA CROSSING AND ASSOCIATED SITES, banks of the Colorado River, 18th and 19th centuries. This area was a significant communication and transportation hub during the Spanish colonial period and the western expansion movement. The Yuma Crossing, a narrow, fairly tranquil point in the raging Colorado River, was traversed by almost every person entering southern California from the southeast during the turbulent days of the gold rush. The surviving buildings of Fort Yuma, on the California side, were erected during the height of the rush, in 1850. The fort is now headquarters for the Yuma Indian Reservation, whose Quechan Indian Museum displays relics of that tribe in one of many structures of the strategically located old military outpost. Open all year, M-F 8-5. Admission 50¢. (714) 572-0661.

The Customhouse Museum, on the Arizona side, is thought to be the oldest Anglo structure in Yuma, dating from the mid-19th century. It was used by the Customs Service for offices and residence until 1955. Open all year, Tu-M, 10-2. No charge. 782-9314.

The fort's Quartermaster Depot (1864) is nearby, not far from the Yuma Territorial Prison State Historic Park (1876). Built by convicts, the prison proper was one of the frontier's most secure jails—breakouts were rare. A museum here displays general history, photographs, Indian artifacts, and memorabilia relating to the prison's unhappy history. NR, NHL. Open all year, daily 8-5:30. 50¢ adults. 783-4771. [image]

YUMA FINE ARTS ASSOCIATION, 281 Gila St. Contemporary Arizona paintings, ceramics, sculpture, photographs, and graphics are housed in the Southern Pacific Railroad Depot, a Spanish Colonial Revival building constructed in 1926, which was the checkpoint for the Transcontinental Railroad's crossing of the Colorado River. NR. Open Sept-May, Tu-Sa 10-5. No charge. 783-2314.

Northeast Canyon Country

Adamana vicinity

PETRIFIED FOREST NATIONAL PARK, southeast of Adamana, off U.S. 180. 180 million years ago, giant pine-like trees fell into what was then a floodplain, decayed slowly under a cloak of mud and silt, and were hardened by siliac deposits into what we call petrified wood today. The phenomenon was discovered in the mid-1800s by Army surveyors; now the Petrified Forest is a sprawling preserve of great interest. The Painted Desert petroglyphs of animals, handprints, geometric designs, and human representations—the early Anasazi and Pueblo Indians method of recording life as they knew it—are here. The 93,493 acres of the Petrified Forest area include pithouse and pueblo village ruins such as

Puerco Ruins, Flattop Site, and Twin Buttes, all of which were occupied by farming or earlier hunting tribes. Hiking and camping information is available at the Visitor Center at the northern entrance or at the Rainbow Museum at the south end, where explanatory natural history and historic exhibits are featured. Be forewarned: there is no water away from the developed areas. NR. Open all year, daily dawn to dusk. $1 per car. 524-6228. [image]

Chinle

CANYON DE CHELLY NATIONAL MONUMENT, AZ 63, 300-1300 Within these steep-walled canyons are ruins of several hundred prehistoric Pueblo dwellings. The best known cliff villages are the **White House, Mummy Cave** with its three-story tower house, and **Antelope House,** named for paintings of that animal done by the Pueblos' Navajo descendants 150 years ago. There are a few present-day Navajos living in summer homes along the canyon floors today. Relics of the ancient Basket-maker Indians are well preserved because of the arid climate. Four periods of Indian culture unfolded within the red walls of this canyon: Basketmaker (early Anasazi), Pueblo (later Anasazi), Hopi, and today's Navajo. Because of the canyon's intriguing but somewhat treacherous topography, travel in the canyons is allowed only if the visitor is accompanied by an authorized guide or park ranger. Commercial jaunts in four-wheel-drive vehicles are organized at **Thunderbird Lodge.** NR. Open Memorial Day-Labor Day, daily 8-7; Labor Day-Memorial Day, daily 8-5. No charge for admission to park. 674-5436. 🏃

Flagstaff vicinity

LOWELL OBSERVATORY, 1 mile west on Mars Hill, 1894. The planet Pluto was discovered through the 24-foot refracting telescope installed in 1896 at the observatory, founded by Dr. Percival Lowell. The first observable evidence of the expanding universe was also seen here, in 1912, by Dr. V.N. Slipher. The museum complex contains an 1894 library of native field-stone, a 1914 administration building, and the telescope's original circular housing. The late 19th-century telescope is still in use. The advancement of planetary science today owes much to discoveries made in the past century at this Coconino County site. NR, NHL. Open all year, guided tours M-F 1:30-2:30; also F 8-10 p.m. from June-Aug (including telescope viewing). No charge. Tickets must be obtained from the **Chamber of Commerce** in Flagstaff, 101 W. Santa Fe. 774-4505. 🏃

MUSEUM OF NORTHERN ARIZONA, Fort Valley Rd., 3 miles north on U.S. 180, 1886. **The Homestead,** believed to be the oldest house in the Flagstaff area, was built of logs by the area's first permanent settler. It now contains a library of natural

sciences, a ceramic repository, Indian textiles, jewelry and art, and an herbarium. NR. Open all year, daily 9-5. $1.50 adults, $1 students. 774-5211.

NORTHERN ARIZONA PIONEERS' HISTORICAL SOCIETY, Fort Valley Rd. The career of Dr. Percival Lowell, founder of Lowell Observatory, is documented here through photographs, manuscripts, and other articles. There is also a wonderful collection of old movie cameras and photos of the first trip on the Colorado River. Rough Riders memorabilia is on display, as are clothing, furniture, letters, farm and lumbering tools, and military objects, all of which give the visitor the flavor of the early Oak Creek/Red Rock area. The museum is housed in the 1907 **Old County Hospital for the Indigent.**

    Ben Dohey Cabin, nearby on North Fort Valley Rd., is a three-room wood-frame house, built in 1882. It is typical of the sort of residence built by territorial settlers. NR. Open all year, M-Sa 9-5, Su 1:30-5. No charge. 774-6272.

SUNSET CRATER NATIONAL MONUMENT, AZ 3, 1064-1250. The park **museum and visitor center** displays archaeological artifacts of the prehistoric Sinagua Indians, including hand tools and domestic items. The monument is notable for its collection of geological specimens of the area; especially well told is the story of the volcanic action which occurred in the San Francisco Peaks Volcanic Field and caused the eruption of the crater in 1064. Open in summer, daily 7-7; in winter, daily 8-5. No charge. 526-0586.

WALNUT CANYON NATIONAL MONUMENT, 8 miles east of Flagstaff on U.S. 66, 100-1200. Having developed the craft of masonry, the Sinagua arrived in Walnut Canyon 900 years ago and put it to use building 300 small cliff rooms in the limestone walls of the canyon. A rather strenuous trip via paved foot trail leads up to 25 of the dwellings; from the trail, about 100 more are visible. The rooms can be viewed from a short trail along the rim of the canyon as well. The **Old Headquarters,** Walnut Canyon's first visitor center, is now a museum. The 1904 log building has a curious recessed rear porch with an alligator cypress tree growing through a hole in its roof. NR. Open May 31-Labor Day, daily 7-7; Labor Day-May 30, daily 8-5. $1 per car. 526-3367.

WUPATKI NATIONAL MONUMENT, 30 miles north of Flagstaff off U.S. 89, 1100-1215. After the eruption of Sunset Crater, black volcanic ash turned the earth into rich farmland, and the Anasazi and Sinagua congregated to take advantage of the fertile lands. One of the longest inhabited villages that resulted from the migration of farming tribes is the Wupatki, from the Hopi word for "tall house." This red sandstone pueblo, and the nearly 800 others nearby, include ball courts, pit houses, and an open-air amphitheater. There are self-guided tours to the ruins and a series of displays with Sinagua and Anasazi artifacts. NR. Open daily in summer, 9-7; in winter, 8-5. No charge. 774-7000.

Fort Apache

FORT APACHE HISTORIC DISTRICT, 10 miles northwest of Cibecue, 1870. The original Fort Apache military post was established in 1870 as a temporary camp; troops and officers took shelter in tents along the south bank of the East Fork of the White River. The site has 18 historically significant buildings, and the ruins of two lime kilns, machinery foundations, and a reservoir, as well as two Apache

Scout camp sites and a military cemetery. The evolution of construction and building techniques from 1870 to 1922 are reflected in the variety of structures here. The fort, which today houses an Indian reservation, has several notable prehistoric petroglyphs and pueblo ruins, the most famous of which is **Grasshopper Ruin,** settled during the drought of 1275-95. About 20 of the 300 rooms have been excavated to date; numerous artifacts and burials have been uncovered. Fort Apache was abandoned as a military post in 1924. The **Theodore Roosevelt Indian School** was established here in 1923, and is still in use. NR.

Ganado

HUBBELL TRADING POST, Navajo Indian Reservation, 1 mile west of Ganado, 1876. The oldest surviving post of its kind, this was begun by John Lorenzo Hubbell, an honest entrepreneur who was the most successful trader with the Navajo. In its heyday a sort of general store and gossip center, the long, low post influenced the revival of rug weaving among the Indians, a craft which became an important means of financial survival for them. Today the Hubbell home displays crafts and paintings and looks much as it did a century ago. Baskets, saddles and saddlebags, silver and turquoise jewelry, rugs, blankets, and water jugs are prominently featured.

Grasshopper Ruin

Fort Apache military cemetery

Surprisingly, the post still operates much as it did at its inception, when John Hubbell opened his doors to travelers and dispensed advice to his Navajo friends. Operated by the National Park Service. NR. Open daily in summer, 8-6; in winter, 8-5. No charge. 755-3475.

Globe vicinity

ROOSEVELT DAM, Salt River, 31 miles northwest of Globe on AZ 88, 1906-11. The world's highest masonry dam is an awesome sight, rising 284 feet and extending for 1,125. It provides water for the **Salt River Irrigation Complex**, a direct descendant of ancient Hohokam irrigation lines, similar Pima Indian projects, and those of thirsty 19th-century settlers. **Roosevelt Lake**, formed by the dam, irrigates over a quarter-million acres of land. NR, NHL.

TONTO NATIONAL MONUMENT, 28 miles northwest of Globe on AZ 88, 14th century. The Salado Indians, who gathered and farmed in the desert, were a Pueblo tribe. Three of their villages, built of masonry and roofed with mud and poles, are preserved at this monument—

and they're extremely accessible compared to some of the other dwellings in the Southwest. It's a pleasant walk to the **Lower Ruins** and their annex through desert vegetation similar to that utilized by the Salado in their medicines and foods. A trip to the 40-room **Upper Ruin**, however, the best preserved of the unit, requires advance arrangements with the National Park Service. Excavated pottery, jewelry, and textiles are on display. NR. The **Visitor Center** and **Museum** are open all year, daily 8-5. Self-guided trails are open daily 8-4. 50¢ per person, $1 per car. 467-2241.

Grand Canyon

EL TOVAR HOTEL AND STABLES, AZ 64, 1905. This truly incredible establishment on the North Rim of the Canyon was designed by Charles Whittlesey in a modified T-shape; its view of the Canyon is spectacular. It has been called a big country clubhouse, been compared to a Norwegian villa, and has a dining room decorated in 15th-century "elegance." Somehow, all the incongruous elements of this stone, frame, log, and clapboard lodge

El Tovar Hotel

work together, and the effect is wonderful. Among its many delights are a private dining room with Indian deer hieroglyphics on its walls, oriental rugs, French-inspired curtains, majestic beamed ceilings, a solarium, and a poetry quotation in metal letters on a porch lintel. Its stables—three frame buildings with board-and-batten lower sections and shingled upper sections—once served as blacksmith shop and barn for horses and mules. The eclectic design of the place is typical of the turn of the century, and happily, not much has been changed. NR. (See also Lodging and Dining.)

GRAND CANYON NATIONAL PARK, Grand Canyon. Once you've satisfied yourself with the astounding views of the Canyon, formed by the Colorado River between 5 and 25 million years ago, and taken a walk on the Canyon desert, explore some of these man-made attractions: Buildings in the **Grand Canyon Village Historic District** (1890-1930), represent such architectural styles as Shingle Mission (**Verkamp's Souvenir Shop**) and the imitation Swiss chalet; the terraced stone **Hopi House** (1905) is especially exotic. The area

retains the ambience of an early 20th-century resort. The **Railroad Station** (1909) saw many train passengers on their way to and from the Canyon after the railroad went through in 1898. Old mine shafts and machinery from 1892 to 1907 may be viewed at the ruins of **Grandview Mine.** Buckey O'Neill, a well-known judge, sheriff, author, reporter and editor, killed in the charge up San Juan Hill, is remembered in the cabin which bears his name (1890s).

One of the earliest **water reclamation plants** in the country is located here: it was established in 1926 to reclaim precious water on the south rim of the canyon, and today displays pre-sedimentation and aeration tanks, storage and holding tanks, and screening boxes.

Red Horse Stage Station, also known as the Old Post Office and the Cameron Hotel, is an integral part of the Canyon area history because it did serve all three functions, from its erection in the 1890s until 1935, when the Santa Fe Railroad bought it and converted it into a two-room tourist cabin. The one-story log house is still used for that purpose as part of Bright Angel Lodge.

The remains of a U-shaped Anasazi pueblo, the **Tusayan Ruins**, have two round ceremonial kivas and a two-story dwelling. Nearby is the **Tusayan Museum**, which interprets the ruins and offers other exhibits on early man. Open daily all year, summer, 9-8; winter, 9-5. No charge.

There is a wealth of history in the Grand Canyon, both ancient and modern, which is interpreted both at the visitors centers and at the **Yavapai Museum**, one mile east of Grand Canyon Village. Open daily, summer 9-8, winter 9-5. No charge.

The south rim of the canyon is most accessible: the north rim is often blocked by snowdrifts in winter. NR. The park is open daily all year, summer, 7-8; winter, 8-5. $2 per car. 638-2411.

Kayenta vicinity

NAVAJO NATIONAL MONUMENT, 30 miles southwest of Kayenta, 1200-1300. In the middle of a Navajo Indian reservation stand the largest and best-preserved of Arizona's cliff dwelling ruins—and given the state's abundance of riches, that's really saying something. Three major Anasazi ruins, one 450 feet in length, were excavated in the 1900s, although a date carved in one of them is, mysteriously, 1661, and all are open to the public. Because of the fragility of these pueblos, however, the number of visitors is restricted to 20 per day, so advance planning is essential. Navajo rugs, jewelry, silver work, and pottery are displayed, and an **archaeological museum** gives further insight into prehistoric Indian culture. NR. Open all year, daily 8-5. $1 per car. 672-2366.

Lee's Ferry

NAVAJO STEEL ARCH HIGHWAY BRIDGE (Grand Canyon Bridge), southwest of Lee's Ferry on US 89A, 1928. 1200 tons of steel were used in the construction of this span across the Colorado River. The bridge is significant in that it

Navajo Steel Arch Highway Bridge

Old Orabi

allowed travelers, for the first time, to enter the Grand Canyon area from either the north or the south, and to traverse the canyon. The steel workers on the project refused to allow a safety net to be hung below the bridge, citing the toll its "mental hazards" would take on their performance. Four men lost their lives on the bridge, which was dedicated in 1929. At that time, it was the highest steel arch bridge in the United States. Its appearance has not been altered in the last fifty years. Open all year.

Oraibi

OLD ORAIBI, Hopi Indian Reservation, 1300-present. Old Oraibi is probably the oldest continuously inhabited pueblo in the Southwest—consisting of seven house rows, with most houses three- or four-stories high; 13 kivas, and a number of enclosed courts. Owned by the Hopi Tribe, it is not accessible to the public at present. NR, NHL.

Page

GLEN CANYON NATIONAL RECREATION AREA, US 89. Its name inspired by the wooden glens along the banks of the

Colorado River, Glen Canyon is a majestic landscape of sandstone cliffs between which Glen Canyon Dam was built in the late 1950s, creating the 186-mile-long Lake Powell. The lake was named for John Wesley Powell, a hero during the Civil War, who led an expedition down the Colorado River in 1869 and was later named director of the U.S. Geologic Survey. Visitors may take self-guided tours of the dam daily. The largest known natural stone bridge, **Rainbow Bridge,** may be toured by boat. There are Pueblo ruins to explore, with artifacts from ancient farming and hunting tribes that once lived on the canyon bottom. NR. Open all year, daily 8:30-5. No charge. 645-2471.

JOHN WESLEY POWELL MEMORIAL MUSEUM, 6 N. 7th Ave. In the 1860s and '70s, Powell mapped the Glen Canyon area and gave names to many of its geographical features. The history of his life is documented at the memorial museum, along with archaeology, anthropology, ethnology, and geography of the area. Indian artifacts, coins, and minerals are displayed, and relevant historical films are often shown. Open in spring and fall, M-Sa 9-5; in winter, M-F 10-4; in summer, daily 8-7. No charge. 645-2741.

Snowflake

Groups of Mormon immigrants from Salt Lake City settled Snowflake in 1879, on instructions from their church leaders. The small community is like many Mormon towns in northern Arizona which were begun to solidify and expand the church's position throughout the Southwest. Among the noteworthy early residences which still stand is the **John Freeman house,** constructed in 1893 by one of the church's most influential business and civic leaders. Freeman lived in the house for 60 years before his death in 1952 at the age of 92. During his lifetime he was actively involved in the Arizona Co-operative Mercantile Institute (ACMI), a business established by the Mormon community to support the settlement of the area. NR. Privately owned.

Whiteriver vicinity

KINISHBA RUINS, 15 miles west of Whiteriver, 1250-1350. The inhabitants of this large pueblo, perhaps as many as 1000 of them, were a blend of Mogollon and Anasazi ancestry. They were primarily farmers, and manufactured storage, table, and ceremonial pottery. The rectangular dwelling consists of two large and seven small masonry buildings, with two enclosed courtyards typical of late 13th- and early 14th-century architecture. The pueblo was abandoned in 1400. It is now operated by the University of Arizona. NR, NHL. Open daily 8-5. No charge.

Window Rock

NAVAJO TRIBAL MUSEUM, AZ 264. Founded in 1961, the museum houses permanent and temporary exhibits on Navajo history, ethnology, herbology, and arts and crafts, as well as collections of manuscripts, maps, and photographs. The geology and paleontology of the Window Rock area is explained. It is an important cultural center for the Navajo, one of the most progressive Indian tribes. Open May-Sept, M-Sa 9-5, Su 1-5; Oct-Apr, M-F 9-5. No charge. 871-4941.

ST. MICHAEL'S MISSION, 2 miles west of Window Rock, 1895. Window Rock is named for a natural bridge which frames the town like a window. The work done at this stone Catholic mission has helped the advancement of the Navajo in Window Rock; it was in fact their first permanent Catholic mission. There is an interesting display of Indian dictionaries and grammar books written by missionaries and general exhibits about local history. NR. Open May-Aug, M-F 9-4, Sa, Su 11-4, and by appointment. Donations accepted. 871-4172.

Lodging and Dining

ARIZONA'S historic tourist hotels and inns or ranches are mainly a 20th-century phenomenon. There are a few surviving Victorian frontier hotels, such as the Cochise and the Copper Queen in Bisbee, but most of the "older" establishments date from the 1920s and '30s when Arizona was unquestionably a safe territory for travelers. During this time Arizona also became a quite fashionable destination for wealthy Easterners and Mid-Westerners seeking the sun and dry climate. The Arizona Biltmore in Phoenix was perfectly designed as a resort complex for the Chicago chewing gum heir William Wrigley, Jr. For those who wished to "rough it" on the ranch, such establishments as the Hermosa Inn in Paradise Valley were opened.

Bisbee

COPPER QUEEN HOTEL, 11 Howell St., 85603. (603) 432-2216. Virginia and Richard Hort. Open all year. Built in 1902 by the Copper Queen Mining Company, this 43-room hotel sheltered the politicians and mining executives drawn to what was then the largest copper mining town in the world. Bisbee retains much of its Frontier charm. Public restaurant. Inexpensive. MC, V.

Chinle vicinity

JUSTIN'S THUNDERBIRD LODGE, 3 miles SE of Chinle and AZ 63 at entrance to Canyon de Chelly National Monument. (602) 674-5443. The lodge is actually located in the Navajo Indian Reservation and is partially built from an old rock and adobe trading post dating from 1896. Tours to the Canyon leave from this site. 34 rooms in lodge and motel. Moderate. MC, V.

Cochise

THE COCHISE HOTEL AND GIFT SHOP, 5 miles south of I-10, 85606. (602) 384-3156. Mrs. Thomas B. Husband. Open all year by reservation only. This 1882 inn contains its original Wells Fargo freight office, an old Greene Cattle Company safe, and a carved wooden sofa reputed to have belonged to Jenny Lind. Meals by reservation. 5 rooms. Inexpensive.

Grand Canyon National Park

EL TOVAR HOTEL, on the rim of the Grand Canyon, 86023. (602) 638-2631. Fred Harvey. Open all year. Constructed in 1904 of native boulders and Douglass firs from Oregon, this rambling 78-room hotel affords one of the world's most spectacular views. The architecture weds elements of a Swiss chalet and a Norwegian villa. Public restaurant. Expensive. AE, D, CB, M, V.

Paradise Valley

HERMOSA INN, North Palo Cristi Rd., 85253. (602) 955-8660. Eckard (Ike) and Angy Bauer. Open Sept-May. The luxurious Spanish Colonial hacienda that Western painter Lon Megargee built for himself in 1930 is the setting for this splendid resort hotel. Megargee, the scion of a wealthy Philadelphia family, is most famous for his painting "A Cowboy's Dream," and, if a Philadelphia cowboy ever had a dream, this is it. 28 rooms and suites. Public restaurant. Expensive. AE, MC, V.

Phoenix

THE ARIZONA BILTMORE, 24th St. and Missouri, 85002. (602) 955-6600. Westin Hotels. Open all year. This lushly landscaped hotel, part of the winter vacation resort of William Wrigley, Jr., of chewing gum fame, was built in 1929. Frank Lloyd Wright's colleague, Albert Chase McArthur, is responsible for the design. 393 rooms. Several public restaurants. Expensive. AE, D, M, V.

Sedona

OAK CREEK LODGE, Oak Creek Canyon, 86336. (602) 282-3343. Gary and Mary Garland. Open Apr-mid-Nov. The setting, in a red-rock canyon with one of the best trout streams in the West flowing by, is spectacular. Housed in a c. 1900 log homestead surrounded by guest cabins, the lodge is a friendly family-run establishment, justly proud of its homegrown food, expertly prepared from scratch. 11 log cabins. MAP. Moderate. MC, V.

Tucson

ARIZONA INN, 2200 East Elm St., 85719. (602) 325-1541. John S. Greenway and Robert Minerich. Open all year. Arizona's only Congresswoman, Isabella Greenway, built the inn in 1930 on 14 acres near the edge of town. It consists of 86 cottage rooms, with fireplaces and private patios, nestled among fragrant gardens in the desert. Expensive. AE, CB, M, V.

HACIENDA DEL SOL, Hacienda del Sol Rd., 85718. (602) 299-1501. This Spanish-style hotel with adobe walls and stark exposed beams, designed in 1929 by Josias T. Joesler, lies in the foothills of the Santa Catalina Mountains. Date palms and citrus trees dot the superbly landscaped grounds. 45 rooms. Expensive.

THE LODGE ON THE DESERT, 306 N. Alvernon Way, 85733. (602) 325-3366. Schuyler W. Lininger. Open all year. Surrounded by 20-foot-high oleander hedges and adobe walls, the lodge, which dates to 1936, is constructed primarily of mud adobe buildings connected by bell-shaped arches. The grounds are carefully tended, with fruit trees and desert palms. 35 rooms. Moderate. M, V.

SUNDANCER SADDLE & SURREY RANCH, 4110 Sweetwater Drive, 95845. (602) 743-0411. Jack J. Jackson. Nov. 1 to May 1. The resort has served as a desert hideaway for film stars and others of note; several TV commercials and fashion layouts have been shot on the well-kept grounds. 14 rooms. Expensive. AP.

5. HAWAII

WHEN the would-be traveler dreams of a trip to Hawaii, waving palms, beautiful beaches and modern seaside hotels are images likely to be conjured. Although this dream vision is in fact reality in today's Hawaii, it is nonetheless only part of the whole picture.

While it would be easy to spend a week or two of total relaxation merely sampling the sun, the surf, and the food, the visitor who wants to delve more deeply into the culture and history of these beautiful islands — so different from the other 49 states — should plan some excursions among them. For Hawaii is, in fact, not one island, but a chain of nine separate land masses, each with its own distinctive appeal. For the purposes of this volume, the state has been divided into four parts: **Hawaii; Maui, Lanai, and Molokai; Oahu;** and **Kauai.**

The history of Hawaii is rooted in the prehistoric past. The Polynesians' ancestors began migrating from Asia several thousand years before the birth of Christ, and gradually settled the western Pacific islands. By the year 700, and possibly as early as the 6th century, this migration had extended to Hawaii. Many remnants of the early settlements remain, principally in the form of *heiaus* (temples) which are scattered throughout the islands. Members of the royal class, the *ali'i nui,* held a privileged position because of their supposed descent from the gods, and exercised total control over land, people, and property. Until the unification of Hawaii under Kamehameha I about the end of the 18th century, control was divided among many royal families. Shortly after British explorer James Cook arrived in 1778, Kamehameha began using English advisors and weapons in his power struggle with other local chiefs and gained overall control in 1791.

The first American missionaries began to arrive in the early 19th century, followed closely by the great whaling ships, whose captains found the hunting in the Pacific most fruitful. Hawaii provided important supply and repair stations for both American and British whalers, and the Islands' economic prosperity became closely tied to these fleets. As was true on the mainland after the Civil War, the whaling industry declined markedly and was replaced in importance by the development of agriculture. Large-scale sugar operations were begun, and owners of the major plantations imported Chinese workers who often moved to urban centers after their contracts expired and established their own businesses, thus adding their individual stamp to the unique character of our 50th state.

There's no denying the allure of almost perfect beaches, distinctive food, and tropical flowers that make Hawaii a vacationer's paradise. But all too few travelers take the time to explore the *other* Hawaii — the tradition-steeped islands that bespeak the mysteries of ancient cultures and their history, so vastly different from anything in the continental United States. The pages that follow will enable you to be added to the ranks of those who do.

Iolani Barracks

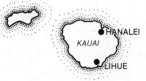

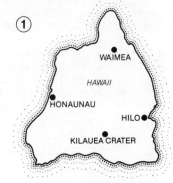

1. Island of Hawaii
2. Islands of Maui, Lanai, and Molokai
3. Island of Oahu
4. Island of Kauai

Island of Hawaii

The "big island," having lent its name to the state, is often mistaken for the complete chain of volcanic and coral islands that make up the state. It is the largest and the easternmost of the Pacific ocean group. More of Hawaii is devoted to agriculture —principally cattle ranching and sugar and coffee bean cultivation—than to any other industry. Hilo on the eastern shore is where most tourists enter the island. The western side, however, is where the principal historic sites are located—Pu'uhonua O Honaunau (Place of Refuge), Pu'ukohola Heiau National Historic Site, Kailua-Kona, and Kealakekua. This coastal region also happens to be one of the most scenic on the island.

Halawa

TONG WO SOCIETY BUILDING, 1886. This finely detailed, well-preserved edifice, the main building of a complex established by and for Chinese immigrants who came to the island of Hawaii after 1860 to work in the sugar fields, is an excellent example of Chinese fraternal society architecture. The oriental feeling of the place is emphasized by serpentine scroll brackets on the floor supports and decorative calligraphic plaques over the doorframes. Societies such as Tong Wo fulfilled many needs of immigrant laborers: religious and political as well as social (gambling and opium smoking were favored activities). This is one of the best preserved buildings of its type in the entire state. NR.

Hawaii Volcanoes National Park

This expansive scenic enclave extends from Mauna Loa volcano, past the Kilauea volcano, to the seacoast near Kalapana. The area is one of giant tree fern forests and weird lava formations; since both volcanoes are still active, you may be able to

Tong Wo Society

witness a minor eruption. Information on the volcanic goings-on is available by calling (808) 967-7977 day or night. When eruptions are occurring, visitors will be directed to special viewing sites.

Numerous trails crisscross the park, such as the **Ainapo Trail,** established in prehistoric times as the customary route to the summit crater of the Mauna Loa volcano. The **Volcano Arts Center,** in an 1877 building near the **Kilauea Visitor Center,** one of two entrances to the park, contains a gallery where seminars and workshops on music, dance, pottery, printmaking, and other arts are given.

The Polynesian volcano goddess Pele is rumored to make her permanent home in nearby **Kilauea crater,** although she reportedly appears at eruptions around the islands. **Volcano House** (see Lodging and Dining) is located on the rim of the crater.

Be sure to glimpse the 18th-century **fossil footprints** believed to have been made by warriors of King Kamehameha the Great and their families; the prints have been well preserved in volcanic ash dating to the 1790 eruption of Kiluaea.

Most of the archaeological sites in the park are located near the coastline, near Pahala, in the rugged Puna-Ka'u area which comprises the **Puna-Ka'u Historic District,** 1300-1900. The area contains many ancient habitation sites, such as **Kamoamoa village,** evidence of whose inhabitants exists from both ancient and relatively modern periods. The village includes an old schoolhouse used as a meeting hall in 1847, a windmill tower, house sites, and some high-walled enclosures probably used by 19th-century goat farmers. The park's largest concentration of ancient petroglyphs (prehistoric rock carvings) may be seen at **Puuloa.** The visible forms are ancient renderings of human forms, fish, sails, and circles.

Another area of interest in the district is the site of a **pulu** (vegetation used for stuffing mattresses) **factory** used from 1850-54. Pulu harvesting was a major industry of the area during the 19th century, as was goat ranching.

There are two public entrances to Hawaii Volcanoes National Park. One is at Kilauea, off HI 11. A visitor center, already described, is located here. The second entrance is at Kupaahu on HI 130. The **Wahaula Visitor Center** is located here and houses displays concerned with the natural and man-made history of the park area. A wealth of Hawaiian artifacts is exhibited.

Both visitor centers are open daily 7:30-5. For more information on park facilities, telephone (808) 967-7311.

Hawi

Heiau in Kukipahu, view to southeast

HEIAU IN KUKIPAHU, SW of Hawi, prehistoric. This massive, terraced temple is considered unique because it is constructed mainly of cut and dressed stone, smoothed manually by Hawaiian craftsmen. It must have been an important holy site to warrant the organization of such large amounts of labor. Influences of Tahitian and Marquesan architecture in this heiau seem to indicate certain Pacific migration patterns. Further archaeological exploration of the surrounding area may disclose large living sites which, in light of this sophisticated structure, are sure to be significant. NR, NHL.

MOOKINI HEIAU, 1 mile W of Upolu Point Airport, northern tip of Hawaii, 1000. This sizable heiau (temple), one of the largest physical remnants of ancient Hawaiian religion, contains ruins of a sacrificial temple with a paved stone open courtyard. The **Birthstone of Kamehameha I** is nearby at Kokoiki, and an actual **sacrificial stone** lies in a field just outside the 20-foot-thick walls.

Hilo

LYMAN HOUSE, 276 Haili St., 1839. This was the home of Rev. and Mrs. David Belden Lyman of Boston, members of that city's fifth group of missionaries to arrive in Hawaii. The oldest frame house on the island, it is two stories high, with wide verandas and doors and floors of native koa wood. The roof of galvanized iron imported from England, dates to 1857. A **museum** adjacent to the house holds period antiques, Hawaiiana, and many scientific displays, as well as ethnic displays of the seven national groups living in Hawaii. NR. Open M-Sa 10-4, Su 1-4. $2 adults, $1 children. (808) 935-5021.

Honaunau

CITY OF REFUGE NATIONAL HISTORICAL PARK, on HI 16, 16th-17th centuries. **Pu'Uhonua O Honaunau** contains 321 structures; it was a cultural and religious center where taboo breakers, defeated warriors, and those seeking safety from war were welcome. The refuge area is encircled by a massive stone wall, built in 1550 of hand-laid boulders, each weighing over a ton. The wall separates the pu'uhonua (city of refuge) from the home of the ruling king. None of the thatched buildings that formed his palace are left, of course, but you can see remains of the royal fish pond and canoe landing, several temples, and a petroglyph. Burial remains and artifacts are displayed. NR. Park open

daily 24 hrs. Visitor center open daily 7:30-5:30. No charge. (808) 328-2326.

ST. BENEDICT'S CHURCH, Middle Keei Rd., 1875. Also known as the Painted Church, this small Roman Catholic church has a rather dull exterior that gives no indication of the interior riches—elaborate neo-primitive illustrations of Bible scenes in wonderful colors. One of this country's finest examples of religious folk art, the paintings are the work of Father John Velghe, a Belgian priest, designer, and painter whose studies in Spain probably influenced this series of work. A panel of Eve with the dying Abel is particularly notable. The island's oldest Catholic church, this is a must-see. NR. Open daily 9-5.

Kahaluu

KAHALUU HISTORIC DISTRICT, off HI 11 near Kahaluu Bay. This historic district is noteworthy because of a concentration of ten major heiaus, massive piles of stacked stones forming temples to the Hawaiian gods. The area is rife with ancient relics: caves, walls, habitation sites, petroglyph fields, wells, and burial platforms. Most of the structures are in good condition, especially the heiaus, many of which have associations with major events in Hawaiian history. ⚐

Kailua-Kona

KAILUA TOWN. "Discovered" by Captain James Cook in 1778, this village on the west coast of Hawaii is tucked between Kailua Bay and the volcano Hualalai, which last erupted in 1801. A favorite resort of King Kamehameha I, who died there in 1819, Kailua has further historic significance in that it saw the arrival of fourteen New England missionaries in 1820—who brought with them diseases which were to fell approximately three-quarters of the natives.

Places of special interest include **Mokuaikaua Church** (originally built in 1826, replaced in 1837, and restored in 1937), one of Hawaii's best preserved New

England missionary churches (NR), and the 1838 **Hulihee Palace** (see below).

HONOKOHAU SETTLEMENT, N of Kailua-Kona, prehistoric-1920. This area was as important in ancient times as in the previous century, and vestiges of both cultures—ancient and modern—remain. There are over 50 habitation sites, several heiaus, tombs, and a holua, or toboggan slide, used for ancient sporting competitions. The **Makaopio heiau** is a fisherman's temple, with two upright stone slabs which served as gods. A few petroglyphs are scattered about. The place is inhabited by Filipino fishermen today, and is accessible by recently completed jeep roads. 🚹

HULIHEE PALACE, Alii Drive, 1837-38, 1884. The brother-in-law of King Kamehameha I built this elaborate dwelling of lava rock with coral mortar and native koa wood interior. It has a two-story Italianate lanai (porch) at the rear, a front second-story centered three-part lancet window, and is decorated in a Victorian manner with Greek and Gothic Revival elements. In 1884 the palace was stuccoed and a kitchen wing was added; restorations also took place in the 20th century. In the late 19th century, King Kalakaua acquired it for his summer residence. It is owned today by the Daughters of Hawaii. Collections displayed in the palace include the famous feathered capes of royalty, tapa cloth, household furnishings, and the distinctive Hawaiian quilts. NR. Open daily 9-4. $3 adults, 50¢ children. (808) 329-1877.

KAMAKAHONU, NW edge of Kailua Bay, 1812. This was the final residence of King Kamehameha, who died in 1819. Remains of the house and his personal heiau are the sole standing buildings of this complex where some of Hawaii's most important agricultural and trade reforms were instituted. Kamehameha's son Liholiho abolished the taboo system here, which left the natives open to the teaching of Protestant missionaries who arrived in 1820. NR, NHL.

Kawaihae

PUUKOHOLA HEIAU NATIONAL HISTORIC SITE, off HI 26, 1 mile SE of Kawaihae, 1791. Puukohola, which means "hill of the whale," was a temple dedicated to the family war god of King Kamehameha I. His workers built the heiau, without mortar, of waterworn lava rocks and boulders. (An original temple on this site, dating to about 1550, was a place of human sacrifice, as was this heiau.) This appeal to his god was successful for Kamehameha, who united the Hawaiian Islands into one kingdom, governed by himself and his family successors, until 1872. Remains of the house of John Young, a British sailor stranded on the island in 1790, who became a favorite of royalty, may be seen nearby. It was originally a compound combining Hawaiian and European influences, with its stone and mortar construction seen so rarely on the island. NR, NHL. The site covers 77 acres. For information regarding park hours, call 328-2336. 🚹

Kealakekua Bay vicinity

KEALAKEKUA BAY HISTORICAL DISTRICT. This is one of Hawaii's most significant historical and archaeological areas. By the time Captain Cook arrived in 1778, there were large villages here at Kaawaloa and Kekua, supported by outlying agricultural fields. Archaeological points of interest include the **town of**

Napoopoo, historic house foundations, religious heiaus, and shrines. NR.

Keauhou

HOLUA SLIDE, E of HI 18, prehistoric. This 1290-foot-long toboggan slide is the best preserved in Hawaii. It was here that the "Olympic games" of the Hawaiian people were performed; the holua race, in which only chiefs could participate, consisted of sliding down a track of rock layered with earth after flinging oneself onto a sled and flying downhill. The chief who slid the farthest in this dangerous pastime was the winner. NR.

KAUIKEAOULI STONE, 1814. Although the pili (grass) hut in which King Kamehameha III was born is long gone, the Kauikeaouli Stone, a 2-foot-high volcanic boulder bearing a bronze tablet, stands to commemorate the event. The stone is situated on a piece of land bordered by a low wall formed of lava stone and mortar. The grounds are well maintained by the Daughters of Hawaii. NR.

Kohala

BOND DISTRICT, SE of Kapaau off HI 27, 1841. This homestead was established by the Rev. Elias Bond of Maine in 1841. He and his wife Ellen Mariner Howell, who bore ten children in Hawaii, lived in these small one-story buildings. The structures, consisting of two residences, a doctor's office, and eleven outbuildings, demonstrate the New England building traditions with which Bond was most familiar. The amalgamation of native and foreign construction techniques has produced a complex of diversity, with both fieldstone and burned coral masonry, heavy timber, and mortise and tenon joints. The homestead has a tranquil air, its structures in harmony with their surroundings, and the grounds are well maintained.

The stone **Kalahikiola Church,** 1855, is located in the southern section of the district and is still used for services. NR.

KOHALA DISTRICT COURTHOUSE, Government Rd., 1889. Built by King Kalakaua's administration, this local landmark was the scene of an historical legal

Kalahikiola Church

drama involving plantation owners and their Chinese immigrant laborers in 1891. It is typical plantation style, with a wide lanai and simple design. Appealing in its spareness, it has a corrugated iron roof—a rare type of building for Hawaii, and a successful application of plantation architecture to that of public buildings. In the yard of the courthouse stands the famous **statue of King Kamehameha,** who was born here. The statue once lay on the ocean floor, for the boat carrying it to Hawaii from Paris, where it was cast, capsized. After a duplicate was produced, the original was mysteriously retrieved and unveiled in the place where King Kalakaua spent his youth.

Waimea

IMIOLA CHURCH, NE of Waimea on HI 19, 1855-57. This is another example of successful architectural unity between native materials and style and that of New England churches. The frame and clapboard Imiola Church shows Greek and Gothic Revival influences; its interior of hand-rubbed koa wood, graceful and plain, is impressive. Dr. Lorenzo Lyons, who came to Hawaii in 1832, was postmaster, school agent, and government physician, as well as Congregational spiritual advisor to the community. He was responsible for the building of fourteen churches in the area. NR.

KAMUELA MUSEUM, Kawaihae-Hohala Junction, HI 19 and 250. Treasures from Iolani Palace and other royal artifacts dating from the period of the monarchy have been gathered at this private museum. It is open daily 8-5. $2 adults, $1 children under 12. 885-4724.

PARKER RANCH VISITOR CENTER, THEATER AND MUSEUM, Parker Ranch Shopping Center. More than 300,000 acres make up the Parker Ranch, the second largest cattle ranch under the American flag. It was founded in 1847 by John Palmer Parker and is still owned and managed by a member of the family. A museum building houses Parker memorabilia as well as a collection of nostalgic mementoes relating to the Olympic career of swimmer Duke Kahanamoku. A fifteen-minute slide show on the ranch is presented in the nearby Thelma Parker Theater. Open M-Sa 9:30-3:30. $1.95 adults, $1.25 children 12-17, free for children under 12. 885-7655. 🕈

Imiola Church

Islands of Maui, Lanai, and Molokai

Maui and its neighboring islands of Lanai and Molokai lie between the island of Hawaii and the populous island of Oahu with its capital city, Honolulu. At one time Lahaina, on Maui, was the capital of the Hawaiian monarchy, and Honolulu a mere minor settlement. The early New England missionaries also made Lahaina their headquarters. Both Lanai and Molokai are much quieter, more remote places that Maui. Molokai, in fact, was considered so well removed from life that it was safe for the monarchy to establish a lepers' colony there in 1866. The settlement of patients at Kalaupapa is long gone, but the memory of the work of a Belgian priest, Father Damien, is remembered at St. Philomena's Church.

Hana, Maui

PIILANIHALE HEIAU, 4 miles N of Hana at the mouth of Honomaele Gulch near Kalahu Point, 16th century. The Garden Isle's largest temple, it is a combination of platform and court-type heiaus, measuring approximately 340 by 425 feet, and it is very well preserved. Piilani, a great ruling chief of the island, is believed to have been responsible for its construction. Within the high, strengthened walls are several stone images and many strange "spirit" holes. NR, NHL.

Lahaina, Maui

LAHAINA HISTORIC DISTRICT, HI 30, mid-19th century. Lahaina's golden days were the 1840s when the whaling industry made the town an important port. Today it retains the ambience of a 19th-century Hawaiian seaport, and for this reason was chosen as a location for the making of the movie *Hawaii*. Lahaina was the capital of the island monarchy from the early 1800s to 1845, and was the gathering spot of the first legislature of Hawaii called by the king in 1841. Among the important buildings in the district are:

The Rev. Dwight Baldwin House, Town Sq., 1834, 1840, 1859. Baldwin was a Harvard-trained medical missionary and arrived in Lahaina with his wife in 1835. As the Baldwin family grew, additions to their house were required. The oldest house on the island of Maui, it has been painstakingly restored and furnished by the Lahaina Restoration Foundation. Baldwin was instrumental in saving many Hawaiians from the smallpox epidemic of 1853. A nearby building served as a missionary center with a reading room for sailors and a lookout. Open daily 9:30-5. $2 adults, $1 children. (808) 661-3262.

Carthaginian II, opposite Wharf St., 19th century. This historic brig is maintained by the Lahaina Restoration Foundation as a floating education museum. The exhibits focus on whale and whaling as well as on Hawaii's wondrous undersea life. Open daily 9:30-5. $1 adults, 50¢ children 12 and under. 661-3262. 🛉

Chee Kung Tong Society, Front St., early 20th century. This is the headquarters of a Chinese fraternal society. The altar fires are kept lit and ceremonies are still performed by descendants of the original members. NR. Private, but visible from the public way. In the same area, on Ala Moana St. is the **Lahaina Jodo Mission** and the **Buddhist Cultural Park,** sites

Courthouse, Lahaina

which form the religious center for the Japanese community. In addition to a temple and pagoda, there is a formidable statue of Amida Buddha which was brought to Lahaina from Kyoto, Japan.

Courthouse, Wharf St., Courthouse Sq., 1859. A two-story coral stone building was constructed from a demolished fort previously on the site. The new building served as a custom house as well as the governor's office and post office. Nearby in the square is the famed banyan tree which was planted in 1873 by the sheriff of Lahaina to commemorate the 50th anniversary of the establishment of the first Protestant mission.

Hale Paahao, corner of Prison Rd. and Wainee St., 1850s. This coral stone building served as Lahaina's prison for many years. The name translates roughly as "stuck-in-irons house," a reference to the iron wall shackles and ball and chain restraints commonly used to keep unruly prisoners in line.

Pioneer Hotel, 658 Wharf St., 1901. The hotel is not a venerable landmark, but any building devoted to lodgings in Hawaii

which has stood for more than a generation or two is worthy of respect. Turn-of-the-century regulations are still posted in guest rooms. For further information regarding accommodations, consult listing under lodging and dining. 661-3636.

Wainee Church (1953) and **Cemetery** (1823), Wainee St., between Chapel and Shaw Sts. The Wainee church, renamed Waiola (meaning "Water of Life") when rebuilt in 1953, is not an insurance man's dream. The first building, put up between 1828 and 1832, could hold as many as 3,000 parishioners and stood until a whirlwind unroofed it; in 1894 royalists protesting American annexation burned the whole building down. It was rebuilt, but then burned to the ground again in 1947. Four years later another whirlwind demolished the building. Perhaps the name change will bring better luck.

Through it all the famous inhabitants of the adjoining cemetery appear to have stayed put. Buried here are Keopuolani, wife of Kamehameha I, one of the first converts to Christianity, and the Rev. William Richards, the first missionary. Other members of the Hawaiian royal family are also interred here.

Pioneer Hotel

Hale Pa'i

Lahaina vicinity

HALE PA'I, Lahainaluna High School, Lahainaluna Rd., c. 1837. Once again, the New England architectural style imported by zealous missionaries is reflected in this building of coral and lava rubble which has been subtly adapted to the Hawaiian climate. This was at first the home of Lahainaluna Seminary, a school for young Hawaiian men. It was also a center where missionaries met with the leaders of the native community and together drafted a Hawaiian bill of rights (1839) and the first constitution (1840).

The first printing press was located here, and such important publications as the first newspaper, *Ka Lama Hawaii* (1834), and the first recorded history of the Hawaiian people, *Ka Moolelo Hawaii,* were printed on this equipment. The building is closed for renovation, but will be opened again by the Lahaina Restoration Foundation when the work is completed. For further information, telephone 661-3262.

LAHAINA-KAANAPALI & PACIFIC RAILROAD, between Lahaina and Kaanapali. The railroad line is a replica of one that ran between these two towns from 1890-1920. It is an especially scenic trip and a convenient one, too, for those staying in the Kaanapali-area hotels who wish to visit Lahaina. It operates daily. One-way fare: $3 adults, $1.50 children 2-12; round trip: $5 adults, $2.50 children. 🚹

Wailuku, Maui

OLD BAILEY HOUSE, Iao Valley Rd., 1833-50. This 2½-story amalgam of four structures is also known as **Hale Hoikeike.** The first building of lava stone was built as a parsonage for the Rev. Jonathan Green, a Congregational missionary. In the 1840s Edward Bailey, principal of the Wailuku Female Seminary and later operator of a sugar mill, expanded the building. It is now a museum maintained by the Maui Historical Society. Among the special objects displayed here are landscape paintings executed by Bailey, a gifted amateur; pre-colonization Hawaiiana of stone, wood, shell, and feathers; and relics from the missionary era. NR. Old Bailey House is open 9-3:30 daily. $2 adults, 50¢ students. 244-3326.

Old Bailey House

KAAHUMANU CHURCH, S. High St., 1876. With an original section built in 1837, this is the oldest Congregational Hawaiian church in central Maui. It is made of stone which has been painted. The church, designed in a combination of Georgian and Gothic Revival styles, is distinguished by its steeply pitched gable roof, buttresses, quoins, and pointed-arch windows. This was the church with which missionaries Edward Bailey and Jonathan Green were associated.

Lanai City vicinity, Lanai

KAUNOLU VILLAGE SITE, on Kaunolu Bay, SW cape, origin unknown. Because of its favorable bay location, Kaunolu was a thriving fishing port until the 1800s. The ruins of the village are extremely well preserved because of the isolated location and dry climate. The remains include **Halulu Heiau**, a temple and small place of refuge, a stone altar to the fish god Kunihi, a canoe shed, graves, house platforms, and a temple. There are also petroglyphs. Kaunolu was the favorite fishing spot of King Kamehameha I. NR, NHL.

Nearby Lanai City is home for many Dole pineapple plantation workers and is beautifully situated on a plateau dotted with Norfolk pines.

Kalaupapa, Molokai

KALAUPAPA LEPROSY SETTLEMENT, 1866, 1911. At one time, victims of Hansen's disease or leprosy were sent to live and suffer on this low island peninsula. The reverend Father Damien, a Belgian Catholic priest who did much to help the lepers in their plight and contributed to research for the disease's cure, made his home here. Damien, himself, died of the disease. Sights include frame and stone structures dating as far back as 1778, with the early leper colony of Kalawa, 1866, also nearby. The area is accessible by mule ride, a hike down the steep cliff, or by small plane.

St. Philomena, the settlement's Catholic church, was built in 1871 and is still standing. NR, NHL.

Ualapue vicinity, Molokai

HOKUKANO-UALAPUE COMPLEX, on HI 45, pre-colonization. This area contains six heiaus, or temples, and two of the island's most famous fish ponds. Molokai itself once had 58 of these ponds, some of which ranged up to 2,000 feet long. The ponds were "royal," that is, built and maintained exclusively for the use of the king and his chiefs. Stone walls with a sluice gate which allowed the entrance of small fish were erected to form shallow ponds. The two remaining here are still used for their original purpose, but are no longer the privileged domain of nobility. NR, NHL.

Island of Oahu

Oahu is the island which is often considered to be Hawaii and Hawaii alone. This is because Honolulu, the capital of the state, is the largest city of the island, the main port of entry, and the center of tourism. Oahu is actually about one-quarter the size of the big island, Hawaii, to the east. Whatever it lacks in geographic strength, however, Oahu more than compensates for in historical and cultural riches. "There are few cities in the world," one writer notes, "that have as many buildings dating from the first quarter of the century of their founding; and all within walking distance of one another." This city is, of course, Honolulu, a settlement which only grew with the coming of the European and the North American in the early 1800s. Eventually, the new Western citizens were joined by others from the Far East in creating one of the great treasures of Hawaii—a true, multiracial society.

Haliewa

KAWAILOA RYUSENJI TEMPLE, 179-A Kawailoa Dr., 3 miles N of Haliewa, late 19th century. One of the best Japanese temples built during the sugar plantation period of Hawaiian history, this one-story elevated wood frame structure sits near the edge of Kawailoa Camp. The camp was established during the late 19th century to house immigrant laborers in the sugar cane fields. The ornamental art of the temple is impressive; it is the only Buddhist temple in Hawaii whose inner shrine ceiling is covered with panel paintings. A particular carved dragon panel over the entrance may well be one of the most priceless pieces of immigrant artwork. In the praying room, which one must enter barefoot, is a Buddha figure in a bell-shaped wooden container. Moveable shoji doors allow for easy indoor-outdoor movement, a tenet of Japanese architecture. NR.

KUPOPOLO HEIAU, Kamehameha Hwy. 3 miles N of Haleiwa, 18th century. This two-terraced rock-paved heiau is noteworthy because of its impressive size, 114 by 275 feet. A heavy stone wall divides the two terraces. NR.

PUU O MAHKU HEIAU, HI 83, 4 miles NE of Haleiwa on HI 83, date unknown. Oahu's largest heiau, it is historically significant because the island's greatest priests came from this district. It contains three adjoining structures which formed the court temple, and two unrelated structures on the ocean side. Puu O Mahku heiau was allegedly the site of a famous human sacrifice, when Captain George Vancouver's men were killed here in 1792 as they tried to get water for their ship, the *Dedalus*. NR, NHL.

Honolulu

ALEXANDER AND BALDWIN BUILDING, 822 Bishop St., 1929. This is the home office of Alexander and Baldwin,

General view of Honolulu and Waikiki Beach

one of Hawaii's "Big Five" corporations. Designed by two outstanding local architects, C.W. Dickey and Hart Wood, it is a four-story, concrete-over-steel building once considered one of the state's most modern. It has inlaid floors of black Belgian marble, and a high tile roof with exposed roof rafters. Chinese in flavor, it also hints of Moorish, Italian, Japanese, and classic Hawaiian influences. Indeed, it is a wonderful combination of Western and Oriental designs, adapted to the mild Hawaiian climate—the closest thing to a masterpiece that exists in Hawaiian archi-

tecture. It sits in a tropical bower of cypress grass, palm trees, and lush plants. NR.

ALIIOLANI HALE, King and Miliani Sts., 1874. Designed by an Australian, Thomas Rowe, this is one of the earliest buildings of concrete block masonry to have been built in a U.S. territory. It is the present home of the Supreme Court of Hawaii and was the scene of the state's declaration of the Provisional Government during the 1893 revolution. Originally planned as a palace, its design reflects the architect's European influences; with its Ionic columns and rotunda with decorative wrought iron elements, it is an early example of the Second Renaissance Revival style. Nearby is an impressive **statue of King Kamehameha the Great** sculpted by T.R. Gould. NR. Open during regular office hours.

ALOHA TOWER, Pier 9, Honolulu Harbor, 1926. With pseudo Gothic and Second Empire styling, the tower is both an amusing and charming symbol of early

Aliiolani Hale

Kamehameha statue

Aloha Tower

Bishop Museum

20th-century tourist-trade Hawaii. The tower is made of concrete and was designed by Arthur Reynolds. It was used during World War II as a control facility for convoy shipping. If a harbor had a control tower like an airfield, this would be it. NR.

BERNICE PAUAHI BISHOP MUSEUM, 1355 Kalihi St., 1889. There is a magnificent library here, with 88,000 volumes illuminating the history of the Pacific Islands through old documents, photos, manuscripts, and periodicals. Be sure to visit the **Hawaii Immigrant Heritage Preservation Center**, the **Hall of Discovery**, and the **planetarium**, as well as an 1878 ship (**Falls of Clyde** — see below) near the museum grounds. This is a resource for information about the natural history of the islands — everything from its mollusks and reptiles to its corals and plants. Open daily 9-5. $4 adults, $2 youth. Planetarium: $1.50 adults, 75¢ youth. 847-3351.

CAPITOL BUILDING, Hawaii Capitol Historic District between Punchbowl, Richards, and South Beretania Sts., 1969. It was designed by Belt, Lemon, and Lo in association with J.C. Warenecke and Associates to be the state's single most dominant piece of public architecture, and it is. Although constructed of modern steel-reinforced concrete and structural steel, it intentionally recalls elements of Hawaii as significant in its past as in its present: an airy interior lobby recalls Hawaii's open society, the conical ceramic tile legislative chambers recall its volcanoes, and 40 reinforced concrete columns remind one of the coconut palm's important role in Hawaiian economy and culture. Open during regular business hours. Free. 🛉

CHAMBERLAIN HOUSE, 553 S. King St., 1831. Known alternatively as one of the Three Mission Houses (see **Mission Houses Museum**, following), this was begun in 1821 by missionaries who transported the pieces of this prefabricated house from New England, and was finished ten years later. Its construction was delayed by a lengthy bureaucratic process occasioned by the fact that it was larger than the king's palace. In excellent condition, the former home of mission business agent Levi Chamberlain and his family was largely reconstructed of new materials in 1935, but looks much as it did in the last century. Original clapboards, cupboards, shutters, floorboards, and windows remain. The Mission Children's Society assumed ownership in 1910. NR. Open daily 9-4. $2.50 adults, $1 children 6-15. 531-0481.

CHINATOWN HISTORIC DISTRICT, bounded by Beretania St., Nuuanu Stream, and Nuuanu Ave., early 20th century. After Hawaii's early Chinese immigrants had fulfilled their contracts to work in the sugar fields, many of them moved to this area, buying land and opening small businesses. Few of the earliest buildings are left after the devastation of two fires, one in 1886 and another in 1900; most structures, dating from 1900 to 1920, are in an "American main street" vernacular, with storefronts and a unifying street facade with individual sidewalk canopies. Oriental elements include bright primary colors, tiled roofs with upward-turned eaves, detailed doors, windows and window grills, and other decorative elements. Most buildings are of cut blue stone, brick, and wood. Chinatown's close proximity to Honolulu Harbor contributed to the area's successful trading career. It is still an enclave for oriental people today, with numerous restaurants and ethnic shops. NR.

DILLINGHAM TRANSPORTATION BUILDING, 735 Bishop St., 1929. Mediterranean and Spanish Mission Revival styles, which were extremely popular in Hawaii during the 1920s, are evident in this structure, affording a magnificent view of Honolulu Harbor. It is a memorial to B.F. Dillingham, scion of Honolulu's Dillingham Corporation, and the founder of the Oahu Railroad and Land Company. This is an imposing structure, with a first-story arched arcade and a low tile roof; one

of the city's most significant landmarks, it is well preserved. The lobby is of marvelous design, with "modernistic" cast-aluminum elevator doors, multitoned glazed brick, and buff and red marble walls with gold mosaic tile. Like Honolulu's Alexander and Baldwin Building, it is a graceful, tangible monument to the old industrial families. NR. Open to the public during regular business hours.

FALLS OF CLYDE, Pier 5, Honolulu Harbor, 1878. Anchored near Honolulu's Bishop Museum, this is the only four-masted, full-rigged sailing ship whose hull is still afloat. The work of Clyde of Glasgow, Scotland, she was used originally as a tramp freighter (one of nine, all named after Scottish waterfalls), then as a sugar trade cargo vessel sailing back and forth to San Francisco. This iron-hulled ship is 266-feet long, with a 40-foot beam. *The Falls of Clyde* was purchased by the people of Hawaii in 1963 for over $25,000 and towed here, where it serves as a floating museum and has undergone extensive renovation. NR. Contact the Bishop Museum for information regarding hours and admission. 847-3511. 🕴

HONOLULU ACADEMY OF ART, 900 S. Beretania St., 1925. Although designed by a New Yorker (Bertram Grosvenor Goodhue), this complex of galleries, encircling five open courts, has a serenity about it that is uniquely Hawaiian. Wide lanais, thick walls of hand-laid lava rock, and a high pitched roof lend a quintessentially tropical air. The Academy, founded by

Iolani Barracks

Iolani Palace

Mrs. Charles M. Cook, is housed in a splendid vernacular structure combining island, Chinese, and Spanish styles in a tranquil, satisfying manner. The museum contains the James A. Michener Collection of Japanese prints, traditional Asian, European, and American paintings and sculpture, and the Kress Collection of Italian Renaissance painting. A stroll through the occidental and oriental gardens, in which grow monkeypods, pandanus, and coconut palms, is immensely soothing. NR. Open Tu-W and F-Sa 10-4:30, Th 11-4:30 and 7-9, Su 2-5. Free. 538-3693.

IOLANI BARRACKS, Richards and Hotel Sts., 1871. The building was originally located in a different spot and was moved in 1965 to make way for the new Capitol. Theodore Heuck, a German architect who also designed the Royal Mausoleum, was responsible for the monumental stone buildings. It housed the Royal Household Guard. NR. It is part of the Iolani Palace complex. See Palace listing for hours and admission fees.

IOLANI PALACE, King and Richards Sts., 1878-82. America's only royal palace, the Italian Renaissance-style Iolani

Iolani Palace, Throne Bay, Throne Room

was built by King Kalakaua to serve as his official residence and that of his sister Queen Liliuokalani until the overthrow of Hawaiian monarchy in 1893. An important ancient heiau once stood on the site of this glorious Victorian mansion. The interior is dominated by a majestic central staircase of polished koa wood; many of the palace's doors and paneling are of rare native woods. The decorative work, all restored, is of etched and cut glass, cast iron, and molded plaster. Elaborate stenciling, chandeliers, and lighting fixtures embellish a veritable wonderland of architecture and decor. Iolani Palace is the work of Thomas J. Baker of San Francisco, a former builder and bricklayer. The divergent elements he employed (French Rococo, Italian Villa, Second Empire) all work wonderfully together in this, perhaps Hawaii's best-known historic edifice. Be sure to glimpse Kalakaua's **coronation pavilion** and **bandstand** in the yard, as well as the site of the **royal burial tomb.** The palace serves as a museum of artifacts from the period of Hawaiian monarchy, 1882-1893. NR, NHL. Open W-Sa 9-2:15; res-

Iolani Palace bandstand

ervations required. $3 adults, $1 children 5-12, children under 5 not admitted. 536-2474. ⚇

KAWAIAHAO CHURCH, King and Punchbowl Sts., 1836-42. It's not surprising that
this simple church is reminiscent of neo-
classical New England architecture, for its
designer, the Rev. Hiram Bingham, was
born in Vermont and came to the islands
with the 19th-century wave of missionaries. Within the walls, formed of some
14,000 "reef rocks," or blocks of coral
from the reef that ends at Pearl Harbor,
church services in both English and Hawaiian are still conducted. Nearby are
three frame mission houses (see **Mission
Houses Museum** below) from 1820-30, an
adobe schoolhouse (1835), and a cemetery, including **King Lunalilo's Tomb**
(1876). Many historically significant
events took place here, including the marriage of Kamehameha IV and Emma
Rooke in 1865, and the inaugurations of
kings Kamehameha IV and Lunalilo. This
church is the fifth on the site. The gray and
white building is plain and dignified, with
only four front columns and a steeple for
adornment. NR, NHL. Open for worship.

Adobe schoolhouse

MERCHANT STREET HISTORIC DIS-TRICT, Merchant St. vicinity, 19th century. This group of buildings, some dating to 1854, serves as an illustration of Honolulu's industrial and economic development in the area between Bishop and Nuuanu Sts. Constructed mostly of brick and stone in a variety of Victorian styles, some particularly noteworthy structures are the 1854 **Melchers Building** (now the Honolulu prosecutor's office), the oldest existing commercial building in the city, built of coral blocks; the 1896 Richardsonian Romanesque **Bishop Estate Building,** made of dark gray lava stone quarried from Bishop Estate land, and resembling a fortress; and the **Kamehameha V Post Office** at the corner of Merchant and Bethel Sts. Built in 1870-71, the latter was Hawaii's first building of concrete blocks and reinforced concrete, as well as the state's first post office, and it exhibits influences of English architecture in the Second Renaissance Revival style. Also worth a visit in this district is the **Kapuaiwa Building** on Queen St., the 1884 work of architect George Lucas. Originally intended as a fireproof repository for government documents, it is a two-story affair of rusticated concrete blocks, Italian Renaissance Revival in feeling. The Italianate **Yokohama Specie Bank** (1909) and **T.R. Foster**

Building, once known as Alfie's Pub, contribute greatly to the fine historic tone of the district. NR.

MISSION HOUSES MUSEUM, 553 S. King St., 1852. This is an important place to visit for anyone interested in the history of the islands; the museum contains 19th-century toys, clothing, and artifacts of American Protestant missionaries, and a fascinating working replica of the Ramage printing press in the 1841 **Printing House,** built of coral blocks, where copies of mission tracts were produced. The three original missionary houses, which include the **Levi Chamberlain house, Kawaihao Church** (see separate listings), and Honolulu's **oldest frame house** (1821), successfully recreate the lifestyle of the early 19th-century Boston missionaries sent by the American Board of Commissioners for Foreign Missions to spread God's word among the "heathen." NR, NHL. Open daily 9-4. $2.50 adults, $1 children 6-15. 531-0481.

OUR LADY OF PEACE CATHEDRAL, 1183 Fort St., 1843. Honolulu has many historic reminders of the influx of Protestant missionaries, but this is one of the few buildings contributed by French Catholics who arrived here in 1828 and remained for only a short time before being expelled by the Protestants. In 1839, Kamehameha declared religious toleration, and the Catholics returned. This church, in a simple rectangular pattern, its facade divided in three by large Doric columns, is still one of Hawaii's oldest buildings. It has been gradually added to over the years, with a Gothic porch in 1910 and buttresses in 1940, long after Hawaii's dramatic religious struggles had cooled. NR. Open for worship.

LA PIETRA, 2933 Poni Moi Rd., 1921. Designed by David Adler of Chicago for the wealthy descendant of an early missionary family, the **Walter F. Dillingham Home,** as it's also known, sits on the slope of Diamond Head overlooking Waikiki Beach—a most perfect location for this series of Mediterranean stucco villas ringing a central court with an arcade. Presently operated by the Hawaii School for Girls, and serving as a school, La Pietra retains its

Punahou School

red tile roof and ceramic tile floors. Open M-F 8-4, weekends by appointment. 922-2744.

PUNAHOU SCHOOL CAMPUS, 1601 Punahou St., 19th-20th centuries. This was the first school west of the Rockies where the English language was taught; it's a complex of stone buildings at the edge of Honolulu, established in 1842 as a school for the children of foreign missionaries. Original buildings include **Pauahi Hall,** 1898, with its Richardsonian Romanesque influences; **Old School Hall,** 1851, in Hawaiian vernacular style; and the 1908 **Cooke Hall.** The land on which it stands was provided by a royal grant to the missionaries in 1829. NR.

QUEEN EMMA'S SUMMER PALACE, 2913 Pali Hwy., 1849. Also known as **Hanaiakamalama,** this recalls contemporary Deep South plantation houses with high ceilings and wide verandas. Originally built by an American minister to the Hawaiian Kingdom, Henry A. Peirce, it was used as a cool mountain retreat by Queen Emma, consort of King Kamehameha IV. Since the island of Oahu was not equipped with enough sawmills to do

the job properly, the palace's timbers and woodwork were prepared in New England and shipped to Honolulu. Built in a modified Greek Revival style, it has fluted Tuscan columns, six rooms, and a center entrance with transom. The frame clapboard house was purchased by the Daughters of Hawaii in the early 1900s, and serves as a museum of original furnishings, personal effects of Queen Emma and her family, and Hawaiian feather work, all recalling the heyday of the beloved royal family. NR. Open daily 9-4. $3 adults, 50¢ children. 595-3167. 🚻

ROYAL MAUSOLEUM, 2261 Nuuanu Ave., 1865. This coral block necropolis of the Kamehameha and Kalakaua families was designed in the Gothic Revival style by Theodore C. Heuck, a Germany architect. It is in the form of a Latin cross, with corner buttresses and decorated cast-iron double gates. In 1904 arched Gothic windows and interior frame trusses in tracery form were added. The mausoleum was consecrated as a chapel in 1922 and is the burial place of the 19th-century Hawaiian minister of foreign affairs, R.C. Wyllie. Eighteen coffins containing the remains of Hawaiian royalty were moved from the royal palace and interred here. NR. Open M-F 8-4, Sa 8-12. 536-7602.

ROBERT LOUIS STEVENSON'S GRASS HOUSE, 3016 Oahu Ave., 1880s. Near the end of his life, the famous author spent six months of each year here among the tropical plants and birds, as the guest of Princess Kaiulani, whose family once owned the property. Stevenson's possessions and period artifacts are displayed, and the grass roof is replaced every four years. The idyllic house is operated by Waioli Tea Room. Open daily 8-4. Free. 988-2131.

THOMAS SQUARE, King, S. Beretania, and Victoria Sts., 1843. Named for Rear Admiral Richard Thomas, this was the site of ceremonies in 1843 to restore the rule of Kamehameha III after British forces seized the government buildings nearby. Rear Admiral Thomas, an envoy of Queen Victoria, implemented the restoration. Surrounded by mock-orange hedges, the 6½-acre park is a lovely spot for strolling. Banyan trees and a fountain decorate the well-tended lawns. The site was enlarged in 1850. NR.

U.S. ARMY MUSEUM, Battery Randolph, Kalia Rd., Fort DeRussy. Historic Fort DeRussy was one of the U.S. Army's earliest posts in Hawaii. Exhibits of domestic and foreign military equipment and paraphernalia fill Battery Randolph, a pre-World War I artillery defense bastion, and the role of the Army in the Pacific islands is well documented. Open T-Su, 10-4:30. Free. 543-2639.

WASHINGTON PLACE, 320 S. Beretania St., 1846. Originally built as the residence of merchant sea captain John Dominis, it was named in honour of our first president in 1848. It presently is the official governor's mansion, as it has been since 1922. Washington Place is a large two-story colonial mansion of coral stone and clapboard originally constructed in the Greek Revival mode and added to in the 20th century. It is Hawaii's oldest continuously occupied house. Operated by the state, of course, it is open to the public on special occasions. NR.

Honolulu vicinity

NATIONAL MEMORIAL CEMETERY OF THE PACIFIC, Punchbowl Crater, at the top of Puowaina Dr. Thousands of Korean, WWII, and Vietnam veterans are buried at this ancient "hill of sacrifice" overlooking Honolulu and Pearl Harbor. NR. Open daily 8-5.

Kahaluu

KAHALUU FISH POND, off Kamehameha Hwy., NW of Laenani St., prehistoric.

Washington Place

The semicircular walls of this pond are built of stacked stone and extend 1200 feet out to sea; this is one of only four such ponds left on Oahu. It was a form of ocean farming, illustrating the ancient Hawaiians' resourcefulness and conservation-minded engineering. So successful was this particular example of a sea husbandry laboratory, in fact, that it was operational until 1960. NR.

Kahuku

KAHUKU SUGAR MILL, Kamehameha Hwy., near NE tip of Oahu, 1890. Superannuated by the mechanization of the sugar cane industry in 1971, this mill was tranformed into a museum with original machinery and displays. The various processes used to produce sugar are color-coded, and a film on the sugar-making industry and its Portuguese, Filipino, Chinese, and Japanese immigrant workers is shown regularly. The exporting of raw sugar (usually then sent to California to be refined) is one of Hawaii's major economic activities, and a guided tour through the mill accurately recreates the technology and sheer volume of sugar production. There are seven restaurants and 20-odd shops on the grounds—but this remains a valid excursion into Hawaii's industrial past. Open daily 10-6. $3.95 adults, $1.95 children. ⫙

Kailua

ULA PO HEIAU, off Kailua Rd., prehistoric. This is another well-preserved heiau, the construction of which is attributed to the legendary Menehune people, who supposedly passed stones from hand to hand over long distances, rather like a bucket brigade. Whether or not this process was implemented here, this large open terrace temple, 140 feet wide and 30 feet high, is one of the largest remaining on Oahu. Some interior portions may be viewed in the south central part of the area; other portions are seen from above on walkways. NR.

Kaneohe vicinity

KUALOA AHUPUA'A HISTORICAL DISTRICT, Kamehameha Hwy. Hawaiian legends about Pele, Kamapua, and Haloa are set in this sacred area, the training ground for newborn children of chiefs, who were raised here. The holy district was an area of sacrifice and protection, a common symbol of sovereignty and independence which was held in the highest esteem. Several fish ponds in the immediate surroundings are worth visiting: **Milii Fish Pond,** three of whose sluice gates are still used to net fish between the pond and Kaneohe Bay as they were in prehistoric times. And the **Heeia Fish Pond,** with an amazing 5000-foot wall, averaging twelve feet in thickness, was an important food-gathering source for the ancient Hawaiians, who built several watch houses along the wall of this 88-acre expanse of water. NR.

Laie

POLYNESIAN CULTURAL CENTER, off HI 83. On land they purchased in 1865, members of the Mormon Church of Jesus Christ of Latter-day Saints established this non-profit educational center in the 20th century. It contains, in a lush tropical setting, superb architectural recreations of each of the seven cultures which contributed to Hawaii's unique ethnic background: Tonga, Samoa, Tahiti, the Marquesas Islands, New Zealand Maori, and old Hawaii are recreated in "villages." Although the building styles are somewhat similar—thatch over wood is most common in a simplified A-frame style—each is subtly different. Accuracy is ensured through documents and drawings left behind by Captain James Cook's artist companion John Webber and a surgeon, both of whom recorded remarkably lucid and detailed observations for history. The process of thatch-making may be closely observed, with ti leaves, sugar-cane leaves, pandanus, pili grass, and banana fibers among the mediums used. Ancient songs and dances, Polynesian cuisine, and sporting events are also part of the center's program. Open from 10 to dusk for the general program; a special evening show, "Invitation to Paradise," begins each day at 7:30 p.m. Admission for the day-time

events is $9 for adults, $4.50 for children. Admission includes tours of all the villages, a "Music Polynesia" program at noon, and the "Pageant of the Long Canoes" at 3:30. The evening program costs $8.50 adults, $4.25 children. For reservations or information, 293-8561.

Pearl Harbor

PEARL HARBOR NAVAL BASE, 3 miles S of Pearl City, HI 73, 1911. Everyone knows what happened here on December 7, 1941, but seeing it is an unforgettable jolt into history. The U.S.S. *Arizona* is spanned by a memorial bridge dedicated to the slain servicemen—more than 1,100 of them, entombed within the ship as it sank after the Japanese attack. Pearl Harbor remains one of the world's finest harbors, protected from the ocean by coral reefs and headlands. An active base, it cannot be toured except for the *Arizona* memorial area, on a controlled cruise which takes advantage of Hawaii's splendid sun and sea winds. Its involvement with American naval history may be traced to 1887, when the U.S. government gained exclusive rights to establish a refueling and repair station for its navy at the harbor. It became Naval District headquarters in 1916, and soon afterwards became command center for the Pacific fleet. To visit the memorial area, you can take one of the National Park Service tours which leave regularly from 9-3 Tu-Su. Free. Children under six are not permitted.

The **Pacific Submarine Museum** on the base contains battle flags, missiles, and torpedoes from World War II, as well as a working snorkel trainer device and assorted submarine memorabilia. NR, NHL. Open W-Su 9:30-5. Free.

Wahiawa

KUKANILOKO BIRTHSTONES, off HI 80 NW of Wahiawa, 12th-18th century. When the wife of a high-ranking chief was about to give birth, she was brought to one of these natural boulders located in a spot suitable for the birth of royalty, or so the

U.S.S. Arizona *Memorial*

ancient Hawaiians believed. Many of the 1½ to 6½-foot stones have large surface depressions which served as "sitting spots" for the woman, and some even had natural backrests of rock. The Hawaiians believed that birth in such exalted spots would further enhance the power and prestige of children of already high birth.

Island of Kauai

Kauai, the westernmost major island in the Hawaiian group, is appropriately called the "Garden Isle." A great deal of the land is maintained for agricultural purposes or is held in its natural state. When one speaks of a Pacific island paradise, it is Kauai that most often comes to the mind of the experienced traveler. It was here that the movie version of the musical *South Pacific* was filmed.

Kauai was the first of the islands to be discovered by Captain Cook, and there are historic reminders of his visit in the south-shore Waimea area. Most of what is left to be discovered of the past, however, is either prehistoric or dates from the mid-19th century. The heiau or temple ruins complex at Waioli is particularly rich in Hawaiian lore. As to the history made by North American colonists and their immigrant laborers, this experience can be relived at such places as the Grove Farm Homestead.

Hanalei

WAIOLI MISSION DISTRICT, off HI 56, 19th-20th centuries. This complex of missionary buildings combines elements of Gothic, Colonial, and Hawaiian architec-

Mission House, Waioli

ture in the main mission house, garage, and two caretakers' cottages. The mission district was once the center of life in Hanalei Village. The mission hall, which dates to 1841, is the **Old Waioli Church** which now serves as a community center, built in the Hawaiian vernacular with heavy plastered walls and a well-pitched thatch roof. The main mission house was built in 1836-37 by the Rev. W.P. Alexander, who laid the sandstone chimney himself. It houses a museum containing antique furniture and an engaging exhibit of Hawaiian horticulture. The house was restored in 1921 along with Old Waioli Church-mission hall. NR. Open Tu-Sa 9-3. Free. 245-3202.

Also in Hanalei is the **Hanalei Museum,** housed in a c. 1880 plantation house. The Hanalei Hawaiian Civic Club that maintains the museum also cares for the original **Japanese Community Church,** c. 1920. The museum collection illuminates the history of this agricultural center where missionaries planted cotton and sugar cane to provide funds for a church and bell and a school for their own and native children. Open Tu-F 10-5, Sa-Su 10-6. Donations accepted. 826-6267.

Lihue

KAUAI MUSEUM, 4428 Rice St. The island's principal historical and art museum is located in the chief city and port of entry. It is housed in the **Wilcox Building,** an early 20th-century edifice, designed by Hart Wood. It contains a rich collection of Hawaiiana relevant to Kaui. Open M-F 9:30-4:30, Sa 9-1, $3 adults, no charge for children through age 17 if accompanied by an adult. 245-6931.

Lihue vicinity

GROVE FARM HOMSTEAD, on HI 501, 1 mile SE of Lihue, 1864. Of the historically significant places in the Lihue area, this early sugar plantation complex is by far the most interesting and important. It was founded in the 1860s by George N. Wilcox, one of Hawaii's most influential men, and operated by his family until the early 1830s. There is a main residence (dating from 1915), guest cottage, office building, several outbuildings, and the Wilcox cottage. All are of frame construction. The workings of a sugar plantation may be reviewed in full historical detail here. In addition, there is a fine collection of original household furnishings and family artifacts which add considerable detail to the life on such an expanse from the mid-19th century to the 1930s. NR. Tours by advance reservation: M, W-Th 10 and 1:15. $3. adults, $1 children 5-12. 245-3202. ♠

MENEHUNE FISH POND (Alekoko Fish Pond), S of Lihue on Huleia River, prehistoric. The fish pond, probably the oldest one in Kauai, is attributed to the tiny legendary race, the Menehunes, thought to predate the Hawaiians. The stone-faced wall of the pond is 900 feet long and cuts off a bend in the Huleia River. NR.

Wailua vicinity

WAILUA COMPLEX OF HEIAUS, Lydgate State Park, Poliahu State Park, and a county park; HI 56 and 580 and area around Wailua Bay; prehistoric. The series of stone heiaus and other prehistoric ruins found in this area is historically significant in the Hawaiian Islands, for it encompasses many aspects of aboriginal culture and takes in an unusually long period of Hawaiian prehistory. Although these are ruins, they are very well maintained and easy to view; vegetation has been cleared away around them.

Lydgate State Park. This nearly 40-acre site on the harbor contains the remains of a **heiau** and of a **city of refuge** known as **Puuhonua Hikinaskala,** which served as a shelter for those accused of crimes or escaping from battle. The setting for these ruins is a particularly beautiful one and is shaded by a coconut grove.

Across HI 56 from Lydgate Park is a small, 2.75 acre plot which is owned by the state and contains a **heiau.** This was a platform temple, and the great stone walls, eight feet wide and from six to eight feet in height, remain standing.

Poliahu State Park. This 13-acre area beyond the Coco Palms Hotel includes a court type of *heiau* which is 57 by 96 feet in size. It was restored in 1933 by the Kaui Historical Society and the Bishop Museum. The temple holds a priest's house and three replicas of Polynesian idols. Further into the park is a **sacred coconut grove** which was a residence for early Hawaiian royalty, and the birthplace of kings. Nearby are royal **birthstones** and a **sacrificial rock.**

County park. About 1½ miles upstream along the Wailua off HI 580 is a 54-acre area administered by the county of Kauai and owned by the state of Hawaii. Here one finds the *Poliahu heiau* situated on a high precipice overlooking the river. This temple is a paved and walled rectangular enclosure. The view from the site is quite spectacular.

The entire complex of Wailua heiaus is listed in the National Register of Historic Places and constitutes a National Historic Landmark.

Waimea

KAMUELA MUSEUM, Kwayaihae-Kohala Junction, HI 19 and 250. Antique objects — both royal and ancient Hawaiian — have been gathered here. There are also objects on display which date from a later period of immigration. Open daily 8-5. $2 adults, $1 children under 12. 885-4724.

Waimea vicinity

COOK LANDING SITE, 2 miles SW of HI 50, 1778. Captain James Cook, the first European to reach the islands, reportedly hit terra firma here on Waimea Bay. As the story goes, he named the islands after his patron, the Earl of Sandwich. Cook, who was on his way to North America from the Society Islands, remains an invaluable source of information about the early days of Hawaii. His observations of natives and their customs are extremely useful, as are the drawings of his companions. The Cook Landing Site, maintained as a recreational park by the county of Kauai, may be as infamous as it is famous, for the men who landed here supposedly gave venereal diseases to the natives, thus decimating their ranks. NR, NHL.

RUSSIAN FORT, HI 50, 200 yards SW of bridge over Waimea River, 1816-17. Ruins of a hexagonal stone fort built by an agent of the Russian American Company of Sitka, Alaska, are all that remain today. The fort was intended as an important imperial Russian foothold in the islands. Although the resident agent, Georg Anto Scheffer, succeeded in making Kauai a Russian protectorate in 1816, he was expelled the next year by King Kaumaulii, and his troops went with him. There are remnants of barracks and a magazine inside the heavy piled-stone walls. They are 15 to 30 feet wide and 20 feet high. The remains of a stone wharf lie on the riverbank; the fort is now surrounded by sugar fields. After being held by Hawaiian troops after the expulsion of the Russians, it was abandoned in 1853. NR, NHL.

Lodging and Dining

No one goes to Hawaii for its history. But once there, why become entrapped in the slickly modern, the all too familiar bland expanse of plastic and polyester which is the same in Maine, Missouri, and a few miles from Mauna Loa? An unfortunate number of Hawaii's accommodations are about as genuine and satisfying as paper leis. If Hawaii is not that different in many respects from many other tourist areas, neither is it a cultural desert. Honolulu has some fine old hotels which survived the Depression, use by the Navy during World War II for rest and relaxation, and the stampede of tourists to the Waikiki beach since the war. The Royal Hawaiian and the Moana stood for years as the undisputed "great ladies" of Honolulu. There have been many changes in the décor and various additions to both buildings, but the essential form and style of both establishments is intact. On the other islands, the traveler seeking something more than pretty postcard scenes has only a few obvious choices to make. There is no other hotel in the world quite like Volcano House, and the Pioneer Inn would pass muster by a summer resident of Nantucket. These are but a few selections. The visitor may discover other outposts of traditional Hawaiian culture. If so, he is best advised to keep the secret to himself and friends so as not to invite a swarm of tourists.

Hawaii Volcanoes National Park, island of Hawaii

VOLCANO HOUSE, 40 miles S of Hilo, 96718. (800) 325-3535. Phil Lee. Operated by the Sheraton Corp. for the National Park Service. Volcano House was constructed in 1941 to replace an earlier hotel with the same name which had burned to the ground. The first hotel, built in 1846, was little more than a grass hut, but it offered a tremendous view of the steaming crater of Kilauea. The present building has an air of a friendly hunting lodge, and when Kilauea begins to bubble, it fills up rapidly. Volcano House is a National Register landmark (for further information see listing). 37 rooms. Public restaurant. Moderate. AE, CB, M, V.

Kaupulehu-Kona, island of Hawaii

KONA VILLAGE RESORT, 96740. (800) 367-5290. A very luxurious oasis in a desert of lava, Kona Village only pretends to be historic, but it does it very well. Guests stay in handsomely and comfortably appointed thatched huts; breakfast and dinner are served in the Hale Moana, a New Hebrides longhouse. Some of King Kamehameha I's mysterious fish ponds are nearby. 100 cottages. Expensive. AE, CB, M, V, D.

Lahaina, island of Maui

PIONEER INN, 658 Wharf St., 96761. (808) 661-3636. Built in 1901, the Pioneer was pressed into service for the movie *Hawaii* and is often cited as one of the island's most historic lodgings. It is a miracle, of course, that such a modest hostelry is still standing. There are old and new wings, the former being the cheaper and without air conditioning. The Old Whaler's Saloon is a local landmark. The Pioneer is included in the Lahaina Historic District (see listing). 48 rooms. Inexpensive. AE, CB, D, MC, V.

Honolulu, island of Oahu

MOANA HOTEL, 2365 Kalakaua Ave., 96815. (800) 325-3535. A Sheraton Corp. hotel. Designed in 1901, the Moana is one of the earliest high-rises on the island. In the heart of Waikiki Beach, it is an oasis of classic South Seas turn-of-the-century charm, a place where life moves as slowly and sedately as the tropical ceiling fans. 388 rooms. Public restaurant. Moderate. AE, D, CB, MC, V.

ROYAL HAWAIIAN HOTEL, 2259 Kalakaua Ave., 96815. (800) 325-3535. A Sheraton Corp. hotel. The sensational "Pink Palace of Waikiki" was built in 1927 and is a stunning example of pre-war tourism in the islands. Designed by Warren and Wetmore, it has been variously termed Moorish, Mission, and Spanish Colonial Revival in design. The building stands on the site of King Kalanikapulis's home. 568 rooms. Public restaurants. Expensive. AE, D, CB, MC, V.

Index